W9-ACI-048

Inside the Soviet Writers' Union

Inside the Soviet Writers' Union

John and Carol Garrard

THE FREE PRESS
A Division of Macmillan, Inc.
NEW YORK

Collier Macmillan Publishers
LONDON

The Free Press
A Division of Macmillan, Inc.
866 Third Avenue, New York, N.Y. 10022

Collier Macmillan Canada, Inc.

Printed in the United States of America

printing number

1 2 3 4 5 6 7 8 9 10

Library of Congress Cataloging-in-Publication Data

Garrard, John Gordon.
Inside the Soviet Writers' Union/John and Carol Garrard.
p. cm.
Includes bibliographical references.
ISBN 0–02–911320–2
1. Soi͡uz pisateleĭ SSSR. 2. Russian literature—20th century—History and criticism. 3. Russian literature—20th century—Political aspects. 4. Russian literature—20th century—Social aspects. 5. Glasnost. 6. Russian literature—20th century—Censorship. I. Garrard, Carol. II. Title.
PG2920.S68G37 1990
891.7′06′047—dc20 89–23594
CIP

This book is dedicated
with love to our children,
Richard, Alex, Michelle, and Alison.

TO THINK of the political problem as a problem of finding the true form of organization leads either to political despair, if one knows one has failed to find it, or, if one thinks one has been successful, to a defense of tyranny for, if it is presupposed that people living in the wrong kind of order cannot have a good will and people living in the right kind cannot have a bad one, then not only will coercion be necessary to establish that order but also its application will be the ruler's moral duty.

W. H. AUDEN

THE Union of Writers has become a terribly bureaucratic organization, repeating in miniature the way in which all organizations work in our country—from the Party on down.

VITALY KOROTICH

Contents

Preface and Acknowledgments

Our main purpose in writing this book was to discover what it is like to be a Russian writer in Soviet society, that is, a Russian writer, as distinct from other Soviet writers. How does the literary environment in Moscow differ from that of London or New York, or indeed from that of St. Petersburg a century ago? Can Russian literature revive and flourish within Soviet society? We are much less concerned with text than with context, that is, the social, economic, and political environment in which the writer must function. Literary works are treated insofar as they illustrate trends and conflicts in the literary environment.

We had expected to base our study on the three pillars of the Soviet literary system: Socialist Realism, Glavlit (the censorship organization), and the Union of Soviet Writers. However, during our interviews with recent émigré and exiled Russian writers, and with writers, editors, and cultural officials in Moscow, we discovered that Socialist Realism and Glavlit, whatever significance they might have had in the past, have faded into the background and now play a relatively minor role in the daily life of the Russian writer. Even before glasnost nobody paid much attention to Socialist Realism, and a study of the formal censorship could never provide an adequate understanding of the complex relationship between writer and regime that evolved after Stalin's death.

It is the Union of Soviet Writers that dominates the Russian writer's professional and even personal existence—as it does that of his non-Russian Soviet compatriots. Hence our focus on the Union: its organizational machinery and its rules and regulations, its formal structure, and its "inner face" behind the scenes. The Union is a remarkable organization, the centerpiece of a unique effort by government not simply to control writers, but to harness them in service to the state. To this end, the Union does not use force as much as psychological and material inducements. Its forms and rituals provide members with a sense of community and status that anchors them in Soviet society. The Union serves the interests of the Communist Party, while managing and meeting the needs of its members. In a collective society that means a great deal.

We concentrate on the national organization, headquartered in Moscow, and on the Russian Republic branch. Although the human and material resources available to us contoured our approach, a brief examination of the activities of non-Russian and regional branches of the Union suggested that their policies and procedures have mirrored those of Moscow over most of the Union's existence. However, Mikhail Gorbachev's campaign for glasnost and perestroika has revealed sharp differences in attitudes and priorities between the Union apparatchiks in Moscow and their brethren in some, although by no means all, of the Republic writers' organizations. Union officials in some areas have pressed forward with reforms in a particularly aggressive manner, threatening confrontations with the Kremlin and with the powerful Russian nationalist movement. Theirs is a vitally important story that should be told, but by those with the necessary linguistic background.

The Union of Soviet Writers has configured the political, social, and economic environment in which Russian writers must function. It represents the most extensive and longest-running cultural experiment in any major society since the Middle Ages; yet, as a subject, it falls between disciplinary boundaries. Literary specialists are concerned with the published text, while social scientists naturally focus attention on more traditional centers of political and economic power. We have tried to bridge the gap by showing that the non-esthetic context can have an important impact on creative writers. At the same time we suggest that the Union, as a Soviet-type organization, holds much interest for the social scientist. Other than the Party itself, it is the only Soviet enterprise that publishes stenographic reports of its congresses. It offers useful insights into the mechanisms used by the Party to control a non-Party organization.

When Max Weber outlined his classic description of bureaucracy at the turn of the century, he was describing an "ideal type" of rational efficiency. Weber recognized that his model was hypothetical rather than factual. He did not foresee that the Communist Party of the Soviet Union would attempt to bring the ideal down to earth and implement it for the profession of writing. The Party has tried to achieve a utopia with a utopian concept of organization, one that discounts accident, personality, rivalries, and greed. How has the Union worked in practice? How successful has the Party been in promoting its policies through the Union? What type of literature, and what type of writer have flourished within the Union, and conversely, what literature and what type of writer have been suppressed? And what impact has Mikhail Gorbachev's campaign for glasnost and perestroika had on the Union's structure and procedures? These are the questions we address in the chapters that follow, because the future of Russian literature depends on the answers.

While researching and writing this book we received help from many individuals and institutions (though we alone are responsible for the views expressed).

A Sesquicentennial Grant from the University of Virginia in the fall of 1983, and a research fellowship from the Hoover Institution in the summer of 1984 (both to John Garrard), supported much of the initial research into published sources.

The book could never have been completed without a year-long research fellowship for John Garrard in 1984–85 at the Kennan Institute of the Woodrow Wilson International Center for Scholars in Washington, DC. The help and encouragement given to both of us by the Institute's staff were much appreciated. Herbert Ellison of the University of Washington, who was Secretary of the Kennan during that period, and James Billington, then Director of the Wilson Center and now Librarian of Congress, made the year particularly rewarding.

In its early stages our work also received much invaluable support from the Soviet Interview Project, directed by James R. Millar at the University of Illinois and funded by the National Council for Soviet and East European Research in Washington, DC. The Soviet Interview Project facilitated interviews with recent émigrés to the United States and provided released time for research.

Travel grants from the Earhart Foundation of Ann Arbor, Michigan, and the Institute for Foreign Policy Analysis of Cambridge, Massachusetts, enabled us to conduct interviews with Russian writers and critics now living in Western Europe. The experienced staff at Radio Free Europe/Radio Liberty in both Paris and Munich gave us generous help in setting up some of these interviews. The staff in Munich allowed us access to their superb archives of Soviet *samizdat* (self-published) sources.

Travel grants from the International Research and Exchanges Board (IREX) of Princeton, New Jersey, allowed us to interview within the USSR in 1983 and 1985. Our special thanks go to friends and colleagues at the Gorky Institute of World Literature (IMLI) and the Union of Soviet Writers. Soviet officials at related enterprises, the State Committee on Publishing (Goskomizdat), and the Soviet copyright organization (VAAP), also consented to be interviewed. While the statements of Soviet executives should be placed in context, they provided much valuable information, and they have a right to have their side of the story heard.

We want to express our special gratitude to the Rockefeller Foundation for offering us a joint residency at the Villa Serbelloni in 1988 at a critical stage in the editing of the manuscript. The idyllic setting and superb facilities at Bellagio allowed us to do much-needed intense work. Bob and Gianna Celli were unfailingly gracious hosts.

We are extremely grateful to the many Russian writers and editors in the United States, England, France, Switzerland, Germany, and Canada, who consented to be interviewed. Many friends and colleagues in this country also gave generously of their time and expertise. Walter Connor, Alex de Jonge, Martin Dewhirst, Leonid Vladimirov, Maurice Friedberg, Paul Goble, Radomir Luza, Robert Maguire, and Savely Senderovich read earlier rough drafts and offered much sound advice. Peter B. Maggs gave us help with Soviet legal codes. Rosa Simkhovich did a fine job transcribing many of the interview tapes. We are also grateful to Alex Dunkel for sharing his unrivalled knowledge of Russian culture and his extensive library.

Chris Johnson and his staff at the Arizona Humanities Research Center helped us grapple with the mysteries of computers and laser printers.

Joyce Seltzer, Senior Editor and Vice-President at The Free Press, and Project Editor Roz Siegel labored with great patience to get our manuscript into final shape. Whatever blemishes remain are our own responsibility.

And finally, we owe a special debt to our parents, John and Ella Garrard of Ottawa, Canada, and Clarence and Rose Hamersen of Green Valley, Arizona. Throughout the research and writing of this book, their love and support—as parents and as grandparents—were a constant source of encouragement.

Sabino Canyon, Arizona
July 4, 1989

A Note to the Reader

In transliterating Russian, our main concern has been readability for the non-Russian speaker; anyone knowing Russian should have no problem restoring the original Cyrillic, or discerning the rules and exceptions we have used.

The Union of Soviet Writers (*Soyuz Sovetstikh Pisatelei,* or *SP SSSR*) is referred to as the Writers' Union or simply the Union.

The Communist Party of the Soviet Union (*Kommunisticheskaya Partia Sovetskogo Soyuza,* or *KPSS*) is referred to usually as the Party.

Republic (always capitalized) refers to one of the fifteen constituent Republics of the Soviet Union.

Only central or national bodies of the Union are capitalized, for example, Board, Secretariat. Parallel bodies in Republic or other regional bodies are not capitalized.

Glasnost and perestroika are not italicized.

All translations are our own, except where indicated. When published translations are used, they have been checked against the original Russian, and adapted where necessary.

Prologue

52 Vorovsky Street

I write at the bidding of my heart, and my heart belongs to the Party.

MIKHAIL SHOLOKHOV

Just around the corner from the American Embassy in Moscow runs one of the most charming streets in the city, Vorovsky. It cuts a fairly straight line through the heart of Moscow's embassy district, an area favored by foreign delegations due to its convenient location west of the Kremlin, and also because it retains some of the charm and flavor of pre-revolutionary Russia. No. 52 Vorovsky is occupied by a particularly striking example of Russian neo-classical architecture. Beyond imposing pillars, set wide apart to accommodate the horse-drawn carriages of tsarist days, the visitor follows a circular driveway framing a handsome central building set between two symmetrical wings. The entire Palladian facade in pale yellow, trimmed with white, is reminiscent of villas in Lombardy—a natural resemblance since northern Italy and the Ticino in Switzerland provided many of the architects and builders who created the imperial style in both Moscow and St. Petersburg. A statue of Leo Tolstoy graces the forecourt, lending credence to the long-standing rumor, now officially accepted as fact, that the mansion served as Tolstoy's model for the Rostov home in *War and Peace*. But where once horses and carriages filled the driveway, now cars—Ladas, Volgas, even a rare Zil or Chaika limousine—compete for parking. The presence of so many cars—more so than the beauty of the building—would alert any Soviet citizen that this must be an important enterprise. Appearances do not deceive: this gracious mansion houses the administrative headquarters, known as the "Secretariat," of one of the most prestigious organizations in the country, the Union of Soviet Writers.[1]

Of less architectural interest, but still impressive because of its size and its handsome portico, is a second Writers' Union building located right next door, and connected to the Secretariat by an underground passageway much appreciated in the severe Russian winters. This enormous structure, which extends all the way back to Herzen Street, is the Central House of Writers (*Tsentralny Dom Literatorov*, or *TsDL*), usually known as the Club. It contains a well-stocked bar, a pleasant cafeteria, and a spacious reading lounge, plus a library, a barber shop, and a variety of large meeting rooms, one of which is used to show recent Soviet and foreign films to members and their guests. But the Club's main attraction is its excellent restaurant, probably the best in Moscow, and that means in the whole country. The prices are heavily subsidized, and the service is quick and polite—a great contrast to other restaurants in town, as any Western tourist (and many a Russian) will be quick to verify.

The Writers' Union is a great deal more than just an association of writers in the Western sense of the term; over the years, since its inaugural congress in 1934, the Writers' Union has become an exclusive club to which not only bona fide writers but also members of the Soviet elite belong. According to Soviet literati, in terms of prestige and perks, membership in the Writer's Union ranks second only to the august Academy of Sciences. Officials in the Party and in government who deal with literature, as well as chief editors at leading journals, display "Member of the Writers' Union" on the business cards they exchange with foreigners. Anyone showing such a card will be treated with special deference by Soviet police, local Party officials, and the KGB, since top officials of the Union will certainly have influential contacts in the Party and possibly in the KGB as well. It testifies to the high prestige and unique status of the Writers' Union that it was selected as one of very few locations to be visited by President Ronald Reagan on his brief summit trip to Moscow in May of 1988.

This picture of official favor and privilege does not jibe with the Western image of Soviet writers as browbeaten by the authorities, struggling in isolation and in straitened circumstances against attempts to censor their works, and speaking out boldly for intellectual and creative freedom. Such writers do exist, and their courage and dedication deserve respect. But over the years rebels like Alexander Solzhenitsyn and Vladimir Voinovich have proven to be exceptions to the general rule; they constitute a tiny percentage of the membership. Union members are pampered by the Soviet authorities, treated with a great deal of respect by the population at large, and given many material advantages not enjoyed by ordinary Soviet citizens.

This surprising relationship between writer and régime is a logical outcome of decisions taken by Stalin in the early thirties—for the Writers' Union was not formed by writers themselves, but created by the Party. This is a union established and run by management. The Soviet state, even before the Union came into existence, set out not simply to censor Russian writers, but to harness them to the Marxist cause and put their talents to good use. For more than fifty years the Party has been conducting a unique experiment in its attempt to serve as both patron and Muse of all the arts. It has gone to a great deal of trouble and expense to mobilize writers because it recognizes literature as a potent force in Soviet society. The Writers' Union, with all its prestige and privileges, is the result of this unprecedented effort. As an example of state subsidy and mobilization of creative writers, it has no parallel in history.

From the beginning the Writers' Union has been linked to the program of the Communist Party. When the Union celebrated its golden anniversary in September of 1984, the lavish ceremony took place in the Kremlin and was attended by the entire Politburo. While this event marked a particularly auspicious occasion, the attendance of the Politburo was not all that unusual. It has become customary for the General Secretary and nearly all Politburo members to attend at least the opening sessions of the Union's national congresses; it is only a short walk from their offices in the Kremlin.

The Writers' Union is a national organization, but like the Party it is heavily centralized in its command structure and dominated by Russians. It has branches in each of the fifteen Republics (unlike the Party, which has no branch in the Russian Republic), as well as in smaller administrative units and in major cities and towns. The Moscow branch, founded in 1955, has more than 2,000 members. It forms part of the Russian Republic branch, which, although it was only created in 1958, now has some 5,000 members, about half the overall total, and plays a leading role in the organization. In any case, whatever his national origin, whether his chapter is in Leningrad or Chita (a small chapter of eleven members in eastern Siberia), in Armenia or in one of the Baltic republics, the writer's professional life is scripted by the Union's Secretariat at No. 52 Vorovsky Street.[2]

Although its structure and procedures are similar to the Party's, the Writers' Union is not officially designated a Party organization; one does not have to be a Party member to be admitted. However, the percentage of Party members in the Union has been increasing steadily since 1934, and is now close to 60 percent.[3] The ratio of Party members among delegates to the Union congresses has always been even higher. It too has been increasing slowly but steadily with every congress; it is now over 80 percent. Like the Party, the Union is totally dominated by males. Although the percentage of males in the membership has been dropping very slowly, as of 1986 it was still almost 85 percent. Among delegates to national congresses the percentage of males has remained even higher (over 90 percent). Hardly any women are included in the Union's governing bodies; there are none at the apex of the organization, the Litburo, just as there are no women serving as full members of the Politburo of the Party.[4] The Writers' Union is a rapidly aging organization, with more than one-third of its members aged 61 or older.

The Union has become so prestigious and dominates Soviet literary life to such an extent that the word "writer" connotes "member of the Writers' Union."[5] Virtually all writers aspire to belong. Those struggling to gain admission, and they are legion, are regarded as mere apprentices, people who have not yet made the grade. Membership in the Writers' Union is highly prized and difficult to come by, not only because it offers an impressive range of benefits, but also because vast numbers of Soviet citizens are striving to be writers—far more than in the United States. To some extent, this phenomenon results from conditions peculiar to a society where whole professions—financial services, management consulting, commercial advertising, insurance, stockbroking, for example—hardly exist. Such professions swallow up tens of thousands of upwardly-mobile college graduates in the United States every year. But in the Soviet Union a similarly impressive pool of intelligent, well-educated men and women must look elsewhere. Far more of them than in the United States become engineers and scientists. However, it is also true that many others follow careers in writing, journalism, and literary criticism. The Writers' Union cannot absorb all would-be members, so that large numbers of people find themselves occupying lower rungs on the ladder, working—in Soviet parlance—as "literary slaves" (*literaturnye negry*).

While a writer can make a living by his pen outside the Union, once he becomes a member his situation takes a dramatic turn for the better. The Union functions as a kind of medieval guild and guards its privileges jealously. In Marxist terms this organization controls (on behalf of the Party) the very "means of production" of the craft of literature. It operates printing presses, runs a major publishing house, and all the major literary journals and periodicals throughout the country; the last official count listed a total of 120 literary journals as being "under the jurisdiction of" (*podvedomstvennye* or *v vedenii*) the Writers' Union.[6] These so-called "thick journals" (*tolstye zhurnaly*) appear every month, not just every quarter, and play an essential role in Soviet literary life because they, rather than publishing houses, print new novels and plays as well as short stories and verse. The chief editors of all of these journals belong to the Union, as do most members of each editorial board; the rest are cultural and ideological specialists appointed by the Party. All literary journals must submit every two or three years to a full-dress review and evaluation of their operations by the Union's Secretariat. In cooperation with Goskomizdat (the State Committee on Publishing) and the ever-present Party ideological specialists, the Secretariat makes the day-to-day decisions on what works of literature will or will not get published, and in how large a print-run. Manuscripts that do not pass muster have little chance of ever reaching Glavlit, the formal censorship organization.

Although membership in the Union has numerous advantages for a writer, the majority of its privileges and perks bear no direct relationship to the profession of writing. The importance of the Union to its members, and hence the reason why so many people are constantly trying to be admitted, cannot be fully understood without taking into account the unique conditions of Soviet life. In a society where the individual has traditionally counted for less than the collective, and where consumer goods and services are in chronically short supply or absent altogether (*defitsitny*), belonging to an organization, and especially one as powerful as the Writers' Union, is as crucial to one's livelihood as it is to one's professional career. In Soviet society the main problem is not money, but access. Union members have a special advantage when it comes to buying goods and services. The Writers' Union has virtually limitless resources, provided by the Party, to determine a member's quality of life: the size and location of his apartment, the freshness and variety of his food, the length and location of his vacation, the type of medical care both he and his family receive.

Membership in the Union means even more than prestige or privilege—it offers writers both economic and legal status. A membership card is the full-time writer's sole proof that he is employed, or "working under contract" (*rabotayushchy po dogovoru*). As a result of the Soviet claim of full employment, no male (unless he is a full-time student) is permitted not to work, that is, not to be engaged in "socially productive labor." Indeed, to be unemployed in the Soviet Union is to be a "parasite" and that is a criminal offense. Article 21 of the Criminal Code of the Russian Republic cites a series of punishments, including a sentence of one to two years to a corrective labor camp, for those who become beggars or peddlers, or otherwise lead "a parasitical existence" (*paraziticheský obraz zhizni*); repeat offenders can receive three years in a camp.[7] Membership in the Union provides the professional writer, traditionally engaged in the quintessentially individual enterprise, with the guarantee that he cannot be arrested for this violation of the Soviet penal code. Members do not automatically receive a salary (though in 1988 one member proposed that they should), but the Union offers writers many opportunities to lead a comfortable existence.

The Writer's Union is clearly an extraordinary institution, and also something of a legal anomaly. It is formally considered to be a voluntary, non-governmental association, yet members' dues and royalty contributions could not come near paying the costs of all the privileges and services members enjoy. The Union receives funds from the Ministry of Culture, which has authority over all theaters and cinemas in the Soviet Union (but not over the Writers' Union), and income from other sources designated by the Party and guaranteed by law. Furthermore, the Union has been delegated functions that, to a Westerner at least, belong to the state. A collaborative volume by Soviet legal experts, published in 1970, revealed that it is the Union that determines the amount of its members' retirement pensions, and how much disability income they may receive.[8] In fact, the Union has been given the authority to verify and approve the length of full-time employment (*trudovoi stazh*), which in turn determines the retirement and disability income, of *all* Soviet citizens who claim to have made money in the profession of writing, even if they are not members of the Union. In this instance the Union has subsumed the authority that within the United States belongs to the Social Security Agency.

The anomalous position of the Writers' Union as a quasi-government organization has been exacerbated by the fact that it is a "legal entity" (*yuridicheskoe litso*). The Union is thus capable of signing contracts and making legal arrangements with similar entities. But the single most important fact about the Writers' Union, from a legal standpoint at least, is that it has been granted the special status of a "creative union" (*tvorchesky soyuz*). This is a unique designation, quite unknown outside the Soviet bloc.[9] An exploration of its ramifications is crucial to understanding the organization and the literary environment in which Soviet writers must function.

The Writers' Union is the oldest and certainly the most prestigious of the creative unions which the Party has established over several decades, to both guide and subsidize the work of writers and other professionals in the arts—a group known formally in Soviet parlance as the "creative intelligentsia." Creative unions now exist for composers (1932), artists (1932), architects (1932), journalists (1959), cinematographers (1965—but an organizational committee had been formed as early as 1957), theatrical workers (1986), and designers (1987).[10] These unions are all slightly different in their structure, procedures, and benefits. The Union of Journalists was, in fact, one step below the level of a true creative union until its Sixth Congress in March of 1987 when, as Radio Moscow-1 reported on March 16, a new version of its rules was passed, stating for the first time that the Union of Journalists was a "creative union," like the Unions of Writers and Composers. The Soviet listener knew exactly what the addition of that word *tvorchesky* meant: journalists would henceforth be allocated access to more goods and services, better sanatoriums, and longer vacations in more prestigious locations; perhaps at Pitsunda on the Black Sea, where the Union of Journalists and the Writers' Union had already cooperated on the construction of a lavish resort hotel. The perks and privileges allocated by the government for journalists' work would go up several notches. Since the Union of Journalists has about 80,000 members, the switch represented a considerable investment on the part of the Soviet authorities.

The material privileges and legal protection granted to members of the Union result partly from the traditional respect for writers and literature in Russia. As the émigré novelist Anatoly Gladilin noted:

> If in the United States you say to somebody that you are a writer, people will say, "That's nice." But they will not be too impressed. In Russia it's entirely different; being a writer is very prestigious, it is a high honor. It's really like being in the nobility (*dvoryanstvo*).[11]

This is a remarkably suggestive historical parallel: one of the most desirable advantages of achieving the legal status of personal or hereditary "noble" (*dvoryanin*) in Peter the Great's Table of Ranks was that you could protect yourself, your family, and possibly all of your descendants from physical abuse by the forces of law and order, and from other "cruel and unusual punishment." That phrase was carefully placed in the United States Constitution as a safeguard against the physical punishment widely practiced by British authorities in the eighteenth century, and later. The "Table of Ranks" provided the same sort of protection. It consisted of fourteen ranks, not all of them used, for military, civil, and court service.

These special benefits are granted by the Party not merely because of its respect for writers, but more specifically as part of a calculated strategy to encourage and reward loyalty. Similar preference is shown to other professionals and skilled personnel. The Party has adopted the old tsarist tactic of offering privileges to the classes of people it needs to maintain its power and prestige. Creative unions serve its purpose for writers and other artists. They continue to meet the needs of the Party, otherwise it would not have continued to permit various professional groups to create them, or to spend such huge amounts of money subsidizing them.

It has in fact been the Party's official policy, openly declared since the 1920s, that is, even before the Union was established, to exercise what is described as "guidance" (*rukovodstvo*) over literature.[12] As early as 1928 the Party's Central Committee noted:

> The basic objectives of the Party in the field of literature and the arts can only be achieved by increasing the Party's influence within the organizations of writers and artists and by strengthening Marxist communist criticism.[13]

Here encapsulated is Stalin's future program: a combination of organization and method (or theory). Four years later the Party's Central Committee found a way to strengthen Marxist communist criticism by introducing the obligatory method of Socialist Realism, and at the same time established the Writers' Union as the organization through which it would implement its policy.

The policy of Party "guidance" exercised within the arena of creative unions remains unchanged to this day:

> Its [the Party's] guidance cannot be effective if it involves direct interference into the creative activity of artists, but only when it is carried out through their own organizations, that is, the creative unions.[14]

The latest edition of the official Party Program, approved at the 27th Party Congress in March 1986, reaffirms the longstanding policy whereby the Party "guides (*rukovodit*) the literary and artistic process by relying upon (*opirayas na*) the creative unions."

The Party does not want to be seen as interfering directly in the literary process, nor does it see itself in this role. It prefers to influence the work of writers through an intermediary: the Union of Writers was established for that very purpose. But the Party maintains that it did not create the Union; it was created voluntarily by writers themselves. This myth is necessary to comply with Article 47 of the Soviet Constitution, which states that the Union is merely one of several "voluntary societies" which ensure the "freedom of scientific, technical, and artistic work." Article 51 guarantees the right of citizens "to associate in public organizations that promote their political activity and initiative and the satisfaction of their various interests." The Soviet Constitution requires the government to provide material support for these "voluntary societies": to protect authors' rights, to offer moral support, and "to respond to these societies' social initiatives." The Writers' Union is viewed as "a social institution, acting under the ideological guidance of the Party in cooperation with other public organizations, the Komsomol, the trade unions, and other unions of workers in the arts."[15] It is because the Union is a "voluntary" organization that the government and the Party are legally allowed such an important role in its activities.

This concerted effort at total control over the creative process is a natural outgrowth of the Soviet belief, inherited from Lenin, that "Socialism is an organized society . . . organized on the collectivist principle. Literature and art are no exceptions, existing as they do in society and for society." Writers, therefore, have an obligation to help in the common purpose of improving man's lot and creating communism. The Party ideological specialists base their approach to the Union on a seminal article by Vladimir Lenin entitled "Party Organization and Party Literature" (1905), which continues to be referred to as "the manifesto of socialist culture" in much the same way as Americans might quote Alexander Hamilton or James Madison from *The Federalist Papers*. In his article Lenin stated that, with the triumph of the proletariat, writers would voluntarily produce ideologically correct works, without coercion.

In reality, Party guidance has come to mean pervasive control of the writer's total activity, far more extensive than mere censorship. The activities of the formal censorship organization, Glavlit, whatever their intrinsic interest, are inadequate to explain the true nature of the Soviet literary situation. It is true that all works must receive the Glavlit stamp of approval, but the Party's guidance system has already affected the creative process long before the manuscript reaches the Glavlit censor's desk. If the Party relied passively on censorship, its system would be no different from that of the tsars in the past or more recent dictatorships around the globe.

Whereas traditional censorship focuses on the end product of writing—the manuscript—guidance targets the author; it aims at influencing the creative process from the moment of inspiration. In the West an author might take Virgil to be his guide, like Dante in *The Inferno*, or declare "Nature" to be "the anchor of my purest thoughts and soul of all my moral being," as did Wordsworth in "Tintern Abbey." A Soviet author is not allowed to seek such private inspiration. The Party is to be the writer's Muse, leading him obediently by the hand, guiding the creation of a literature that exemplifies *partynost*, *ideinost*, and *narodnost*. The meaning of these crucial terms can only be suggested by approximate paraphrases in English: Party-mindedness or Party spirit, correct ideological stance or content, and ready accessibility to the people (*narod*).

The Party's goals are intended to be present in the writer's mind even before he decides what to write about. The Party is not interested in the creative expression of individual feelings or impressions; the writer's responsibility is to illustrate, to provide artistic images that will project the Party's policies and appeal to the Soviet reading public. Consequently, Party ideological experts have tried to change the way authors think about themselves and about their work. The Party aims to make them feel they have a duty to perform, that they owe something—everything—to the people, and therefore to the people's representative, the Party. In return, the Party is ready to demonstrate the people's deep appreciation by supplying authors with material incentives, "to each according to his work."

The bureaucracy of the Union is crucial to implementing the Party's objectives. Without the Union, the Party would find it virtually impossible to intervene so early in the creative process, and at the same time maintain the myth that writers are really independent. The Union is the agency through which the Party can most efficiently use both stick and carrot, or as the Russians say, "whip and gingerbread" (*knut i pryanik*). Since the death of Stalin, the Party has found that distributing gingerbread is much more effective than administering the whip in persuading writers to serve the state and its ideology.

A few writers have managed to maintain some measure of artistic independence within the Party's system of guidance. However, it is very difficult to escape completely because of the Union's pervasive influence. As an agency of the Party, it is supposed to set the writer's agenda, and monitor his adherence to the current Party policies, that is, *partynost*. The Union no longer hands out assignments, as it did in the early days of the first five-year plan and the collectivization of agriculture. The system has grown much more complex and sophisticated. It aims to persuade the writer to produce what is desired without actual coercion. The Union's job is to encourage its members, through appeals to loyalty and patriotism, and the promise of material rewards, to support the Party's program. It is the Union that will pay for the writer to take a *komandirovka* (creative trip) to Latvia or Siberia, and arrange the "latheside" chats with workers to ensure *narodnost*—ready accessibility to the ordinary folk—in the ensuing piece. Finally, after the author has written up his "task," it is the Union that will recommend him for a prize sponsored by either the USSR Ministry of Transportation or the Latvian Ministry of Agriculture.

The Union is the transmission belt to worker-writers, ticking off the Party's expectations that they create a "positive hero" in their works, and be optimistic and upbeat about the progress Soviet society is making toward achieving communism. These are the parameters of Party literature; their "just circumference" is set by the Union using its bureaucratic compass.

Thus, the distinguishing characteristic of creative unions is their social and ideological purpose. Membership may be voluntary, but those who join the Writers' Union are supposed to be united by a common objective, which is not to improve their own working conditions or wages, as is the case with Western associations of writers. In fact, there is no need for them to do so, because the Party is not officially viewed as being hostile toward writers, as are publishers or press barons in the capitalist West. The contrast is set in sharp relief if we compare the constitution of a Western association of writers with that of the Soviet Writers' Union. For example, the constitution of the Writers' Union of Canada reads in part:

> The purpose of The Writers' Union of Canada is to unite Canadian writers for the advancement of their common interests. These interests include: the fostering of writing in Canada; relations with publishers; exchange of information among members; safeguarding the freedom to write and publish; and the advancement of good relations with other writers and their organizations in Canada and all parts of the world.[16]

Soviet writers, according to Marxism-Leninism, have no need to be concerned with "relations with publishers" or with "safeguarding the freedom to write and publish," because they are said to enjoy those rights already. Instead, the main purpose of Soviet writers is to work toward the greater good of the Soviet people, and indeed of all mankind. And they can only perform this noble task properly under the guidance of the Party.

This stress on the political role of Soviet writers and other artists is laid out by the authors of the 1970 collaborative volume on the creative unions, to which reference has already been made:

> Soviet creative unions are social organizations which unite professional writers and artists on the basis of the ideological and creative method of Socialist Realism, with the aim of producing works of high artistic quality, of promoting the organizational initiatives and political activity of their members, and of defending their rights and interests.[17]

This approach is based on notions and assumptions of the function of literature and the arts, and the role of the artist, that are quite different from those that are generally accepted in Western countries today. The introductory essay to a volume of essays by Union officials states this unambiguously:

> The Writers' Union, we stress this always, is based on ideological principles. The Charter [i.e., Statutes] of the USSR Writers' Union has been revised four times . . . but the principles on which the writers were united remained immutable. The Writers' Union, according to the Charter, is a voluntary, public, creative organisation uniting the professional writers of the Soviet Union who participate with their work in the struggle for the construction of communism, for social progress, for peace and friendship between nations.[18]

The opening statement in the Writers' Union Statutes, formally adopted in 1971, emphasizes the same purpose:

> Soviet multi-national literature, the literature of a new historical epoch, is struggling for the high ideals of socialism and communism, for the creation on earth of a truly just society, one whose banner will be peace, work, freedom, equality, brotherhood, and the happiness of all nations.[19]

Both these quotations illuminate the two important ideas, entwined one within the other like a cadeusus, that have underpinned the Party's subsidy of the Writers' Union. The first is that literature should serve the state; the second is that the objective is the creation of a *future* state, the utopia of global communism. Therefore literature's educative role is crucial.

The Party proclaims that communism is a viable goal, for men and women can be trained and shaped to build such a society. Literature is one of the most important tools by which the "new Soviet Man" is to be reshaped out of the lumps of proletarian clay. All the perks and privileges of membership in the Writers' Union—the medical care, special foodstuffs, apartments, vacations, loans and outright grants, funds for domestic and foreign travel, as well as unique contacts and opportunities—all are ostensibly awarded on the basis of how well the writer fulfills this task. In order to inculcate, monitor, and reward the production of socialist literature—to be not only patron but Muse—the Party needs an organization, and thus it has created and subsidized the Writers' Union.

The current Western view of the function of literature in society is so very different from the Soviet view that it is easy to forget that both share a common source in the European intellectual tradition. Indeed, one of the fascinations of Russian studies is to trace the often startling ways in which Russians adopt Western ideas. The notion that literature should serve an extrinsic purpose—whether it be moral, spiritual, or the greater good of society as a whole—has a long and honorable tradition in the West. It is, for example, a commonplace of Romantic attitudes—Percy Bysshe Shelley termed the model poet an "unacknowledged legislator" to mankind. Further, some tenets of Socialist Realism recall central notions of French neoclassical esthetics, such as the recommendation to poets that they focus on "beautiful nature" (*belle nature*) and be guided by "verisimilitude" (*vraisemblance*) rather than by vulgar reality. This is not so very different from the Soviet view that artists should portray reality "in its revolutionary development," which means not what is but what should be, or what is becoming, according to Marxist-Leninist theory. Hence writers are invited to seek out what is "typical," rather than the insignificant realia of the moment.

Entering the Soviet literary world is like stepping across a threshold into a time-warp. Western opinion has abandoned the Romantic faith in inevitable progress, in political utopianism, and in a political role for literature, whereas Marxism-Leninism harks back to an earlier age when such notions dominated European intellectual and cultural life. Contemporary Western writers embody another variant of the Romantic tradition, one that praises individualism: "To thine own self be true." Their works are offered and received as the creative expression of personal feelings, of a private, even idiosyncratic view of the world and of the societies in which they live, and which they often portray in harsh, ironic colors. Western writers prefer pricking balloons with their pens rather than waving flags and joining the parade.

But the Communist Party has instructed Soviet writers to help organize a perfect society. What are the sources of this utopian vision? What are the reasons, unique to Russian and Soviet history, that caused the Party to band writers together in an organization, rather than allow them to operate as individuals or in informal groups? To answer these questions, we must track the origins of the Union in Russia's tsarist past, and in the beliefs of Vladimir Ilyich Lenin, the man who created the Russian revolution and laid the cultural, as well as political, foundations of the Soviet state.

1

Organizing Utopia

*I*n sharp contrast to bourgeois customs, to the profit-making, commercialized bourgeois press, to bourgeois literary careerism and individualism, "aristocratic anarchism" and pursuit of profit, the socialist proletariat must promote the principle of *Party literature.*

LENIN (*1905*)

The notion that literature should play a special role in creating a new social order took root in St. Petersburg and Moscow well before Marxist thought fertilized the intellectual soil of Russia. It drew from the same source that Marx himself tapped a little later in the nineteenth century—German idealist philosophy. In his influential essay "On Naive and Sentimental Poetry" (1795–96), Schiller insisted that a poet does not describe a landscape for its own sake; he uses it as a vehicle to describe the "ideal," a timeless realm of being beyond the limited world of the senses. This transcendental cosmos can be apprehended only through the poetic imagination. Hence the mind does not depend solely upon sense impressions from the world of experience; it can create experience as well.

When these ideas were imported into Russia, they combined with domestic social and intellectual conditions to produce revolutionary notions about the function of literature. Since language could create its own reality, a visionary role was accorded to the writer—he was to transform society with his pen. Russian writers have enjoyed enormous prestige because of the unique role that literature has played in the intellectual and social life of their country. Pushkin, Lermontov, Dostoevsky, Tolstoy, Turgenev, Chekhov—the catalogue of Russian writers in tsarist times who became not only literary but moral heroes to the public is long and honored. Almost by default, as the regime allowed few other forums to discuss contemporary ideas, creative literature became a sounding board for the burning political and social issues of the time.[1] The majority of writers in the nineteenth century followed the influential critic Vissarion Belinsky (1811–48) in believing that a Russian writer had a civic duty to help his readers become better citizens. This belief in its turn resulted in a positive enrichment of Russian fiction. Since ideas had to be discussed tangentially in literature, in "Aesopian language," because of the strict tsarist censorship, Russian writers avoided overt preaching while they poured into novels, poems, and plays their moral passion and concern for the "accursed questions" of the human condition. However much the great novelists of the nineteenth century might differ amongst themselves, they were linked by a desire—owed to Belinsky—to examine moral and philosophical issues.

The sowing of German ideas in Russian soil produced a sense of moral and social responsibility in writers that gave their works great force. As Russian literature became both vessel and catalyst for Russian national consciousness, creative writers gained increasing stature. However, they also acquired new obligations when Belinsky's ideas were intensified a generation later by Nikolai Chernyshevsky (1828–89), leader of the so-called radical or civic literary critics, who demanded that writers involve themselves much more directly in promoting revolutionary change. Writers rejected this threat to their creative independence. They continued to portray a passionate search for solutions, but maintained an esthetic distance. Only rarely did narrators advocate the hero's beliefs, or show him triumphant in his search for solutions. Frequently the hero came to realize that his quest should be for spiritual enlightenment rather than for political or institutional goals. Writers stuck closer to Russian reality than Belinsky's heirs, increasingly radicalized as they were by tsarist obduracy, would have wished.[2]

Since neither Dostoevsky nor Turgenev, nor any other major writer, would produce the type of fiction that he and his friends demanded, Chernyshevsky himself produced a novel, *What Is To Be Done? Tales about New People* (*Chto delat? Iz rasskazov o novykh lyudyakh*), designed to inspire readers to greater efforts in the revolutionary cause. Chernyshevsky wrote the novel in 1863 while awaiting trial in the Peter-Paul Fortress in St. Petersburg. He had been arrested for making inflammatory remarks about the predicament of the serfs. Like many young radicals at the time, he was bitterly disappointed by the 1861 Emancipation Proclamation, which freed the serfs from slavery, but obliged them to pay large sums of money to landowners until the end of the century and deprived them of the opportunity to own land. The novel was published in a journal Chernyshevsky edited himself. It was quickly suppressed by the embarrassed authorities, but the damage was done; pirated copies circulated widely through the remainder of the century. It was this obscure novel that later became the model for the type of literature promoted under Socialist Realism.

What Is To Be Done? traces the trials and tribulations of a group of "new people" and describes their plans and dreams for a communist society that the reader is meant to understand will follow the inevitable revolution in Russia. Chernyshevsky devotes much attention to the need for revolutionary disciples to give themselves totally to the cause, even if family and friends must be cast aside. In exemplary fashion his heroine, Vera Pavlovna, escapes what she regards as the stifling environment of her home. She contracts a marriage of convenience with Lopukhov, a medical student. The marriage is not consummated because Lopukhov respects Vera Pavlovna's independence. Indeed, when she falls in love with another medical student named Kirsanov, Lopukhov fakes suicide and flees to America. Vera Pavlovna and Kirsanov get married, although she is still tormented by what she believes to be her responsibility for Lopukhov's death. She has a series of dreams, which show her concerns and her hopes for the future. In Vera's fourth dream a "Radiant Beauty" (*svetlaya krasavitsa*), with many quotes from Rousseau, Goethe, Schiller, and from Russian writers, escorts her on a visionary tour of a future world that is bright and glowing. The Radiant Beauty, who plays Fairy Godmother to Vera Pavlovna's Cinderella, concludes the vision by exhorting Vera to continue her struggle until she achieves her goal:

> You have seen the future, you know what it will be like. The future is radiant and beautiful. Tell everyone that the future is radiant and beautiful. Urge people to love the future and work towards it, to hasten its coming, to take from tomorrow as much as they can today. Tell everyone that if they do that, then their lives will be bright and good, full of happiness and joy. Tell everyone to struggle and work for this future. . . .[3]

At critical moments in the story a mysterious young man named Rakhmetov arrives to encourage Vera Pavlovna and the other "new people." At one point he announces that Lopukhov is alive and well; Vera Pavlovna rejoices that Lopukhov is living in America, the land of opportunity.[4] At another epiphany Rakhmetov resolves the heroine's doubts about her chosen path to liberation, organizing a dressmaking collective. Vera Pavlovna and her husband live happily ever after.

Their fictional fate, however, is not nearly so important as the significance of Rakhmetov in the destiny of Russian society. Weak as the novel is, Rakhmetov is an exciting character, and one can easily understand how he caught the imagination of young readers searching for a way to give purpose to their lives, a way to attack the tsarist regime. He embodies Chernyshevsky's personal ideal of the dedicated revolutionary, who will carry out the transformation of Russia into the ideal society pictured in Vera Pavlovna's fourth dream. Rakhmetov is only 22 years old when we are introduced to him, but has already traveled the length and breadth of the country and visited Western Europe. It turns out that Rakhmetov is an aristocrat, descended from a thirteenth-century Tatar named Rakhmet, and that his ancestors had played a distinguished part in major events throughout Russia's history. Rakhmetov himself owns large estates, has 400 serfs and enjoys an annual income of 3,000 rubles. However, he has resolved to devote his wealth and energies to improving the lot of his less fortunate compatriots; he puts several young men and women through university. He restricts himself to 400 rubles a year, and his only serious indulgence is quality cigars, on which he spends as much as 150 rubles out of his annual allowance—the narrator points out that it would be too much to expect someone of Rakhmetov's background to be satisfied with cheap cigars. To toughen himself up and thus become more acceptable to the simple folk, Rakhmetov adopts a "boxer's diet" (*boksyorksaya dieta*), consisting chiefly of beef. He also spends a great deal of time on physical exercises and gymnastics. To test his willpower, he even sleeps on a bed of nails, which puncture his body and leave him covered with blood.[5] This ruthless devotion to the cause of revolutionary change was adopted by countless disciples in Russia and echoed in the proletarian literature of the early Soviet regime.

Chernyshevsky himself had acted on his theory that literature should be a servant of social change, aimed at the betterment of society. For his pains, the tsar's justice sentenced him to twenty-five years in Siberia. He was only permitted to return to his birthplace, Saratov, a short time before his death in 1889. But while Chernyshevsky endured harsh punishment, his ideas spread like wildfire. He came to embody in his own person the model for a new type of writer, who would not simply expose the tsarist regime—the poverty and brutality of Russian life—but also portray for his readers an idealized future society so as to inspire them to greater efforts in the revolutionary cause. Moral obligation now became a social task. Writers were expected to forget their interest in the doubts and failures of what Turgenev described as "superfluous men," and to present heroic figures like Rakhmetov, role models larger than life. The young radicals had no time for tragedy, they wanted inspiration and the promise of a happy ending.

There was much to admire in Chernyshevsky's motives, and much to pity in his fate. Nevertheless, the great writers of the time objected strenuously to this new form of prescriptive censorship. Fyodor Dostoevsky wrote *Notes from Underground* (*Zapiski iz podpolya*, 1864) as a satire on Chernyshevsky's novel and other writings. Dostoevsky ridiculed Chernyshevsky's cardboard characters, and has his own absurdly unheroic Underground Man describe the human species as "ungrateful bipeds," whose wayward fancy and contrary nature will always prevent them from serving as model inhabitants of a utopian society. The idea that all men and women would automatically do what is right and good, if invited to do so, angered Dostoevsky, who considered it hubristic, as well as a dangerous misunderstanding of human nature. For him the main problem with utopian socialist ideology, which he had himself embraced in his youth, was that it ignored the existence of evil. Dostoevsky insisted on greater modesty, a recognition that man must struggle against temptation. Man is not automatically perfect or perfectible; if he were, he would not need God, and the Devil would long have faded from human memory.

Compared to the complex and tormented characters in the great novels of Dostoevsky, Rakhmetov seems little more than a comic book hero. However, there is no denying the fascination he exercised over several generations of Russian readers, especially those living in the reign of Alexander III (1881–93), who suppressed all hopes for peaceful change after the assassination of his father, Alexander II.[6] Young men used Rakhmetov as a model as they tried to steel themselves for the struggle against an all-powerful and brutal regime. Vera Pavlovna too had an enormous impact on countless young women, inspiring them to abandon their comfortable bourgeois or even upperclass homes for a life of self-sacrifice and danger.[7] Women threw themselves into revolutionary activities and participated in several assassination attempts, some of them successful, on the lives of tsarist officials.

Although Chernyshevsky appears not to have read Marx (Marx did read Chernyshevsky), his novel influenced several of the early Russian revolutionaries who became leading Marxists. The father of Russian Marxism, Georgy Plekhanov, stated that he switched professions from engineering to medicine because he was so impressed that Kirsanov and Lopukhov were doctors. Plekhanov's whole life changed at a famous rally at the Kazan Cathedral in which he galvanized the crowd by demanding Chernyshevsky's release. Plekhanov got away in the ensuing melee, but he had just dedicated himself to Chernyshevsky's cause. There are many other examples of major figures in the revolutionary movement of the time who were inspired by *What Is To Be Done?* But Chernyshevsky's most significant disciple by far was a teenager named Vladimir Ulyanov. He read the novel at a critical moment in his life—just as he was preparing to enter the University of Kazan to study law in 1889, and not long after his adored older brother Alexander had been hanged as a terrorist involved in a juvenile, failed plot to assassinate Tsar Alexander III. The novel had inspired his brother to become a revolutionary; now it inspired young Ulyanov to take the same course. Like so many young radicals, he came from a good family. He was the son of a civil servant who held a government rank equivalent to major-general, and used to sign himself "Vladimir Ilyich Ulyanov, nobleman (*dvoryanin*)." After receiving a short sentence in Siberia, Ulyanov assumed the revolutionary name Lenin. He gave up a comfortable career as a lawyer to dedicate his formidable intellect and nerve to destroying the corrupt Romanov dynasty. He was equally dedicated to replacing it with a better world, as envisioned by the Radiant Beauty in *What Is To Be Done?* Lenin spoke on several occasions about his fondness for the novel, which he once said provides "a charge to last a lifetime." According to his wife, Nadezhda Krupskaya, Lenin read *What Is To Be Done?* at least five times, and kept a copy with him during his brief Siberian exile, in a place of honor together with works by Plekhanov, Marx, and Engels.

A Western parallel to this instance of fiction's impact upon a nation's destiny is Harriet Beecher Stowe's *Uncle Tom's Cabin,* which appeared just a decade before *What Is To Be Done?* Within a year of its 1852 publication, it sold 300,000 copies in the United States alone. It enjoyed equal renown abroad, including Russia: Chernyshevsky mentions *Uncle Tom's Cabin* in his own novel as one of the works that Kirsanov narrates to the young ladies in Vera Pavlovna's dressmaking collective. When President Lincoln met the diminutive Mrs. Stowe in 1862, he remarked: "So you're the little woman who wrote the book that made this great war."[8] The energies unleashed by Mrs. Stowe were resolved in a bloody conflict, and while her novel merits at least a footnote in historians' discussion of the war's causes, no one puts forward *Uncle Tom's Cabin* as an exemplar of how American authors should write. The case is quite different for *What Is To Be Done?*, which became the model for Soviet literature through the influence of Lenin.

In Chernyshevsky's novel Lenin had found not only an inspiration for his own revolutionary career, but also a perfect illustration of an activist role for the creative writer and the successful socializing impact of literature. However, it was Marxism that provided the "scientific" basis for linking literature to class warfare and revolutionary change. Marx himself emerged from a utopian tradition, one inspired by creative writers. Like them, Marx drew upon the two sources of utopian fiction—faith in the perfectibility of man, and alienation from contemporary society—to fashion his own theories. But he differed from his predecessors by abandoning the creation of fictional utopias to insist that a real utopia on this earth was both practical and inevitable according to the laws of history.[9]

Like Plekhanov and so many others, Lenin too became a radical after reading a novel, and several years before he had read Marx. But Lenin was too much the pragmatist not to have seen the weakness in Chernyshevsky's revolutionary agenda. True, Rakhmetov is all business; he has a horror of wasting time on secondhand ideas and general discussions that lead nowhere. However, it is never clear what exactly he is doing to further the cause. Rakhmetov has no unified theory, no concrete strategy to achieve his ideal society. He can only say rather enigmatically that Newton's *Observations on the Prophecies of Daniel and the Apocalypse of St. John* merits careful study. Lenin understood that Rakhmetov, or even several Rakhmetovs, could not bring about revolution as long as they acted as individuals. Lenin paid Chernyshevsky the compliment of borrowing his title *What Is To Be Done?* for one of his own crucially important works, published in 1902. Without alluding specifically to the novel, Lenin restated Chernyshevsky's question, but answered it differently: it is not enough for individuals to labor for the cause, to encourage sewing collectives, to give informal instruction to young women. What is needed is an *organization*, a tightly-knit group of revolutionaries dedicated to a common purpose. Lenin himself created that organization, a "party of a new type" that could implement both Marxist ideas and domestic Russian notions about the role of literature.[10]

In his *What Is To Be Done?* Lenin argued that one should not sit idly by while, in Marxist terminology, historical materialism took its inevitable course. He drew a seminal distinction between what he called ideological "consciousness" (*soznatelnost*) and revolutionary "spontaneity" (*stikhynost*). Workers might possess the latter, but not the former. In fact, they were not capable of making the transition to full "consciousness" without outside help, which must be provided by a dedicated band of revolutionaries, the "vanguard" (*avangard*) of the revolutionary movement.[11] Lenin called for the Social Democratic Party to lead society in its transformation and demanded that each member's activities be imbued with the concept of *partynost*, which initially was related to the English term "partisanship," but assumed its current, narrow meaning under Lenin's influence. Though he does not allude to Chernyshevsky's hero by name, the implication is clear: only a united and ideologically "conscious" party of Rakhmetovs, disciplined and dedicated, could achieve the radiant society set forth in Vera Pavlovna's dream.

Lenin's choice of the Party's socialist consciousness over the workers' spontaneous revolutionary activity had a decisive impact on literature, because it led to a sharply increased role for propaganda, that is, the use of the mass media, including literature, as a means of inculcating revolutionary consciousness not only in the workers but among all groups and classes in society. That task would require that both the press and literature fulfill a critical mission in educating the people (*narod*). Lenin made this link to literature explicit in a short but equally crucial 1905 article, "Party Organization and Party Literature."[12] *Partynost* was now to be a guiding principle not only in revolutionary tactics but also in all publishing activity. Without explicitly naming them, Lenin outlined two further principles, *ideinost* (correct ideological stance and content) and *narodnost* (ready accessibility to the people), to form what later became the Soviet cultural trinity; these notions continued to dominate orthodox Soviet thinking about the purpose of literature and all the arts until the Gorbachev period.

For Lenin, Party literature is first and foremost literature which exemplifies *partynost*. He explains: "Publishing and distribution centers, bookshops and reading-rooms, libraries and similar establishments—all must be under Party control."[13] But this is not control for its own sake. The overriding objective in wresting literature (and the press) from random, individual control, as well as from the hands of the class enemy, is to make it serve the proletariat, whose interests are the Party's prime concern:

> For socialists, proletarian literature cannot be a means of enriching individuals or groups; more than that, it cannot be an individual undertaking at all, independent of the general proletarian cause. Down with non-Party writers (*literatory bespartynye*)! Down with literary supermen! Literature (*Literaturnoe delo*) must become an integral part of the common cause of the proletariat, "cog and screw" of one single great Social Democratic machine that is set in motion by the entire [politically] conscious vanguard of the entire working class. Literature must become an integral component of organized, planned work in the Social Democratic Party.

This is *ideinost* in action.[14] Literature must be ideologically motivated and function as part of a political platform in favor of everyone who is "conscious" (*soznatelny*), that is, who possesses socialist or proletarian consciousness.

For Lenin, freedom was derived from the Hegelian (and Marxist) "recognition of necessity," a necessity bred of history and of economic forces. He set forth in his article an important element of Soviet cultural policy: an insistence that Party literature will be truly free because it will be "a literature *openly* linked to the proletariat" (*deistvitelno-svobodnuyu,* otkryto *svyazannuyu s proletariatom literaturu*):

> It will be a free literature because the idea of socialism and sympathy with the working people, rather than greed or careerism, will win over increasing numbers to its ranks. It will be a free literature because it will serve, not some satiated (*presyshchennoi*) heroine, not the bored "upper ten thousand" suffering from obesity, but millions and tens of millions of workers, those people who make up the best part of our country, its strength and its future.[15]

The belief that literature must serve the ordinary working people, rather than an elite, constitutes the basis of *narodnost,* the third element of Socialist Realism. It is his adherence to the notion of *narodnost* that led Lenin to reject forms of Modernism and abstract art that seemed "highbrow" and difficult for the average person to understand. In so doing, he rejected many outstanding achievements by Russian artists at the turn of the century. At the same time, Lenin rejected the arguments of other Marxists, notably Karl Kautsky, who coined the phrase, "total control over the means of production, but total anarchy in culture."

Whether Lenin meant his words to refer only to official Party literature is still an issue. Whatever his original intention might have been, Soviet literary critics have taken Lenin's 1905 article as the cornerstone for their esthetic imperative, Socialist Realism. They continue to quote it as the main justification for creating the Writers' Union, and the article's anniversary is regularly celebrated in the literary periodicals published by the Union. Furthermore, all anthologies for secondary school and college literature courses throughout the Soviet educational system begin with Lenin's article, so its arguments and phraseology are part of every literate Soviet citizen's cultural vocabulary.

Lenin anticipated objections to the suggestion of control over literature (*literaturnoe tvorchestvo*) and justified his own case by drawing a parallel between freedom of expression and freedom of association:

> Some intellectual, an ardent champion of liberty, will shout: What, you want to impose collective control over such a delicate, individual matter as creative writing! You want workers to decide questions of science, philosophy or esthetics, and by a majority vote! You are denying the absolute freedom of absolutely individual ideological creativity!
>
> Calm yourselves, gentlemen! First of all, we are discussing Party literature and its subordination to Party control. Everyone is free to write and say whatever he likes, without any restrictions. But every voluntary association (including the Party) is also free to expel members who use the name of the Party to advocate anti-Party views. Freedom of speech and the press must be complete. But then freedom of association must be complete too. I am bound to accord you, in the name of free speech, the full right to shout, lie, and write to your heart's content. But you are bound to grant me, in the name of freedom of association, the right to enter into, or withdraw from, association with people advocating this or that view. The Party is a voluntary union (*dobrovolny soyuz*), which would inevitably break up, first ideologically and then physically, if it did not cleanse itself of people advocating anti-Party views.

Lenin's non-Marxist contemporaries seem to have been in no doubt as to the implications of Lenin's arguments for all creative literature. Since Lenin's article had appeared in the legal Russian press, this was one of those rare occasions when his opinions could be challenged by someone outside the revolutionary movement. As a rule Lenin engaged in polemics with other Marxists. He and his usual opponents disagreed on interpretation and tactics, but they shared a base of Marxist assumptions. In this instance Lenin's views were contested by someone belonging to a different wing of that special Russian institution called the intelligentsia, intellectuals of all classes and kinds who opposed the tsarist regime. At the time Lenin was writing his article (1905) members of this non-radical wing of the intelligentsia had helped Russia take the lead in advancing new forms and styles across all the arts, from painting to music and ballet. And it was one of the leading figures in the Symbolist movement, himself a prolific writer and critic, Valery Bryusov (1873–1924), who reacted at once to Lenin's arguments. His response, suggestively titled "Freedom of Speech" ("Svoboda slova"), appeared in *Vesy* (*The Scales*), which had been founded the previous year and was to become the leading literary journal of the Symbolist movement until it closed in 1909, as the Symbolist movement itself lost momentum.[16] There could be no greater contrast to the anti-Western views of Lenin and his Bolshevik wing of the Social Democratic Party than the cosmopolitan, Westward-looking outlook of *Vesy*. Bryusov was a product of two centuries of St. Petersburg culture, a culture that sought to make Russia a participant in Western civilization, not to regard it as alien or threatening.

Bryusov countered Lenin's arguments by pointing out that people would hardly think of submitting their work to a publication holding radically differing opinions from their own. Hence Lenin was really saying that there could be no difference of opinion within the Social Democratic Party. Bryusov condemned this as "fanaticism" and suggested that Lenin was merely proposing a new type of censorship, reminiscent of Catherine the Great's ambiguous declaration: "Freedom is the possibility to do anything that the laws allow." According to Bryusov, Lenin had rephrased the tsarina's definition to read: "Freedom of speech is the possibility to say anything that agrees with the principles of the Social Democratic Party."

As Bryusov suggests, Lenin had not addressed, let alone resolved, the conflict between two rights, those of speech and of assembly, either in specific cases or as a general principle. Lenin insisted: "Freedom of thought and freedom of criticism within the Party will never make us forget about the freedom of organizing people into those voluntary associations known as parties." But how much freedom could exist within a Party where *partynost* was the guiding principle? In response to Lenin's claims, Bryusov wondered what would happen in a "voluntary" association when it became the only one permitted by the party in power.

Bryusov zeroed in on what he evidently saw as the main danger of Lenin's approach, its denigration of the individual writer's freedom of personal expression:

> These are at the very least frank admissions! One can not deny that Mr. Lenin is bold: he does not shrink from drawing extreme conclusions from his ideas. But one searches in vain for any genuine love for freedom.

Bryusov was not impressed by Lenin's argument that "Absolute freedom is a bourgeois or anarchist phrase," or with his contrast between a captive bourgeois literature and a truly free proletarian literature:

> The real meaning of [Mr. Lenin's] definitions is that neither literature is free. The first because it is secretly tied to the

> bourgeoisie, and the second because it is openly tied to the proletariat. One may see the advantage of the latter in its more open admission of its enslavement, not in its greater freedom. . . . A slave belonging to the learned Plato was no less a slave, and not a free man.

Without realizing the full extent of the threat, Bryusov still sounded a warning:

> For us the type of freedom [proposed by Mr. Lenin] is simply an exchange of old chains for new. It is true that in the past writers were shackled in irons, whereas he is now offering to tie our hands only with ropes of soft hemp, but a man cannot be free even if his chains are made only of roses and lilies.

The brief exchange between Lenin and Bryusov in the fall of 1905 shows the extremism to which both sides had been led by tsarist intransigence. Here was a replay of the great debate conducted almost fifty years earlier between Chernyshevsky and Dostoevsky. Lenin's demands on writers summarized and sharpened the demands of his intellectual ancestors in Russia. But Bryusov had taken to the extreme Dostoevsky's criticisms of the civic critics; in his way Bryusov was just as extravagant in his search for "absolute freedom" as Lenin, and just as hostile to the "bourgeoisie," as they both called bearers of the mainstream Western tradition of pluralism and tolerance. In what now seems a poignant phrase, Bryusov described what he must have thought of as only the remotest possibility:

> We, seekers of absolute freedom, consider ourselves just as hostile toward the Social Democrats as toward the bourgeoisie. And, of course, should there ever come into existence a "non-class" or so-called "truly free" society, then we would become outcasts and *poètes maudits* in that society, just as we are in the bourgeois society of today.

Far from becoming a *poète maudit*, Bryusov switched sides and joined the Bolshevik Party, once it was clear that they had won the Civil War against the Whites. His article "Freedom of Speech" has never been reprinted since the twenties, although it is scheduled to appear in 1989 in *Voprosy literatury*, and is not available in English. On the other hand, Lenin's "Party Organization and Party Literature" became the Bible of the Soviet literary system.

Only twelve years after his 1905 article had appeared, the successful Bolshevik coup put Lenin in power. Lenin's preference for Chernyshevsky's style and theories naturally affected his answer to the two major cultural questions facing the infant Soviet state: What type of literature and art should it promote? What approach should be taken toward the ideologically obsolete and perhaps harmful culture of Russia's bourgeois past? Lenin insisted that the new dictatorship of the proletariat should have a traditional literature, in the style of Chernyshevsky, rather than modernist or experimental. There would be no room for Bryusov and other *poètes maudits.* Nor did Lenin have much time for the revolutionary art and literature of the time, even when they were produced by Bolshevik sympathizers, such as the poet Vladimir Mayakovsky, later canonized under Stalin as one of the founders of Soviet literature. Lenin had been brought up on the verse of Nikolai Nekrasov, a celebrated "civic poet" of the nineteenth century who was a great ally of Chernyshevsky and the radical critics. Nekrasov wrote straightforward verse describing in an idealized fashion the sad fate of the common Russian folk under tsarist rule. Lenin insisted that literature and art had to be easily understood if they were to serve as propaganda, that is, to help educate and enlighten the masses, to change their outlook and raise their political consciousness. He always argued against "elitist" art and in favor of a "populist" approach (*narodnost*). His remark in January 1923 to the German Marxist Clara Zetkin is typical of his outlook:

> Art belongs to the people. . . . It should be understood and loved by the masses. It must unite and elevate their feelings, thoughts, and will. It must stir them to activity and develop the artistic instincts within them. Should we serve exquisite sweet cake to a small minority while the worker and peasant masses are in need of black bread?[17]

Lenin's talks with Clara Zetkin capture perfectly the combination of utopianism and paternalism that marked his approach to art and to the masses, who could not be relied upon to find their own way and make their own choices.

With regard to the literature of the past, Lenin rejected the extreme theories of Proletkult, an organization of Bolsheviks who wanted to throw overboard all of bourgeois culture and create a totally new proletarian culture. He adopted a "two streams" approach, arguing that every national culture produces not only reprehensible and worthless works by bourgeois artists, but also works of lasting value that should become part of the proletariat's heritage. It was the responsibility of the Party to sort out which was which. This strategy enabled Lenin to rationalize the retention of carefully selected and interpreted works of pre-revolutionary Russian literature.

Lenin did not have a chance to implement fully his ideas on culture and art, chiefly because he was preoccupied with fighting the Civil War and then trying to preserve Soviet power, in the midst of appalling social and economic conditions caused by that internecine conflict and Lenin's own extreme policies. However, a fanatical faith in his own recipe for revolutionary change prompted him to take a series of actions that curtailed the freedom of thought that nourishes literature, and to limit the range of opportunities for readers (and writers). He created the Cheka, forerunner of the KGB, and established "terror" (his word) as a governing principle in the dictatorship of the proletariat.[18] He reintroduced the censorship, which had been extremely light from 1905 until the abdication of Tsar Nicholas II, and was abolished by the Provisional Government in April 1917. He started the Soviet state on the path toward the politicization of culture by arguing that writers can never simply express their own subjective viewpoint; they are bound to reflect their class and ideological backgrounds (the "theory of reflection," borrowed from Engels).

Lenin demanded that literature educate the *narod* and serve as an ideological arm of the Party. He adopted the same pragmatic approach to all forms of art, from poetry to architecture. Anatoly Lunacharsky, People's Commissar for Education from the Bolshevik seizure of power until he was removed from the post by Stalin in 1929, recalled in his memoirs:

> One day in 1918 Vladimir Ilyich called me in and spoke to me about the need to promote art as a means of agitation. He set out two plans he had. The first was to have revolutionary slogans inscribed on the walls of buildings, fences and other places where posters were usually hung. He suggested some of the slogans right then and there.
>
> His second plan was to erect temporary plaster monuments to great revolutionaries in both Petrograd and Moscow, and to do it on an extremely large scale. . . . Vladimir Ilyich called it "monumental propaganda."[19]

Lenin realized that the masses were illiterate and would not follow abstruse ideological disputation; they needed basic education and visual images. Here in its simplest form is the implementation of *partynost, ideinost,* and *narodnost*—art must belong to the people, and be readily accessible to them, because the Party wants its propaganda to have as immediate and effective an impact as possible. But Lenin's pragmatism was motivated by utopian dreams. One of the slogans he suggested to Lunacharsky was "The Golden Age is coming." It was this utopianism that convinced Lenin that all means he deemed necessary to achieve his dreams were justified.

Lenin did not live to see the promised land of communism, or the terrible destruction wrought by his successors. He fell ill after a stroke in 1922, and died in January 1924 at the age of 53. During the next four years, while his successors jockeyed for position, a relatively liberal period for writers continued, associated with the New Economic Policy (NEP), a compromise initiated by Lenin himself in 1921 to maintain the Bolsheviks in power. Various literary groups sprang up, ranging from the apolitical Serapion Brotherhood to the Russian Association of Proletarian Writers (RAPP), which was full of Trotskyites, who soon adapted to the new Stalinist doctrines. In 1928, when Joseph Stalin had outmaneuvered his rivals, he signalled through a Central Committee decree that the time of relative freedom for writers had come to an end:

> Literary art must be developed, its social contents must be made deeper, it must be made completely understandable for the mass reader, its circulation enlarged, etc. We must struggle for the hegemony of proletarian literature.

At first Stalin gave free rein to RAPP, headed by Leopold Averbakh, to bully other writers into submission and to force the dissolution of most other literary groups. But then on April 23, 1932 (by coincidence the anniversary of Shakespeare's birth) the Party's Central Committee announced a decision "On the Restructuring of Literary and Artistic Organizations."[20] The announcement was brief, no more than a few short paragraphs in length, but it marked a critical turning point in the cultural life of the country. The Central Committee rejoiced in the fact that "new writers and artists have come forward from the plants, factories, and collective farms," to take the place of the "alien elements" who had exercised much influence in the twenties.

Stalin had resolved that the Soviet state needed socialist literature and socialist art. No other type of art or literature, and indeed no other type of artist or writer, would be permitted. When Stalin put into place the twin pillars of the Soviet guidance system for literature—the Union of Soviet Writers, and Socialist Realism—he was in effect closing down a century-long debate about the nature of literature and the role of writers in society. By adopting Lenin's program for literature he capped a process that had begun with Belinsky and then intensified with Chernyshevsky. The notion that writers should serve the cause of improving society had been modified by Lenin to mean that they should serve the Party, since it was leading the people to a better future under communism.

The introduction of Socialist Realism as the official literary dogma in 1932–34 was part of Stalin's overall policy to declare the Soviet Union a socialist state. In a report to the Sixteenth Party Congress in 1930 Stalin had declared that the culture built by the dictatorship of the proletariat would be "socialist in content and national in form, and would continue to exist as such until the global victory of the proletariat, at which time both of its aspects would become socialist."[21] Stalin then persuaded the first session of the 17th Party Congress, which met January 30–February 4, 1932, to make the achievement of socialism part of the official Party program. A resolution was passed which called for converting the "entire working populace" into "active builders of a classless socialist society."

By abandoning the notion of the Soviet Union as a dictatorship of the proletariat, Stalin dispensed with the necessity of defining proletarian literature—a subject of endless, bitter arguments throughout the twenties. Here too Stalin showed himself to be a faithful follower of Lenin, who thirty years earlier had argued in *What Is To Be Done?* that the Social Democrats should try to raise the political consciousness of all classes of society, not just that of the industrial proletariat. Stalin now implemented Lenin's program by declaring that the new socialist state would need a socialist literature, one produced by and for all Soviet citizens. Since the bourgeoisie had been defeated, only two classes officially remained: the industrial workers and the peasants, with a "stratum" (*prosloika*) made up of the intelligentsia. However, there no longer existed any class conflict, since everyone was united with and behind the Party. This in turn meant that all professionals, including those of bourgeois origin, and writers whom Trofsky had called "fellow travellers" must now be incorporated into the new socialist society and encouraged to participate in the great work that lay ahead.

Like Lenin, Stalin adopted an organizational approach. Just as Lenin had created "a party of a new type" to implement Marxism, so too now Stalin created the Writers' Union, organizing writers in a new comprehensive way to implement Socialist Realism.[22] Maxim Gorky, longtime friend of Lenin and sometime supporter of the Bolshevik Party, was named as honorary president of the Organizing Committee, which was chaired by Ivan Gronsky, chief editor of the newspaper *Izvestia*, with Valery Kirpotin of the powerful Communist Academy in the more important position of Organizing Committee secretary. The latter two men, neither of whom was a creative writer, were assigned the task of finding *ex post facto* ideological justification in the works of Marx, Engels, and Lenin for Stalin's decisions.[23]

From the outset, official spokesmen stressed that Socialist Realism was not a new method or style, and that it had certainly not been imposed by the Party on writers. Maxim Gorky was proclaimed the major progenitor of Socialist Realism, and his novel *Mother*, written in the Catskills of New York State and published in Russia in 1906, was proclaimed the leading examplar of the method. The novel tells the story of a mother and son struggling heroically against tsarist oppression. Stalin must have been well aware of Lenin's views on literature and the arts, and probably had read the 1905 article on "Party Organization and Party Literature." However, since Maxim Gorky enjoyed respect among writers of all social backgrounds and political persuasions, Stalin used him to lend prestige to the new organization and its literary credo. In return Stalin permitted Gorky to think that the new style would be very close to his own.[24]

Gorky, like Lenin, was a direct cultural descendant of Chernyshevsky. His prose fiction, written in a straightforward style, combined pity for the suffering poor with idealistic hopes for the better life to come. It was chiefly through Gorky's influence that Soviet literature returned to the domestic tradition initiated by Belinsky and Chernyshevsky. Following in their footsteps, Gorky wanted to create an idealistic literature, a literature of social uplift—a style better named Red Romanticism than Socialist Realism. Gorky gave the new method its distinctly optimistic bent. In his essay "The Old Man and the New," he described the type of "new Soviet man" that the times required and that literature should portray:

> A new type of man is springing up in the Soviet Union. He possesses a faith in the organizing power of reason. . . . He is conscious of being the builder of a new world, and although his conditions of life are still arduous, he knows that it is his arm and the purpose of his rational will to create different conditions and he has no grounds for pessimism.[25]

The allusion to the "old man" and the "new man" recalls St. Paul's insistence that believers should "put off the old man" and "put on the new man" (Ephesians, 4:22 and 24). Like St. Paul, Gorky wanted converts to his faith. He worked tirelessly to support beginning writers, as long as they wrote in the style he approved.

The Statutes of the Writers' Union, published in the verbatim report of the First Congress, confirmed that Socialist Realism was the basic method of Soviet literature and criticism, and laid out in considerable detail the various ways in which members were expected to fulfill their tasks and responsibilities in socialist construction. Only at the end of a long list of requirements were writers urged to produce works "of lofty artistic importance," but immediately afterwards they were reminded that they should give pride of place to "the great wisdom and heroism of the Communist Party."[26]

Providing they met their obligations and promised to abide by the rules, creative writers in all genres (fiction, poetry, drama) and literary critics were eligible to join. Purely literary qualifications were left rather vague. Applicants merely had to show that they had published works, but these works could have been "posted on walls in institutes and clubs." As a result the ardent Stalin loyalist Vesevolod Vishnevsky was able to report on behalf of the Credentials Committee (*Mandatnaya komissia*) that fully 42.6 percent of the delegates were of peasant origin and 27.3 percent of worker origin, while 18.4 percent were from the "working intelligentsia" (the remaining 11.7 percent were listed as "other").[27] In short, the statistics tell a chilling demographic tale: the pre-Soviet intelligentsia, descendants of the Europeanized gentry who produced the great literature, art, and music for which Russia is known today, had been killed off, forced to emigrate, or were simply being excluded from playing a role in the new organization.

There was no problem in attracting members of the now triumphant class of workers and peasants to join the Union. In his report to the Congress on the proposed Statutes, which were approved without any discussion, another young Stalinist, Pavel Yudin, was rather vague about exact figures; he stated that "about 4,000" people had applied for admission to the Union, with "about 2,500" being accepted; of these "over 1,500" were admitted to full membership, and "the rest" were admitted as candidates, that is, probationary members, as in the Party itself. In fact, the ethnic breakdown of the membership provided by Yudin himself adds up to a total of about 2,200 rather than 2,500.[28]

Without a doubt, many applicants were genuinely enthusiastic about the idea of assisting in the creation of a new society. However, others must have been attracted by the obvious material advantages that membership would bring. These were laid out in the Statutes, making it clear to everyone that this would be a powerful organization with enormous resources at its disposal. The Union was declared to have the "rights of a legal entity" and thus empowered to own property and sign contracts. It could establish subsidiary institutions to provide "cultural and material services for writers (housing, clubs, retreats, restaurants, museums, libraries, reading rooms, bookstores, courses, exhibits, competitions, publishing houses, journals, etc.)." In a decree dated July 28, 1934, the Council of People's Commissars ordered the establishment of a Literary Fund (Litfund) to administer and finance these services to writers.[29]

The Union was established as a national organization, with

branches in each of the Soviet Union's seven Republics at that time, with the sole exception of the Russian Soviet Federated Socialist Republic (RSFSR) which, as in the Party, was given the honor of being governed by the central apparatus. Members from the Russian Republic in fact dominated the Union, accounting for 1,535 of about 2,200 members (of course, not all of these were ethnic Russians). Most writers' organizations in the Republics were formed before the First Congress of the Writers' Union; they held their own congresses in 1934, in part to elect delegates, and to receive instruction in Socialist Realism.[30] All these Republic organizations were controlled by local Party secretaries and were run from the center by an apparatus in Moscow, consisting of a Presidium and Secretariat, formally elected by the Board (*Pravlenie*), as well as a Central Auditing Committee (*Tsentralnaya revizionnaya komissia*), whose responsibilities were to review the Union's financial affairs periodically and make a report to the membership at congresses. The branch organizations had a structure and chain of command similar to that of the central Writers' Union in Moscow. Both the organizational structure and the centralized control by the Party echoed patterns already established for trade unions, councils (or soviets), and other organizations in the country.

The assembled delegates were called upon to elect the "governing organs" (*rukovodyashchie organy*) for the congress: these were (and remain) a Presidium, a Secretariat, a Credentials Committee (*Mandatnaya komissia*), and an Editing Committee (*Redaktsionnaya komissia*) to produce the stenographic report. The procedure, still followed, is for someone to propose that each body consist of a specific number of people. Once that proposal is approved unanimously, the same person then reads out a list of names to fill that body, and again the proposal is accepted unanimously by delegates raising their *mandaty* or *udostoverenia*, that is, their congress credentials or identity cards. The Leningrad poet Nikolai Tikhonov, who was not a Party member but a model of the non-Party functionary totally loyal to the Party, proposed the number and membership for all the congress governing organs, even including his own name for inclusion in the Presidium. Later it became customary for a different person to be called upon for each body. It is also the rule that each person will say that he is offering a proposal or slate of candidates on behalf of a series of delegations from various parts of the country. Tikhonov himself declared that he was speaking for the delegations from Moscow, Leningrad, the Ukraine, Belorussia, and the three Caucasian Republics. His proposals all received unanimous approval by the delegates without any discussion or additional names being suggested. Nor did any delegate wonder, at least not out loud, why the Presidium should consist of 52 people, the Secretariat of 15 people, and so forth.

The same procedures were followed at the conclusion of the Congress, when delegates were called upon to elect the organs that would run the Union (as opposed to the organs elected to organize the Congress itself). This time a Ukrainian poet, Ivan Kulik, who had been a Party member since 1914 and was president of the Ukrainian Writers' Organization, served as proposer. His moment of glory was short-lived, because he was arrested in 1937 and died in 1941 (apparently in the Gulag), thus sharing the fate of several of the writers whose names he was proposing. Kulik declared that he was speaking on behalf of the delegations from Moscow, Leningrad, the Ukraine, Belorussia, the Caucasus, and the Central Asian republics. He proposed a Board of 101 members and an Auditing Committee of 20 members. On this occasion the chairman of the session actually asked the delegates if they wanted to vote on the lists of names "as a whole" (*v tselom*), rather than "individually" (*personalno*). Delegates obligingly shouted "*v tselom*." A few delegates did object from the floor that they thought 20 people were too few for the Auditing Committee, but cries of "That's fine" (*Khorosho*) drowned out these objections and the voting proceeded smoothly without further interruption.[31]

As soon as Gorky had made a brief opening statement and elections to various bodies had been briskly processed, the keynote address was given by Andrei Zhdanov, Stalin's chief spokesman on cultural affairs in the Party Secretariat (and later the Politburo) from 1934 until his death in 1948. Adopting Stalin's favorite technique of controlling the agenda by asking rhetorical questions, Zhdanov made it clear that the Party was expecting quick results: "Comrade Stalin has called our writers engineers of human souls (*inzhenery chelovecheskikh dush*). What does that mean? What responsibilities does that title impose upon you?" He answered his own questions by declaring that Soviet literature would be openly tendentious, it would abandon old-fashioned romanticism for a new "revolutionary romanticism" that would show the way to the communist future. He warned writers that they should be guided by the new method of Socialist Realism, which required them to portray not mere "objective reality in a scholastic or lifeless manner," but in its "revolutionary development." Repeating the exact phrasing of the draft Statutes, which had been published six months earlier, Zhdanov explained this meant that "the truthfulness and historical concreteness of the artistic portrayal should be combined with the ideological remolding and education of the people in the spirit of socialism."[32]

The First Congress lasted for two weeks and consisted in a seemingly endless stream of more than 200 speeches, reports, and declarations; the verbatim report of the congress runs to 700 double-columned pages. Time and again, speakers returned to a few basic themes and motifs: the direct link between writers and the people, hostility toward the bourgeois West, a sense of pride and specialness in being Soviet and of exciting opportunities open to writers, simmering divisions between pre-revolutionary writers and the creatures of Stalin, and lavish praise of Stalin himself as an all-wise leader. For example, Ivan Lezhnev declared that "comrade Stalin has shown himself to be the outstanding figure of our age." Alexander Fadeyev, destined to lead the Union later, described Stalin as "that mighty genius of the working class."

The proceedings were frequently interrupted by a series of carefully staged floor demonstrations and visits from delegations of workers, collective farmers, and military detachments—all greeted with "stormy applause" (*burnye aplodismenty*) by nearly 600 delegates from across the country. Each delegation declared its support for the writers, but also announced that it expected works of fiction, drama, and verse devoted to its members and their heroic struggles for socialism. During one session chaired by Boris Pasternak, a group of Moscow Pioneers (a children's organization) marched into the hall with bugles blaring and band playing, then sang a song of welcome to the delegates, urging them to produce more inspiring works.[33] Once the enthusiastic Pioneers had marched out with fife and drum, like characters in a Shakespeare play, Pasternak, who was chairing the session, remarked with studied calm: "Comrades, after that truly exciting scene, permit me to introduce the next speaker." In his memoirs, Ehrenburg describes Pasternak as sitting thoughtfully throughout with a beatific smile on his face, even when he was being attacked by one of the speakers he had himself introduced.

Later in this same session a contingent of soldiers from the Moscow garrison entered the hall to the accompaniment of bugles and shouts of "hurrah!" A representative pledged his comrades' undying loyalty to the Party and the people, declaring that they and the writers were all warriors in the service of the working class. After cheers for the Motherland, for the nation and for "great Stalin" the contingent departed singing, garlanded with flowers. Then Vsevolod Vishnevsky read out a formal greeting to Klim Voroshilov, Politburo member and People's Commissar of Defense. Not to be outdone, a contingent of naval reservists entered the hall; once again a representative wished the delegates well, but on this occasion gave them a brief lecture on their unjustifiable neglect of the sea and sailors as exciting subjects for future novels, plays, and poems. The military and anti-Nazi tone of the congress faithfully reflected official Soviet concern about the rise of Hitler, who had become German Chancellor the previous year.[34]

In keeping with Stalin's professed conciliatory attitude, writers of all persuasions were permitted, indeed encouraged to speak at the Congress. Even a few of Stalin's political foes such as Bukharin and Radek spoke. Bukharin gave the keynote address on contemporary Russian poetry, displaying his familiarity with a wide range of poets as well as with European literature.[35] He praised the efforts of many new proletarian poets, but showed with frequent quotations that the general level of Russian poetry was embarrassingly low and needed much improvement; poetry was more than simply rhyming the latest editorial in Pravda. Bukharin focused on Pasternak's poetry, implicitly contrasting it to that of Mayakovsky, the Stalinists' choice as poet of the age. However, he carefully avoided mentioning three of the most celebrated Russian poets of the time, Anna Akhmatova, Nikolai Klyuev, and even Osip Mandelshtam, whom he had helped keep out of serious trouble on several occasions. As he well knew, Akhmatova (whose first husband, Nikolai Gumilyov, had been shot by the Cheka in 1921) remained a "non-person" in Russian literature, while Mandelshtam and Klyuev were already under arrest. (Both later died in the Gulag.)

The century-long debate over the purpose of literature and the function of writers had now become one-sided, a foregone conclusion: the descendants of Chernyshevsky were in control. The tone was set by Maxim Gorky who, as the designated head of the Soviet literary world, dominated the Congress. At one point he even asked delegates to stop praising him so lavishly. In a lengthy opening address, Gorky specifically attacked Chernyshevsky's chief opponent Dostoevsky as the most hostile writer to the Bolshevik cause, and then asserted that Western literature had been in decline since the Renaissance. Gorky's speech was a diatribe against Western culture and, by implication against much of nineteenth-century Russian literature. Gorky rejected "European Russian literature" because of its "superfluous heroes," who failed to take action against tsarist conditions. Here Gorky is echoing almost word-for-word the critical articles of Chernyshevsky and his fellow critics, adding a Nietzschean twist.

Supporters of the opposing view of the writer's role, that is, the followers of the great Russian writers of the pre-revolutionary period like Dostoevsky and Turgenev, who had opposed the civic critics, or of Bryusov, who had taken exception to Lenin's 1905 article, did not dare to speak out publicly against Gorky. However, some of the Western writers present, chiefly those from France, felt obliged (and secure enough) to challenge Gorky personally and more generally the overall tone and approach that prevailed at the congress. André Malraux tried to establish a few basic distinctions between art and reality, specifically between great art and mere documentary copying. As a foreigner he could afford the luxury of criticizing Zhdanov, and by implication Stalin himself:

> It may well be true that writers are engineers of souls, but let us not forget that an engineer's highest calling is to invent. Art is not submission, art is conquest (*Iskusstvo—ne podchinenie, iskusstvo—zavoevanie*).[36]

Malraux's statement was greeted with applause, as was his remark that Soviet culture would only gain prestige abroad through works of genuine artistry, such as those of the late Mayakovsky and the living Pasternak. Doubts and concerns such as these expressed by Malraux, Mauroix, and other Western guests carried unusual weight since they were being advanced not by bourgeois foes, but by celebrated writers with pronounced Soviet or at least leftist sympathies.

However, it was one of the lesser known French authors, Jean-Richard Bloch (1886–1947), who offered the most incisive critique of the new Soviet literary dispensation. Bloch, a longtime Communist sympathizer, continued to believe in the possibility of a proletarian literature, although this notion had now been abandoned by Stalin. Bloch began by confirming Gorky's portrait of Western bourgeois literature, especially in his own country, as part of a culture in imminent decline (repeating in a minor key a major refrain that echoed throughout the Congress, and was of course an article of faith in Nazi pronouncements at this same time). He pronounced Soviet culture both young and lively, whereas French culture, though it had a long tradition, was merely surface brilliance with no substance or vigor. Bloch praised his Soviet hosts for "smashing the barrier between the mass reader, even though he may be poorly educated, and the most progressive members of the intelligentsia." In a rather involved metaphor, he likened the Soviet masses to a Sleeping Beauty, destined to be awakened by the handsome Princes of the Writers' Union.

Bloch then proceeded to disagree directly with Maxim Gorky, who had argued that Soviet writers, unlike those in the bourgeois West, were not in an adversarial relationship with their society and government. No, said Bloch, even here in the Soviet Union a writer would have to adopt a contrary stance, although naturally not in the sense of class conflict:

> A writer is not merely a "poet-laureate" as in old England. If he were, then he would be fulfilling a role that is certainly important, but rather comical. He would actually be playing the part, as the ironical French phrase says, of the "inspector of work already done." The writer would risk gradually becoming a social parasite, as happened in Classical Antiquity or in the royal courts [of renaissance Europe] when a writer's job was simply to repeat to the monarch: "How handsome you are, how wise, how great, and how just."[37]

Bloch closed his speech with a reminder that writers address different audiences; one may write for a relatively small audience, while another might address a mass audience. Both writers are worthy of support; it is not necessary for all writers to be exactly the same. This call for pluralism was greeted with polite applause, not the standing ovation that followed the speeches of many foreign guests.

The only Russian writer to speak in the same forthright manner as Bloch and other foreign guests was Ilya Ehrenburg (1891–1967), who had translated and delivered Bloch's address. He may have been emboldened to do so because at that time he lived in France and served a very useful role as a respected and sophisticated representative of Soviet literature abroad. Ehrenburg first attacked what he called the "dying world" of Western capitalism, then switched his focus to the contemporary literary scene in the Soviet Union. Bourgeois novels portrayed the modern hero from one side only, as a romantic lover, without any reference to other aspects of his life. But, said Ehrenburg, Soviet novels err at the opposite extreme by telling us only about the hero's work; we need to know more about characters as human beings. He went on to attack the tendency to link literary works too closely with authors' social beliefs, so that artistic failures become viewed as crimes, and successes as a reason for "rehabilitation." Ehrenburg went out of his way to defend both Yury Olesha and Isaak Babel, two non-Party writers who had come under repeated attack for writing too little since Stalin had assumed power. He said that he himself was as prolific as a rabbit, but he insisted on the right of other writers to stay pregnant with works as long as an elephant. He regretted that "social command" often became simply "command" and called for an end to the "administrative approach to literature" (*vedomstvenny podkhod k literature*). Ehrenburg charged that much in Soviet culture was provincial and eclectic, reminding his listeners that simplicity could only be achieved through great art. He was interrupted several times by applause and laughter, and received loud cheers at the end of his speech.

The few remaining Russian delegates who shared Ehrenburg's views spoke with a great deal more circumspection. Pasternak, who was verbally abused on a number of occasions by other delegates, gave a very short speech, in the enigmatic style he adopted at difficult moments in his life. He declared that the truly "lofty poetical language" heard at the Congress had been pronounced not by delegates, but by members of the various delegations that had visited to express greetings and hopes for the future of Soviet socialism. He recalled wanting to help a woman working on the construction of the Moscow Metro, who had come to the congress (as part of a delegation) carrying a heavy piece of equipment. Another writer on the podium had laughed at him for displaying the "delicate sensibility of a member of the intelligentsia" (*intelligentskaya chuvstvitelnost*), said Pasternak, but at that moment he had felt as though the woman were his sister, someone he had known for a long time. Pasternak then went on to say that the poetry heard at the Congress was really prose: "Poetry is the language of organic fact, i.e., of the fact with living consequences." He closed by expressing the fear that all the warmth with which the people and the state had surrounded writers might turn them into "literary dignitaries" (*literaturnye sanovniki*). Writers must take care to stay close to their sources of inspiration; they must love the people and the Motherland.

Viktor Shklovsky, one of the leaders of the Formalist movement in Russian literary criticism and therefore equally vulnerable to attack, also adopted an enigmatic style, but one leavened with irony. In very brief remarks, Shklovsky simply took the statements of Gorky and others to extremes, in a curious way making use of the device of "estrangement" (*ostranenie*), which he had claimed in his Formalist days was a fundamental technique of a writer seeking to shock the reader into paying attention to his works. He recalled Gorky's attacks on Dostoevsky and declared that, if Dostoevsky had attended the Congress, then the delegates, as the descendants of humanity with responsibility for the world's future, would have had the right to condemn him as a traitor: "Dostoevsky cannot be understood outside the Revolution; he can only be understood as a traitor." Shklovsky called upon the new Soviet writers to express their feelings more, to be sentimental, but they must be sentimental in a better and stronger way than the bourgeoisie. He praised Mayakovsky and then regretted that the poet had shot himself at the wrong time (1930); the Revolution needed songs now, not sacrifices. Shklovsky declared that writers must have a plan, they needed a vision of the future: "We must write for the whole world, in the name of humanism, against the rise of a new Dark Age."[38]

The prose writer Yury Olesha gave a touching speech, in which he confessed that he was confused by the new demands of Socialist Realism and doubted whether he would be able to respond to them adequately. He tried to explain that a writer creates, uses his imagination; he must try to picture what it is like to be poor or young. Olesha confessed that he himself had found that he could not imagine being a young construction worker or revolutionary:

> This was not my theme. I could have gone to a construction project, lived at a factory among workers, described them in a sketch, even in a novel, but this was not my theme, it was not in my bloodstream, not a part of my breathing self. I would have lied, invented; I would not have had what is called inspiration.[39]

Olesha summed up the position of the "fellow travelers" (*poputchiki*) still struggling to adjust to Soviet realities.

But these were voices crying in the Stalinist wilderness, swamped by the enthusiastic shouts of the worker and peasant delegates, direct beneficiaries of Stalin's cultural revolution of 1928–31. Most of the delegates were full of confidence about the future of the new Soviet literature, whose horizons and potential seemed limitless. The sense of flexing muscles, of realizing new opportunities, pervaded most of the speeches. Konstantin Fedin, a member of the apolitical Serapion Brotherhood in the early twenties who was just beginning his career as a leading Union functionary, described a collective commitment to building socialism: "We have found a broad theme that is common to all socialist literatures: the contemporary theme, the theme of the reality around us." Leonid Leonov, another former Serapion, declared that he and his colleagues had the great good fortune to live in "the most heroic period of world history." Vsevolod Vishnevsky, who within a year or so would be denouncing countless colleagues to the NKVD, the People's Commissariat of Internal Affairs, that is, Stalin's secret police, exclaimed: "Our Congress is proof that what Lenin bequeathed us and conjured us to complete has been done."

Leonid Sobolev began his speech with a phrase that continues to be quoted approvingly by orthodox Soviet critics to this day: "The Party and Government have given the writer everything, and taken away from him only one thing—the right to write badly." He ended his remarks on the same exultant note: "I believe that . . . we can create a truly great literature, that is, fulfill the task assigned to us by the Government and the Party."[40] Gorky quoted with approval Sobolev's remark about the "right to write badly" and added a classic example of self-deception and wishful thinking:

> The Party and Government are also taking away from us the right to order one another what to do, offering us in return the right to teach one another. To teach, meaning to share with one another our experience. That is all. That is all, nothing more.[41]

In a speech laced with wit and subtle irony, the prose writer Isaak Babel said that he would like to follow Gorky in praising Sobolev's remark, but noted with tongue in cheek that the right to write badly was "a very important right, and to take it away from us is no small thing. (laughter) It is a privilege that we were taking full advantage of."[42] Babel's reactions to Socialist Realism were exactly the same as Olesha's, but he adopted a different tactic in trying to defend himself. He explained his own failure to write suitable works by declaring that he himself had decided to cultivate a new genre, the "genre of silence."

The overall mood at the Congress was euphoric. Even today one of the very few survivors of those times looks back at the First Writers' Congress as "a celebration of Soviet literature."[43] Gorky spoke for the majority with his enthusiastic description of the emerging energy and power of writers: "The Union is being created not only to unite writers in a physical sense, but so that a professional union should make them aware of their collective strength." In his closing address Gorky admonished his fellow writers that they should cast aside old bourgeois habits. Their task was not to follow their own individual paths, but to work together—in groups if necessary—to portray the "new reality" according to a single unified method. He criticized Ehrenburg for his "skepticism" with regard to collective writing; if brigades of workers can produce concrete, then why, he asked, should a brigade of writers not be able to produce literary works? "I feel emboldened to say that it is precisely the method of collective work on literary material that will help us understand better what Socialist Realism really ought to be."

In response to the speeches by Pasternak, Babel, Olesha, and other fellow travellers, Gorky said he felt highly optimistic:

> Those who were considered non-Party men, who were "wavering," have recognized—with a complete sincerity I cannot doubt—that Bolshevism is the single most active (*boevoi*) idea guiding their work and, in a word, their art.[44]

Gorky declared that readers [rather than Stalin] were calling writers "engineers of souls" and demanding that they describe the workers' thoughts, feelings, and heroic deeds "in simple language and in truthful images." Again adapting slightly a Stalinist phrase, Gorky said that the new literature should "remain individual in its forms, and Socialist-Leninist in its fundamental governing ideas." He also expressed the hope that the phrase "non-Party writer" would become merely a formal designation without any real meaning.

Apparently stung by the critical remarks of several Western writers at the Congress, Gorky argued that doubts about the place of the individual personality within a classless society had no foundation; such doubts were merely "academic and philosophical" since the matter had been resolved in the Soviet Union. Soviet writers were in a much more favored position than their Western counterparts. In phrases that would sound like black humor in less than three years, Gorky claimed:

> In Europe writers feel the ever increasing weight of bourgeois oppression, they fear the revival of medieval barbarism, which will in all likelihood involve a new inquisition to root out heretical thoughts.
>
> In Europe the bourgeoisie and governments are treating honest writers with increasing hostility. We do not have a bourgeoisie, and our government leaders are our teachers and our comrades, comrades in the fullest sense of the word.

Gorky urged delegates to join the struggle, for "books are the most important and most powerful weapons in socialist culture."[45] He reminded his fellow writers of the enormous debt of gratitude they owed to the Soviet government for allowing the Congress to take place and for providing the necessary facilities and funds to make it such a glorious success. Gorky then led a series of cheers ending with: "Long live the Party of Lenin, leader of the proletariat, and long live the leader of the Party, Joseph Stalin!" The delegates then joined together in the singing of the revolutionary hymn, the Internationale.

Set against the backdrop of one hundred years of extraordinary achievements by Russian writers and of genuine debate about the proper function of literature, Gorky's final address makes melancholy reading. The transcendental cosmos of the poetic imagination, adumbrated by Schiller and the German idealists, has been brought down to earth, reified as industrial projects and collective farms. Instead of being free to create their own reality, the writer is now instructed to describe an idealized reality, to gild the Potemkin villages erected by the state. The epigones of Chernyshevsky were no longer exiled to Siberia, but sitting on the podium of the Writers' Congress in Moscow, prepared to run the organization that the Party had contoured in order to help make Vera Pavlovna's dream a reality. Writers were expected to play the role of the "Radiant Beauty" and show Soviet readers a vision of the ideal world of the future.

Nevertheless, it is not hard to see why, in the euphoria of the moment, so many writers looked forward to helping Soviet society with their literary talents. According to the testimony of the Danish writer Martin Andersen Nexo, who was also present as a delegate:

> It's a fine thing to be a writer in Soviet Russia. . . . Representatives of Soviet literature are an energetic, joyous tribe, unlike Western European writers, even those who are revolutionary. Their very bearing shows that they are children of the triumphant class, and they themselves are participating in the country's construction, assisting in the general push forward.[46]

In his memoirs, published during the Khrushchev period, Ilya Ehrenburg confirmed this rosy picture: "In general, it was a good time and we all thought that in 1937 when, according to the rules, the Second Congress of Writers was due to meet, we would be living in paradise."[47]

In fact, many of the delegates, and millions of other Soviet citizens, would be either dead or dying in the Gulag by 1937, the height of Stalin's Great Terror. The show trials of Bukharin, Radek, and of other speakers at the First Congress would be held in the very same building as the first Congress, the eighteenth-century Assembly Mansion of the Nobility (*Blagorodnoe dvoryanskoe sobranie*), renamed the Union Building (*Dom soyuzov*) by order of Lenin in 1919, and the site of Lenin's lying-in-state on his death in 1924.[48] All evidence that the first Congress had ever taken place was "suppressed": the verbatim account of the First Congress was quickly removed from circulation and has never been reprinted.

2

Whip and Gingerbread

Poetry is respected only in this country—people are killed for it. There's no country in which more people are killed for it.

OSIP MANDELSHTAM

The two decades separating the First and Second Congresses represent an extraordinary timeframe in the life of the Union. Simultaneously, the Union acted as an agency of Stalin's Terror against its own members, and as a cornucopia of privileges and luxuries that set them apart from the rest of the population. Members of the Union suffered proportionately just as many losses as did the Party and the military, and yet those who managed to survive formed part of a new cultural elite, enjoying quality housing, food, clothing, opportunities to travel abroad, and other material benefits unavailable to ordinary citizens. Whether its members were pampered or persecuted, the Writers' Union offered a classic example of Stalin's "principle of institutionalized insecurity."[1] With writers, as with other professionals, Stalin made effective use of whip and gingerbread (*knut i pryanik*). While his policy was a deliberate and calculated one, Stalin executed it on such a vast scale and so capriciously that the Terror swept away many people who were not only innocent but also personally loyal to him and to the Party. The devil not only took the hindmost, but those at the head of the line too, as many Soviet citizens denounced neighbors and friends in a frantic effort to save themselves.

Just as the Soviet government did not function according to its 1936 Constitution, so too the Writers' Union ignored its own Statutes. The national congress was stated to be the "highest organ" of the Union; it alone could elect the Board and Presidium, which served as the legislative and executive branches of the organization between congresses, scheduled to take place every three years.[2] But delegates at the First Congress had not even been consulted about the formation of the most important ruling organs of the Union—the Presidium and the Secretariat—whose membership was chosen at a closed meeting of the Party group of the Congress (*Partgruppa syezda*), held on the last morning of the Congress (September 1). At a plenum of the Board on September 2, Ivan Kulik (head of the Ukrainian Republic branch of the Union) announced "on behalf of the Party group" that the Presidium would consist of 37 people and the Secretariat of five people, with Alexander Shcherbakov as First Secretary.[3] Kulik became a member of the Secretariat, so he was proposing his own name for "election." Shcherbakov was not a writer, but a full-time Party apparatchik, and had not even been a Congress delegate.

Since the Second Congress was not held for twenty years, and the members of the Board and Presidium were shuffled in and out according to Stalin's whim, none of the Union's official decisions were statutorily legal during this entire time. The Statutes also stated that the Board in Moscow was to hold a plenary session or plenum at least three times a year. This rule too went by the wayside. Only fifteen such plenums were held between 1934 and 1954.[4] Very little business was enacted even at the few meetings of the Board and Presidium that did take place, because writers were afraid that anything they might say would be used as evidence against them. At most sessions a majority of the speakers were not members of the Union, but various officials from the Party and government apparatus, who lectured writers on their responsibilities or argued for the expulsion of Union members, and even members of the Board and Presidium. As at the First Congress, meetings of the Board were frequently interrupted with cheers and singing, but now only at the mention of Stalin's name—and nobody wanted to be the first to stop clapping.

For the first few months following the 1934 Congress, the Presidium, with Maxim Gorky as President (or Chairman, *predsedatel*), did meet to discuss and resolve various procedural matters. The Presidium consisted of 37 people chosen from the Board and was dominated by Stalinists and ideological apparatchiks, such as Lev Kamenev, Valery Kirpotin, Ivan Kulik, Alexander Shcherbakov, Vladimir Stavsky, and Pavel Yudin, and malleable writers, such as Maxim Gorky himself, Konstantin Fedin, Vsevolod Ivanov, Leonid Leonov, Mikhail Sholokhov, Fyodor Panfyorov, Alexander Serafimovich, Aleksei Tolstoy, Alexander Fadeyev, and Demyan Bedny (whom Max Eastman described as the "poetic staff-officer of the Stalin clique").

The loyalty of the Presidium to Stalin and his policies was unquestioned. However, with 37 members it was too large to act as a true executive body, and the much smaller Secretariat, of which Gorky was not a member, soon became the dominating authority within the Union. This may have been Stalin's intention all along, since he had himself risen to power by using the Party Secretariat to gain authority over the Politburo. The Union Secretariat consisted of only five men following the 1934 Congress, and it remained quite small throughout Stalin's reign. It grew to 13 members in 1946, but had dropped to 11 by the Second Congress in 1954.[5] Alexander Shcherbakov served as First Secretary and was joined by two other full-time Party bureaucrats, Vladimir Stavsky and Ivan Kulik.[6] The two other members of the Secretariat were genuine writers, devoted to the Bolshevik cause, but without any political authority: Vsevolod Ivanov (1895–1963), whose reputation rested on his early Civil War novella, *Armored Train No. 14–69* (*Bronepoezd 14–69*) and other tales set in Siberia; and an Iranian poet, Abulkasim Lakhuti (1887–1957), a leftist who had lived in the Soviet Union since 1922 and had worked to promote the creation of a new Soviet Tajik literature.[7] He had been added to the Secretariat as a gesture to the Central Asian Republics.

While Gorky was alive, his great prestige and the personal favor of Stalin allowed him to resist the apparatchiks' attempts to preempt decisions. In his memoirs Nikita Khrushchev characterizes Shcherbakov as a "poisonous snake" who angered Gorky by trying to impose his will over the Union's affairs: "Gorky wasn't the sort of person Shcherbakov could boss around and Shcherbakov ended up being transferred at Gorky's request."[8] Gorky may have won this round, but he had already permitted the Presidium to expel members from the Union for "lack of ideological vigilance." Not long after Shcherbakov's departure to head the Leningrad Provincial Committee (*obkom*) in early 1936, Gorky fell ill and died on the operating table. Gorky certainly passed from the scene at a most convenient time for Stalin, having fulfilled his purpose in blessing the creation of both the Union and Socialist Realism. Nikolai Bukharin, putative author of the famous "Letter of an Old Bolshevik," suggested that Gorky's departure left Stalin free to mount an all-out attack on the friends and colleagues of Lenin, the leading figures of the Bolshevik movement.[9]

Whatever role as inhibitor Gorky may have played, after his death the arrests and executions of members of the Union accelerated at an incredible rate. It is almost certain that from 1935 to 1938 more people were expelled from the Union than were admitted to its ranks. New members had to be sponsored; what if the proposed member should then be arrested as a "Trotskyite wrecker"? Stalin operated on guilt by association, and the crime of having nominated a "traitor" to Writers' Union membership meant not only dooming oneself, but one's whole family, as well as friends and associates. Even if a writer was proposed and admitted to the Union, it was no guarantee of safety. On some occasions writers became members and were then arrested almost at once. The weekly magazine *Ogonyok* reported the fate of one momentary member:

> On February 23, 1938, D. I. Gachev was admitted into the Union, then arrested the following day and accused of Trotstyite counter-revolutionary activities. He served eight years in the camps of Kolyma, but a few months before he was scheduled for release his sentence was rolled over for another ten years. He died at the beginning of 1946, but how exactly is not known.[10]

Members new and old, famous and obscure, were all swept away indiscriminately. One of the more prominent victims of the Terror in Leningrad was the poet Nikolai Zabolotsky (1903–58). He was arrested in 1938 but survived torture and later terrible deprivation in the Gulag to be released in 1946. He was accused, incredibly, of participating in a counter-revolutionary plot with several other Leningrad writers, headed by Nikolai Tikhonov—the same non-Party loyalist who had figured prominently at the First Congress of Writers. Other names mentioned during Zabolotsky's interrogation were those of Konstantin Fedin and Samuil Marshak. All three were left untouched, but many other writers and critics were arrested, as the circle of "criminals" widened.[11]

Just how many writers were "repressed" (*repressirovany*) may never be known. Reliable facts and figures are difficult to obtain because the NKVD concealed the true fate of many of its victims. Families of victims were told that their loved ones had been sentenced to "ten years without right of correspondence" (*10 let bez prava perepisi*); it was only much later that they understood that this was a code phrase for immediate execution.[12] Under Mikhail Gorbachev's campaign for glasnost, it came to light that for five years, beginning in 1937 and continuing until the German invasion, the NKVD carried out executions day and night outside Kiev and Minsk; the bodies were discovered in mass graves similar to those used by the Nazis.

Long before glasnost, private Soviet citizens attempted to gauge the numbers of Union members arrested and killed during the Great Terror. In 1974 the historian Roy Medvedev, who remained a Marxist but was at odds with the Brezhnev regime, reported some estimates suggesting that between 1936 and 1939 "more than

600 writers were arrested, that is, almost one-third of the Union membership."[13] Shocked by this figure, Eduard Beltov, an editorial assistant at the literary journal *Druzhba narodov*, began collecting data from published and unpublished sources on Stalin's victims.

After nearly 15 years of research, by 1988 Beltov had assembled a card catalogue of some 17,000 public figures in political, military, and cultural life. His data showed that the number of writers, chiefly members of the Union, arrested during the whole Stalin period had been about 2,000, of whom half died in prisons or camps.[14] Beltov was quick to stress that all national literatures, large and small alike, were affected. Some of the smaller national literatures (Udmurt, Bashkir, Ossete) were virtually wiped out, but more established literatures also suffered terrible losses. In ratio to population, Russians suffered less than most nationalities, particularly the Ukrainians and Jewish writers living in the Ukraine. Only 300 of the 1,000 writers who died were Russians; another source suggests that 100 of the 1,000 arrested came from Leningrad, and 60 of these died. However, about 500 writers were arrested in the Ukraine, and 150 of those died or were murdered. In 1948–49 almost all Jewish writers, notably those writing in Yiddish, were annihilated—many of them lived in the Ukraine. At least 41 Armenian writers perished, even some in their seventies and eighties, among them founding members of the Union.[15]

Beltov's figures show that the arrests of writers in all Republics began in earnest only after Kirov's murder, but dozens of Ukrainian writers were arrested already in 1930, well before the Union was established. The arrests of Ukrainian (and Jewish) writers dropped off slightly in 1936, then picked up again in 1937, mounting to a crescendo, as writers were mowed down by what Beltov calls "an artillery barrage" (*shkval*). He concludes that nearly all writers arrested in 1937 were shot forthwith; hardly any were sent to the Gulag.[16]

Many participants in the First Congress were swept away in the fire storm. The Writers' Union Board elected in 1934 comprised 101 members. Only 18 people from that group would be repeated in the slate proposed at the 1954 Congress. According to Soviet figures, only 123 of the nearly 600 delegates to the First Congress of Soviet Writers were still alive to attend the second.[17] Though some of the deaths were natural or caused by World War II, this is still a fatality rate of nearly 80 percent. In late 1988 an authoritative source at the Union itself declared that fully 90 percent of those who joined the Union in 1934 were "repressed"—that is, sent to the Gulag or shot.[18] It is difficult to translate this astonishing percentage into a concrete figure because the exact number of people who joined in 1934 has not been revealed. It seems likely that a majority of the membership announced at the First Congress in late August (close to 2,200) had joined in 1934; others would have joined through the rest of the year. The figure of 90 percent appears to corroborate Eduard Beltov's data, or it may have been extrapolated from his research.[19]

The role of Union officials in the decimation of their own membership remains, understandably, a sensitive topic at No. 52 Vorovsky Street. Current members of the Secretariat have dragged their feet in investigating the impact of the Great Terror on the Union, and have made no attempt at a full recovery of the organization's past history. Eduard Beltov notes that in his long quest for information the Union was "the only organization that paid no attention to me whatsoever." Only after Beltov and other private individuals began in 1988 to publish data about Stalin's victims among the cultural elite did the Union manifest concern about examining its membership records. The Union was conspicuous by its absence when, in August 1988, the magazine *Ogonyok*, the newspaper *Literaturnaya gazeta*, and five other creative unions (Architects, Artists, Cinematographers, Designers, Theater Workers) joined together to form a voluntary society named "Memorial," whose aim is to establish a center for the exchange of information and to collect donations for a monument to all of Stalin's victims.[20] The co-chairs of the "Memorial" Organizing Committee are Ales Adamovich, Yevgeny Yevtushenko, Yury Karyakin, and Academican Andrei Sakharov. Other members include prominent writers Grigory Baklanov and Vasily Bykov, as well as Vitaly Korotich, chief editor of *Ogonyok*, and Bulat Okudzhava, whose own father disappeared in 1937.

Finally, in December 1988 the Union Secretariat claimed incorrectly that it was joining "Memorial" as a founding member, and announced a contribution of 100,000 rubles for the monument: this large amount is testimony to the Union's enormous wealth. The Secretariat also announced the creation of a National Commission on the Literary Heritage of Repressed and Deceased Writers, which would press for the publication of their works, many of them confiscated and hidden for years in state archives (and the KGB's vaults).[21] The commission is chaired by Vladimir Karpov and consists of 42 members, with a fair cross-section of opinion, including Bulat Okudzhava.

Although the Union joined "Memorial" and listed Eduard Beltov as one of those assisting its own efforts (!), the Secretariat introduced a subtle change in focus. First, it quickly dropped "and Deceased" from the official title of its Commission. Second, the Commission is concerned with recovering manuscripts of persecuted writers, rather than with compiling detailed information about the circumstances in which these writers met their fates, particularly those who were tortured and murdered, or died in the Gulag. The rationale behind its shyness is not hard to seek. Some older writers and apparatchiks are anxious to keep their own past activities out of the public eye. Other members of the Secretariat, even if they have nothing personal to hide, may prefer to keep secret the fact that the Union itself was directly involved in the persecution of writers during the Stalin period.

Beltov's research threatened the comfortable notion that the Union in the thirties consisted merely of victims, persecuted by outside forces. He painted a nightmare picture of writers scrambling to save themselves by attacking others, and revealed several cases in which writers had denounced fellow members and were then denounced by others in their turn. He mentioned the "terrible" activities of Vsevolod Vishnevsky in 1937 and asked why and how men had come to behave in such a ruthless, brutal manner to their fellow writers. And how could they then declare themselves proud of their actions? This, said Beltov, was "a separate, enormous, and melancholy issue." As he well knew, Vishnevsky not only escaped the fate of his many victims, but is still honored in all literary histories as a great hero of Soviet literature. To follow Beltov down this path of investigation to the trail's end would mean at the very least a complete rewrite of the Union's own official history. He had probed beneath superficial accounts of the Great Terror as the actions of an evil, deranged Stalin and his cohorts—this is the version presented by Anatoly Rybakov in his popular novel, *Children of the Arbat,* and by the Marxist historian, Roy Medvedev. Beltov hinted that Stalin's Terror had gained such momentum in part because it found many willing collaborators, in the Union itself, and throughout society—people quick to believe in the guilt of others, through greed, envy, ambition, or ideological fanaticism.

Beltov's most serious challenge to the Union's self-image was his direct attack on Vladimir Stavsky as "literally the executioner (*palach*) of Soviet literature." He did not elaborate. The Union's own official history, published in 1981, alludes only once to Vladimir Stavsky, saying that he arranged for members of the Union to send extra rations, including oranges, to their compatriots in Leningrad during the Blockade.[22] Stavsky's role in the Union was in fact much less benign. In 1936, when Stavsky took over Alexander Shcherbakov's position as the Central Committee's liaison at the Union, he assumed the title of General Secretary (the same title Stalin held in the Party), rather than simply First Secretary. But with authority came responsibility. In 1937 the Politburo passed a secret resolution requiring the "responsible official" at every enterprise and institution to countersign the arrest warrants for all those picked up by the NKVD.[23] Stavsky thus became the "executioner of Soviet literature" because he authorized the arrests of so many members of the Writers' Union. Given Stavsky's background as a commissar in the Civil War and as an active participant in the brutal grain confiscation units during collectivization, he probably had few scruples about supporting the arrest of anyone designated "an enemy of the people" (*vrag naroda*). This phrase, introduced by Stalin in the early thirties, was designed to isolate prisoners and deny them sympathy from the rest of the population.

As Beltov is certainly aware but was not able to say for public consumption, Stavsky did not act alone. He was closely assisted throughout the thirties by Alexander Fadeyev, whose career path had paralleled and then crossed Stavsky's from the beginning of the Soviet period. Stavsky was born in 1900, Fadeyev in 1901. Both joined the Communist Party in 1918, fought for the Revolution, and eventually became Party bureaucrats in literature. Like Stavsky, Fadeyev served as a military commissar in the Civil War, and wrote about his experiences in fictional form. He differed from Stavsky in having more literary talent. His short novel, *The Rout* (*Razgrom*, 1927), is still respected as a gritty account of the Civil War in Siberia. A man of proven physical courage, Fadeyev was wounded in 1921 during the assault on the Kronstadt sailors, whom Lenin and Trotsky crushed for demanding more democracy in Party decision-making. During the twenties Fadeyev began to devote himself more and more to administrative work for the Party. From 1924 to 1926 Fadeyev served in Krasnodar and Rostov-on-Don, where he may have met Stavsky, who was editing a Rostov journal at that same time. Fadeyev became a leader of RAPP from 1926 (Stavsky moved to Moscow and joined RAPP in 1928). Like Stavsky and several other leading RAPPists, he quickly adjusted and was appointed vice-chairman of the Organizing Bureau that prepared the First Congress of Writers in 1934. Both men served at the front during World War II as editors and correspondents. Stavsky died at the front in 1943 (reference works give no details as to the circumstances), but Fadeyev survived the war and became the Union's boss, Stalin's commissar for literature. He ruled with such a rod of iron that writers nicknamed him "the marshal."

The participation of Alexander Fadeyev in Stalin's crimes against Union members remained one of the most closely kept secrets of the Secretariat until late in 1988. Soviet reference works for many years have tried to separate him from any connection with Stavsky, or with the "repression" of Union members during the Great Terror. They list Fadeyev as simply a member of the Board and Presidium from 1934 until 1939, that is, just as the Great Terror had begun to subside. The Soviet *Short Literary Encyclopedia* notes that in 1939 he suddenly became a member of the Party's Central Committee (a very important appointment), and at the same time joined the Union Secretariat. Only in 1946 is he listed as taking over the title of General Secretary, left vacant by Stavsky's death in 1943.

By contrast, the testimony of witnesses and survivors of the period, which came to light only fifty years after Fadeyev's public promotion to the Secretariat in 1939, implies that Fadeyev had already taken over major responsibilities in the Secretariat much before that time, and that he served as Stavsky's close associate as early as 1937, perhaps even 1936, when Shcherbakov moved to Leningrad. One of the strongest pieces of evidence in favor of placing Fadeyev at center stage during the Great Terror appeared in the Union's own official weekly newspaper, *Literaturnaya gazeta*, in mid-November 1988.

The publication of the reminiscences of an early member of the Union, Ivan Uksusov (b. 1905), may have been connected with the Secretariat's decision to join the "Memorial" and to found its own Commission on the Literary Heritage of Repressed and Deceased Writers. If so, it represents a sophisticated attempt at damage-control. Although Uksusov never draws conclusions or attempts to generalize from personal experience, his memoir offers a valuable insight into Fadeyev's role and personality. More than that, Uksusov provides information about the Union's newfound power to punish and reward in the thirties, its use of both whip and gingerbread on behalf of the Party. He also gives a rare eyewitness account of the prelude to the Great Terror, since he was arrested and tortured in 1935. His account illustrates the fact that many, if not most, of its victims were not only innocent of any "anti-Soviet activities," but were in fact completely loyal to the Soviet regime.[24]

Ivan Uksusov was himself a man with an exemplary working class background in Leningrad, and had been a beneficiary of the Soviet regime's campaign to encourage proletarian writers in the late twenties. In 1930 he published two prose works in the Gorky style about Russian workers during the Civil War, *The Sisters* (*Syostry*) and *The Twentieth Century* (*Dvadtsaty vek*). He was immediately accepted into RAPP, the forerunner of the Union, and elected to its Presidium. The Leningrad Party boss, the same Sergei Kirov whose assassination on December 1, 1934 foreshadowed the Terror, personally ordered Alexander Fadeyev, then in charge of the Leningrad RAPPists although he lived in Moscow, to take Uksusov with him to the international writers' conference in Kharkov in the late fall of 1930. This conference is described sarcastically as a Stalinist fandango by Max Eastman in his 1934 book, *Artists in Uniform.*

Kharkov was at that time the capital of the Ukraine, where Stalin (with the assistance of Vladimir Stavsky and other commissars) had initiated a campaign to starve the whole peasant population for resisting collectivization. One must picture a group of Soviet RAPPists, and "progressive writers" from 23 different countries (including the United States), assembling in Moscow to board a "special train" (*spetspoezd*) with luxurious accommodations and service, for a trip through the impoverished Ukraine to Kharkov, where the assembled delegates discussed over a period of nine days—in between lavish banquets—the role of writers in critiquing the decadent West.

Uksusov's fate was sealed at what seemed his moment of greatest triumph. At a banquet given by Ukrainian government officials, the Danish author, Martin Andersen Nexo (the same man who, as an enthusiastic foreign guest at the First Congress of Writers four years later would term Soviet writers "children of the triumphant class"), suddenly turned to Uksusov and proposed a toast to him as the youngest writer present. Nexo then gave Uksusov an autographed copy of one of his books. This gesture encouraged other writers to do the same, and by the end of the conference Uksusov had a total of 58 autographed copies of volumes written by all the leading writers in the world communist and leftwing movements. Fadeyev himself also mentioned Uksusov's novel, *The Twentieth Century,* in his speech, as did Leopold Averbakh, the head of RAPP, so that the young author became the toast of the conference. On the return journey to Leningrad, in the same special train, Fadeyev jokingly expressed some envy of Uksusov's extraordinary collection of autographed volumes: "You are taking back home with you the revolutionary literature of the whole world."

For the next five years Uksusov's literary career continued to gather momentum. He gained further fame when his work, with other Soviet books, was selected for ceremonial burning by Hitler's Brown Shirts in 1933, and he was quickly accepted as a member of the new Writers' Union. Suddenly, on April 5, 1935, just over four months after Kirov's murder, Uksusov was arrested at one o'clock in the morning by two young men in leather overcoats, members of the NKVD. He was held in jail for 62 days, during which time he was alternately interrogated and beaten, losing all but eight of his teeth, which were left as broken stumps, causing him excruciating pain whenever he tried to chew food or even to talk. The interrogator began by asking him which country or countries he was spying for. As evidence for this charge he mentioned only the fact that Uksusov had attended the Kharkov conference and had received many books autographed by foreign authors. Uksusov steadfastly denied all the charges and refused to name any of his fellow Soviet writers as close friends, realizing that anyone he named would also be arrested and interrogated. Finally, at the beginning of August 1935, Uksusov was rewarded for his courage by being sentenced to only three years of "administrative exile" in Omsk Province in distant Siberia, rather than being sent directly to the camps. As was the custom in those innocent times, he was even offered a choice of three equally dreary Siberian towns where he would spend his exile: Omsk, Tyumen, and Tobolsk (he chose the last). Soon no choice of location was offered to those arrested and the basic sentence for the innocent jumped from three to ten years. Yevgenia Ginzburg in her memoir about her experiences in the Gulag, *Journey into the Whirlwind* (*Krutoi marshrut*), tells the story of someone complaining about a ten-year sentence; the response from a guard was: "That's for nothing, for something you get twenty-five."

Uksusov started his journey among a sizable group of Leningraders in five freight cars. There were 37 men packed into his car, but no one said a word because, as Uksusov later realized, each was innocent and thought all the others were guilty. In these early days Leningrad may have been a special target as Kirov's power base, but at a transit station in Sverdlovsk, and later on the journey to Omsk, Uksusov saw other freight trains full of prisoners from all over the country. At Tobolsk, Uksusov observed a column of about 100–150 old men and women and younger women, some carrying babies, and children. These were relatives of men like himself who had been arrested by the NKVD; they had been forced to walk along a 320-kilometer road from Tyumen to Tobolsk (there was no railroad). As the column halted near a stream, a woman stepped toward it and began drinking thirstily. One of the vicious guard dogs, an Alsatian (*ovcharka*), pounced on her and ripped off her left breast. The dying woman was picked up and dumped at the end of the column.

Uksusov was one of the lucky ones; he stayed in Tobolsk, and got an easy job working on the local newspaper, even though he says everyone there viewed him as "an enemy of the people." During his exile Uksusov saw countless numbers of other prisoners gathered together in columns, then piled like sardines onto large barges and towed by steamer up the Irtysh River to deserted areas hundreds of miles from the nearest habitation. Uksusov learned that they were then left to fend for themselves, at the mercy of the numbing cold, wild animals, birds, and, in the short summers, swarms of midges and mosquitos, large and persistent enough to drive men insane.

In December 1938 Uksusov was released and returned to Leningrad. This was just about the time that the mass arrests were coming to an end, otherwise he would certainly have been shipped to the camps himself or executed. Almost at once Uksusov's old friend Fadeyev invited him to Moscow. When he learned that Uksusov had been arrested because of the autographed books, he seemed stunned: "As I finished my story, his face was red from ear to ear, and his small bluish eyes were brimming with tears." After a long silence Fadeyev begged Uksusov not to blame the Soviet government for his suffering. When Uksusov asked who then should he blame, Fadeyev launched into a strange monologue, seeming to take the question as a personal accusation:

> Oh, come now. . . . I have always tried to be kind to all writers. But what a time it was. It was a terrible thing for a man to be in charge of the Writers' Union at such a time. When they started arresting many of our writers, I called the Party Central Committee and left word that I wanted to see Genrikh Yagoda [head of the NKVD]. . . . His Lordship (*barin*) refused to see me; he did not even deign to give me a reply of any kind. I am not surprised he turned out to be an enemy of the people and was shot. Now Yezhov [who succeeded Yagoda in 1936] was quite different, more straightforward. He sent word that he could only see me in a month's time. So a month later I went to his office and we spoke for about an hour. Ivan, you have to understand what it was like then, last year. How could I know exactly why each writer had been arrested? I am not Jesus Christ. Even so, in nine cases, including yours, I practically staked my own life that these people could not possibly be enemies of the people. Yezhov made no effort to conceal the fact that he did not believe me. He cross-examined me on each of the people I named: Who were they, what had they published? He wrote six of the names in a notebook. I told him that you came from a family of mineworkers in the Donbass. . . .

Again, Uksusov draws no conclusions, but Fadeyev's remarks reveal that he was already deeply implicated in Stalin's repression of writers. He speaks of being "in charge of the Union" and of going to see Yagoda on behalf of "many of our writers" who had been arrested. That means that Fadeyev already held a high position in the Union by 1936, before Yagoda was replaced by Yezhov that fall. It seems likely that Fadeyev's responsibilities were further increased in 1937, when Stavsky was appointed chief editor at *Pravda*, the Party's leading newspaper. Stavsky continued as General Secretary of the Union, but could hardly have had much time to devote to its affairs once he started working at *Pravda*.

Although Fadeyev was supposedly not even a member of the Secretariat until 1939, in speaking with Uksusov in December 1938 he did not mention having to consult with Stavsky. Fadeyev's comments on Yagoda's fate (yet another "enemy of the people") and his own lack of divine omniscience show that he was ready to believe in anyone's guilt, unless proven otherwise. The bizarre statement—"I am not Jesus Christ"—suggests that Fadeyev thought of himself as a victim, rather than an accomplice. But he was careful not to tell Uksusov about the 1937 Politburo resolution requiring responsible officials at all institutions to sanction or countersign the arrest warrants of people working there. By December 1938 Stavsky (and perhaps Fadeyev too) had already authorized the arrest of many hundreds of writers, knowing that they were sentencing them to immediate execution or to the Gulag.

In addition to suggesting Fadeyev's involvement in the Terror, Uksusov's account illustrates the new power of the Union to dispense material benefits and privileges. Having claimed the credit for Uksusov's release, Fadeyev again revealed his special prerogative in the Soviet literary world by offering (on his own personal authority) to have Uksusov's novel *The Twentieth Century* republished, "in a mass edition with the highest royalty possible." He explained to Uksusov that all works by "repressed writers" had been destroyed, but he had a copy (another mark of unusual privilege, since possession of books by enemies of the people would normally bring immediate arrest). Uksusov remarked that first the Germans and then the Soviets had burned his novel, and he refused to have it republished while Stalin was alive (this was a remarkably bold remark, which could have got him arrested again). But he did follow Fadeyev's suggestion and go to see Konstantin Fedin, at that time chairman of the Board of Litfund, and a powerful dispenser of all benefits and privileges to members of the Union.

As a man of working-class origin, Uksusov felt awkward with Fedin, a member of the pre-revolutionary intelligentsia. In addition, he could still only mumble incoherently because of his painful teeth. After a brief greeting, Fedin, who had clearly been forewarned by Fadeyev, handed Uksusov an envelope containing 1,000 rubles (a considerable sum in those days, before the devaluation of the ruble in 1960), a free pass to one of the Union's resort hotels in the Crimea, and told him that the Litfund Board would order its

Leningrad branch to pay him 500 rubles per month for a period of six months; the money did not have to be returned. Uksusov does not say what happened to the 58 autographed books that caused all his problems; nor does he speculate on a possible connection between Fadeyev's 1930 expression of envy and his later emotional reaction to Uksusov's story.

The memoirs of Nadezhda Mandelshtam, which have not yet been published in the Soviet Union, confirm the important role played by Fadeyev in the Great Terror of the mid-thirties, as well as the Union's activities as a dispenser of goods and services to the new cultural elite. She recalls that in 1937, on their return from three years' exile, her husband Osip was strongly advised by Valentin Kataev and Viktor Shklovsky to ask Fadeyev for help in getting some kind of work as a translator.[25] The choice of Fadeyev as intercessor suggests that knowledgeable writers considered him a person of literary judgment who had the authority to assist even a writer just back from exile. Fadeyev promised to do what he could and wept on hearing Mandelshtam recite some of his poems (Nadezhda Mandelshtam remarks that Fadeyev was always "emotional").

The sequel to this story shows Fadeyev's character in mixed hues of light and shade, and suggests that, whatever power Fadeyev held, Stavsky still retained supreme authority in the Union Secretariat. The Mandelshtams heard nothing for several months. Then quite suddenly, in the early spring of 1938, Mandelshtam was summoned to a meeting with Stavsky, still officially General Secretary of the Union, and offered Litfund coupons to go to a rest home at Samatikha, a few miles outside Moscow. In the meantime Fadeyev had apparently tried without success to get help for Mandelshtam from Andrei Andreyev, a member of the Politbouro. Friendly as ever, Fadeyev offered the Mandelshtams a lift in his chauffeur-driven car from the Writers' Union to the center of town. When he learned that Mandelshtam was being sent to Samatikha, which was a Party rest home, not one belonging to the Union, he seemed surprised and ill-at-ease. However, he wished them well and gave Mandelshtam a warm embrace. Soon after, the Mandelshtams went to Samatikha and on May 1, the day following their arrival, Mandelshtam was arrested and disappeared for ever. He died in December 1938 at a transit camp outside Vladivostok, emaciated and half-mad, from a brutal beating inflicted by criminal prisoners.[26]

After World War II, Nadezhda Mandelshtam bumped into Fadeyev in an elevator. He ignored her, but just before stepping out he leaned over and whispered: "That business with Osip Emilyevich was handled by Andreyev." She noticed that he was a little drunk (he had long since become a very heavy drinker), and therefore could not be sure how to interpret his remark: had it really been Andreyev, or was Fadeyev trying to excuse himself? Judging from Nadezhda Mandelshtam's account, Fadeyev was cut out of the loop in this case. However, he failed to alert the Mandelshtams to their danger and obviously made no move to intercede. It was this failure of writers to support one another that made things so easy for Stalin.

Mandelshtam had perceived earlier than most that the new Writers' Union would not protect writers from Stalin, any more than RAPP had. And he saw certain members of the Union as a greater threat to him than even the secret police. According to his wife Nadezhda: "He preferred to die not at the hands of the writers' organizations who had initiated the process of his destruction, but rather at those of the 'punitive organs'."[27]

Mandelshtam was first arrested in the spring of 1934, and, like Uksusov, was given the opportunity to choose a permanent place of exile for three years—in this case any town except the largest twelve cities in the country; this sentence was known as "minus twelve." Mandelshtam chose Voronezh, simply because he had visited there some years before. In her memoirs Nadezhda Mandelshtam notes that Osip had to report in Voronezh not only to the secret police, but also to the local branch of the Writers' Union. This was late in 1934, only a few months after the First Congress, but the Union had apparently begun to assume some bureaucratic responsibility for all writers, even those in exile. At this early date the local Union officials were extremely nervous about making decisions, and first made sure of their ground by checking with the secret police. Once they received assurances that the Mandelshtams were entitled to residence permits, they became very obliging and wished the exiles well. Union officials in Moscow were much more sure of themselves and treated both Mandelshtams with barely concealed hostility, as befitted enemies of the people.

Even before the Mandelshtams left for Voronezh, they had noticed the power of Union officials to dispense privileges and material benefits. Very soon after the new organization was created, before the First Congress, writers began to pay far less attention to being independent and more to the benefits of toeing the line:

> At that time, as we saw all around us, there was furious competition among the writers for the good things of life, among which the greatest prize of all was an apartment. A little later country villas were also handed out "for services rendered."[28]

In 1937, when the Mandelshtams returned to Moscow, they were surprised to find that members of the Writers' Union had become "a privileged caste" (*privilegirovannoe soslovie*). Some of the better-known writers—Ilya Ehrenburg, Konstantin Fedin, Valentin Katayev, Viktor Shklovsky—had just moved into a splendid new apartment building, constructed by Litfund, on Lavrushinsky Street, across the river from the Kremlin. The building, which had an impressive foyer of expensive marble (labradorite), also housed literary bureaucrats, such as Vsevolod Vishnevsky, who commandeered the apartment allocated to Ehrenburg while he was abroad. Kataev drove the Mandelshtams around Moscow in a new American car brought back from a recent trip, and offered them wine with ice cubes produced by another American trophy—Osip Mandelshtam called it "the first writers' refrigerator." The Mandelshtams were also impressed by the transformation in the writers' appearance: members of the Union had abandoned the drab dress of previous days and now wore imported suits. Writers enjoyed these material advantages at a time of tremendous hardship for most of the Soviet population, who were struggling to achieve Stalin's dream of rapid industrialization.

In spite of their more comfortable circumstances, by 1937 all members of the Union had to endure the constant threat of sudden arrest. Nadezhda Mandelshtam describes the atmosphere as "like the Last Judgment (*Strashny Sud*), with some being trampled underfoot by demons, and others being celebrated with paeans of praise." The writers living in the new apartment building recognized their good fortune, as did other survivors:

> Everybody could hope for speedy advancement because every day somebody was plucked from their midst and had to be replaced. Of course, everybody was also a candidate for prison and death, but during the day they did not think about that, giving full rein to their fears only at night.[29]

Shimon Markish, whose own father, the poet Perets Markish, died in Stalin's anti-cosmopolitan campaign, lived as an adolescent through the post-war years up to Stalin's death. He gave a telling description of the impact of living with constant anxiety:

> For me, the very essence of the Terror was that you never knew when you were guilty. All of us were guilty! Everybody. It was Kafkaesque. When I first read Kafka, I was astonished at Kafka's ability to explain the Soviet situation. . . . Life was a shapeless fear. . . . People breathed it in. Where could literature exist in such an atmosphere?[30]

The Great Terror finally abated in 1939, but only in the sense that mass arrests subsided. Parodoxically, it was the German invasion of June 1941 that banished temporarily the atmosphere of terror and the fear of denunciation. The war was a catastrophic event for the country, and yet it also blasted away the lies and malice. It created a new atmosphere of mutual trust in Soviet society, as Stalin found he needed to unite the country against a common foe. This decision in turn improved literary life. Boris Pasternak in a haunting sentence towards the end of *Doctor Zhivago* describes how the war "broke the spell of the dead letter." The relief from the fear of a denunciation conducted by one's friends, colleagues, and even family members explains people's otherwise puzzling sense of exhilaration and joy. The country was united, the enemy was no longer neighbor or relative, or some unknown police informer, but the easily recognizable foreign invader.[31]

Having arrested and killed off hundreds of the Union's members, Stalin now ordered that writers, especially prominent ones or those in ill health, should be evacuated to the East out of harm's way. In the fall of 1941, when the Germans were threatening to capture both Moscow and Leningrad, the authorities went to the extraordinary trouble and expense of transferring some members of the Union to a small provincial town called Chistopol (others were moved to Alma Ata, Tashkent, Kazan, Kuibyshev, and Sverdlovsk—the latter city became briefly the provisional capital). Anna Akhmatova, who had been admitted to the Writers' Union in 1940 during a period of relative calm following the Terror, was airlifted out of Leningrad on the same plane that carried Dmitry Shostakovich, whose opera *Lady Macbeth of Mtsensk District* had been attacked in the opening salvo of the Great Purge in 1936. As a Union member Akhmatova was entitled to an additional 20 square meters of living space; she immediately invited her lifelong friend, Nadezhda Mendelshtam, now Osip's widow, to live with her.[32]

The evacuation of writers hundreds of miles to the east, particularly at a time when the regime was fighting for its life, reflects the bizarre world of privilege and menace in which members of the Union lived during the thirties, and in the post-war years prior to Stalin's death. By the time the Germans invaded in 1941, writers in Moscow and Leningrad had become so spoiled, and so removed from the hard life of ordinary citizens, that they were genuinely shocked at the poor living conditions in their temporary quarters. Boris Pasternak was one of several dozen Union members evacuated to Chistopol during that first terrible winter, before they all returned to Moscow in 1942 and to Leningrad somewhat later. During the evacuation, Pasternak and all the other writers received a regular living allowance from the Soviet government, since they could not earn money for themselves.[33]

The war years witnessed a conflation of propaganda with patriotism. Censorship and ideological controls remained, but most writers now found their own literary stance coincided with an expanded definition of Socialist Realism: their works were to be of service to their country, which needed all the patriotic fervor that could be marshalled. The new mood was enhanced by a measured loosening of literary restrictions; certain works were published that would have never seen the light of day before the war. The poetry of Olga Berggolts fortified her fellow citizens in Leningrad, starving in the Nazi blockade. Her husband had already died in Stalin's Terror; now no longer a non-person, her voice was needed for the siege. Anna Akhmatova wrote some fine patriotic lyrics which were printed in *Pravda*. Her verse had not been published within the Soviet Union since 1925—the day she was expelled from Soviet literature by a resolution of the Party's Central Committee. On February 9, 1944 the Soviet military newspaper, *Red Star* (*Krasnaya Zvezda*), published two poems by Pasternak.

Although members of the Writers' Union were officially exempt from military service (another extraordinary privilege), many gave unstintingly to the war effort. The official Soviet account says that a total of 417 members of the Union fell during the war, with 962 receiving decorations for war service.[34] Many writers went to the front to give talks and read their works to the troops, or became war correspondents for *Pravda* or *Red Star*.[35] Others volunteered for active service and were killed or wounded in the fighting. A marble tablet listing 81 members from Moscow who lost their lives in the war is the first thing one sees inside the Club entrance. The value of writers to the war effort is impossible to quantify, but they had an enormous impact on morale. Stalin himself said once that Ilya Ehrenburg, who displayed tireless energy and talent as a wartime journalist, was worth at least two army divisions. And that may well be the reason Ehrenburg survived the postwar purges.

Though the victory over Germany in May of 1945 meant the end of the hemorrhaging of Soviet lives, it also brought a return to domestic repression in the name of the Soviet state. Once more, working through the organizations that he had created, Stalin clamped down on the creative energies loosed by war. The blow fell in 1946, when the Central Committee issued a series of draconian resolutions on literature and the other arts. Andrei Zhdanov, who had promulgated Socialist Realism at the 1934 Congress, launched a vicious attack on Boris Pasternak, Mikhail Zoshchenko, and Anna Akhamatova, whom he called "half nun and half whore." Zhdanov was head of the Leningrad Party organization, and, since the summer of 1944, Central Committee Secretary with responsibility for ideology. He accused all three of being anti-Soviet, of undermining Socialist Realism, and being unduly pessimistic. To put some teeth into the decree on literature, the journal *Leningrad* was simply abolished. *Zvezda*, another culprit, was put under the direct command of a member of the Central Committee of the Party. Zoshchenko and Akhmatova, but not Pasternak, were thrown out of the Union. Surprisingly, none of the three writers was physically harmed, although the psychological pressures on them can only be imagined.

In 1988 the government daily *Izvestia* published a partial transcript of a meeting to which Leningrad writers and editors were summoned at the Kremlin to explain their errors of judgment. Stalin and Andrei Zhdanov took the lead in condemning Akhmatova and Zoshchenko in harsh terms. Stalin said in part:

> Writers think that they are not concerned with politics. . . . Why don't I particularly care for people like Zoshchenko? Because they write stuff that's like an emetic. Can we tolerate having people in leadership positions who permit all this to be published? . . . In our country a magazine is not a private enterprise.[36]

Stalin's comment underlines the sorry fact that the "collectivization of literature" had come to mean collective guilt as well.

The period from 1946 to Stalin's death in 1953, the bad times under Zhdanov, or *zhdanovshchina*, witnessed the loss of the modest room to maneuver that writers had gained during the war years. Serious writers with an independent sense of their rights and responsibilities were badly affected. However, large numbers of writers quickly adapted to the new conditions and went to further and further extremes to demonstrate loyalty to Stalin's line.

In retrospect, the whole Stalin period, and particularly the *zhdanovshchina*, looks like a cultural wasteland; little of any lasting esthetic value was produced and hardly any works published at that time are remembered today, with the notable exception of Mikhail Sholokhov's *Quiet Don*. But a semblance of literary life continued in the postwar period, as it had during the Great Terror itself. Many writers, often former combatants, wrote heroic accounts of the war—the Soviet equivalent of British and American movies on the same subject. There was also a ready market for fiction about the rising bureaucratic class, many of whom had made dazzling careers by taking the places of those killed in the Great Terror and then in the war itself. Like the old bourgeoisie in its time, this "new class" enjoyed reading stories about itself.[37] And the authors of these works not only received generous royalties, but also qualified for honors, awards, prizes, and opportunities to enjoy the luxuries of the decadent West.

However, members of the Writers' Union were expected to earn their keep by playing a part in the cultural crackdown. The malleable Nikolai Tikhonov, a Leningrad poet who had been First Secretary from 1944 to 1946, was summarily dismissed, and replaced by the more aggressive Fadeyev. Ominously, Fadeyev took over Stavsky's title of General Secretary. More Soviet writers and critics were "illegally repressed" (notably Jews), and many of these would have to be "posthumously rehabilitated" after Stalin's death. The Union Secretariat continued to play a leading role in these persecutions, and there can be no doubt Fadeyev personally signed the warrants for those writers who were arrested. He was also directly responsible for preventing works from being published, thus condemning authors to financial hardship. For example, Andrei Platonov, now regarded as one of the major prose writers of the Soviet period, told a British journalist a few years before his death in 1951 that "Fadeyev has now been sitting on my manuscripts for years."[38]

Fadeyev himself did not escape public humiliation. He was obliged to rewrite his war epic, *Molodaya gvardia* (*The Young Guard*), not once but twice, to correct his failure to demonstrate the central role played by the Party in the Soviet triumph over the Nazis. The obligation to rewrite published works, a literary equivalent of the public confessions during the purge trials of the thirties, became one of Stalin's favorite tactics in the post-war period. He spared none of the leading official writers or literary bureaucrats. Not only Fadeyev, but even Mikhail Sholokhov had to comply, rewriting sections of the Soviet classic *Tikhy Don* (*The Quiet Don*) and of his patriotic epic *Oni srazhalis za rodinu* (*They Fought for Their Motherland*).[39]

To all appearances Russian literature had been destroyed and writers had been cowed into submission. Yet the great traditions of the past merely lay fallow. New shoots began to sprout forth from the frozen soil within weeks of Stalin's death on March 5, 1953, as liberal writers—that is, those who wanted more creative freedom—attacked the status quo, which was vigorously defended by conservative writers and apparatchiks.[40] Articles appeared stating, at first tentatively, a few basic truths about the literary process: the code words were "self-expression" and "sincerity." The ice started breaking up, and the more liberal atmosphere soon acquired its name from Ehrenburg's novel *The Thaw* (*Ottepel*), the first part of which appeared in 1954. Before long the Union itself became a target, as bolder spirits publicly attacked the activities of the Secretariat. Fadeyev was obliged to resign as General Secretary, to be replaced by Aleksei Surkov, but with the less Stalinist title of First Secretary.

The post-Stalin leaders allowed (or ordered) the Union to hold its Second Congress in December 1954, more than seventeen years after it should have taken place. The decision to hold the Congress so soon after Stalin's death marked an important break with previous tradition, since Stalin had not needed Writers' Union congresses, preferring to rule by fiat, behind the scenes. It was also a singular tribute to the growing importance of the Writers' Union as a public institution that its Second Congress was held more than a year before the Party held its own 20th Party Congress in February 1956. It seemed that Khrushchev planned on using the Writers' Congress as a trial balloon, testing the political atmosphere before laying out in the open his revolutionary, anti-Stalinist policy.

The great uncertainty of those days in December 1954, less than two years after the death of Stalin, was symbolized at the very start of Congress when the elderly novelist Olga Forsh called upon the assembled delegates to "express deep respect for the memory of Joseph Vissarionovich Stalin by standing." All members of the Party's Politburo (at that time called the Presidium) attended this opening session and were soon unanimously elected an "Honorary Presidium"—continuing a tradition that began in 1934 and survives to this day. One wonders what thoughts were passing through each of their minds during this moment of silence—they must have remembered that the Party itself had suffered the highest percentage of casualties during Stalin's purges.

Forsh went on to pay respects to Maxim Gorky and to all those members of the Writers' Union who had died in the twenty years since the First Congress in 1934, but she mentioned only World War II as a cause of their disappearance. Again everyone was asked to stand and remember the fallen.[41]

The Second Congress, even though it had been delayed seventeen years, conducted its business in ways very like the First. Again delegates were obliged to vote unanimously for whole slates of candidates to various bodies, including important officials who were evidently not even members of the Union. The new man in charge, First Secretary Aleksei Surkov, gave a long, self-congratulatory speech on the great achievements over the past twenty years, spiced with quotations from Lenin and warnings that these remarkable triumphs had to be protected against the continued machinations of the capitalist West. His example was followed by countless other loyalists who saw no reason to alter their standard boilerplate. In scenes eerily reminiscent of meetings of the Union Board at the height of the Great Purges, the proceedings would occasionally be interrupted by "spontaneous" demonstrations such as a marching band of Young Pioneers who recited long poems urging the delegates on to greater efforts.

Ehrenburg notes in his memoirs that some writers attending the 1954 congress referred to it sardonically as "Twenty Years After," echoing the title of Dumas' sequel to *The Three Musketeers*—both novels then and now enormously popular with Russians.[42] In fact, a few of the major speakers in 1954 had also figured in the First Congress, notably Ehrenburg himself. But the terrible damage done to Soviet literature by twenty years of Stalinism was also painfully evident, not simply in the absence of countless "repressed" writers, but in the need for writers to reclaim the elementary rights of a creative artist.

The Leningrad poet Olga Berggolts returned to one of the major themes in her pre-congress articles by declaring: "Poets can achieve nothing if they do not express their own personalities. Impersonality—that is yet another reason for the backwardness of our poetry." Berggolts' modest suggestion that "self-expression" was essential to lyric poetry aroused almost as much controversy as had Alexander Pomerantsev's advocacy of "sincerity" in a famous *Novy mir* article exactly one year before the Second Congress. The conservatives opposed both self-expression and sincerity since they threatened to divert attention from *partynost*—from the celebration of public triumphs, industrial projects, and the like. Members of the Secretariat understood that what lay behind Berggolts' call for self-expression was a revival of lyricism, of the personal and private over the public. Such a revival would threaten establishment poets, who had made handsome careers from rhyming *Pravda* editorials and celebrating Soviet triumphs with occasional odes, much like court poets in the time of Catherine the Great during the late eighteenth century.

Berggolts scored some palpable hits on the Union bosses, charging that poor works had been praised as a result of "directives issuing straight from the Union Secretariat."[43] She condemned the suppression of works by important poets and the attempt by Union bureaucrats and their spokesmen to force every poet into a single mold, and to reduce all poetry to a uniform style, preferably "one that would send readers to sleep" (this remark caused what the stenographic report of the congress calls a "stir" in the hall). Only this kind of poetry, she claimed, would set the Union secretaries' minds at ease. The Leningrad poet called for an end to what she described as "ex cathedra criticism" (*direktivnaya kritika*).

Once again, as in 1934, Ilya Ehrenburg, the leading spokesman for liberal writers, had to renew his crusade for fundamental human values and literary standards, but on this occasion there were no foreign guests to back him up, and certainly no Party leaders of Bukharin's intellectual range to lend support. Ehrenburg focused on the use of whip and gingerbread by the Secretariat: "Writers should not be regarded as members of some select caste, but neither should they be whipped like naughty schoolchildren (*ne nuzhno ikh sech, kak provinivshikhsya shkolnikov*)."[44] Ehrenburg spent most of his time arguing against the whip. He condemned capricious judgments of literary works, especially in the case of young writers, whose careers were sometimes decided by non-writers, by "people on the periphery of literature" (*'okololiteraturnye' lyudi*), an obvious hint at the continued influence of cultural and ideological specialists in the Party. And he went on to suggest that the atmosphere of tsarist Russia just prior to 1917 had been more open than it was at the time they themselves were meeting, when he asked what reception Mayakovsky might receive today "at No. 52 Vorovsky Street" if he were to present his early, experimental poems to the Secretariat. This comment again provoked laughter and applause in the audience because Mayakovsky, following his suicide in 1930, had been deified by Stalin as the leading poet of the revolution.

Ehrenburg challenged by implication the dogma of Socialist Realism and called for the de-criminalization of literary life:

> Where is the law that states one can only write in a certain way? Where are the scales that can measure precisely whether a fictional hero is "typical" or not? It is right and proper to disagree about these issues, but discussing a book is not like arguing a case in court, and the judgment of this or that Union secretary should not be regarded as a sentence, with all the consequences that flow from such a verdict.

The aim of literary criticism, Ehrenburg reminded his audience, was simply to compare differing points of view, not to come to a definite conclusion binding on everyone. And he added—quite aware that he was advancing arguments totally unacceptable to the Secretariat—that in any case readers would be the ones who ultimately decided what they did or did not like.

Ehrenburg made the most searching comment at the Congress when he contrasted the contemporary literary situation of Soviet society with that twenty years earlier at the First Congress of Writers:

> What has in fact happened? Readers have overtaken many writers. Just think how things were at our First Congress. At that time we faced tens of millions of new readers, who had never looked at a novel before in their lives. . . . From the beginning of the revolution to the thirties, culture had expanded its boundaries; in those days we needed to bring that culture to the masses. It was a time when writers were justified in complaining about a certain lack of sophistication in their readers. But now Soviet readers look down on these same writers; their fictional characters seem far less sophisticated, less complex, and less spiritually rich than the readers themselves or many of their friends.

He pinpointed the paternalistic attitude of the Party toward Soviet citizens when he complimented the Union's Section for Children's Literature for producing many worthy works, then said he often wondered, while he read recent Soviet novels, whether it might not be a good idea to create a Section for Adult Readers. This remark was greeted with applause, and he received an ovation at the close of his remarks.

The prose writer Vladimir Ovechkin opened up one of the major liberal themes in the post-Stalin period by zeroing in on the special privileges of the top bureaucrats, and hinting strongly at widespread corruption among members of the Secretariat. Their only concern, he charged, was for "positions, meetings, receptions, and banquets." He suggested that, while administering the whip to writers on behalf of the Party, the "literary generals" were also taking most of the gingerbread for themselves.[45] Ovechkin deplored the fact that their mediocre works received awards and prizes, often very soon after publication, before they had been widely reviewed or even read by the general public. Some multi-volume works had received prizes, one for each part or section that appeared. Ovechkin claimed that certain writers arranged to have their works published in journals during August and September so as to maximize their chances of winning an annual prize. Works appearing in the first half of the year tended to be forgotten by December.

Ovechkin charged that the awarding of prizes and bonuses (*premirovanie*) to selected writers had become a scandal. But the hunt for prizes was part of a more general problem that had become particularly serious over the past decade. Leading writers traveled rarely, and then mostly abroad. Now and again they would go on a *komandirovka* somewhere in the Soviet Union; they stayed perhaps for a month at a construction site, passing most of the time in the dining room of the local hotel, then rushed back to Moscow to write a novel or poem about the life of workers. Ovechkin condemned this manner of gathering material as "ersatz" and "armchair research" (*gastrolnoe izuchenie zhizni*)—literally, "studying life while on tour." He recalled that in pre-revolutionary times famous writers used to live all over the country, but now the best-known authors all congregated in the same apartment building in Moscow, or at Peredelkino—Ovechkin did not have to tell his audience that he was referring to the building on Lavrushinsky in Moscow, where luxurious apartments were provided free or at nominal cost by the Union's own Litfund. If writers wanted to focus their works on Moscow, that was fine. There was plenty to write about in Moscow, "But you will not find it at No. 52 Vorovsky Street, in the Writers' Club, or in meetings."

Ovechkin did not limit his attacks to the corrupt and luxurious lifestyle of the "literary generals." As the founder of an important school of writing that flourished later in the sixties and seventies under the name of "village prose" (*derevenskaya proza*), he took particular exception to Aleksei Surkov's sliding over serious problems by quoting average figures. Ovechkin pointed out that this had been the same technique used to conceal the terrible truth about the disastrous situation on collective farms. He also pinpointed Surkov's other tactic, much favored by Soviet officials in all areas, of admitting mistakes but claiming that they were not typical: "No, comrade Surkov, it is not a matter of isolated errors." Of course, agreed Ovechkin, it was true that the past twenty years had witnessed the appearance of some major works, but everyone should face the fact that many poor works had also been published, and he mentioned specifically works by Yelizar Maltsev and Fyodor Panfyorov. Ovechkin noted that the past few years in particular had witnessed a sharp drop in literary standards and the publication of many boring, humdrum (*serenkie*) works. He charged that Surkov had ignored this dangerous phenomenon, and that Konstantin Simonov had also said too little about it in his address on Soviet prose fiction.[46]

Ovechkin's speech attacking the privileged lifestyle of the "literary generals" aroused more anger than did the critical remarks by liberal writers on Socialist Realism and bureaucratism. He was not only subjected to several formal attacks, but also lampooned in satirical verses posted on noticeboards during the Congress, accusing him of trying to get an official position in Moscow. In his response Ovechkin noted:

> I have heard the sharply critical speeches made at this congress described as "cliquishness" (*gruppovshchina*). Apparently, some of our comrades here, those in administration (*v apparatnoi*

> *zhizni*), have so lost touch with ordinary human give-and-take that they cannot even accept the fact that someone might make a sharply worded speech because he loves literature, because he wants our literature to be great and good. (applause)

Ovechkin stated his determination to remain in his home town of Kursk and to decline any invitation to move to the capital. He received more applause for saying that he would not accept any official post, even one that paid him a salary for turning up in Moscow once a month to attend some conference or meeting—a sharp dig at the practice of the secretaries of regional Union branches.

If there had been an applause meter at the congress, it would probably have shown that the liberals had a majority among the delegates. However, the conservatives also received much applause and were not about to yield without a fight. They arranged for Alexander Fadeyev to give a final major address at the congress, even though he had been removed as General Secretary. His speech was an extraordinary performance, an atavistic relapse. Like Surkov, Fadeyev began with a quote from Lenin's 1905 article "Party Organization and Party Literature," specifically the utopian section where Lenin dreams of a truly free proletarian literature, unlike the elitist commercialized literature of the corrupt bourgeoisie. Fadeyev started a post-Stalin tradition whereby Union leaders would use it to buttress their own positions when threatened. Now and then throughout his long speech Fadeyev would return to Lenin's article, paraphrasing and reinforcing its arguments:

> Comrades! The most important aspect of our understanding of what constitutes a free literature is our open acceptance as writers, whether we belong to the Party or not, of the Party's leading role in all fields of life, including literature.
>
> Bourgeois writers are subject to bourgeois political parties, whose bosses are the wheeler-dealers (*vorotily*) of the financial and industrial world of capitalism. Bourgeois writers are subject to capitalist publishing houses and the press. The so-called political independence (*bespartynost*) of the bourgeois writer is a sham.[47]

Fadeyev used the Party's formal greeting to the congress in the same way as he did Lenin's article. The greeting had listed a series of expectations and tasks that the Party was imposing upon Union members. He mentioned or paraphrased it at least a dozen times, as though it were a mechanism to trigger his own thought processes. Throughout his address Fadeyev used all the old code words and phrases associated with the worst abuses of Stalinism: "survivals of capitalism," "imperialist ideology," "the transforming and educational role of our literature," "decadents," "positive and negative images," "aggressive and reactionary circles," "leftovers of hostile ideology," "hacks and lipservers (*khaltushchiki i prisposoblentsy*)," "the ideological enemies of Soviet literature," "petty cliquishness," and so forth. He spoke of the major new tasks that writers must tackle as Soviet society made the transition from socialism to communism, recalled the golden years of the First Five-Year Plan, took some comrades to task for lagging behind on their obligations to the Party and the people, and argued that Soviet writers must keep up their ideological guard because the enemies of socialism were just waiting for the right moment to attack. Fadeyev mouthed these cliches like an automaton programmed by Stalin and Zhdanov. It seemed that neither he himself nor anyone else knew how to reprogram him, or to turn him off.

Fadeyev did mention criticisms of the Union Secretariat and admitted some errors in the past, but he employed Lenin's rhetorical trick of appearing to give ground, then quickly taking it back again (for example, "Everyone is free to write whatever he likes, but . . .). He agreed with Olga Berggolts, but then suggested she should find a term other than "self-expression" because it recalled the views of "decadents of all stripes." He agreed with Ovechkin, but then advised him not to "play the coquette because of his knowledge of provincial life"; it did not matter whether a writer lived in Moscow or elsewhere. Fadeyev came down hard on Pomerantsev, and received applause when he played on wartime memories by declaring that nobody had the right to accuse Soviet writers of "insincerity" when they had fought and struggled so hard for Soviet society. Then he continued:

> As you can see, the motive of the writer of that article in *Novy mir*, in taking the line he did, was also political. He was [prompted by] the desire, perhaps unconscious (*neosoznannoe*), to have our great Soviet literature renounce the inspiring ideas of communism and become instead the agent (*provodnik*) of an alien ideology.

One can imagine many of the delegates getting a shiver up and down their spines as they heard these all-too-familiar threatening phrases. However, Fadeyev's day had passed. The Politburo decided that he should play no further role in the affairs of the Union. The post of President or Chairman (*predsedatel*) of the Board was abolished, perhaps deliberately, so that Fadeyev could not retain the position he had acquired in 1946, together with the title of General Secretary.[48]

The Union bureaucrats had hoped Fadeyev would help restore

their authority and set the tone for the future. But Khrushchev now embarked on an anti-Stalin campaign that was to shake the entire political and cultural system to its foundations. More humiliations were in store for Fadeyev himself. He was reduced to candidate membership of the Party's Central Committee, a sure sign that he was out of favor. Then, at the 20th Party Congress in February 1956, Mikhail Sholokhov, the only writer permitted to address the delegates, launched into a virulent personal attack on him. This was the prelude to Khrushchev's attack on Stalin himself, the man to whom Fadeyev had given his life.[49] Khrushchev portrayed Stalin as having virtually destroyed the Party, torturing and murdering its membership according to his own caprice.

Khrushchev's revelations junked what had been the Party line for almost thirty years. Lecturers were sent across the country to help the Party faithful understand this new picture of the man who had been idolized for a generation as the savior of the Soviet Union and the best hope for all mankind. Closed Party meetings were held in all institutions and enterprises across the country so that Party members could then explain the sudden change to their flocks. Fortunately for our understanding of the effect this bombshell had within the Writers' Union itself, there exists a unique partial transcript of a meeting of the Party organization of the Moscow chapter in March, less than one month after the 20th Party Congress. Aleksei Surkov's opening report seemed most concerned to rebut Sholokhov's charge that the Writers' Union had become a Union of Dead Souls.[50] But Surkov's colleagues cheered the remark and criticized Surkov's lack of candor. They demanded a more forthright discussion of the sins of the past: the groundless attacks on loyal writers and their works, informing on others, denunciations, and the conniving with widespread anti-Semitism by such officially approved writers as Anatoly Sofronov. Others such as Nikolai Gribachev, Alexander Chakovsky, and Vasily Smirnov were also attacked by name for their participation in campaigns of abuse and innuendo against respected writers.

The transcript shows a pastiche of charge and counter-charge. Some writers tried to put all the blame on Stalin, claiming that they had behaved honestly, that their genuine love for Stalin had been betrayed. Others condemned such talk as hypocrisy and pointed out that Stalin had created his cult of personality with the eager help of many careerists and timeservers:

> Instead of a socialist apparatus, a bureaucratic apparatus has been built and trained to worship rank, mindless careerism, and the pursuit of the soft job. [It is] an apparatus that has lost all

sense of responsibility. Stalin held the place of the tsar, and his power rested on this apparatus.

Other speakers recalled the tragic fates of fellow writers and members of the Union, who had been persecuted and sometimes died in poverty, while the top Union bureaucrats lived in luxury. A couple of people mentioned the extraordinary case of a high Party ideological expert, Georgy Fyodorovich Aleksandrov (1908–1961), who had recently been revealed as "the key figure in a den of debauchery at a dacha where orgies were held." Like Pavel Yudin, Aleksandrov was a typical product of Stalin's cultural revolution of 1928–31. Throughout the Stalin years Aleksandrov served as a leading Party spokesman on cultural affairs. As head of the Central Committee's powerful Propaganda and Agitation Administration (*Upravlenie propagandy i agitatsii*) from 1940 to 1947, he participated in the 1946 meetings at the Kremlin, when Stalin initiated the post-war crackdown in literature and the arts. Aleksandrov was serving as the Soviet Minister of Culture in 1955, when his sexual shenanigans were exposed.

The pressures all these events placed on Fadeyev can be well imagined. On the night of May 13, less than three months after Khrushchev's secret speech, and two months after the recriminations at the Party meeting in the Union, he committed suicide at the writers' colony of Peredelkino just outside Moscow. The contents of a long farewell letter Fadeyev addressed to the Central Committee have never been revealed. The chief reason, according to a statement attributed by Mikhail Sholokhov to Stalin's longtime crony Klim Voroshilov, was that it was a "terrible letter" in which Fadeyev had "made personal attacks on members of the Politburo!" (*na lichnosti chlenov Politburo pereshel!*).[51]

It would be useful to have Fadeyev's final thoughts made public, but his motives for committing suicide can hardly be in doubt. The official announcement mentioned only alcoholism, but it was common knowledge that Fadeyev began to drink very heavily in the post-war period, well before Stalin's death. Indeed, Khrushchev says in his memoirs that Fadeyev drank to the point that he was often hardly able to stand up when making recommendations for the Stalin Prizes in literature and the arts. Stalin frequently had to send the police and the NKVD to search for Fadeyev in what Khrushchev describes as his favorite "dens of vice" (*po zlachnym mestam*), and bring him to the Kremlin to make his reports.[52]

In 1989 a flood of reminiscences and re-evaluations of Fadeyev began to appear in the Soviet press. He remains a troubling figure for many Russians, in part because he believed so completely in the October Revolution and yet committed so many crimes in its name. He is often pictured as a tragic character, a man who sacrificed his talent and his conscience for the cause. Fadeyev is generally viewed more favorably than his successors in the Brezhnev period, who had no talent and apparently believed in nothing but their own welfare. And yet, whatever the peculiar circumstances of the Stalin period, it is hard to understand, let alone excuse, Fadeyev's behavior on many occasions, which have so far not appeared in the Soviet press. For example, one evening in 1937 he stopped by the apartment of the writer Ivan Kataev, who had belonged to different literary groups than had Fadeyev, but was a member of the Party and enjoyed friendly personal relations with him. Kataev's wife was bathing their baby. In great good humor Fadeyev joined in the splashing and playing with the baby, then left. Only after Stalin's death did Kataev's friends and family learn that on that very same day Fadeyev had counter-signed documents approving his friend's arrest. In the early hours of the morning Kataev was arrested, and died in the Gulag in 1939.

Fadeyev was able to live with his own behavior, chiefly through self-deception and heavy drinking, until Stalin's death in 1953. Then at last he was brought face to face with his Stalinist past. His only justification—serving a noble cause—was stripped away by Khrushchev's speech at the 20th Party Congress in 1956. By that time many writers and their families who had survived the Gulag returned to Moscow as part of Khrushchev's amnesty of political prisoners; they confronted Fadeyev and accused him of complicity in their arrest, and in the deaths of countless comrades.

One such confrontation came to light in April 1989. Ivan Makaryev was a literary critic and, like Uksusov, had unimpeachable class and revolutionary credentials. He and Fadeyev met in 1924 and worked together for a decade or more, first in RAPP and then in the Union. When Makaryev was arrested and sent to the Gulag, he wrote to Fadeyev appealing for his help, then simply asking for some pencils and paper; he received no reply. On his return to Moscow after 19 years in the camps, Makaryev discovered that Fadeyev had co-signed the warrant for his arrest. Confronted with this evidence of treachery, Fadeyev admitted that he had received Makaryev's letters and tried to explain his betrayal: "Forgive me, I got scared. . . . Ivan, spit in my face."[53] Makaryev seems to have been crushed by this confession of betrayal; like Fadeyev, he committed suicide—by cutting his veins.

Fadeyev's personal and professional fate illustrated the bankruptcy of the entire policy of whip and gingerbread that had brought Russian literature to a virtual standstill. The task of the post-Stalin leadership would be to find a way out of the Stalinist dilemma that destroyed Fadeyev and so many of his victims, and to discover what role the Union of Writers should play in reforming and reviving the Party's guidance system.

3

Party Guidance

Our creative unions—the unions of writers, artists, composers, and others—have achieved a high level of ideological and political maturity. They are able to find a principled Party solution even for the most complex ideological and political problems.

CENTRAL COMMITTEE (1957)

Gradually and painfully, as the Party once again resumed its leading role in Soviet society, the Writers' Union rode its coattails to new authority and prestige. The Union became one of the main beneficiaries of the Party's decision to dispense with terror and to replace one-man autocratic rule with a new *modus operandi*—bureaucratic rules and procedures. The transition from coercion to "organized consensus" raised the stock of the Union as a mobilizing agency, but the process took several years to accomplish.[1] It was not until the late sixties that the Party revealed its decision to rely on the Writers' Union as one of the main agencies through which it would try to create Brezhnev's new society. The Union's prominence was acquired at a price: its procedural and structural links with the Party were tightened to such a degree that within a few years both organizations marched in lockstep. This was a price the literary apparatchiks were happy to pay because their own position was secured.

The foundations for these changes were laid by Nikita Khrushchev: he ended mass terror, and restored the Party as a "primary instrument of direction and coordination." In specific terms Khrushchev resuscitated the Central Committee, long moribund under Stalin, as "an organ to legitimize the daily decisions of the Secretariat and the Presidium."[2] And yet, in spite of these accomplishments, Khrushchev replicated, albeit in a minor key, one of

Stalin's most disturbing characteristics, unpredictability. Shimon Markish describes the bizarre atmosphere of those years:

> Khrushchev was very contradictory and whimsical. We never knew what would happen the next day. In this he was like Stalin. But with the one existential and very important difference: we knew that whatever happened, it would *not* be arrest and death.[3]

The newly confident Party apparatchiks should have been Khrushchev's main constituency, but he failed to give them what they most wanted after surviving years of shapeless fear under Stalin: bureaucratic order.

Within the microcosm of the Union of Soviet Writers, Khrushchev repeated this same approach, with even less success. He tried to revive the organization, but he had no literary "policy" other than anti-Stalinism. When liberal writers turned out to have more than that on their own agenda, he lost his temper and tried to bully them back into line. Once he harangued writers in the Kremlin with such ferocity that a woman fainted; on another occasion he grabbed the Union's First Secretary by the lapels and shook him thoroughly. On one memorable day, he became so enraged with liberal writers in the capital that he dissolved the entire Party organization within the Moscow chapter. Markish recalls what happened next:

> You cannot be a member at large in the Communist Party. You have to belong to a "cell." So the Party members in the Moscow branch had to find the closest one, geographically, to the Union. It turned out that the closest one was at the Moscow zoo. So that's where they ended up.[4]

Khrushchev's behavior resulted in scenes much closer to *opera buffa* than Stalinist tragedy, but this switch in genre did not endear him to the victims of his tantrums. Khrushchev's meddling with the Party bureaucracy on the much broader political and economic stage led to his downfall in October 1964.[5]

The new General Secretary, Leonid Brezhnev, substituted bureaucratic legalism for Stalin's autocratic rule and Khrushchev's caprice. Guidelines were set up; a chain of command was clarified; a system of "checks and balances" was implemented. The new leader's reforms did not mark a break with the Stalinist past, except in the vitally important abandonment of mass terror. Rather, they refined bureaucratic procedures that had lain dormant in Stalin's time. Brezhnev played by the rules, both written and unwritten. Within the Writers' Union, the gingerbread would be dispensed predictably, and the whip would fall only when the miscreant had ignored standard operating procedures. This would prove to be a very reassuring and satisfying arrangement for the vast majority of the membership throughout the Brezhnev period.

First, however, Brezhnev had to end the heady and unsettling atmosphere of the cultural Thaw. Opposition from the liberal intelligentsia, reluctant to give up the spasmodic gains made under Khrushchev, lasted a long time. The Union Secretariat continued to delay the Fourth Congress, which should have been held in 1963 even before the removal of Khrushchev. A congress of the more pliant Russian Republic branch of the Union was held in 1965. (In a classic example of the zigzagging that finally brought him down, Khrushchev had established the Russian Republic branch in 1958 as a conservative balance to the Moscow branch, which he had himself founded in 1955 to placate the liberals.) However, it was not until May of 1967, four years later than required by the Statutes, that the Fourth Writers' Congress finally took place. This was the last tense national arena for disagreement among Soviet writers during the Brezhnev years.

Liberal writers struggled to salvage some of the freedoms and options obtained during the Thaw. Alexander Solzhenitsyn, though not a delegate, sent an open letter to the Congress demanding an end to censorship and attacking the Union Secretariat for not protecting its own members. Solzhenitsyn's letter was ignored, even though nearly one hundred writers signed a second open letter in support of his views. The volume containing the stenographic report of the Fourth Congress is less than half the size of those for the preceding and following congresses: the Party wanted to get it over with as smoothly and quickly as possible. The proceedings were completely dominated by conservative and hardline writers. None of a handful of liberals present as delegates addressed the delegates. The printed speeches are a steady repetition of self-congratulation and abuse of the United States and its allies. The one jarring note in this litany was sounded by a foreigner, the Italian writer Carlo Levi, author of the novel *Christ Stopped at Eboli* and other works of fiction and social commentary. As an official guest Levi was polite, but he did insist, in the spirit of André Malraux a generation earlier, that "concepts such as 'formalism', 'dogmatism', 'modernism' and so forth, which are contrasted to a narrow type of realism, have now grown obsolete; they are out of date and have lost any real meaning."[6]

The three years following the Fourth Congress saw the Party use the celebration of several important anniversaries to pound home its message that the Thaw was over. The rest of 1967 was taken up with celebrations marking the fiftieth anniversary of the

October Revolution. The Party ordered a joint plenum of the Boards of all the creative unions on October 21, where devotion to the Party and its Leninist principles became the main agenda. Hardly had the echoes faded from the 1967 celebrations than the centenary of Gorky's birth occurred in June 1968, and preparations began to mark the one hundredth anniversary of Lenin's birth in 1970. The new hard line was also implemented in Eastern Europe. In August of 1968, Soviet and Warsaw Pact tanks rolled into Czechoslovakia: the "Prague Spring," harvest of the Thaw, was forcibly blighted.

The Party used these occasions to reassert its primacy and to demand ideological conformity to the old trinity of *partynost, narodnost,* and *ideinost.* But this revival of Leninist principles was not matched by a return to Stalinist terror. In 1965–66, the Party flirted briefly with show trials and jail sentences for writers in the celebrated case of Andrei Sinyavsky and Yuly Daniel. But the universal outrage that was expressed in the West, even among European communists, at the harsh sentences imposed on the two writers made it reconsider this policy. Yury Andropov, appointed head of the KGB in 1967, implemented a sophisticated new strategy for punishing "dissidents"—individuals who wrote and distributed materials in *samizdat* ("self-published") or sent works abroad to the West as *tamizdat* ("published there"). A few hardcore dissidents were jailed, but for the most part writers—and particularly members of the Writers' Union—were left untouched. Instead of being arrested and sent to Siberia, several writers with international reputations were shipped to the West as exiles or encouraged to emigrate, sometimes through KGB harassment.

Brezhnev's new system of guidance for literature, which stressed organizational control through the Union's bureaucratic procedures and structures, was based on a thorough review of the Soviet cultural scene, including the proper function of all creative unions. It may have been this review that led legal specialists at the Soviet Academy of Sciences' Institute of State and Law to publish in 1970 a collaborative study of the creative unions. This is still the only book-length analysis of these unique institutions published in any language.[7] There is no way of knowing what direct influence this volume may have had on Brezhnev's thinking, but it did provide the legal foundation for a more bureaucratic approach to Soviet professionals in literature and the arts.

The Brezhnev guidance system dominated Soviet literature throughout his lifetime and to some extent still endures in the Gorbachev period. He encouraged the Union to extend its authority over writers, and assured the Secretariat of personal security—he adopted the same approach in the much larger arena of the Party bureaucracy. As the Union's role increased, that of the other two pillars of the guidance system declined in importance. The official literary credo, Socialist Realism, was declared to be a flexible method for writers, not a dogmatic, exclusive style. The formal censorship organization, Glavlit, had already assumed secondary importance as a backstop to prevent the revelation of state secrets, or the mention of people, places, and events considered taboo.

In taking these decisions the Party demonstrated a remarkably pragmatic approach, while not abandoning either centralized control or its overall objective: the publication of works that illustrated and supported the Party's policies. Party ideologists could not wait until the finished manuscript was presented to the Glavlit censor; to do so would be to revert to traditionally passive tsarist censorship. At the same time, the Party had learned from its experience with the Sinyavsky and Daniel trial that it could not rely on Socialist Realism to "guide" the creative intelligentsia. If the threat of physical force could no longer be effective in controlling writers, then Socialist Realism was of little value. Hence the Party switched instead to a more sophisticated organizational approach, the use of bureaucratic procedures.

The "Brezhnev solution" involved bringing the Writers' Union onto center stage. Following the 1967 Congress highly placed literary bureaucrats and ideological specialists discussed the need for the Union to take a much larger part in Soviet literary life. They noted that its members already occupied influential posts in such key agencies as the State Committee for the Press, which Khrushchev had established in 1963. Union members also sat on the editorial boards of most literary journals throughout the country. In fact, members of the Secretariat served as chief editors of nearly half the so-called "central" journals. The purpose of these discussions was to increase the Secretariat's control over all major literary journals, including *Novy mir*, whose liberal chief editor, Alexander Tvardovsky, was forced to resign in 1970 (he died of cancer the following year).

To balance this increased authority, structural and procedural links were tightened between the Party and the Union. These were announced at a key plenum of the Board on November 3–4, 1970. This meeting did not make any headlines in the West, and has passed almost unnoticed ever since. But its decisions guided the Writers' Union's relationship vis-à-vis the Party into the age of glasnost and perestroika. The most significant action of the Board at this plenum was the creation of a new "Bureau" (*byuro*), called the Litburo in this book. The Litburo consisted of only nine men, selected from among members in the Secretariat. The formation of this small executive unit brought several managerial advantages. Until 1959 the Presidium had served as a representative body for the first secretaries or presidents of Republic and other regional branches. When the Third Congress abolished the Presidium, these representatives joined the Secretariat, which had grown almost tenfold from its original size and had thus lost its exclusive character. Regional officers of the Union were now invited to become temporary members of the Litburo during their regular sojourns in the capital. But they lost their permanent status in the ruling organ of the Union. On the other hand, the Litburo had effectively created internships for its far-flung bureaucracy, while at the same time reserving to itself the power to make decisions affecting the whole Union.

The emergence of the Litburo represented a significant operational congruence between the administrative machinery of the Party and the Union, a final stage in the growing symbiotic relationship between the two organizations, which had begun at the Union's inaugural congress in 1934. At the apex of the Union now sat a small group of men paralleling the Politburo. The outer rim of the inner circle in the Union would remain, as it did in the Party, the Secretariat. The Union Secretariat of over 60 people is itself drawn from a Board (*Pravlenie*) of about 300 members, which might be compared roughly to the Party's Central Committee in its functions. There are one or two formal differences. The Union Secretariat is larger than the Party Secretariat, and the Litburo membership must be drawn from the Secretariat. By contrast, it is possible to be a member of the Politburo and not a member of the Party Secretariat, and vice versa. These apparent anomalies have no great significance and result simply from a different historical development in the Party, and specifically from Stalin's use of the Secretariat as a power base to outmaneuver his Politburo rivals in the twenties.

Like the Party, although on a much smaller scale, the Union has an extensive bureaucracy assisted by a large support staff. The most important units are the Foreign Commission (*Inostrannaya komissia*), the Creative Personnel Department (*Otdel tvorcheskikh kadrov*), the Planning and Finance Department (*Planovo-finansovy otdel*), the Department of Administration and Management (*Administrativno-khozyaistvenny otdel*), the Protocol Department (*Protokolny otdel*), and the Archives (*Arkhiv*). The Union also provides "consultants" on literary questions in general as well as on the literatures of the Soviet Union. While not identical, the Party's organs—its Central Committee departments—function in much the same fashion on its own organizational chart.

The establishment of the Litburo, and the other plenum decisions, were formalized at the Fifth Congress of Writers in late June–early July 1971—the first congress ever to take place in the year stipulated by the Statutes. In his report to the 1971 Congress on proposed revisions to the Statutes, Sergei Sartakov, a member of the Secretariat, requested formal approval for the creation of the Litburo, although it already existed and he himself was serving as its vice-president. Sartakov described the new Litburo as a "work team" (*rabocheye zveno*), necessary to take care of everyday questions because other members of the Secretariat would be occupied elsewhere, serving the enlarged membership in the Union, and assuming extra duties as a result of the organization's growing international exchanges and contacts. During his report Sartakov also announced a proposal to follow other creative unions in extending the gap between Union congresses from four to five years (it had at first been only three years). Sartakov suggested that the main reason for the change was that it took so much time and effort to prepare congresses, and everyone needed more breathing space.[8]

In fact, Sartakov's proposal was almost certainly prompted by the Party's desire to tighten the links between the Union and its parent organization. The Party planned to avoid a repetition of the unruly atmosphere of the 1954 and 1959 Congresses, and to make them "work" in a more positive sense than the sullen 1967 Congress. The Fifth Congress was timed to take place four months after the 24th Party Congress the previous February. In the interval, two Republic branches held their congresses, at which attention was focused on the major policy statements made at the Party Congress, and delegates were briefed and elected to attend the Union Congress to be held in June. In this way the Party established an effective sequential pattern, which had been laid out during a special meeting of the Union's Secretariat on April 12 of 1971, shortly after the 24th Party Congress. The meeting was devoted to an extended discussion of the decisions and tasks set forth by the Party Congress. It concluded with a formal resolution outlining the ways in which the Union would work to implement them. This resolution, announced with great fanfare in the press, linked the Union more closely to the Party's program. It directed the membership to fulfill tasks specifically assigned by the Party, as in the early thirties, when writers were urged to produce five-year plan novels. Henceforth, the Union was to serve more overtly as the Party's agent, with the exclusive power and authority that had been denied RAPP.

The Party immediately made effective use of the timing. Since

Party congresses are held to announce and lay out the nation's economic five-year plans, the revised schedule made it easier for the Party to set the Union's ideological agenda for the next five years. Each year, in between congresses, the Union (like the Party) holds plenary sessions or plenums, which are designed to refine and discuss Party policy in the arts. At one stroke, the problem of defining Socialist Realism was solved. What was Socialist Realism but the Party line at any given moment? Each Party Congress announced a new five-year plan. The slogans and targets in that plan could now be promulgated on a regular basis through the Union's own machinery, in the congresses and plenums that followed shortly afterward. A flexible operational definition was substituted for previous efforts to dress up *partynost* as an esthetic theory: Socialist Realism is that literature which fulfills its tasks in light of the decisions of the preceding Party Congress. Specific issues on the Party's agenda became the menu for new literary works. As a theory, Socialist Realism had always been interpreted by the Party to meet changing circumstances. Now the Party had given this elasticity organizational shape.

The 1971 revision of the Union Statutes proposed by Sergei Sartakov reinforced a trend already noticeable in the 1967 version, by mentioning Socialist Realism only toward the end of the opening preamble, almost as an afterthought. And it emphasized the official view that Socialist Realism was an "open system," offering possibilities for "the appearance of individual talents, and for innovation in all literary genres." Thus Socialist Realism as a literary theory had become less dogmatic, and much less central to the concerns of the Union itself and its members. These changes were officially justified because Soviet literature had entered "a new historical epoch." The socializing and educative role of literature was still stressed, but now homogenized into a rather vague assignment: "The spiritual formation of man in a new society." Such language was directly linked to the claims of the Brezhnev regime that Soviet society had reach a new plateau called "advanced (or mature) socialism" (*razvitoi* [*zrely*] *sotsializm*), itself barely a step or two away from full communism. This policy was less extravagant—and less quantifiable—than Khrushchev's promise in the 1961 Party Program that the Soviet Union would overtake the United States' GNP and achieve communism by 1980.

The rescheduling of the Union congresses resulted in a rapid increase in ideological decorum. In sharp contrast to the two congresses held in Khrushchev's time, and even to the First Congress in 1934, the remaining two congresses in the Brezhnev period sounded like a Party-Union diapason. The 1976 Congress heard

235 delegates speak from the rostrum, but all their speeches were variations on the same theme: the Party and the Union were in complete harmony. First Secretary Georgy Markov addressed the delegates in language alluding to Lenin's phrase "Calm yourselves, gentlemen!," used in his 1905 article "Party Organization and Party Literature":

> Well, comrades, we can calm the foreign gentlemen by telling them the truth: it's true, there are many commissars in the Union of Writers: eight thousand! All of us Soviet writers, both by conviction and in spirit, and in our way of life, are indomitable Red commissars, for whom there is nothing more dear on this earth than Leninist truth, than the great cause of our heroic people and of our own Communist Party! (applause)[9]

With its writers described as commissars for the Party, the Union's role as a Party clone under Brezhnev was made abundantly clear.

By the Seventh Union Congress in 1981, the formal unity of the two organizations was complete: writers had become Party apparatchiks, and vice versa. In April 1979 First Secretary Georgy Markov had awarded General Secretary Leonid Brezhnev the Lenin Prize for Literature. In his 1981 report Markov extolled the Party leader's literary talents:

> Heartfelt thanks to Leonid Ilyich Brezhnev for his books *Malaya zemlya*, *Rebirth*, and *Virgin Land*, which in recent years have given us fine lessons in service to the people, and have had enormous influence on all types and genres of literature.[10]

There was little to choose between General Secretary and First Secretary. Brezhnev had become a writer and Markov had become a Party apparatchik; indeed he was a full member of the Party's Central Committee, as Alexander Fadeyev had been in his time.

Establishing the ideological reliability of Union congresses was but one part of the overall Brezhnev plan. Congresses only occur every five years, and plenums usually twice a year, in direct imitation of the Party's Central Committee plenums. The Party still needed to make personnel changes, to find people to conduct the day-to-day operations of the Union in a more effective and reliable manner. Accordingly, Georgy Markov was appointed first vice-president of the new Litburo at the November 1970 plenum. For the time being, Konstantin Fedin was named president of the Litburo, and retained his position as First Secretary of the Union. The remaining members of the Litburo were: S. V. Sartakov (vice-president), S. A. Baruzdin, Yu. N. Verchenko, S. V. Mikhalkov, V. M. Ozerov, N. S. Tikhonov, and A. B. Chakovsky. These men were all longtime Party stalwarts; some had taken an active part in attacking Pasternak and Sinyavsky and Daniel, and had been richly rewarded for their loyalty. The total domination of Russians in the Litburo demonstrated the Brezhnev administration's sharp turn toward Russian nationalism, and its heavy reliance on literary bureaucrats from the Russian Republic branch of the Union.

Markov, author of interminable, propagandistic novels about World War II and Soviet diplomatic history, had come to the Party's attention as one of the "Siberian mafia" active in the Russian Republic branch of the Union. He had been moved to the forefront of the Union during the implementation of the Brezhnev reforms of 1970–71. For several years he had given major addresses at Union plenary sessions, and had been a central figure in the crackdown at the 1967 congress. Markov was evidently being groomed as a reliable functionary to take over Fedin's place as First Secretary. The Secretariat effected this change on July 20, 1971, at its first meeting following the Fifth Congress, when it formally established an expanded Litburo, consisting of thirteen men rather than nine. Fedin was dropped entirely from the Litburo and moved from his position as First Secretary of the Union to the purely honorary position of President of the Board. He was replaced as president of the Litburo and First Secretary by Markov, who was assisted in the Litburo by three vice-presidents, all of whom were holdovers: Yu. N. Verchenko, V. M. Ozerov, and S. V. Sartakov. New additions to the Litburo were A. P. Keshokov, V. M. Kozhevnikov, M. K. Lukonin, S. S. Narovchatov, K. M. Simonov, and N. T. Fedorenko. None of these men was a writer of the first or even second rank, with the partial exception of Simonov; some were not writers at all. However, all were reliable Party supporters and all were Russians, except for the russified ethnic Alim Keshokov, originally from what is now the Kabardin-Balkar Autonomous Republic.

Although in a position of great trust as First Secretary, Markov was not left to run the Union alone. The Party had long been aware of the potential conflict between ideological control and professional expertise, most obviously during the Civil War. To combat the danger of Bonapartism, it adopted the system of military commissars, that is, political officers attached to each military commander. During the late twenties and early thirties the Party introduced ideological commissars to work with other professionals. In this way the Party always had its own man working side by side with the specialist, and reporting directly back to the Central Committee in Moscow, or to an appropriate Party organization outside the capital. The Writers' Union from early days followed the same practice, with Vladimir Stavsky serving as the ideological commissar and Alexander Fadeyev offering professional expertise and support, as well as helping to preserve the myth of the Union's independence as a voluntary association of writers.

The usual title of the Party's representative in any organization or institution is "responsible official" (*otvetstvenny rabotnik*) or "responsible secretary" (*otvetstvenny sekretar*) or—in the publishing world—"responsible editor" (*otvetstvenny redaktor*). In Soviet parlance, the adjective "responsible" always indicates that the person answers to the Party authorities, not that he or she is accountable in any sense to colleagues and the general public.[11] In the Writers' Union the term "organizational secretary" (*orgsekretar*) came to be used to designate the ideological commissar. The position of *orgsekretar* has always been held by a full-time apparatchik, who is not a writer and usually not even a member of the organization he supervises on behalf of the Party. Dmitry Polikarpov, who held the position during the forties and fifties while Fadeyev was General Secretary, was offended by an interviewer who thought he was a writer. "What fiction of mine have you read?" he asked. "If none, why do you call me a writer?"[12] Polikarpov thought of himself as a *politruk*, or *politichesky rukovoditel*, that is, a political apparatchik.

Over the years, occupants of this post have displayed greater ambitions to be considered writers. Whether this desire prompted a change in title is not clear, but under Brezhnev the Central Committee's man in the Union came to be known by the more expansive phrase, "secretary for organizational and creative questions" (*sekretar po organizatsionno-tvorcheskim voprosam*), later "secretary for organizational and creative work" (*sekretar po organizatsionno-tvorcheskoi rabote*). The transition from "non-writer" to ostensible author began under Konstantin Voronkov, who served prior to 1970. Voronkov fulfilled the requirement for Union membership in a unique fashion. The rules stipulate that the candidate, if he is a prose writer, must have published at least one book, and preferably two. Voronkov submitted his sole literary output: he had put together the telephone directory of the Union. Since the Soviet Union lacks residential (as opposed to government) telephone books, this directory, including name, address, and phone number for each member, was much more widely used than the great tomes produced by many of his colleagues in the Secretariat. An updated version is published every five years in connection with each national congress.[13]

In spite of this contribution, at the November 1970 plenum of the Union Board, Voronkov was transferred to the Soviet government's Ministry of Culture as deputy minister. On the surface,

Voronkov's appointment was a promotion, but transfers from Party to government positions, at least since Malenkov lost power by selecting the state bureaucracy, have constituted the twilight of a political career. In reality Voronkov was being kicked upstairs because of his perceived failure to keep rebellious writers on a tighter rein over the past decade. The Board then "confirmed" (*utverdil*) the appointment of Yury Verchenko as "secretary for organizational and creative work" to replace Voronkov. Only confirmation was necessary because the appointment had already been made by the Party Central Committee, which was assigning Verchenko the job of whipping the Union membership into shape as part of Brezhnev's reforms.

Verchenko is not listed as a member of the Union; presumably he has other sources of special privilege. Everyone understands his role and the source of his power. He is the Party's chief liaison and authority in the organization, holding a position roughly equivalent to that of a Chief Executive Officer or CEO at an American corporation. The émigré writer Anatoly Gladilin emphasized: "In practice, he [Verchenko] runs the whole show at the Union." Another émigré, Alexander Gershkovich (now working at Harvard's Russian Research Center), remarked that Verchenko "cannot put two words together in a newspaper article, but . . . has used his privileged position in order to become a 'literary general.'" On the other hand, two of the more liberal writers who have worked directly with Verchenko—Vitaly Korotich, chief editor of *Ogonyok*, and Grigory Baklanov, chief editor of *Znamya*—both gave him good marks for doing his job in a decent way, unlike his precedessors.[14]

Verchenko's career is typical of most Party ideological specialists assigned to media and culture. He rose through the Komsomol to become a secretary of that organization, then he served as director of the Komsomol's Molodaya Gvardia Publishing House. (One émigré pointed out that "at the top levels, the Komsomol and the KGB are very close.") Party apparatchiks in all fields often cut their teeth on full-time work in the Komsomol before switching to the Party itself. Prior to his 1970 appointment to the Writers' Union by the Central Committee, Verchenko was a secretary of the Moscow City Party Committee or *gorkom*, an important position. His move to the Union represented a promotion, or at least a lateral move to gain further experience. Verchenko's true power—as the *éminence grise* of the entire organization—illustrates a familiar Soviet pattern, whereby the second-in-command actually makes decisions, while the nominal head gives speeches and exercises overall general supervision. So, for example, the second secretaries of Republic and other regional Party committees, who run things, are usually Russian, while the first secretaries are often members of the local nationality.

Since Verchenko was not even a member of the Union, he could hardly have been legally elected to any office in the organization, let alone to the Litburo itself. How, then, did the Central Committee of the Party appoint him to this extremely powerful position, which he still occupied twenty years later? The answer to this question illuminates a dark corner of the Soviet universe: the *nomenklatura* system. Put simply, the position of "secretary for organizational and creative work" does not belong to the Union membership. It is not a post open for election; the occupant can only be appointed through the *nomenklatura* system, which is controlled by the Party and its chief executive organ, the KGB. It does not matter that Verchenko, the most powerful official in the Union, the *orgsekretar*, is not a member of the Union. What matters is that his position is on the *nomenklatura* list, and that he himself is a *nomenklaturny rabotnik* (*nomenklatura* official) or, as Russians put it more colloquially, *nomenklaturshchik*, that is, "one of the *nomenklatura* crowd."

The word *nomenklatura* itself is borrowed from the Latin *nomenclatura*, that is, list or catalogue. No Soviet dictionary provides an operative definition of the term, but every Soviet citizen understands its true meaning and enormous importance. The Party maintains two lists (as does the KGB). The first is a list of positions that it has the authority to fill. The second is a list of the people who occupy these positions and their level of service. There is also a third list of "potential appointees"—a sort of back-up list.[15] Collectively, these lists make up the *nomenklatura* system. The Party uses the lists for both patronage and as a means of controlling appointments. The *nomenklatura* system is the Soviet equivalent of the "old boy network," or of the Freemasons, in the sense that it operates behind the scenes. Its lists recall the so-called Plum Book of political appointments in Washington, DC, which hopefuls pore through during every Presidential election year, except that neither the *nomenklatura* lists nor their procedures are made public.

The *nomenklatura* system, based on Lenin's insistence on Party control over personnel decisions, was formally introduced by Stalin. Nevertheless, it has deep roots in the traditional Russian method of rule, specifically the feudal system of personal allegiance to the tsar, and later to the service nobility or *dvoryanstvo*, established by Tsar Peter the Great at the beginning of the eighteenth century. Then as now, each individual's career prospects, privileges, and social standing depended totally on his position in an elaborate ranking system maintained by the state.

Members of the *nomenklatura* are all appointed or approved by Party personnel specialists. They have been called the "second pillar" of the ruling Party bureaucracy—the first pillar being the elected officials in the Central Committee and Central Auditing Commission of the Party.[16] Each level of the Party (and of the KGB) has its own *nomenklatura* lists of the people and positions over which it has authority. The most important lists are those under the direct control of the Politburo itself, but the Central Committee's lists contain many of the top positions in Soviet society, including the chief editors of all so-called "central" (national) publications. One can assume that the great majority of names in the *nomenklatura* lists are those of Party members, since joining the Party is the usual (but not exclusive) prerequisite for advancement in all fields.

Whether or not a man or woman is in the Party, membership in the *nomenklatura* guarantees a person virtual security for life; whatever he does, it is very unlikely that he will be fired, although he might be demoted if he makes too many mistakes or loses out in a bureaucratic power struggle. Even then, he will probably be reappointed to a position of some authority, with plenty of privileges and clout. In any case, it is common practice to rotate these men and women around to various jobs, especially in their younger and middle years, so that they can gain broad experience. The usual pattern for an apparatchik in media and culture is to start working in the Komsomol, perhaps as a secretary for ideological matters, then to move to a similar position in a Party organization, with assignments on the editorial board of a journal or newspaper, in the State Committee for Publishing (Goskomizdat), and finally in the Central Committee Departments of Culture and/or of Propaganda (coalesced in 1988 into a new Commission for Ideology). If less successful, he or she will perform these functions at the Republic or regional level over many years, and perhaps never reach Moscow.

Like all executives and managers in the Soviet Union, both the Union's First Secretary (Vladimir Karpov since 1986) and Yury Verchenko, its "organizational secretary," are members of the *nomenklatura*, as are other top members of the Union Secretariat. All were carefully vetted by the Party before receiving their appointments. According to Michael Voslensky, a high-ranking Soviet official who defected to West Germany, the position of Union First Secretary is *nomenklatura* of the Politburo.[17] This suggests that the leadership considers the Union a very important organization, one that must be led by elite members of the Party.

Several former members of the Union declared that Verchenko's position is on the *nomenklatura* list of the KGB. This would certainly explain why Verchenko is free to travel so much and to greet foreign writers and delegations in Moscow, and why he was put in charge of a special Council for Afghan Literature following the Soviet invasion of that country. The KGB connection is also confirmed by the fact that a former Lt.-General in the KGB, Victor Ilyin, served for many years as the organizational secretary of the Moscow branch of the Writers' Union. However, these close ties do not mean that the KGB "commands" in the Union—it is simply that the KGB has oversight responsibility in Soviet society for all matters concerning foreigners and foreign travel. Verchenko's appointment could not have been made without Party approval. The counterweight between the position of First Secretary as *nomenklatura* of the Politburo, and the position of *orgsekretar* as *nomenklatura* of the KGB, offers a fascinating illustration of the Soviet version of checks and balances.

While Verchenko actually "runs the show" at the Union, the First Secretary possesses a great deal of authority. Presumably both make an effort to avoid conflict, which would oblige them to submit their differences to higher arbitration, and also create an unfortunate impression in the Central Committee. Personalities and professional contacts must play a role in determining how decisions are made, but networking at the upper levels of Soviet society remains a mystery. It was common knowledge that Georgy Markov enjoyed an unusually warm relationship with Leonid Brezhnev and would have been a dangerous man to cross. But émigré and exiled writers, who seemed knowledgeable about these matters, insisted on the superior operational authority of Verchenko because of the nature of his position and because the full-time ideological bureaucrat, not the professional writer (however devoted), always has the final say in practical matters. Although he stayed in the background during the Brezhnev period, Verchenko has become more outspoken, and has played a more public role since Markov retired as First Secretary in 1986.

Verchenko is assisted in running the Union by a number of secretaries, both within and without the Litburo. It appears that all members of the Litburo are considered "working secretaries" (*rabochie sekretari*), that is, they occupy a full-time, salaried position (*shtatnaya dolzhnost*) in the Union; such people are sometimes called *shtatnye sekretari*, meaning that they are part of the *shtat*, or regular staff, of an institution. The salaried staff of the Union runs to several hundred people (the exact figure has not been made public), but it is only the top secretaries who have final decision-making authority. Membership in the Litburo has ranged from nine to sixteen. Following the Eighth Union Congress in 1986, the Litburo consisted of nine men, but two years later Verchenko stated that the number of "working secretaries" had been reduced to eight. Georgy Markov, at that time President of the Board and a member of the Litburo, had himself requested that his duties be curtailed, and was therefore working "on a voluntary basis" (*na obshchestvennykh nachalakh*).[18] In a word, Markov had lost his monthly income; in January 1989, again officially at his own request, Markov was removed from his position as Board President.

The remaining eight "working secretaries" in the Litburo as of 1989 were: Vladimir Karpov (First Secretary), Yury Verchenko (Organizational Secretary), Chingiz Aitmatov, Grigory Baklanov, Yury Bondarev, Vasily Bykov, Oles Gonchar, and Sergei Zalygin. While it is clear that Karpov and Verchenko by virtue of their *nomenklatura* positions exercise general supervision of the Union's affairs, the precise role of the other members of the Litburo is less obvious. Baklanov, in an interview in August 1989, said that the 1986 Litburo was "stillborn." It hardly ever meets and conducts no business, chiefly because its members hold diametrically opposed views on so many fundamental issues.

Since the Litburo was established in 1970 its membership has gradually changed in two ways. First, as of 1989 it included more established writers than mere literary apparatchiks: Aitmatov, Bykov, and Zalygin are respected writers, and Baklanov and Bondarev each scored some popular successes with World War II novels, although they are now on opposite sides in the debate over glasnost and perestroika: Bondarev is a Russian nationalist and an extreme conservative—a frequent combination in contemporary Soviet society. Baklanov has lent his support to glasnost and perestroika as chief editor of *Znamya*. Second, the Litburo is less dominated by ethnic Russians, even though the representatives from other literatures write frequently or even exclusively in Russian: Aitmatov is Kirghiz, Bykov is Belorussian, and Gonchar is Ukrainian.

These changes suggest that during the Brezhnev period the Litburo gradually lost effectiveness as a governing body, leaving the actual day-to-day executive operations to the so-called "released secretaries" (*osvobozhdyonnye sekretari*). The term "released" refers to those full-time Party functionaries who are released from other duties, in this case the obligation to write, so that they may be paid to devote themselves to organizational affairs and Party liaison. Although there had been earlier references to the great authority of "released secretaries" in Soviet publications, it was not until the era of glasnost that their names were listed. The account of a meeting of the new Board, following the Eighth Congress of Writers in June 1986, referred to nine men as "released secretaries," apparently for the first time: G. Borovik, Yu. Gribov, N. Gorbachev (not a family relation, as far as is known), Ye. Isaev, Al. Mikhailov, P. Proskurin, A. Salynsky, K. Skvortsov, and Yu. Surovtsev.[19] Both Isaev and Surovtsev had been members of the Litburo, but now moved over to become "released secretaries"; there appears to be no overlapping membership between the two groups.

All of these men are long-time functionaries with many years of devoted service to the Party in media and cultural affairs. None of them could be considered creative writers, although they have published books, or "non-books" as many Russians call them. These publications are designed to give some justification to their authority in the Union and also to provide them with substantial incomes, since they can arrange to have their books published in large editions. Pyotr Lukich Proskurin, for example, is widely viewed as a hack, and has enthusiastically persecuted writers and editors who show any sign of departing from a strict Party line. Genrikh Aviezerovich Borovik is more of a journalist than a creative writer; he is a *mezhdunarodnik* (a foreign affairs specialist who enjoys the privilege of travelling abroad frequently) and is certainly a man with close KGB ties, if he is not a KGB officer himself. Yury Tarasovich Gribov, among other duties, served as joint chairman with Yury Verchenko of the 1987 commission to revise the Union Statutes. Nikolai Andreyevich Gorbachev was the head of Litfund in 1989. Georgy Aleksandrovich Isaev (pen-name Yegor Isaev) is a reactionary poet, an old campaigner, like Afanasy Dmitrievich Salynsky (chief editor of the journal *Teatr*), Konstantin Vasilievich Skvortsov, and Yury Ivanovich Surovtsev (who chairs the Bureau of Councils on Literatures of the Peoples of the USSR). These are the men who give speeches on the tasks of Soviet literature "in light of" the latest Party congress, plenum, or decree. In October 1987 Alexander Alekseyevich Mikhailov became the new first secretary of the Moscow Writers' Organization. He won an election (reported in the press) over Yevgeny Yevtushenko, a poet who has been an outspoken advocate of glasnost.

All the "freed secretaries" belong to the Moscow chapter of the Union, except for Skvortsov who comes from Chelyabinsk. But in fact, nearly all of them are provincials, who came to the capital as part of Brezhnev's campaign to swamp the Writers' Union with reliable authors. It is these men who form the central *apparat* of the Union. They, and the consultants and instructors assigned from the Central Committee, are said to make the important day-to-day decisions affecting the lives and professional careers of Union members.[20] They also have a quite extensive clerical and administrative staff at their disposal, although Verchenko has promised publicly that the Union is planning to reduce its staff by one quarter, while not mentioning any actual numbers.

The so-called working and released secretaries are responsible for law and order in the Union; their job is to keep everyone in line, to make good reports to their superiors in the Central Committee, and to demonstrate that people are writing approved works, which display *partynost, ideinost,* and *narodnost*. They perform various bureaucratic functions, attending meetings, welcoming foreign delegations, travelling to give speeches throughout the country, and consulting with functionaries at other institutions both in the capital and elsewhere. Rather like members of the Politburo dividing up responsibilities for various departments or areas of government, the full-time working secretaries take charge of one or more of the administrative bodies or the commissions and "social councils" (*obshchestvennye sovety*) in the Union.[21]

The situation of the First Secretary, the *orgsekretar*, and the other top secretaries is very like that of management executives in a Western corporation; they must produce results and report regularly to their board, which in this case is the Party Central Committee, not the Ministry of Culture. In cultural affairs, as throughout Soviet society, the power of the state or government apparatus is subordinate to that of the parallel Party apparatus. Several former members of the Union pointed out that the Ministry plays no part in the organization's affairs. One added bluntly: "The Ministry is in charge of such things as workers' cultural clubs and musical concerts. It is considered one of the most despised ministries," because it lacks politicial clout.[22] The Ministers of Culture and of Education (or their representatives) do participate in plenary sessions of the Union Board, but have no real decision-making authority.

Although it has been reorganized on several occasions over the years, the Central Committee apparatus has always retained primary responsibility for the Union.[23] However the titles change, ideological specialists from one or more departments of the Central Committee have always controlled the activities of the Union of Soviet Writers, and of all the other creative unions. Throughout the Brezhnev era the Department of Culture and the Department of Propaganda shared responsibility. The Department of Culture also supervised movies, music, and theaters, while the Department of Propaganda took care of publishing houses, newspapers, magazines, television, radio, and sports. The Department of Propaganda exercised final authority over publishing, and it had more staff than the Department of Culture, and broader responsibilities: while the

Department of Culture's top executive staff consisted of only a head (*zaveduyushchy*), first deputy, and deputy, the Department of Propaganda included a head, two first deputies, and four deputies.[24]

The head of the Department of Culture (that is, until the restructuring in 1988) was Yury Petrovich Voronov, first appointed in 1986 under Mikhail Gorbachev. Officials in the Central Committee Department of Culture may or may not have been members of the Writers' Union, or any other creative union. Yury Voronov was listed as a member as early as the 1976 *Directory* (*Spravochnik*). He is referred to as a poet; predictably, he previously served in the Union Secretariat. Voronov oversaw the work of the Union, but hands-on control was exercised by his deputies, who were not Union members.[25] Voronov has a reputation for being relatively liberal, stemming from his behavior as chief editor of the Soviet youth newspaper *Molodaya gvardia* in the mid-sixties, until he was removed by Brezhnev and went into limbo. The even more powerful position of head of the Department of Propaganda was, until the fall of 1988, Yury Aleksandrovich Sklyarov. This department saw some of its "comers" vault to membership in the Central Committee Secretariat or the Politburo itself.[26]

The Central Committee's Department of Culture exercised its authority over the Union with great discretion, and the new Commission for Ideology will doubtless follow its example. The Department of Culture had a special literature section (*sektor literatury*), headed for several years by V. A. Stepanov. His name used to crop up at the end of accounts of many major and minor meetings of the Secretariat and the Board, and on numerous other occasions. Stepanov's comments were hardly ever quoted; it was simply stated in a ritualistic phrase that "V. A. Stepanov, section head in the Central Committee Department of Culture, attended (*prisutsvoval*), or took part (*prinyal uchastie, uchastvoval*), or spoke (*vystupil*) in the discussion." Under glasnost it became quite common for the names of other Party bureaucrats from this Department to be quoted in similar contexts. Its head, Yury Voronov, was present only at the more important gatherings, but the Party's spoor was apparent from phrases such as a "responsible official (*otvetstvenny rabotnik*) of the Central Committee Department of Culture, A. S. Filin," took part in the discussions of a meeting of the Litburo.[27]

The Central Committee Department of Culture did not have exclusive control; its officials had to consider, for example, the authority of the Department of Propaganda and of Goskomizdat over questions of publication, and also the views of Glavlit (the censorship organization), and of course of superiors in the Politburo and Party Secretariat. Nonetheless, Voronov had an extensive staff to "guide" the Union, and the other organizations and groups that came under his purview. In addition to the literature section (*sektor literatury*), he could call upon senior or "responsible" officials (*otvetstvennye rabotniki*), instructors (*instruktory*), and inspectors (*inspektory*), who actually "run things" (*kurirovat*),[28] as well as upon research assistants and lecturers (*lektory*). It is not known exactly how many people were, or are now, involved.

Nor do we know much about the manner and procedures for Party control of the Union Secretariat, chiefly because guidance is exercised through the telephone. This is no ordinary phone; it is the *vertushka* or closed circuit "hotline" with which members of the *nomenklatura* communicate in secret with officials in the Central Committee. The general Party pattern requires that nothing be written down, no records kept. In a personal interview Vasily Aksyonov described the top bureaucrats in the Union as living in their own special country called "Telephonia." In fact, this is the same country in which all Soviet officials live, particularly those in the Party *nomenklatura*. Whenever he wishes to exercise his authority, a Party official can and does pick up the telephone; he can even tell a judge how to decide a court case. The practice is so widespread that this type of interference is known as "telephone law" in the Soviet press.[29]

Vasily Betaki, a poet and translator from the Leningrad chapter of the Union, now living in Paris, corroborated this description of the decision-making process. He explained the difference between appearance and reality in the country at large and the Writers' Union in particular:

> In the Soviet Union there are written laws and then there are laws that everyone knows but they are not written down anywhere. . . . The Soviet system, unlike the old Russian system that was based on written law, has introduced a new method of operating by custom, where nothing is written down. So the way things work is that Party bureaucrats do not use documents; everything is arranged by telephone.[30]

It would be hard to find a better example of what the pioneer American sociologist Charles Page termed the "inner face" of an organization, that is, "the rules, groupings and sanctioned systems of procedure . . . that are never recorded in the codes or official blueprints." As long as the executives of an organization can operate arbitrarily and in secret, the person at the bottom of the ladder has little recourse when decisions are made as to his privileges, obligations, and punishments.

While it is impossible to listen in to telephone conversations between the Central Committee apparatchiks and the top Union secretaries, we can get some notion of how the Party tries to maintain control at more modest levels in the Union, chiefly through reports of meetings of the Party groups that operate within the organization itself, not only in Moscow but in branches throughout the country. Union congresses take place every five years, and plenums once or twice a year, but it is the more modest meetings being held at frequent intervals that constitute the Party's chief method of control and mobilization of writers on a daily basis. What emerges from an examination of such meetings is that the tight links between Party and Union evident at the apex of the two organizations (Central Committee and Secretariat) are maintained in much the same way at regional levels. Everywhere the Party places its ideological specialists in positions of authority within the Union branch, but in addition each branch must report to the parallel Party organization, whether at the Republic level or lower down the hierarchy in the Provincial Party Committee (*obkom*), City Party Committee (*gorkom*), and so forth.

The system of control at the center—that is, Verchenko must report to the Central Committee—is echoed in a minor key through the All-Union Republics. There are Party central committees in fourteen of the fifteen Union Republics; the sole exception is the Russian (*Rossyskaya*) Soviet Federated Socialist Republic, or RSFSR, which is granted the special privilege of being run by the Central Committee of the USSR in Moscow. The Party organization mirrors the government apparatus: a Party committee corresponds to each government unit. A Verchenko clone reports to the appropriate Party official in every Republic. By this additional control mechanism the Party ensures that it, not the Union (or any other Soviet enterprise for that matter), ultimately commands.

Though more elaborate and sophisticated at the national level in Moscow, Central Committee control is the model for regional Party organizations, where propaganda and culture specialists perform the same functions at every level of the Union. Just as representatives of the Central Committee ideological apparatus attend meetings of the Moscow or Russian Republic branches of the Union, so in the Republics local Party officials attend meetings to take the pulse of the branch chapter. Thus *Literaturnaya gazeta* (October 22, 1986) reported that a meeting of the secretariat of the Ukrainian Writers' Organization to discuss "problems of renewal" (a code phrase for Gorbachev's reform) had been attended by Ye. I. Lukyanenko, head of the literature section of the Department of Culture of the Ukrainian Communist Party.

The further down the scale one moves—or the further away from the center of the country, Moscow—the more direct and "naked" Party guidance becomes. Party officials exercise even greater authority over smaller chapters of the Writers' Union, especially those in areas distant from Moscow and Leningrad. As one émigré writer described the situation:

> In provincial cities like Rostov, the chapter of the Writers' Union might have only 25 members, and 5 of them will be members of its secretariat. So the secretary of the *obkom* [Province Party Committee] will come to their meetings and will say directly what they have to do. In very small cities, where they might have just three members of the Writers' Union, nobody will come to their meeting. They will be "invited" to the Party Committee to get all their instructions.

There is no attempt to preserve the fiction that the chapter is self-governing on this small scale, and a great many of the chapters are quite small: in 1987 the town of Perm had only 25 members; Chita in Eastern Siberia had but 11. By contrast, the Moscow chapter has more than 2,000 members. The Russian Republic chapter, housed in Moscow, has nearly 5,000 (this figure includes the Moscow total, as well as the Leningrad chapter's membership of over 400). But whatever the level or size of the Union chapter, the Party always has final control, and that power is wielded by the parallel Party organization. Vasily Betaki described the situation at a major city branch:

> The fate of the entire Leningrad branch of the Writers' Union is controlled by the Committee of the Province Party Committee, or *obkom*. In a regional Party organization, the second secretary of this committee is responsible for culture and ideology. Always. In any regional *obkom* the second secretary is in charge of politics and ideology. He has a sub-department with three instructors in it. One of those instructors will be in direct contact with the first secretary of the Writers' Union (if the regional branch has a first secretary). That is, he will be in charge of that first secretary; the instructor is the first secretary's immediate boss.

Consequently, the organizational life of any branch of the Union cannot be understood by examining the branch alone. The *obkom*, *raikom*, *gorkom*, and Republic Communist Party structures which run them, wield final decision-making power over the branches of the Union through their first secretary and secretary for ideology.

In the various Republics these ideological secretaries will supervise the literary activities of the Union, oversee the output of the print media, and ride herd on the local chapter. The importance to a writer of the opinion of those who supervise culture and ideology in the Party structure cannot be overemphasized. Vadim Nechaev, a former Union member from Leningrad, said:

> There is an ideological atmosphere in society. There are direct controlling organs from the *obkom* and the *gorkom* and the Central Committee. A writer depends on the opinion about him of those top ideological secretaries in the *obkom* and the Central Committee—even more so than on the opinion of the Secretariat of the Writers' Union.[31]

In short, whatever the Union bureaucrats think about a writer or his work, ultimately they listen and heed the judgment of the Party's own *apparat*. All the media and culture officials in the Central Committee report ultimately to the Politburo Secretary who holds the number two position, just below the General Secretary himself, as the member of the Secretariat with prime responsibility for ideology. Since Stalin's death, this position has been so powerful that it is sometimes referred to by Russians as the "number one-and-a-half" (*nomer poltora*) in the Politburo.[32]

These external Party controls complement the internal organizational chart of the Writers' Union to form the Soviet equivalent of "checks and balances." The Union is officially a non-Party organization, but it contains a large number of Party members. As is the case with all professional organizations, the Party makes sure that it has a majority of the membership. Obviously, the Party has much more direct and regular control over members than nonmembers, but it does not permit them to function as individuals. Party rules state that any group of three or more members, in whatever institution or enterprise they might be, must come together to form a Primary Party Organization, or PPO (*Pervichnaya partynaya organizatsia*), with the aim of proselytizing others and trying to have the Party's wishes respected.[33] A group of 300 members, and even as few as 100, may be permitted to elect a Party Committee (*partkom*); this provides status to the group. Once the group has 150 members (sometimes fewer), it is entitled to have its Party Committee members work full-time on Party affairs and receive a salary. In other words, they are relieved of other duties—such people are the equivalent of the released secretaries at the apex of the Union. Moscow, Leningrad, and other more substantial branches have their own Party Committees. However, every branch, once it has three Party members, must have its PPO, as must every council, commission, or section on prose fiction, poetry, and so forth, wherever it is located in the country.

The Party makes a distinction between rank-and-file members and full-time Party workers or apparatchiks. The mere fact that an individual writer is a member of the Party tells very little about his or her personal feelings. As one émigré put it:

> There are many people totally against the regime in the Party. An older member might have joined out of patriotism during World War II. A younger person might say to you, "I have to join this damn Party for my career." But just because people are in the Party, that does not mean they ever personally support it.[34]

Often the Party will court the individual, rather than the other way round, since it likes to claim that all "progressive" people in Soviet society are members. If a man or woman achieves distinction in a given area, as a rule he or she will be strongly encouraged to join the Party. For example, in 1960 when the authorities decided that the celebrated composer Dmitry Shostakovich should become first secretary of a new Russian Republic branch of the Union of Composers, he was inducted into the Party at once.[35] Furthermore, the *nomenklatura* lists of incumbents and possibles may include non-Party members if their loyalty is unquestioned: Sergei Zalygin, chief editor of *Novy mir*, is non-Party, so is Pyotr Palievsky, deputy director of IMLI, the Institute of World Literature in Moscow (an Academy of Sciences institute). But these are exceptions. It is much more common for people to be required to join the Party before being appointed to "responsible" positions, for example, as chief editor of a leading journal.

At the higher levels of the Union the responsibilities of Party members increase markedly, as does the ratio of Party members to non-members. This practice goes back to the very beginnings of the Union's existence. In his report to the First Congress in 1934, Pavel Yudin admitted that no more than one-third of the members of the new Union belonged to the Party.[36] However, his figures showed that Party members made up over half of the delegates, reversing the ratio in the membership as a whole: 49.1 percent of the delegates were members of the Party, with another 3.7 percent being candidate members and 7.6 percent belonging to the Komsomol (the Communist Youth League, which serves in part as a training ground for future Party apparatchiks). Hence, the Party could rely on more than 60 percent of the delegates at this First Congress to vote as ordered. The picture began to change in favor of the Party as one rose up the hierarchy of the Union's governing bodies. In the Board of 101 members, 57 belonged to the Party, 2 were candidate members, and 2 were members of the Komsomol. In addition, of 4 men not listed as delegates to the congress but still appointed to the Board, at least 2 (Lev Kamenev, a member of the Politburo, and Alexander Shcherbakov) certainly belonged to the Party. Thus, 61 members of the Board belonged to the Party, another 2 may have been, and 2 more were members of the Komsomol—meaning that only about one-third of the Board were non-Party, a reversal of the ratio in the Union as a whole.

Even this preponderance of Party members does not tell the whole story, because several of the non-Party writers owed direct allegiance to the Party and could be relied upon to obey instructions or vote as requested.

The ratio of Party members increased steadily above the level of the 1934 Board. At least 25 of 37 members of the Presidium belonged to the Party, including 2 non-delegates—Lev Kamenev, and Alexander Shcherbakov, who became the First Secretary. The non-Party members of the Presidium, the so-called "non-Party Bolsheviks," included Maxim Gorky himself, Vsevolod Ivanov, Leonid Leonov, Leonid Sobolev, Nikolai Tikhonov, and Konstantin Fedin. In the Secretariat itself 4 of 5 members belonged to the Party. Fifty years later the same pattern prevailed. In the Litburo of 9 members elected (or selected) following the Eighth Congress of Writers in 1986, 7 belonged to the Party. Whatever their personal views might have been, they were subject to Party discipline.

Maintaining another custom initiated at the First Congress, Party officials arranged for the delegates at the Eighth Congress to be cut out of the process through which members are selected for the Presidium and Secretariat. In this fashion the Party is better able to place its own people, and people it trusts, into critical positions. At the conclusion of each congress the delegates depart and leave the powerbrokers to plan the Union's activities for the coming five years. When a Writers' Congress ends, at the stroke of midnight, the delegates must rush home like Soviet Cinderellas, and adapt to a much less glamorous existence. The real movers and shakers of the Writers' Union are members of the Litburo and the Secretariat, elected after the ball is over. The session at which these elections are held is "closed"; only its results are reported.

Even under glasnost, meetings of the Secretariat are not open to foreign observers, but it is possible to get some notion of how such elections are conducted through evidence of the procedures followed at lower levels of the organization. As in all Soviet institutions and enterprises, the Union PPOs hold regular meetings.[37] They discuss the work of their Union chapter, review the latest Party statements and announcements of problems and pressing tasks, and correct errors in the activities of Party members.

At the larger branches, such as Moscow itself, the Party Committee (*partkom*) will hold meetings, and these are often reported in the press. Before Gorbachev the accounts were rather bland; since his arrival, reports have been more lively. But even vigorous and open debate is still kept within bounds laid down by the Party, and specifically by the appropriate Party body to which the *partkom* must report. The familiar "responsible" officials from the Party apparatus attend these meetings and keep an eye on the proceedings. For example, a meeting of the Moscow writers' *partkom* in November 1985 was attended not only by V. A. Stepanov, mentioned earlier as head of the literature section of the Central Committee Department of Culture, but also by Ye. P. Ionov, deputy head of the Department of Culture of the Moscow *gorkom* (city committee), and by F. F. Kozyryov-Dal, first secretary of the local district committee, the Krasnopresnensky *raikom*.[38] Since this was a meeting of Party members in the Moscow branch, it became the responsibility not only of the Moscow Party organization, but also of Party officials in the city district where the Writers' Union buildings are located, that is, Krasnopresnensky.

Whatever else is on the agenda of a *partkom* or PPO meeting, if there is an election coming up, controlling its outcome will be the number-one priority. The example of the Leningrad chapter is instructive. As in all large chapters, the lowest organizational unit is the section (equivalent to the council at the national level). In Leningrad, which has over 400 members, there are sections for prose fiction, poetry, criticism, popular science and science fiction, and translation. In Moscow there would be more sections; in a small town, probably none at all. These sections meet once a week in the Writers' Club (*Dom literatorov*), or in any facility they choose. Each section has its own chairman (the position is almost always occupied by a man) and secretary, who are in charge of that particular section. Officially, they are elected. However, former Union members now in the West are unanimous in claiming that the usual practice is for these "elected officials" to have been, in actuality, "selected to be elected."

At the higher levels within the organization, the election of Party-designees is virtually assured. Each section's Party group will already have met to put together their slate. The section's vote, even if it is by secret ballot, will still almost always go the Party's way, because the Party people always vote in a bloc. But even this checkpoint is not the last one. It is always a Party functionary from the Party group who will nominate the slate. For example, during the seventies in the poetry section (40 members) of the Leningrad branch, there were 7 people in the section's Primary Party Organization (PPO). The secretary of those 7 would stand and read the slate of candidates, prefaced by the code phrase, "I suggest" or "I propose" (*predlagayu*). Everyone understood that the names being suggested came from Party officials in the local Party organization, that is, from outside the Union in the Leningrad city (*gorkom*) or provincial committee (*obkom*).[39] Therefore, it hardly ever happens that anyone would oppose the slate or even suggest other names. Thus it is a trio that in fact controls this section of 40 poets in this particular city's chapter of the Union: the secretary of the section (usually a member of the Party); the chairman of the section (usually a member of the Party), and the secretary of the section's Primary Party Organization (by definition, a member of the Party).

Just as the Party organization in each section ensures the election of the "right" person, so too it uses its voting bloc strength to elect the Party slate to offices at every level in the Union. Moscow prescribes procedures that are followed in a regional Union branch, above the commission and section levels, although there is some variety in structure, depending on the size of the branch. The Statutes provide for branches of forty or more members to elect a board, and sometimes a secretariat and bureau.[40] A local board is made up of the chairmen and the secretaries of the sections. But other members of the board are elected by the entire chapter membership. The election follows the same pattern as that of the section.

Once a year or once every two years, the entire membership will gather in the local writers' club, whether it be in Leningrad, Kiev, or in distant Alma Ata. This meeting or conference is said officially to be the highest organ of the local branch, just as the congress is for the entire national organization. The conference does carry considerable political freight—members of the board as a rule are Party members. Again, either a member of the outgoing board or a member of the Primary Party Organization will suggest or nominate the new board. Not surprisingly, three-fourths of the "suggested" slate are members of the old board. This election is by secret ballot. However, just as in section elections, before this large membership meeting there will have been a previous meeting only for Party members. And at this meeting there is a review of possible candidates, and Party members are told directly that they have to vote "yes" for the entire designated slate of candidates as approved by Party authorities.

Another inhibiting factor is that the secret ballot used in the membership meeting does not seem to guarantee anonymity. At least during the Brezhnev years, many Party members were afraid that their handwriting could identify them, or "some other method"—frightening but amorphous—could give them away if they voted "No." So the Party members vote as they are told; the rest of the membership, having heard the PPO organizer's list of "suggested" nominees, nearly always vote "Yes" as well. The spirit of compromise or inertia are powerful stimulants to go along with the Party's slate.

After the board has been elected, everybody except the members of the new board leaves the room, in exactly the same fashion as at the national level in Moscow. The secretariat is elected only by the board. The former chairman of the old board suggests the slate for the new secretariat. This time, again mimicking the national model, the election is by open ballot, so that everyone knows who is voting, or not voting, for whom. After the secretariat has been elected, the members of the new board leave too. At last, the room contains the real decision-makers. The secretariat will now meet in closed session, and it will distribute the chapter's responsibilities. Usually, the former first secretary will be a member of the new secretariat. He will have an important voice in deciding who will be first secretary, who will be second, who will be third, who will be responsible for the prose section, who will be responsible for the military literature commission, and so forth, on down the line.

What would happen if the Party had decided that someone should be on the secretariat, but this person was not elected to the board? Though extremely rare, a few cases have occurred. The board is elected in secret balloting by the entire membership of the local branch; only people already elected to the Board are eligible for election to the secretariat. Thus, there is a tiny chink in the Party's armor. In Leningrad, such a case actually happened. The longtime first secretary of the chapter had been Alexander Prokofyev; among his other services to the Party was his participation in the vicious denunciation of Alexander Tvardovsky in 1970, when the embattled chief editor of *Novy mir* was forced to resign.[41] Prokofyev was not elected during the secret ballot to the new board, despite all the efforts and all the pressures from the Party Committee (*partkom*) in the Leningrad writers' organization itself and even of the provincial Party organization, or *obkom*.

Although writers have rebelled and scored some successes, these have remained only temporary. In late 1963 the Moscow branch of the Union managed, against the express wish of the chapter's Party organization, to expand the official slate of candidates for the board, thus making it very likely that all the hacks and timeservers would be replaced with popular and honest writers. Unfortunately, it was late and so the meeting was adjourned with the promise that the vote would be announced later. But this democratic election was quickly overturned the next day by the Party bureaucrats at a hastily called meeting that was not announced to the membership. Naum Korzhavin, now living in Boston, heard about the meeting by chance and has provided us with a rare glimpse of the Party with its claws showing. Literary bureaucrats such as Vsevolod Kochetov and Nikolai Gribachev (whom Khrushchev once called "machine-gunners of the Party"—*avtomatchiki partii*), together with other Party stalwarts like Sergei Mikhalkov, Konstantin Simonov, and Felix Kuznetsov, quickly changed the rules and announced that all candidates receiving at least 50 percent of the vote would be elected to the board. The motion was passed because the meeting was packed with literary apparatchiks, but even so, fifteen members, including Korzhavin, voted against. As he says, this was the twilight of the Thaw.[42]

In sum, the Party "guides" the activities of this ostensibly non-Party organization through a complex web of interrelationships between Party members in Union branches and corresponding Party organizations. The Party uses the *nomenklatura* to put its own men into powerful positions within the Union, and it uses the Primary Party Organizations to ensure the "election" of its own candidates. Then it subordinates the entire Union bureaucracy to its own authority by forcing, at every level from the country's capital down to the smallest chapter in Chita, Eastern Siberia, the relevant Union official to answer to a Party apparatchik. The lines of authority go from the first secretary of the branch to the secretary of the branch's Party Organization. Another line goes to the branch's unofficial second secretary, who is the KGB's man. These three, the first secretary, the secretary of the Party Organization, and the second secretary, will be in charge of any given branch of the Union. It is the same trio of positions that acts to control the chapter's individual sections; they are lower down the organizational ladder, but the balance of forces is the same.

One émigré said, "The Party is interbound with everything. It is everywhere, like a cancer." It is certainly there in the Union's lymph nodes. The Union has become the distillation of Lenin's cherished principles as explained in his 1905 essay. Next to the Party itself, it is the quintessential Party organization. But what has been the impact of this pervasive external influence in the affairs of the Union, and how have the writers themselves responded to Party guidance?

4

Soviet Parnassus

*F*riendly togetherness, studios, desks, and first-class gossip about the apparat and colleagues (elements of an intense yet also tranquil creative atmosphere) await us. There are flowers in the park, a lake for the poet, a glade for the novelist, picturesque peasant houses in the village—nor is the capital too far away either.

MIKLOS HARASZTI, *The Velvet Prison*

With the Party's control of the Union's affairs so obvious and pervasive, it might seem that Russian writers, usually pictured as an ornery breed, would shy away from applying for membership, or would resign in protest as soon as Party officials or Union apparatchiks attempted to "guide" their work. Since Stalin's death, writers have not had to fear torture or death at the hands of the secret police; some might have been expected to display a little independence. In fact, the Union is overwhelmed with applications for admission, and only a handful of members have ever resigned voluntarily. The Union dominates the literary environment to such a degree that anyone who wants to make a living as a creative writer has little choice but to belong, or hope to belong, to this unique organization. The Union is the writer's full-time employer, giving him a job description and setting him tasks. But, at the same time, the Union provides its members and their families with social and medical benefits of a quality that places them instantly in the upper-middle class of Soviet society.

One émigré estimated that Union members enjoy the social prestige and material benefits of a colonel or lieutenant-colonel in the Soviet army. This parallel, although impressionistic, has the merit of setting in relief the rank-consciousness of Soviet society and, incidentally, the Party's attempt to mobilize its "artists in uniform" in the struggle for full communism. But an army cannot be made up only of officers. If Union members constitute the officer class in this ideological crusade, and the Central Committee is the General Staff, then who are the hundreds of thousands of non-members, the enlisted men and women fighting in the trenches? They are the part-time editors and writers, the freelancers and would-be creative writers struggling to make a living with their pens, and hoping perhaps some day to become members of the Writers' Union.

Such people shore up the whole literary system; they perform the lowly tasks that keep the presses rolling, and thus help maintain Union members in their privileged positions. Many work part-time on the staffs of a vast number of journals and publishing houses that are designed to meet the ever-increasing demand for reading material. The traditional Russian passion for literature has been expanded by the Soviet government's long-term investment in education, which has created almost 100 percent literacy. To the Western visitor, it seems that half the population is reading and the other half writing. Would-be authors flood journals and publishing houses with a never-ending flow of *samotyok* (literally, "self-flowing"), the Soviet version of the slush pile of unsolicited manuscripts. In addition, every literary periodical and publishing house annually receives tens, even hundreds, of thousands of letters from readers; Soviet law decrees they must be answered, particularly those which level accusations of incompetence or corruption against officials. Someone is obliged to craft responses, which can lead to tough investigative reports and interviews with embarrassed miscreants.

Freelancers can also do translations from Western sources, as well as to and from dozens of non-Russian languages of the Soviet Union. Literary translation has long been an honored profession in Russia, but once again the Soviet multi-national state has greatly increased demand for translated works. Freelancers earn money by doing literal translations, called "inter-linear translation," from non-Russian Soviet literatures, which more senior writers then polish. But the greatest demand is still for Russian translations of contemporary Western literature of all types, particularly popular American fiction. Translators are said to display a great deal of enterprise and energy in trying to persuade publishers and journals to give them contracts for the latest bestsellers in the capitalist West.

There is no byline associated with freelance work, and little creativity, but a person can earn enough rubles to get by, since the staples of life are heavily subsidized. Perhaps even more important is the possibility that, by laboring in the trenches of Soviet cultural and intellectual life, freelancers might also obtain the precious police stamp (*propiska*) in the internal passport that each citizen must have to prove that he or she has a regular job, and is thus a legal resident of Moscow or another large city. All major cities in the Soviet Union are "closed," because they offer much better living conditions and supplies of food and clothing than the rest of the country. One émigré said: "You can go to the journal where you review reader letters and simply say, 'Look, I do this work for you, so please give me a certificate.' And they will." However, other former citizens disagreed. It is not that simple; you have to be both lucky and well connected to get a certificate and then persuade the police to stamp your passport.

Nevertheless, the position of the freelancer is now institutionalized. For decades those with the precious *propiska* could even obtain some fringe benefits through special "professional writers' committees" (*profkomy literatorov*), which in turn reported and submitted requests to the Writers' Union. It is not clear how and when these committees came into existence and exactly what relationship they bore to the Writers' Union, but they obviously spread fast. As of 1970 there were four *profkomy* in Moscow alone.[1] Under glasnost and perestroika they came under attack for corruption. In August 1987 an investigative reporter uncovered a "profkom scam" that led six months later to the abolition of all the *profkomy* in Moscow. The reporter revealed that the Moscow *profkomy* had 1,700 members, but no Party organization—an extraordinary revelation of the decline in ideological vigilance during the late Brezhnev years. She also claimed that many of the people assisted by the *profkomy* were receiving benefits quite illegally, since they were not writers or editors. The most famous illegal recipient of benefits was the celebrated, and very wealthy, pop singer, Alla Pugacheva, who has toured the United States on more than one occasion.[2]

Although the *profkomy* have been abolished, it appears that tens of thousands of freelance writers and editors can still obtain some benefits by belonging to one of two trade unions—the Union of Literary Workers (*Profsoyuz literatorov*), or the Union of Cultural Workers (*Profsoyuz rabotnikov kultury*). It is fairly easy to join these trade unions, as opposed to the creative unions. According to a Moscow writer in 1985, all you need to do is demonstrate that you have earned a minimum of 70 rubles per month from your work over a period of three years. Even though these trade unions do offer limited benefits, they cannot compare with the impressive privileges and cachet provided by creative unions, which rest on the summit of the Soviet Parnassus. The Writers' Union is not really a trade union at all, but more like the associations of doctors, lawyers, or engineers, which demand proof of professional expertise and standing of all applicants.

Getting into the Union presents a Catch-22 situation: you cannot simply declare you wish to become a member, pay your dues, and join. In fact, Union dues are not onerous. Following Party practice, they range from below 1 percent to a maximum of 3 percent of monthly income, once that income reaches 300 rubles, that is, $450 at the official exchange rate.[3] However, what started out as a "voluntary union," in Leninist terms, has now become an exclusive club, whose rules for admission are deliberately left somewhat vague, so that an applicant can be rejected without specific reasons. The 1971 edition of the organization's Statutes, still in effect as of 1989, states that the applicant should present a written application, and include published literary works with reviews, and other materials demonstrating "social approbation of these works" (*obshchestvennoe priznanie etikh proizvedeny*).[4]

The applicant must also present letters of recommendation from three current Union members who have direct personal knowledge of him and his work. Since 1967 there has been growing emphasis on the need for writers of such recommendations to take more care about what they say. In his report on the work of a special committee set up to propose revisions to the Statutes, a Union secretary, the Belorussian author Petrus Brovka, recommended an immediate tightening of admission standards and procedures. He noted that the Union contained many members who lacked any real literary talent and were little more than "dependents" (*izhdiventsy*): "And what a lot of grief some of these people have given to our publishing houses and editorial workers by insisting that, just because they are members of the Union, their works should be published come what may!"[5]

The Statutes go on to state that voting on new members is conducted by secret ballot.[6] Successful applicants must receive two-thirds of the votes at regional branches, but only more than one-half of the votes in the board or secretariat at the Republic level. The candidate still has one more hurdle to go: the Secretariat in Moscow, at 52 Vorovsky Street, retains veto power, except in the case of the Moscow and Leningrad branches, which in 1988 managed to regain their independent right to admit applicants.[7] The Statutes refer to more detailed regulations given in the Secretariat's "Instructions" (*Instruktsia*). Perhaps these "Instructions" mention further requirements cited by émigré writers: the submission of five copies of the standard five-page questionnaire, or *anketa*, which all Soviet citizens must submit when applying for jobs, for entrance to a university or institute, and on numerous other occasions. One copy always goes to the KGB for its extensive files.[8] Also required is a character reference, or *kharakteristika,* which may be written by one's university or institute, or by a current member.

Except for the *anketa* and *kharakteristika,* admission to the Union is rather like trying to get admitted to a private club in the West, or to attain tenure in an American university. Certain types of publications are given more weight than others, and to a much greater extent than in the United States it is just as important who you know as what you know. In practice, according to former members in the West, if you are a poet, one book is the absolute minimum for admission. If you are a fiction writer, two books will be required. Playwrights will have to have several pieces staged and published; the same guidelines apply to writers of movie and TV scenarios, who may belong to the Writers' Union as well as to the Union of Journalists or of Cinematographers. Literary critics (or scholars, who are also admitted) might be accepted after publishing a few articles, particularly if they adopt an orthodox ideological orientation. Science fiction writers probably have to have more than two books, and translators had better have translated as many as five or six books before applying for admission.[9]

Quality, however, is left off the list of requirements. The Writers' Union is no exception to the general rule in Soviet society, where corruption and favoritism play a big part in decisions on appointments and admissions to educational institutions and other organizations. Émigrés cited many cases of mediocre writers who were admitted just because they had fulfilled the minimum publication requirement and had influential friends. They stressed that a book, for the purposes of Union admission, could be "almost any piece of garbage as long as it was printed between hard covers." Even allowing for bias among some critics of the Union, there is much hard evidence to back up claims that the Union's own rules are often bent when the "right" person comes along, especially one with political connections.

The national admissions committee (*priyomnaya komissia*) consists of 25–30 Union members, but their names are not published as far as is known.[10] This committee submits its recommendations to the Secretariat, which as of 1989 was still dominated by the "literary generals" brought in from the provinces during the Brezhnev period. They made it difficult for anyone with unorthodox ideas to enter the Union. However, in 1983 a former member of the national admissions committee at the Secretariat in Moscow seemed more concerned about the lack of professional competence among applicants than with their social or political outlook. He reported that he and his colleagues had become increasingly tough on applicants over the past few years, especially spouses of existing members. He felt that such couples had caused a lot of trouble by applying relentless pressure on members of the admissions committee. Even worse were those members who tried to get their relatives and friends admitted, even though they were obviously unqualified.

Whether justified or not in specific cases, the Union's deliberate exclusiveness runs counter to the Party's objective, which is to proselytize as many budding writers as possible, to harness the next generation in the cause of creating communism. The Soviet press constantly reminds all citizens that they have a responsibility to bring up their children to serve as replacements (*smena*) in the continuing struggle. To help it meet this responsibility, the Union has a Council for Relations with Young Writers and offers "consultation" for those who need advice. It also organizes seminars and groups (*obyedinenia*) for aspiring authors; these are conducted by established writers. The émigré novelist Vasily Aksyonov regularly led such seminars (without pay) and enjoyed doing it; he felt it was a professional duty. The Union also runs four-year courses for aspiring authors at the Gorky Institute for Literature in Moscow, a Soviet equivalent of the writing programs at several American universities. The Institute was founded in 1933 with Gorky's assistance and advice.[11] In its first fifty years it produced 2,921 graduates, and nearly half of that number (1,350) became members of the Writers' Union. Some of the better known writers studied at the Literary Institute during the Thaw years, but several either dropped out or had problems with official guidelines.

Occasionally, not content with this formal path to membership, the Party will step forward and urge the need to revitalize the Union with younger members. Criticism about the "aging of the Union" has been repeated at every congress since 1954. The result will be the sudden admission of several "young" writers, who often turn out to be at least forty years old, although some very young people have been admitted on rare occasions, for example, during Khrushchev's Thaw. As a rule writers have to wait for a long time to be admitted. Beginning authors have little chance of having their work accepted in the national journals in Moscow and Leningrad, and so must be content with provincial publications, which receive little attention from the literary opinion-makers in Moscow.[12] The situation of the beginning writer is much the same anywhere; it is hard to get that first break.

Sergei Yurenen, now living in West Germany, was one of the youngest men ever admitted to the Writers' Union. His story illustrates the importance of mentors, as well as the crucial role the

Party Central Committee's decrees can play. In 1974, after the expulsion of Solzhenitsyn from the Soviet Union, the Party decided to take a new approach in working with young writers, who had been driven to publish underground, because no one would publish them officially. In 1976 the Party's Central Committee issued a resolution calling for improved work with the young creative intelligentsia. It was an official campaign:

> The Party organized a "literary studio" which was controlled jointly by the Moscow writers' organization and the Moscow Komsomol Committee, the latter providing Party control. I sent my stories to this literary studio and was accepted. I went there once a week for two years, and in the studio I got to know the celebrated playwright, Mikhail Roshchin, who was one of the instructors there.

Yurenen explained that being accepted in the literary studio was the major turning point in his career:

> The literary studio also helped me get a job as an editor for the magazine *Druzhba narodov* (*Friendship of Peoples*), which sent me to Tajikistan as a special correspondent. Then I was sent on a trip to Hungary as a member of a Moscow youth delegation which consisted of 300 people. During this same time I participated in three big, important meetings—a national meeting of young writers, then those in the Moscow region, and finally one in Moscow itself; the latter two were organized by the Moscow writers' organization. The purpose of these meetings was to select good works and recommend them for publication. So even there it was not one particular person who recommended that my works be published, but a group of writers.[13]

Yurenen's story shows that political decisions taken at the very top can nudge the Union into admitting a pool of young writers, who have been carefully vetted through the meetings and the literary studio he describes. Yurenen's talent as a story teller was recognized early, but he still had to wait five years for admission to the Union. Even then he was only successful because of the personal interest of Mikhail Roshchin. He had no political connections; he was not a member of the Party. It was, as he put it, "a very hard and a very long process."

Yurenen was fortunate enough to be living in Moscow. The situation of young writers in the provinces is much more difficult. In 1986, Zamira Ibragimova, a writer in Siberia, told a rare success story; she had received invaluable encouragement in the sixties from two established Siberian authors, Viktor Astafyev and Semyon

Shurtakov, in publishing her first works. Ibragimova claimed that beginning authors no longer received that type of assistance, and that the situation had become extremely difficult, not least because provincial areas had so few publishing outlets of their own; a number of journals that did exist were closed down in the seventies. The steadily increasing centralization of Russian culture, according to this author, had proceeded apace since the sixties, that is, during the Brezhnev period. Statistics bear out her claim: one fifth of the total Union membership now lives in Moscow, and that figure has been increasing steadily. Ibragimova noted a recent list of 220 poets from Eastern Siberia, which revealed that only 34 still lived there; the rest had moved to Moscow.[14] She did not mention the fact that the Russian Republic branch of the Union, founded in 1958, had been filled with Siberian and other provincial writers during the late fifties and early sixties, and that some of them, notably Georgy Markov, had acquired enormous power and wealth in the organization under Brezhnev.

Once admitted to the Writers' Union, the new member has access to an impressive array of fringe benefits and special privileges, most of them having little to do with the profession of writing but a great deal to do with making life easier in the peculiar circumstances of Soviet life. That is why many non-writers are eager to join, as the celebrated émigré novelist Vladimir Voinovich has noted:

> Many people have long since realized that the Union of Writers is really "fat city" in a big way (*ochen bogataya kormushka*); and that is why this organization now counts among its members the directors of stores, public baths, theaters, and sports stadiums; ministers; Party bureaucrats of every rank; generals of all the services, including the KGB and the MVD; and even marshals of the Soviet Union.[15]

Although such non-writers belong to the privileged elite of Soviet society, they are still eager to enjoy the prestige and material benefits of Union membership. The Union has in fact been a special cornucopia of privilege from the very moment the creative unions were first established.

As early as 1930 Stalin had already decided to give preferential treatment to professional experts as a way of encouraging them to support his new socialist state. The differential in incomes and privileges between the rising professional class and the rest of the population began to widen as Stalin argued that members of the intelligentsia should be treated with special consideration. In 1931 he launched an attack on "levelling" (*uravnilovka*), that is, the argument that all citizens should be treated equally and receive the same wages. And at the same time that Stalin introduced food rationing (a direct result of his failed collectivization campaign), he also established "closed stores," well-stocked with quality foods for the privileged new class, including members of RAPP; later, special stores were opened for foreigners, chiefly those with diplomatic status. Similar preferential treatment continued to be offered to members of the new Union of Soviet Writers, and it had the desired effect. Nadezhda Mandelshtam reports that when she and her husband Osip returned to Moscow in 1937 after three years' exile in Voronezh, they were both astonished by the new affluence surrounding Union members, more particularly those who had performed valuable services for the Party: "At the time we left Moscow for exile, the writers had not yet become a privileged caste, but now they were putting down roots and figuring ways of keeping their privileges."[16]

Mikhail Bulgakov in his novel *The Master and Margarita,* which was completed in 1940, satirized the Writers' Union in its early years under the Orwellian acronym MASSOLIT, and the Writers' Club as Griboedov's, suggesting that most members were concerned about getting as many perks as possible:

> Every visitor to Griboedov's, unless of course he was a complete dolt, realized at once how good life was for the lucky members of MASSOLIT, and black envy would immediately begin to gnaw at him. At once, too, he would hurl bitter reproaches at heaven for not having endowed him at birth with literary talent, without which, of course, no one could so much as dream of acquiring a MASSOLIT membership card—that brown card known to all Moscow, smelling of expensive leather and embellished with a wide gold border.[17]

Over the past fifty years the material benefits and perks allocated to members have increased enormously, but an even more important privilege conferred by membership in the Union has been granted: freedom from capricious arrest and harassment by the KGB, or by regular police in the MVD.

If a KGB official causes a writer problems, he or she can complain to one of the top secretaries in the Union, who could well have excellent contacts with the KGB. Indeed, it is quite likely that he will have a higher KGB rank than the official who is investigating one, since the Union Secretariat contains its share of KGB majors and colonels, and an occasional general. Even if the Union secretary does not hold KGB rank, he is likely to know people high up in the Party; and a Party official has higher authority than a KGB official of equivalent rank. Furthermore, the Writers' Union, like all Soviet organizations, has a certain esprit de corps—its top officials guard their independence from what they see as unwarranted interference by rival bureaucracies. Therefore, the writer might well find his case suddenly dropped by the KGB, provided he has not committed a truly seditious act.

Union members in good standing are protected from the irritating harassment often inflicted by the "insect authority" of petty bureaucrats and by the despised *militsia* (the militia, or civilian police).[18] As one former Union member put it:

> The militiamen could knock on my door any day and ask me, "How come you don't work? You are a parasite." If I answer that I am a writer, they would say, "So what! Everybody can write. You'd better get yourself a job in two weeks." And that would be it. But if I show them my membership card in the Writers' Union, then they tip their hats and off they go.

Another émigré told virtually the same story. If your apartment was a little larger than the limits provided by law, or if you had some possession that had caused your neighbors to envy you, they would denounce you to the appropriate authorities. Then the *militsia* would come by. You could try to put them off by showing something you had managed to publish. But they could keep coming back to your apartment, month after month, to see that you were still producing.

From the time he was expelled from the Union in 1974 until his forcible exile from the Soviet Union in 1980, Vladimir Voinovich was visited at frequent intervals by the police, who politely inquired as to his reasons for "not working anywhere and living at the expense of the people." Now and then the authorities would harass Voinovich in various ways, trying to break down his resolve. On one occasion KGB officers even poisoned him with doctored cigarettes. But Voinovich was always a tough opponent, like Solzhenitsyn, and the Soviet authorities were never quite sure how to handle him.[19] If he had not been expelled from the Union, Voinovich could not have been treated so cavalierly. A Union membership card provides proof of employment, at least to the satisfaction of Soviet law, so one can no longer be charged with "living at the expense of the people." With a Union membership card a person has no need to be gainfully employed at any regular job. Thus, the Union has helped to create a new leisure class; instead of clipping coupons, these people simply collect their royalties and enjoy fringe benefits provided by the state.

Union membership can also protect its members from harassment by a special branch of the police, known by the acronym OBKhSS, which stands for "Department for the Struggle Against the Misappropriation of Socialist Property" (*Otdel borby s khishcheniyami sotsialisticheskoi sobstvennosti*). Since the state owns everything, it focuses its attention on preventing theft of state property, which is nonetheless very widespread. OBKhSS has the right to poke its nose into anyone's personal affairs. For example, its representatives can ask someone with a car how he came by the money to purchase it—this is part of the drive against corruption.[20] However, anyone with a Union card will immediately be given a smart salute and waved on his way, because Union members are considered part of the elite and therefore expected to own cars. Membership in the Union means one does not have to wait in turn for years in order to buy a car, as do less privileged citizens.

Former Union member from Leningrad, Vadim Nechaev, gave an example of how the Union can help in dealing with the police. Late one night he was with a group of friends making a noise on the street after a party. They were approached by a *militsioner*, but Nechaev stepped forward, showed his Union membership card, and said they were all members of the Union. The *militsioner* simply saluted, did an about-face and marched away. Had Nechaev not been a member of the Union, he and his friends could very easily have been whisked away to a "sobering-up station" (*vytrezvitel*) for a day or two, where they could have been roughed up without benefit of legal advice.

The émigré translator and writer Shimon Markish offered a similar illustration of the surprising privileges that belonging to the Union can bring, and the petty jealousies it can arouse:

> [In Moscow] I had an apartment with two rooms, and in one room there was a telephone. Other people in the building wanted me to move the telephone into the hall so all could use it. I refused. So they denounced me to the telephone station, saying that the telephone was in the name of the previous tenant. "He is cheating you!" they proclaimed. So I went to Ilyin, who had once been a general in the KGB, but who, after being arrested and put into a camp, was now serving as organizational secretary in the Union. Ilyin called the Central Telephone Station, and said, "Shimon Markish is a member of the Union of Writers. His profession requires him to have a personal telephone. Please transfer the telephone to the name of Comrade Markish." And in three weeks it was put in my name.[21]

This incident illustrates several aspects of Soviet life. First, ordinary consumer services are difficult to come by; in order to obtain them, you need influence (*blat*). Second, the busybody has been institutionalized and encouraged by Soviet law and mores. Any citizen who happens to get interested in your affairs can make them his business whenever he feels like it; you cannot respond by telling neighbors to mind their own business, or by threatening a law suit. Third, citizens have become accustomed to the idea of "denouncing" neighbors to the authorities; in fact, they are urged to do so. And fourth, freedom from such irritations is one of the most cherished daily privileges the Union offers its members.

Just as important to a Union member as the legal protection and the considerable prestige or "psychic income" of membership is a range of perks and privileges, which go far to ameliorate the many discomforts of ordinary Soviet life. The purely material advantages that the Union can provide to its members may be seen most readily in a visit to the Central Writers' Club or *Tsentralny Dom Literatorov*, which is located on Vorovsky Street next to the administrative building, known as the Secretariat. Given the fact that the Union constitutes the main difference between the situation of writers today and that of their Russian forebears in pre-revolutionary times, it is ironic that both the building and the street have such important links with tsarist Russia, and especially with Russian literature of the nineteenth century. The Soviet authorities chose the location deliberately for these echoes and for the elegance of the buildings: it remains official policy to stress the continuity of Soviet Russian literature and the great classics of the nineteenth century.[22]

Vorovsky was known as Povarskaya, or Street of Cooks (that is, to the tsar), prior to the eighteenth century, and had been the main thoroughfare from the Kremlin to Novgorod.[23] In the eighteenth century, after the capital was moved to St. Petersburg, the street became a favorite location for the aristocracy. Many famous families lived on Povarskaya, including the Shakhovskois, the Miloslavskys, the Dolgorukys, and the Gagarins. Later, in the nineteenth century, wealthy merchants built beautiful town houses along the same street. The lovely linden trees that still line the street on both sides and add so much to its discreet charm were planted in 1899. Somehow they have survived the ravages of time and the early Soviet passion for destroying everything created in pre-revolutionary times.[24]

Povarskaya has many significant literary associations. The Romantic poet Mikhail Lermontov lived there for two years (1828–30) with his wealthy grandmother, Madame Arsenyeva, while attending school and preparing to enter Moscow University. Alexander Pushkin's father lived on the street, as did Colonel Gartung, husband of Pushkin's daughter Maria. Gartung shot himself after being found guilty of certain shady dealings as master of the Moscow state horse stables; Maria herself is rumored to have served Leo Tolstoy as the model for his heroine Anna Karenina. The fine building at No. 52, which serves as administrative headquarters for the Union Secretariat, has next door to it No. 50, the enormous building that houses the Central Writers' Club. Some members claim that it served as the setting for Pierre Bezukhov's entry into a Masonic lodge in *War and Peace*. True or not, the building did belong to Prince Svyatopolk-Mirsky, ancestor to Dmitry Mirsky, a distinguished professor of Russian literature at the University of London in the twenties before he returned to the Soviet Union and disappeared in the Great Purge.

In 1924 Povarskaya was renamed after Vatslav Vorovsky, a now long-forgotten Bolshevik literary critic, journalist, and later diplomat, who was murdered in 1923 in Lausanne by anti-Soviet exiles.[25] The Writers' Club occupies an enormous building and its excellent appointments give a pretty accurate impression of the Union's financial clout. The Club is used chiefly by members living permanently in Moscow, but members of the Union visiting from another city or Republic are entitled to use the facilities at any time. The main entrance is on Herzen Street, but the rear entrance on Vorovsky is useful for scholars and critics from the Gorky Institute of World Literature, a branch of the Academy of Sciences located further down on the other side of the street, toward the Kremlin, at No. 25; this building was erected in 1827–29 for one of the Gagarin princes. Union administrators who have offices at No. 52 do not have to use the Vorovsky entrance; a tunnel links the headquarters building with the Club.

Immediately inside the entrance to the Club are some steps, and a large marble plaque on which are the names of some eighty Moscow writers killed in World War II; then comes the obligatory cloakroom guarded by someone's stern grandmother, who can warm quickly to a friendly word or two. Beyond the cloakroom through the double doors is a large, high-ceilinged room with geometrically patterned and brightly colored stained glass windows rising high above dark-panelled walls (the Moscow writers' organization has its offices upstairs). This large room now serves as the main hall of the Union restaurant, mentioned nostalgically by many émigré writers, and not only for its culinary delights. One writer explained:

> If I wanted to have a girl, all I had to do was say, "Would you like to have dinner with me in the Writers' Union restaurant tonight?" And that night, she would be mine, absolutely.

Not quite what the Party had in mind when establishing the Union, certainly, but still persuasive evidence of the organization's social prestige. Members go to the Club to eat, chat and socialize with friends, attend meetings, lectures, and showings of films that are often very hard to see elsewhere in Moscow—or impossible, in the case of some Western movies.

The Club is the visible symbol of a complex organization that provides a vast range of benefits and privileges to its members. Other administrative units and institutions that report to the Writers' Union Secretariat are the Gorky Literary Institute (which gives advanced courses to aspiring writers and critics); the All-Union Bureau for the Propagation of Literature (*Vsesoyuznoe byuro propagandy khudozhestvennoi literatury*), which sends members on well-paid lecture tours throughout the country; and the Library and the Reference Room (*Bibliografichesky kabinet*), which are both located in the Club. Members claim that the Reference Room gives better research service than the Lenin Library itself. The Writers' Bookshop (*Knizhnaya lavka pisatelei*) in Moscow and in other major cities offers members the opportunity to buy books that are unobtainable, except on the black market at many times their retail prices.[26]

By far the most important part of the Union for members is the Literary Fund, or Litfund (*Litfond*). With a budget running into tens of millions of rubles, Litfund is the main source of benefits and privileges. A writer normally becomes a member of Litfund at the same time he joins the Union, although it is possible, if unusual, to be admitted to Litfund without prior Union membership. The Soviet Litfund has tsarist connections, as do the buildings occupied by the Union and its agencies. Litfund was grafted onto the pre-revolutionary Society for Financial Aid to Needy Writers and Scholars (*Obshchestvo dlya posobia nuzhdayushchimsya literatoram i uchenym*), but has grown into a bizarre hybrid with many significant differences. The Society was a private organization, founded in 1859 by a group of writers and critics led by Druzhinin, and including Turgenev, Tolstoy, Nekrasov, Ostrovsky, and Chernyshevsky—it was by no means unusual for Russians of sharply opposed political and philosophical views and of differing social and financial status to agree on a joint course of action. This charitable society was governed by a committee of twelve elected writers, with a turnover of four members each year. Reports on its finances and operations were published in the press on a regular basis. In sharp contrast to the current situation, the Society was completely independent of tsarist government control and gave assistance to writers according to need, quite irrespective of their political views or social origin. Among the beneficiaries of the Society's generosity and their colleagues' good fortune were the widow and family of the critic Belinsky (who had died in 1848), and both Dostoevsky and Gorky—it would be hard to think of two Russian writers more opposed in their political and philosophical views.

After the Bolshevik coup in November of 1917 and the subsequent emigration of many writers, artists, and other members of the intelligentsia, the traditions of Litfund were revived among Russians in the West. Independent branches of Litfund continue to exist in Europe, and in North and South America. Perhaps the best known of its beneficiaries was Ivan Bunin, who was awarded the Nobel Prize for Literature in 1933.[27]

In the Soviet Union, Litfund was revived in 1924, and ten years later it was co-opted as part of the Writers' Union. The organization's Statutes were approved in early 1935 by the Council of People's Commissars (now called the Council of Ministers), and have remained basically unchanged since that time. In 1981 Alim Keshokov, then chairman of the Litfund Board, stated in his report to the Seventh Union Congress that Litfund is not a charitable organization, but one that offers assistance to working writers, who for some reason or another are temporarily incapacitated. That may well be part of Litfund's original mission, but it is quite clear that Litfund has indeed become a massive welfare and mobilizing organization. From its modest beginnings as a volunteer organization to help writers and their families in tsarist days, Litfund has grown into a bureaucracy with its own separate national headquarters, located in Moscow along the Leningrad Highway, not far from a major concentration of Union apartment buildings.

Litfund is subject to formal control by the Union Board and Secretariat, and, like the Union, it has branches in all fifteen Republics. It operates in part like a trade union for Union members, in part like a private foundation, in part like a division within a giant multinational corporation. And yet it is at the same time an agency of the Soviet government. Litfund builds and operates apartment complexes, vacation resorts, writers' retreats (*doma tvorchestva*), hospitals and clinics, and retirement homes. Union membership fees could never provide sufficient income for this purpose. Litfund is able to offer lavish perks and benefits because it is heavily subsidized by order of the Party; that is, the Party plows back into Litfund millions of rubles that it could otherwise commandeer itself, or allow other enterprises to use for their own purposes.

Litfund derives the bulk of its impressive income from contributions (*otchislenia*) provided by Soviet publishing houses and other organizations that are under its jurisdiction and control. According to a resolution (*postanovlenie*) of the Council of People's Commissars on July 28, 1934, just two weeks before the Writers' Union held its inaugural congress, Litfund receives a sum equivalent to 10 percent of the fees and honoraria paid to authors by all Soviet publishing houses and literary journals; plus 2 percent of receipts from all performances in large theaters, and ½ percent of receipts from all performances in small theaters.[28] In addition, the Soviet copyright agency, The All-Union Agency for Authors' Rights or VAAP (*Vsesoyuznoe agentstvo avtorskikh prav*), is required by law to contribute some portion of royalties it receives from the publication of Soviet works abroad. A further boost to the Union's income follows from its tax-exempt status, which was established by the Council of People's Commissars in 1935 and confirmed by the Council of Ministers in 1987.[29] The Union is considered under Soviet law to be "not pursuing the aim of making a profit" (*ne presleduyushchy tselei izvlechenia pribyli*). Thus the Writers' Union has become the Soviet equivalent of a non-profit institution.

Litfund provides its members with both material and professional benefits, but the former are more extensive and probably more valuable to the average member. The latest figures, reported at the Eighth Congress of Writers in 1986 by the Central Auditing Committee (*Tsentralnaya revizionnaya komissia*), revealed that during the preceding five years, Litfund had increased its expenditures on "improving the living conditions of writers" by 19 percent. Over the five years since the previous Congress in 1981, it had spent 70.9 million rubles (more than $100 million), of which 32 million had been allocated to cover the "social service needs of writers, and subsidies to writers' retreats," and 23 million rubles had been expended on "capital construction and reconstruction."[30]

While Litfund reported total receipts of 47 million rubles from 1981 to 1986, the overall income and expenditures of the Union are impossible to estimate, and have never been revealed. Their magnitude can be imagined from the fact that, from 1981 to 1986, the Union gave Litfund a total of 30 million rubles for capital construction and purchases. Every year Litfund has been spending over 3 million rubles in "material aid" to writers who are in financial difficulties for a variety of reasons: delays in publication of their works, ill health, or some personal or professional problem. Given the Litfund (and Union) membership of about 10,000 in 1989, this statistic suggests that each member was receiving an average of 300 rubles each year, that is, much more than a month's salary for most Soviet workers.

Of the material benefits that Litfund can provide to Union members, the most significant is certainly housing, which remains a very serious problem in an economy characterized by poor or nonexistent consumer goods and services.[31] Some establishment writers are provided housing free of charge in special buildings reserved for prominent figures in various fields. But Litfund has also been constructing cooperative apartment buildings for sale to its members, at a rapidly increasing rate, ever since Nikita Khrushchev decided to permit the purchase of property as a way of putting people's savings into circulation. The Union has long since extended its activities beyond Moscow and Leningrad to a score or more other Soviet towns, constructing hundreds of these coop apartments.

The privileged position of the Union with regard to housing is written into a law that grants its members an additional 20 square meters of living space beyond the allotted norm for every Soviet citizen, which is 12 square meters per person (up from the 9 square meters decreed by Lenin). If a citizen should happen to have more than 12 square meters in the form of a separate room, and if he is not a Union member, the Soviet government is entitled to take the extra space away and give it to someone else—more than likely the person who reported the excess to the authorities in the first place. If the extra space were not in the form of a separate room, then the citizen would be required to pay a threefold additional payment for the "excess" space (*izlishki*). But if the fortunate citizen is a member of the Union, then the space is his to keep, for free.

These legal guarantees are not always observed in practice, either for Soviet citizens in general or for Union members in particular. According to an article in *Pravda* (January 22, 1989), there are still about 14 million Soviet families and individuals unable to find an apartment to live in. The housing shortage is so great that Russians use the phrase *vybivat kvartiru*, which means literally "to get an apartment by pushing and shoving." In the fall of 1986, as a delegate to the Supreme Soviet (the Soviet proto-parliament), the newly appointed First Secretary of the Union, Vladimir Karpov, did some old-fashioned politicking on behalf of his colleagues. He noted that Union members often do not receive the additional 20 square meters to which they are entitled: "This decree is not observed in many cities: If you have 6 to 9 meters per person, they won't even put you on the waiting list [that is, for a larger apartment]."[32]

Nonetheless, Union members have a much more reliable guarantee that any Party declaration; they can call upon the authority and resources of their organization to obtain adequate, and often more than adequate, living space. They also have a good chance of obtaining decent apartments even for close relatives. A well-known writer in Moscow told of his efforts to obtain, through the Union, a suitable apartment for his son and new daughter-in-law; the young couple would have no chance for anything other than a communal flat in a distant suburb without adequate shops and facilities, were it not for the connections (*svyazi*) and influence (*blat*) provided by the father's membership in the Union.

Adequate living space has been a perennial problem in Soviet society ever since the Bolshevik coup, and was made much worse by the destruction caused by the German invasion in World War II. But the situation would have been a great deal better than it is had the Party not continued to focus most of its resources on heavy industry and military production, while ignoring housing and consumer services and products. There continue to be squabbles over space at all levels of the society to this day. Though the Party has been constructing enormous numbers of huge apartment buildings since the mid-fifties, the pace of construction dropped under Brezhnev.[33] Housing problems have become a staple of Soviet fiction, but the most amusing treatment of the problem is based on fact. Vladimir Voinovich's hilarious satire, *The Ivankiad* (*Ivankiada*), published only in the West thus far, but soon to appear in the Soviet Union. Voinovich explains how he managed to prevent Sergei Ivanko (a Soviet literary bureaucrat with powerful Party and KGB connections) from commandeering a small room that Voinovich's family was entitled to under the law. Ivanko wanted to turn the space into a second bathroom (an unheard-of luxury) to house some American Standard fixtures that he had brought back from his days working with the Soviet mission at the United Nations in New York. The mock-heroic deeds in this Soviet epic show how serious the quarrel over square meters is inside the Soviet Union.

The main center for Union apartments in Moscow is near the "Aeroport" Metro (subway) station on the Leningrad Highway, where Litfund has its own headquarters. It is a prestigious area that also contains apartments occupied by people in the Soviet movie industry and the theater. In fact, friends will point out one building or group of buildings in the complex and tell you what type of artist lives there. The outside of the buildings, like most in Moscow, is dilapidated and in need of repair and cleaning, but the apartments have high ceilings and are quite spacious by Soviet standards. Furthermore, the inner courtyards of the buildings contain an unusual number of private cars—a rare sight even in Moscow. The envy that these upperclass apartment buildings provoke among ordinary people has given rise to the anti-Semitism that lies just beneath the surface in Russia, even if only at the level of jokes. Val Golovskoy, a former editor at the journal *Soviet Screen* (*Sovetsky ekran*), says that this area has been nicknamed *zhid-massiv* or "Yid Quarter" instead of *zhyl-massiv* or "residential district."

Probably the second most important material benefit of Union membership is low-cost, quality medical care, which is provided by the Central Medical Center (*Tsentralnaya poliklinika*) and similar facilities throughout the country. The Central Polyclinic in Moscow is attached to a hospital. As of 1989 Litfund also ran nine *polikliniki;* these are equivalent to the outpatient departments of an American hospital, where patients can come to be treated by various specialists. Treatment is provided at minimal cost; perhaps the closest approximation in the United States would be a Health Maintenance Organization (HMO), serving employees of a university or other institution. Doctors at these facilities treat not only members of Litfund but also their families. Between 1976 and 1981 Litfund spent 2.9 million rubles on medical assistance to members (76.6 percent of the members had received such assistance). As of 1987–88 the cost of delivering these services had risen to an average of 949,000 rubles each year, of which 592,000 rubles were spent on the Central Polyclinic and its hospital in Moscow (where members from all over the country can come for treatment). In addition, Litfund allocates 1.5 million rubles each year for assistance to temporarily disabled or incapacitated writers, and a further 675,000 rubles for care in sanatoria and at vacation spas. No doubt, the rising costs of medical care, still infinitesimal compared to those in the United States, result partly from the steadily increasing average age of the Union's membership.

The general level of medical care in the Soviet Union is amazingly low for an industrialized nation, with often unsanitary conditions (staph infections are not uncommon, even at hospitals reserved for the elite), poorly trained staff, disregard of patients, and a lack of basic medicines and even bandages. Hence the possibility of obtaining quality care through Litfund is an extremely valuable fringe benefit. Through his membership in Litfund a writer can obtain for himself or any member of his family a *byulleten* (doctor's certificate) or a *kursovka* (permit for treatment and meals at a sanatorium). A *byulleten* pays insurance money to the patient at a rate determined by his or her average earnings. Litfund also provides special maternity and childbirth facilities. One writer mentioned that he had been able to arrange his wife's Caesarean delivery only through the private hospital run by the Union, since the operation is quite rare (fewer than 3 percent of all live births, according to a Moscow obstetrician in 1985).

In addition to housing and medical care, Litfund is the source of many other benefits—all of which help to smooth the course of life in a society where the consumer has traditionally taken a back seat. Litfund provides Union members with pensions and retirement assistance; it is easy to imagine how important membership is for those without any other income or institutional support.[34] Litfund members are entitled to special allocations of foodstuffs from restricted distributing centers (*raspredeliteli*) that are not open to the general public. Most of the Soviet elite has access to such privileges, at carefully graduated levels according to rank, through their place of work or some organization.[35]

Litfund runs twelve *pansionaty*, or resort hotels. In 1987 maintenance costs for these buildings exceeded receipts by 2.72 million rubles. Litfund owns and operates several bookstores (which contain rooms or sections open only to Union members, who thereby have access to newly published books unobtainable on the open market), no less than 30 writers' clubs (smaller versions of the Central Club in Moscow), plus nurseries and other facilities for children. Each year it spends an estimated 1,625,000 rubles on grants to members (about 75 percent of the membership are said to receive grants ranging from 100 to 300 rubles each). Litfund gives both loans and outright grants (*bezvozvratnye ssudy* or *posobia*) to members in financial difficulty. The maximum loan or grant during the seventies was 300 rubles; outright grants of 100–150 rubles are apparently quite common, and greatly appreciated (this figure would be close to a month's wages for the average citizen).

With some membership benefits, the line between material and professional is blurred. This is the case, for example, with a score or more "writers' retreats" where Union members (and their families) can stay for as long as two or three months at minimal cost while they think and create. The retreats are used for both vacations and creative work. Anatoly Gladilin explained that the retreats tended to be used for different purposes at different times of the year:

> The greatest demand for space was in the summers, when people used to bring their families for vacations. But it was very nice in the winters too. The winters were really the time to write. I used to enjoy going to retreats particularly in the wintertime. . . . I'd have my own room, usually a nice one, with everything provided; maid service and three meals a day, and as a rule the food was pretty good.

The best known of these retreats is Peredelkino, the first to open in 1935; it is located a few miles outside Moscow, and is easily reached by train. Also just outside Moscow is another widely used retreat, Maleyevka. Some of the more established writers and critics live at Peredelkino on a permanent basis, but this is not the norm at retreats. There is a writers' colony at Krasnaya Pakhra, outside Moscow beyond the Lenin Prospekt (the pre-revolutionary Kaluga highway along which Napoleon advanced toward Moscow in pursuit of General Kutuzov), where successful writers—for example, Yury Nagibin (and the late Yury Trifonov and Alexander Tvardovsky)—have large houses in picturesque surroundings, featuring innumerable silver birches that make the colony look like a nineteenth-century Russian painting by the great landscape artist, Isaak Levitan.

Over the past twenty or thirty years, new writers' retreats have been opened or expanded along the Black Sea—at Koktebel, Gagra, and Pitsunda. The older Chekhov Retreat at Yalta, where the writer spent his later years after falling ill with tuberculosis, is being renovated. Other retreats exist at Alma Ata in Central Asia; on the Baltic coast at Dubulty; near Leningrad (Komarovo); in Armenia; near Baku; at Frunze; and also at Khabarovsk and Baikal in the Far East. Litfund has three additional writers' retreats under construction or planned for near Leningrad, Sochi (a famous resort on the Black Sea), and in Kirgizia (Central Asia). Extensive repairs and additions are planned in several retreats, including the renovation of three "cottages" (*kottedzhi* in Russian—one wonders how they compare to dachas), and a wing for writers with children at Peredelkino. This wing is to be named after the former First Secretary and later President of the Union, Konstantin Fedin, a writer much despised during his day by liberals, since he was a man of talent and education who went out of his way to prevent the publication of literary works, even when the Party itself was ready to approve them.[36]

Another privilege of membership that might be considered both a material and professional benefit is the *komandirovka*, that is, a fully paid trip within the country to gather creative material, or to give lectures and meet workers. Many émigrés confessed that these trips are often used creatively by writers in ways not envisaged by Litfund; they become short holidays, a chance to visit friends, to do some shopping. This is all the more true of "creative trips" taken abroad, particularly to the West, although the non-convertible ruble remains a serious obstacle. As of 1989, Soviet citizens were permitted to change only 200 rubles into foreign currency. Litfund has no authority over *komandirovki* outside the country. Traditionally, all matters pertaining to foreign travel and contacts with foreigners are controlled by the KGB, in this case through the Foreign

Commission of the Union (*Inostrannaya komissia* or simply *Inokomissia*). However, under Gorbachev Soviet citizens have been offered the right to travel and even to work abroad, for a period up to one year, without loss of citizenship.

The Foreign Commission organizes receptions for visiting writers, usually delegations of writers, from all over the world. The Foreign Commission has access to the Union's special "foreign currency account" (*valyutny fond*), which writers must draw upon in order to travel abroad.[37] Foreign travel is the highest, most desirable, privilege in the Soviet Union today. The desire of top apparatchiks to travel abroad probably has as much as anything to do with the Union's persistent desire to join the PEN Club, which holds annual conferences and occasional meetings in various countries throughout the world. However, Vitaly Korotich, chief editor of *Ogonyok*, stated in an interview in August 1989 that the newly formed Soviet PEN branch would play an important role in helping reform and liberalize the Union.

While most of the benefits of Union membership pertain to the material or social aspects of ordinary life, there are other important advantages that have more to do with the writing profession. Members actually become employees of the Union, which provides them with income, directly or indirectly, through its pervasive influence in Soviet cultural life. The most important professional benefit is privileged access to journals and publishing houses. Although he has no guarantee, a Union member is much more likely to get published than a non-member, especially in the national periodicals, which are swamped with manuscripts. And once he is published, a member will receive higher rates, or a larger advance, than a non-member. Members usually get first refusal to give lectures, not only at universities, but also at factories, plants, and other institutions. The Union's own All-Union Bureau for the Propagation of Literature has the authority and funds to send members on well-financed lecture tours, which can gain them considerable extra income. Another major sponsor of such lectures is *Znanie* ("Knowledge"), a nationwide organization that promotes general education and is also used to inform the public of government decisions and policies. Members not only have an inside track on public lectures, but they get paid higher fees, sometimes double those of non-members. One émigré said that in the seventies, when the average monthly salary in the Soviet Union was not much more than 100 rubles, a Union member would get 14 rubles for such an average lecture: a non-member would get only eight.

A Union member certainly has a much better chance to receive a literary prize or award, although once again the competition for the top prizes is fierce; they are usually reserved for the secretaries and their friends. Prize winners gain the advantage of having their works republished in vast editions—print-runs of one million or more copies. Émigrés agreed that such an edition of collected works in three or four volumes assured the author of a considerable fortune. Literary prizes bring with them not only prestige but large cash awards. The Lenin Prize pays 10,000 rubles, and the USSR State Prize pays 5,000, while Republic State Prizes usually amount to 2,500 rubles. To put these figures in context, remember that the average Soviet writer earns less than 2,500 per year. Most of the non-Russian Republics have state prizes of equal worth, named after a famous local writer. For example, the Ukraine awards the "Shevchenko Prize," and Georgia awards the "Rustaveli Prize." The State Prizes were established in 1939, and called Stalin Prizes. The name was changed in November of 1961, the same month in which Stalin's body was removed from the Lenin Mausoleum. In 1956 the Lenin Prizes were restored, and now included literature as well as science and art. They are awarded on April 22, Lenin's birthday. No Lenin prize for literature was awarded in either 1958 or 1966, omissions that were quite likely related to the disruption surrounding the Pasternak affair and the Sinyavsky-Daniel trial. In 1967, the decision was made to award the Lenin Prizes every two years, and the State Prizes every year, on November 6, the day before the national holiday celebrating the October Revolution.

Some members of the Writers' Union are so successful in winning prizes, and having their works published in large editions, that even at 3 percent their membership dues are very large indeed. Since the fees automatically reveal the members' monthly incomes, they are a closely guarded secret. However, according to Union members in Moscow, some "fat cats" (literally, "big whales" *bolshie kity*) pay hundreds of rubles per year, suggesting huge incomes by Soviet standards. These successful men (almost no women) are not so much the genuinely popular writers as the "literary generals" in the Secretariat and other official favorites.

Thus there are almost certainly more ruble millionaires among writers than in other legal profession in the Soviet Union, including the prestigious Academy of Sciences. Other members of the Soviet elite, such as world-class scientists, ballet dancers, and athletes enjoy dazzling privileges, including the chance to travel to the West, but as a general rule they do not have the same opportunity to earn such vast sums. Literary millionaires, however, are a small (if unknown) fraction of the Union membership. The great majority of members earn far less extravagant incomes, although the general public views writers as among the privileged elite.

According to Union officials in 1983, a recent survey had showed that on average Union members make only 105 rubles (about $160) per month from writing, whereas the average monthly income for the country as a whole was about 180 rubles (about $270), according to Soviet statistics. But during an interview in 1988, the Union's *orgsekretar*, Yury Verchenko, who was trying to downplay the elitist image of the Union, admitted that the average writer's income was 162 rubles (about $240) a month. This is still less than the official Soviet average monthly income, but does not take "total compensation" into account.[38] It might seem at first glance that the Union member's income is not so very different from that of the average American writer. According to the results of a similar survey prepared at Columbia University and published in 1981, the average annual income of American writers from their writing was only $5,000. However, a majority of the American authors surveyed only wrote as a part-time activity, and supported themselves through a second profession, or by serving as "writers in residence" on college campuses. The material benefits provided by Litfund gave its members an opportunity to be full-time writers.

Litfund is a vital plum for the Soviet writer, perhaps the most important reason for joining the Union itself. Many Western writers, struggling to earn a living from their works, to find room and board, somewhere to sit quietly and write, or to get a travel grant to research a book, would probably envy their Soviet counterparts. However, there have always been many complaints about Litfund, especially concerning its secrecy, its cronyism, and its suspected corruption. Almost without exception, émigrés complained about Litfund, although they were grateful for the benefits they did receive. During the campaign for glasnost, complaints have begun to appear in the Soviet press, with demands for more information about the organization's resources and expenditures, and pointed remarks contrasting Litfund's current secrecy to the much more democratic operation of its pre-revolutionary predecessor.

The Party appears to take far less interest in the operations of Litfund than it does in the operations of the Union itself. However, according to émigrés, the head of Litfund is on the *nomenklatura* list of officials appointed by the Central Committee. He must be a Party bureaucrat; it is immaterial whether or not he is a writer. The chairman of Litfund has a board of directors. Not surprisingly, those making the decisions make sure that the biggest benefits go to themselves and their friends. The possibility of corruption involved in the power to distribute such sums and patronage is very great, particularly because decisions are taken in secret and are not subject to public scrutiny.

Litfund members are obviously curious as to exactly how the organization distributes its millions, and who receives most of the benefits. Furthermore, there is growing dissatisfaction about the lack of proper maintenance in existing facilities. From the report of a meeting of the Presidium of the Litfund Board in late 1986, it seems that several of the writers' retreats were noted as needing "capital repair and reconstruction," and there were calls for the construction of many more apartment buildings for writers and for an improvement in medical services. The head doctor of Litfund's Central Hospital, Dr. Yevgeny Nechaev, was instructed to improve the performance of the hospital, and to do a better job in coordinating medical services with the writers' retreats, sanatoria, and so forth. A new plan was announced to make regular check-ups (*meditsinskaya profilizatsia*) available at writers' retreats.[39]

Literaturnaya gazeta gave an important nudge to the growing desire for more basic facts about Litfund by publishing a lengthy letter to the editor, entitled "What Is Litfund?", by a literary critic named Ilya Konstantinovsky. It was accompanied by an extensive and informative, if unrepentant, response by Litfund's chairman, Nikolai Gorbachev (no relation as far as is known), who was listed as one of the "released" secretaries following the Eighth Union Congress in June 1986.[40] Nikolai Gorbachev's answers provided some useful facts and figures on Litfund's activities. The Presidium consists of 31 and the Board of 101 members. It is not clear if the Presidium is selected only from the Board, but that is presumably the case. New rules adopted at the Eighth Union Congress for the "ruling organs" of all Union and Litfund branches require that the Board shall consist of one representative for every 100 members (Litfund therefore had about the same number of members as the Union, about 10,000); and the Presidium shall consist of one representative for every 500 members in a branch organization, with branches of fewer than 500 members sending one representative to the Presidium. This marks a significant increase in regional representation over the preceding Presidium, which consisted of only 22 people, fully 18 of them coming from Moscow; obviously complaints by writers in the provinces about the centralization of benefits had some merit.

According to its chairman, Litfund in 1987 allocated 2.1 million rubles for the construction of apartment buildings for writers. Nikolai Gorbachev did not say how much finished living space that figure created, but he added that in 1985 Litfund had built 2,000 square meters of living space in Moscow, again without saying how much money that achievement cost. If we divide that figure by 30 square meters (a conservative estimate of the average living space for a member of the Union and his or her family), we arrive at about 70 apartments, which cannot come anywhere near meeting the demand. Gorbachev also revealed that in the near future Litfund planned to build two apartment blocs in Moscow consisting of 135 units, and to allocate half-a-million rubles each year to apartment construction throughout the country. He balanced this bright picture by admitting that construction projects in several cities, including Leningrad, Odessa, Yerevan (Armenia), and Saratov, remained unfinished because local organizations had not contributed their share to the projects, leaving a debt of 3.54 million rubles. Half-finished buildings are a familiar sight in the Soviet Union—and writers and their families still wait to move into their promised apartments. Others give up and prefer to live in cramped conditions in the center of Moscow, rather than try to get a bigger apartment located in the distant suburbs, which often lack even the basic amenities, such as stores, schools, and recreational facilities.

Approval of paid trips (*komandirovki*) also seems to be a sore point with many writers. Nikolai Gorbachev said that in 1987 the Soviet Ministry of Finance had released a total of 256,400 rubles for such "creative trips"—which would average out at 25 rubles ($40) per Union member, hardly adequate. He claimed that allocations are not made according to some preconceived plan (*po valu*), as many writers charged, but to meet the interests of individual writers and, furthermore, that Litfund simply follows the lead of the Union Secretariat and does not make these decisions itself. He also revealed that funds for *komandirovki* are distributed to Republic organizations based on the size of their membership. This means that the Russian Republic gobbles up the major share of these funds, as it does almost everything else.

In answer to the charges of Konstantinovsky, Nikolai Gorbachev insisted that none of the 57 dachas constructed by Litfund at Peredelkino since 1934 had ever been sold personally to any writer; they were rented to older or more distinguished writers. He also rejected all charges of special deals being struck, or of apartments being rented for very small amounts, and claimed that Litfund's plans were realistic, not "vague and mysterious" (*tumanno-abstraktny*). However, he did note that the new Union Statutes would probably include a provision for the election of those serving on the Presidium and Board of Litfund, rather than the current method of appointment by the Secretariat (that is, the Litburo and the released secretaries), as at present.

Several émigré writers insisted that Litfund has indeed been building dachas for members of the Secretariat ever since the Union was established. Nowadays the ordinary writer can get a loan or grant of 150 to 300 rubles ($225 to $450), but a large dacha (really a country house) could have a price tag of well over 50,000 rubles ($75,000). It is still a fact that only the establishment writers and "literary generals" can afford to purchase a dacha; ordinary writers usually rent. The insistence of the current chairman of the Litfund Board that such privileges and deals have not occurred is disingenuous. However, it is very unlikely that any evidence will ever be uncovered. The Party has unlimited sources of funds and privileges; it can provide rewards for Union bureaucrats at any time without anyone knowing.

The Union secretaries and other establishment writers often do not live in the standard writers' colonies, although these are quite lovely and contain very comfortable houses; they have spacious homes provided free or for a nominal charge by the Party in the center of town, or else in villas on the outskirts. Many of the top secretaries and favored authors live in large apartment buildings on Bezbozhny Pereulok (literally, "Godless Lane"), which is located in the Dzerzhinsky District of Moscow to the north of the downtown area. We were told that the average size of these apartments is 100 square meters—enormous by Soviet standards. These are the successor buildings to the first apartment building on Lavrushinsky. "Literary generals" also have lavish dachas and vacation homes made available to them at any time.

The Soviet Union is the land of inconspicuous consumption; the elite guard their privileges and try hard to conceal them from ordinary folk, not least because this is supposed to be an egalitarian society. But the top literary bureaucrats not only live extremely well, they have access to a wide range of quality goods and services at nominal cost, including a chauffeur-driven limousine. The revealing of officials' salaries is still taboo. Émigrés, former members of the Union, stated that the salaries of "working secretaries" were high enough to place their recipients among the elite. In the mid-seventies, the First Secretary of the Moscow Writers' Union chapter, Felix Kuznetsov, was rumored to be making 600 rubles ($900) a month, that is, more than four times the national average. Kuznetsov is now the director of the Gorky Institute for World Literature (IMLI). This "golden parachute" removed Kuznetsov from a politically powerful position, but provides him a comfortable sinecure at the head of an Academy of Sciences Institute, and rewards him with the honor of becoming a Corresponding Member of the Academy. His salary there is considered a state secret, but it is surely very high.[41]

But salaries only convey a partial notion of the enormous income differential between the elite and the masses, since free or heavily subsidized fringe benefits make up a large portion of elite compensation. Top members of the Secretariat can easily arrange to have their works published in vast editions of a million copies and more (and sometimes these works are written by "ghosts," or else edited to such an extent that they are essentially re-written). Georgy Markov, as the Union First Secretary, even had a statue of himself erected in his Siberian hometown, and a small museum dedicated to his life and works.[42] Émigrés said that when Markov became First Secretary, one of his first acts was to request 30,000 rubles from Litfund, claiming that he had to "renovate" his dacha because he would now be entertaining foreign visitors. The rubles were forthwith allocated.

We can take the political temperature of the Union membership from articles and letters in the small-format, four-page newspaper *Moscow Writer* (*Moskovsky literator*), which is published every Friday by the Party Committee, and the board of the Moscow writers' organization. This is purely an internal Union publication, and so the members are, as it were, speaking without pretense or restraint. In the November 28, 1986 issue Vadim Kovda published an article entitled "Are Writers Satisfied?" (*"Dovolny li pisateli?"*), which made it quite clear that the great majority were not, especially with Litfund, but their concerns are exclusively with bread-and-butter issues. In 1987, *Moskovsky literator* (no. 34) published an interview with Yury N. Voronin, described as the Director of Litfund. Voronin, who is not listed as a member of the Union in the 1986 *Directory*, attempted to fend off a whole series of hostile questions about the dilapidated state and total inadequacy of existing facilities in the Moscow region, which had almost reached a point of no return, according to the interviewer. Voronin claimed that repairs and restorations were now under way, and new facilities were under construction or being planned. He promised "reliable" telephone service between the retreats and Moscow, properly stocked libraries, better meals and service in the dining rooms, "special furniture," improved medical facilities, and even promised more convenient opening hours of Litfund offices and the Litfund tailors (*atelye*)—yet another valuable privilege in a land of ill-fitting clothes. Voronin concluded his remarks by objecting to the "offensive tone" of many questions and letters Litfund has been receiving. However, the editors of *Moskovsky literator* seemed unrepentant; they declared that the old days of quiet submissiveness were over and invited further criticism of Litfund, and even of their own newspaper.

Union members have continued to complain about the operations of Litfund under glasnost. But what is most interesting about these complaints is that they focus exclusively on material comforts, not on questions of creative freedom. Obviously, more and more writers have come to expect the Union to provide them with more and more benefits and privileges. They do not see the "costs" of membership—for example, Party interference in their work—as being sufficient reason to forfeit the advantages of belonging to this exclusive club.

Vladimir Voinovich considers all the privileges a sham, since it is the regime itself that has created artificial deficits:

> You do receive a chicken once a week in the buffet there, but here [in the West] you can buy twenty chickens in any store. You do have a little bit better clinics for writers than for ordinary people, but it is better to be healthy than to use this privilege. You get a room in a writers' retreat for a month because you have very bad living conditions and cannot write in your own home. But all those privileges are not privileges at all for a Western person. They are a joke.[43]

The Party never misses an opportunity to remind the writer that he owes his privileged position to his patron, not to creative imagination or talent. The Party doles out material benefits in a measured and hierarchical fashion so as to encourage enthusiasm and obedience. Litfund is itself stratified according to different categories of benefits.[44] The Secretariat ranks writers according to their level of performance in carrying out "tasks." Vladimir Voinovich has provided a perfect example of this bureaucratic grading. He reports that, on one occasion, Litfund suddenly announced it would be distributing fur hats to Union members (these are an absolute necessity in the Moscow winters):

> Eminent writers were given hats of young deerskin, well-known writers received muskrat, noted writers got fox, and the rank and file got rabbit. One person considered himself well-known and demanded a muskrat hat. He was told: "Comrade, your place in literature is determined not by you but by the Secretariat. Go complain to them if you want."[45]

The writer described by Voinovich has become the ultimate victim of the system: he can only think to grumble because he has not been ranked one step higher. This is exactly the same type of "rank-consciousness" described by Gogol, Chekhov, and other leading Russian writers in the nineteenth century, who always prided themselves on their independence from the tsarist court and its bureaucracy.

From day to day, Union members are chiefly concerned with the practical questions of getting something published, of finding a decent place to live, and of making sure they do not miss a chance to take that *komandirovka* to the Black Sea next February, when the weather in Moscow or Leningrad will be too cold for comfort. One writer described the Union as "a mighty faction of corruption. But it is a contract between the writer and the state. They corrupt me, and I accept it."

For the average writer the Union is a haven, an exclusive club that offers him high social status and an enviable range of privileges and perks, many of which have less to do with the profession of writing than with providing its fortunate members with ways of handling the chronic shortage of goods and services that continues to plague Soviet society. All writers are perfectly well aware that the Union is run according to Party ideology. There may well be "dues" to pay—ethical compromises necessary in order to remain members in good standing. Nearly all writers are happy to pay this price of admission, but they have placed themselves in an unenviable position of subservience.

One former member of the Writers' Union, Mark Popovsky, has said with brutal honesty that everyone has purely material motives in wanting to join the organization: "Fat city is fat city (*Kormushka yest kormushka*). So the problem is not the Union of Writers, but us."[46] That is a fair criticism. However, even if a writer decided he could dispense with these perks and privileges, if he decided to be noble and tuck himself off somewhere quietly and tap away at the typewriter, to take his chances of making it on his own, he could hardly do so. The Union of Writers takes care of its own; anyone trying to become a successful author without the benefits provided by the Union and its multiple publishing outlets would be in for a very tough time indeed. And that is exactly what the Party had in mind when it established the Writers' Union more than fifty years ago.

5

Crimes and Punishments

After being criticized . . . at a Writers' Union meeting, Boris Balter once said that mounting the rostrum in that organization was sometimes more terrifying than facing enemy bullets.

VLADIMIR VOINOVICH

While the Writers' Union has a virtual monopoly on the dispensing of Soviet gingerbread, its power in wielding the whip is more restricted. The Secretariat's chief role is to persuade, cajole and bribe writers in order to keep them within the fold. Its fundamental weapon is collective pressure against the individual, brought to bear in closed meetings of the Secretariat as well as in open sessions designed to expose the miscreant to public humiliation and disgrace. But the Secretariat has other powerful weapons of persuasion: the denial (or promise) of the right to publish, to earn a living as a writer, and to enjoy all the fringe benefits of membership. If the writer persists in trying to avoid being "guided," then he or she has committed a literary crime, and is expelled from the Union as an outcast, a pariah. As such, the writer becomes a potential target for the Soviet legal system, and possibly, for the KGB.

Since the concept of literary crime lies outside the purview of Western jurisprudence, the nature of the offense may be puzzling. Literary crimes fall under the general umbrella of "anti-Soviet activities" in the Soviet legal system, particularly Section 1 of Article 70 in the Criminal Code of the Russian Republic, which reads as follows:

> Agitation or propaganda carried out with the purpose of subverting or weakening the Soviet state or of committing particularly dangerous crimes against the state, the dissemination for the said purposes of slanderous inventions that defame the

> Soviet political and social system, as well as the dissemination or production or harboring for the said purposes of literature of similar content, are punishable by imprisonment for a period of from six months to seven years with or without exile from two to five years, or by exile from two to five years.

This section of the Russian Criminal Code turns the state into an individual citizen, who can sue for slander and defamation of character, but does so in criminal—not civil—court. The provisions of the section are so vague and all-embracing that any piece of imaginative literature could be used as evidence against its author.

In practice, a writer becomes subject to punishment under this provision of Soviet criminal law only if he tries to step outside the collective in a public manner, to bypass the guidance system either by sending his works abroad (*tamizdat*) or by circulating them in manuscript form within the Soviet Union (*samizdat*). In either case the writer has effectively sidestepped the elaborate procedures set up by the Party for vetting and approving manuscripts. This action constitutes a direct challenge to the Party and threatens to undermine its dual role as patron and Muse. However, once a manuscript has been published in the regular manner, then as a rule the author is off the hook. The fault in such cases lies with the editorial board of the journal or publishing house which authorized publication. They were the Party's deputies for "guidance" and did not perform their task correctly.

Under Stalin, at least once the Great Terror was initiated, committing literary crimes through *samizdat* or *tamizdat* would have been unthinkable. The slightest hint of disloyalty, even a joke or a careless remark, could bring arrest. But the post-Stalin leadership has made no effort to pry into people's private conversations, and thus Russian writers were placed in much the same position as English Catholics in the reign of Elizabeth I: the outward appearance of conformity is sufficient. The freedom from capricious arrest was part of the "social contract" which the new Party leaders struck with society: play by the rules, and nothing will happen to you. As long as members stay within the Union, then they will be protected. Writers who had been obliged to leave the Soviet Union stressed the importance of the protective shield provided by Union membership, and therefore the pressure not to lose it.

It took the Party several years to find a substitute for the more abrupt customs of the great dictator. At first, Party leaders accepted the advice of top literary bureaucrats in the Secretariat, but when that advice proved counter-productive, they developed a more sophisticated method of monitoring and guiding the creative energies of Union members. For those few writers who refuse to comply with the new rules, expulsion is now used only as a last resort, and the decision to expel is taken by the Party, since it marks a failure of the Union to fulfill its mission. The Party must now step forward and punish the convicted criminal directly, thus tarnishing the Union's image as an independent association of writers. The decision to expel represents failure in a deeper sense; writers are among the most highly favored people in Soviet society and are expected to play a leading role in persuading others to commit themselves to the goals of the state. Given the long Russian tradition of writers as cultural and intellectual heroes, disaffection among members of the Union presents a very serious problem indeed.

The celebrated cases of Boris Pasternak (1957–58) and of Andrei Sinyavsky and Yuly Daniel (1965–66) show both Khrushchev and Brezhnev struggling to get control of events after accepting bad advice from the Union Secretariat. Conservative writers took the lead in persecuting their liberal colleagues and in urging the Party to punish them more severely than the Party itself might have been inclined to do. The tightening of the links between the Party and the Union that occurred under Brezhnev was probably designed to avoid a repetition of these mistakes, that is, to make the punishment fit the crime.

In Pasternak's case, his fellow writers, not Party leaders, hurled the first stones. In September of 1956 the editorial board of *Novy mir* sent Pasternak a long letter rejecting publication of his novel, *Doctor Zhivago*. This letter laid the groundwork for the Party's subsequent press campaign against Pasternak. It was printed in October 1958 in *Literaturnaya gazeta*, which termed the novel "a libel on the October Revolution, the people who made the Revolution, and the building of socialism in the Soviet Union."[1] As the storm of abuse mounted against Pasternak, it became clear that the advice the editors and Union bosses had given to the Party was based as much on professional jealousy and concern for their own privileged position as on ideological principles. Not much had changed since Osip Mandelshtam declared that his chief persecutors were literary bosses. All the top men in the Union Secretariat had made their careers during the Stalin period by sycophantic acceptance of each twist in the Party line, and by pouncing on any writer who revealed the slightest hint of creative talent or independence.

No one was a better exemplar of this type of literary apparatchik than the Union's First Secretary, Aleksei Surkov. He established himself as an enthusiastic supporter of Socialist Realism in the thirties, and became widely popular during World War II for his patriotic songs. But this was the limit of his talents; anything more complicated than patriotism, pity for the fallen, rage at the enemy, was beyond him. The rest of his career he produced drum-beat verse to order and was ready to undertake any task on behalf of his superiors. In 1957, after the camps began disgorging Stalin's rehabilitated victims, he tried to justify his own complicity in their fate: "I saw my friends, writers, disappear before my eyes, but at the time I believed it necessary, demanded by the Revolution."[2] Even after Stalin's death, when he was no longer threatened with severe punishment if he disobeyed, Surkov still found it "necessary" to denounce fellow writers.

As soon as word came of Pasternak's Nobel Prize in October 1958, Khrushchev summoned Surkov to the Kremlin for a debriefing:

> Surkov said that Pasternak was a scoundrel and God knows what else, that his poems were always terribly anti-Soviet and his influence on Russian literature baleful. On the basis of this report the vicious Soviet campaign against Pasternak was launched, and of course it incensed world opinion. When the whole scandal erupted Khrushchev summoned Surkov, grabbed him by the collar, shook him fiercely and gave him a terrible dressing-down for failing to mention that Pasternak was a world-famous author.[3]

The Party's General Secretary had asked the Union's First Secretary for advice, and taken it. For his pains, Khrushchev was rewarded with worldwide protest. Enraged, Khrushchev removed Surkov the following year from his position as First Secretary of the Writers' Union and replaced him with Konstantin Fedin. But Khrushchev's successor, Leonid Brezhnev, was to find that Fedin was no more reliable as an adviser than Surkov.

Unlike Pasternak, whose novel was published abroad without his permission, Andrei Sinyavsky and Yuly Daniel deliberately sent their works abroad for publication under pseudonyms. While Pasternak dealt only with early Soviet history (Zhivago dies of a heart attack in 1929), the fiction and criticism of Sinyavsky and Daniel focussed on the contemporary scene, and satirized established Soviet myths and practices.

According to the recollections of Yevgeny Yevtushenko, published in May 1989, the two writers were arrested in September 1965 without Brezhnev's knowledge. Yevtushenko says that, when news of an impending trial of the two writers began circulating in Moscow, he went personally to P. N. Demichev, then a Central Committee secretary responsible for culture, to urge that the idea be abandoned. Demichev replied that he himself opposed a trial, but it was too late to do anything about it. He went on to say, according to Yevtushenko, that when Brezhnev had asked Konstantin Fedin, First Secretary of the Union, whether Sinyavsky and Daniel should be tried in criminal court or be dealt with through a "comradely investigation" by the Union Secretariat, Fedin "raised his hands in horror and said that it would be beneath the dignity of the Writers' Union to deal with such criminal activities (*ugolovshchina*)."[4] Demichev's statement suggests that Brezhnev would have taken Fedin's advice had the latter recommended a "comradely investigation." Therefore, the responsibility for the trial and sentencing of Sinyavsky and Daniel falls squarely on Fedin's shoulders.

Throughout the post-Stalin period, even when the pressure to conform was not nearly so high as before, there was never any shortage of writers eager to denounce their fellows in the most virulent terms. Fedin was not the only establishment writer to condemn Sinyavsky and Daniel. Mikhail Sholokhov declared to repeated cheers from delegates at the 23rd Party Congress in March 1966, shortly after the trial, that he was ashamed of people speaking up in defense of these two "werewolves" (*oborotni*). In his view their sentences had not been hard enough; in the twenties such traitors would have received much rougher justice. Sholokhov may have been particularly angry because the worldwide outrage surrounding the trial had diverted attention from his reception of the Nobel Prize for Literature the preceding October. In fact, the arrest of Sinyavsky and Daniel had taken place in early September, but was concealed for several weeks until Sholokhov had received the prize.

The Sinyavsky-Daniel trial marked the end of hopes for a more liberal cultural policy under Brezhnev. Indeed, it suggested a calculated return to Stalinist show trials, since it included a ghost from the past—Pavel Yudin, the ruthless philosopher-apparatchik and notorious coward in World War II, who had been rewarded for his zeal with membership in the Academy of Sciences. Still earning his laurels, Yudin served as an "expert witness" for the prosecution. But the role of "public accusers" (*obshchestvennye obviniteli*), as required by the punctilious authorities, was played by two members of the Writers' Union, the prose writer Arkady Vasilyev and literary critic Zoya Kedrina. Even before the trial had taken place, Kedrina published in the Union newspaper *Literaturnaya gazeta* an article, entitled "The Heirs of Smerdyakov" (after the bastard parricide in *The Brothers Karamazov*), indicting the two prisoners for treachery. At the trial itself Kedrina declared that she was presenting her "demand that Sinyavsky and Daniel be punished for their criminal acts . . . at the request of writers' organizations."[5] Vasilyev closed his speech at the trial by stating:

> I am speaking as a representative of the Union of Soviet Writers, of which, I am ashamed to say, Sinyavsky was a member. There's a black sheep in every family. In the name of all our writers, I accuse them [Sinyavsky and Daniel] of the gravest possible crime and I beg the court to punish them severely. Anyone who enters the Central Writers' Club sees a marble slab on which are engraved in golden letters the names of writers who fell in the Great Patriotic War. I accuse [these two men] in the name of the living and in the name of the dead. Their crime must be punished.

The transcript records that Vasilyev's jeremiad was followed by applause in the court, which was packed with Party loyalists. While calling upon the memory of writers in World War II, Vasilyev made no mention of the fact that Yuly Daniel had himself fought in the war and been seriously wounded at the front; he suffered from frail health as a result.

Vasilyev was richly rewarded for his performance as, one must assume, was Kedrina. An eyewitness has reported that Vasilyev paid 360 rubles as his monthly Party dues in the fall of 1965. Since the maximum rate for dues in the Party (and in the Union) is 3 percent of income, this meant that Vasilyev had earned 12,000 rubles in one month—the equivalent of ten years' income for the average worker. Vasilyev claimed that he had been paid for writing a film script, but the witness thought it much more likely that Vasilyev had received advance payment for agreeing to play the role of "public accuser" at the Sinyavsky-Daniel trial.[6]

The eager participation of Union members in the persecution of their colleagues made it easier for the Party to preserve the fiction of the Union's professional independence. However, Party leaders soon learned that this atavistic return to Stalin show trials aroused a great deal more trouble than it was worth. The universal condemnation of the trial and of the harsh sentences obliged the Party to attempt rapid damage control by asking Soviet journalists directly for their help. The top people in the Party abhor such direct and public interference because it suggests a failure of their guidance system; they would much prefer for the organizations they have created to voluntarily follow their lead and lend public support. Leonid Vladimirov, a former member of the Union of Soviet Journalists (a parallel organization to the Writers' Union founded in 1959), said that he could only remember this one occasion, in twenty years of work, when the top brass made a personal appearance. He and his fellow journalists were gathered together in a large hall of the Journalists' Union Club, where movies were usually shown:

> But there was no movie showing. The Deputy Chief of the KGB, Lieutenant-General Bannikov, appeared in front of us, in a well-tailored suit. He said: "Comrades, I'm going to tell you something about a nasty anti-Soviet campaign going on in the West. All the dogs are barking, and all the cats are meowing, about the arrest of these two wretched anti-Soviet types (*anti-Sovetchiki*) who smuggled their so-called 'works', their slanders, to the West. They are now trying the strength of our nerve. I can tell you that our nerves are strong enough, and they will get the punishment they deserve. But *you* must help us."[7]

This extraordinary episode illustrates how desperate the situation had become. Presumably, Party officials demanded that a high-ranking KGB officer make a direct appeal in person because the arrest of Sinyavsky and Daniel was a KGB operation and, according to Yevtushenko's account, Brezhnev had not been informed beforehand. In the aftermath of the trial, it became clear that there was a sharp disagreement in the Party itself about the wisdom of the trial. One émigré reported that a journalist with close ties to the Party hierarchy offered him a complete transcript of the trial in an obvious effort to get it circulated and thus embarrass those involved in mounting it.

Sinyavsky and Daniel were sentenced to 7 and 5 years in strict-regime camps. Both survived. Sinyavsky was permitted to emigrate to the West; Daniel remained in the Soviet Union until his death in late December 1988.[8] In the months prior to Daniel's death the Soviet press was permitted to report impartially on the trial and officials stated that it had been a miscarriage of justice. Looking back, we can see that it was more than that; it was a serious blunder. The Party achieved only a Pyrrhic victory. The trial and harsh sentences gave rise to the Soviet human rights movement, and helped the further spread of *samizdat* and *tamizdat*. Union secretaries continued to excuse and explain the trial of Sinyavsky and Daniel. One said to the British journalist Alexander Werth in June 1967: "Unfortunately it had to be done, since otherwise hundreds of writers would have started sending their works abroad." Werth suggests, nevertheless, that the Party realized it had made a very serious mistake in mounting the trial.[9]

The punishment of Sinyavsky and Daniel for literary crimes merely aroused more criminals to follow their example. Furthermore, in a remarkable display of solidarity, sixty-three writers signed an open letter of protest to the Party Presidium and the

Supreme Soviet. One of these men, now living in the West, spoke of the consequences:

> We were called to the Union Secretariat and asked to retract our signatures. I said "No," and they said "Goodbye," but then I had a whole series of troubles. I wanted to go to Poland—I was refused. There were two in the group who retracted. Viktor Nikolaevich Ilyin, who was an ex-general of the KGB, said to one man, who was very sick, and had been in the camps, "Look, Tolya, do you want to go back there? If not, please, take back your signature." And he did. One other man wanted to go to England, very much. They knew that; so they got him to retract too.

But Ilyin's threats had no effect on the other signatories. With one man, a poet, he tried everything. But the poet said, "Look, if you have fucked a girl, how could it be that she is not fucked, even if you say you didn't fuck her? I have signed this letter—it has been published abroad. So. . . ."

In addition, five scholars sent a protest letter directly to Brezhnev.[10] The writers had perceived the threat that the sentences represented for literary life as a whole. Liberal writers and intellectuals manifested a collective will to resist Party dictates. Even though they failed to save Sinyavsky and Daniel from jail, the phenomenon of jointly signed letters in defense of an individual was a new and serious challenge to the Secretariat. However, the most notable letter provoked by the harsh treatment of Sinyavsky and Daniel was written by one individual to another—Lidia Chukovskaya's letter to the establishment novelist Mikhail Sholokhov in response to his speech at the 23rd Party Congress. She sent copies to the Union of Writers and to the editorial offices of five Soviet newspapers. Chukovskaya, a woman of unshakeable intellectual integrity, took Sholokhov to task, contrasting his behavior unfavorably to that of the great Russian writers of the nineteenth century:

> The greatest of our poets, Alexander Pushkin, said with pride, "I have called for mercy to the fallen." In a letter to Suvorin, who in his paper had dared to blacken Zola, the defender of Dreyfus, Chekhov said, "Even supposing Dreyfus were guilty, Zola would still be right, because it is the business of writers not to accuse or prosecute, but to intercede even for the guilty, once they have been condemned and are undergoing punishment. . . . There are enough accusers and prosecutors as it is."
>
> "It is the business of writers not to prosecute but to intercede.

> . . ." This is what we are taught by Russian literature through those who represent it best. This is the tradition you have broken by loudly proclaiming your regret that the sentence was not harsh enough.[11]

For this public challenge to the Party's favorite writer, Chukovskaya was not physically harmed, but yet another black mark was checked off against her name by the literary bureaucrats. It is entirely possible that Sholokhov, a man with powerful Party contacts, had something to do with Chukovskaya's expulsion from the Union in 1974.

The Party, condemned throughout the world—even by members of Communist Parties—decided it had to avoid a repetition of the Sinyavsky-Daniel trial and yet regain control over writers. Yury Andropov was appointed head of the KGB in 1967 as part of a long-term plan to crush the human rights movement and curtail *samizdat* and *tamizdat* activities. At the same time, the Party made a concerted effort to refine the Union's punishment system and to lend it more of an air of legality, in order to distinguish the new guidance from crude Stalinism. In 1967 the Union's Statutes were made more explicit about both crimes and punishments. In his report on planned revisions to the Statutes at the Fourth Congress (May 1967), the Belorussian literary apparatchik Petrus Brovka noted that the Statutes had until that point been "rather severe in the matter of punishments" since they provided only for expulsion. Reprimands and rebukes had been administered in the past, but "not on the basis of the Statutes." Brovka, representing the new official line, wanted a staggered series of punishments that would bear the imprint of legality in the Statutes and also carry the weight of social rejection:

> We recommend that the following sentence be added to the Statutes: "For actions demeaning the honor and dignity of any branch of the Writers' Union and for violation of the Statutes, a member of the Writers' Union may be subject to public censure or rebuke, administered by the ruling organ of the local branch or higher organs of the Writers' Union."[12]

The granting of punishment powers to local branches was of particular interest: it was quickly invoked two years later when the tiny Ryazan branch met to expel Solzhenitsyn and recommend his expulsion to the Russian Republic organization in Moscow. Brovka also suggested that the first item in a list of violations should be "deviation by Union members from the principles and tasks as formulated in the Statutes of the USSR Writers' Union." To justify these additions, Brovka merely posed one of those rhetorical questions so favored by Stalin:

> After all, what sense is there in having a writer belong to our organization if he does not adhere to its fundamental principles and tasks; if he not only does not defend those principles against our ideological enemies, but even violates them himself?

Brovka did not have to explain, because every delegate knew where to find the answer to his question: in Lenin's 1905 article "Party Organization and Party Literature," which had argued that the right of association took precedence over the right of free speech. At the Tenth Party Congress in 1921 Lenin had insisted on outlawing differences of opinion within the organization; this decision laid the foundation for Stalin's later insistence that anyone who disagreed with him was "anti-Party." This general hostility toward differing opinions had long since filtered down into the Union and throughout Soviet society.

At the 1967 Congress Brovka did not list the censures and rebukes that could now be imposed on Union members. Lidia Chukovskaya lays them out in her book, *A Case of Expulsion* (*Protsess isklyuchenia*), which was published in Paris in 1979 (and has not appeared in the Soviet Union). They are carefully graduated, rising in a crescendo of condemnation, prior to expulsion itself: "caution"; "severe caution"; "public reprimand"; "rebuke"; "rebuke recorded in writing"; "severe rebuke recorded in writing."[13] A student of organizational reprimands might be amused to compare the Union's list to those laid down by St. Benedict for his Order in the sixth century. Disobedient monks were faced with a similar rising scale of punishments, starting with "private admonition," moving on to "public reproof," thence to "silence at mealtime," then up to "scourging," and finally, the same "expulsion" that is the ultimate punishment for the recalcitrant Union member.

This refinement in the schedule of punishments had to be matched with a corresponding refinement in procedures. Although this was never spelled out publicly, evidence strongly suggests that the Party's ideological specialists decided they needed to acquire greater control of writers at an earlier stage in the creative process. The Union was obviously too large and cumbersome to maintain constant surveillance of all its members, so the Party reverted to its favorite mechanism: group pressure through meetings of smaller units. The mechanism for such pressure already existed in the form of various councils and commissions, which had increased significantly in number since 1960. Always sensitive to the ideological threat posed by individual activity, the Party had tried to group writers together into smaller units within the Union itself. This emphasis on group activity and discussion followed logically from the official view that writers should work together to serve the people. Prospective members had to apply for membership as writers in a certain genre—poetry, prose, drama, and so forth. Although there was no specific requirement to do so, it was expected that each member of the Union would belong to at least one "council" (*sovet*), usually organized according to genre, or "commission" (*komissia*), usually organized according to theme or topic. In Republic and other regional branches of the Union, a council is generally known as a "section" (*sektsia*). These sections are often subdivided into commissions. For example, the section on children's literature would have a commission on school literature, a commission on youth literature, and others.

From 1967 on, the Party tried to tighten discipline in these councils, commissions, and sections, determined to avoid a repetition of what had happened at the meeting of the section on prose fiction of the Moscow writers' organization in November 1966—the section had praised Solzhenitsyn's novel, *Cancer Ward*, and recommended its publication. The Secretariat had managed to counter the recommendation with a second meeting. However, the Party learned from this experience, and developed a broad strategy to make better use of these smaller groupings within the Union to achieve two major objectives. The first was to establish agenda control by encouraging members in each group to write on approved topics. If this attempt failed, then the groups could serve as an early warning system and fulfill the second objective, which was to mobilize colleagues to initiate the series of rebukes and reprimands against the recalcitrant individual. In his opening statement to a 1981 volume of essays by members of the Secretariat, Yury Surovtsev declared that all the gatherings arranged by the Union are aimed at "organizing literature." Officially, this "organizing" is not regarded as dictating: rather, it is called "teaching," a verb which picks up and amplifies the etymology of *rukovodstvo* as "leading by the hand," and at the same time recalls Maxim Gorky's programmatic statement at the First Congress of Soviet Writers in 1934—that the government was offering writers a chance to teach one another and share their experiences. According to Surovtsev, teaching and sharing are the main objectives of the Union's heavy schedule of meetings, which occur at "congresses, the plenary sessions of the Board, the meetings of its Secretariat, the numerous sections, . . . at meetings of councils run on a voluntary basis, . . . and at the many smaller units." Surovtsev is pleased that so many meetings take place: "These regular discussions, outspoken and comradely in spirit (at writers' gatherings or in the literary press) have proved to be the best form of mutual exchange."[14]

There is nothing particularly sinister in writers gathering together to discuss their work and exchange ideas. In practice, however, the Secretariat tries to use these meetings and discussions as a means of monitoring the activities of Union members and directing their creative energies into approved channels. The Secretariat's real objectives are seen most obviously in its centralized control of the non-Russian literatures through special councils on the literatures of all fourteen non-Russian Republics. Although a Russian Republic branch of the Union was established in 1958, it continued to enjoy the honor of not having a council to coordinate its work, meaning that it had been granted special distinction. The privileged position of Russians in the Union is also shown by the fact that all the councils for non-Russian Republic literatures are chaired by Russians, with an ethnic serving as vice-chairman. In all cases the Russian chairman is a literary apparatchik or a reliable "non-Party Bolshevik." For example, the Council on Ukrainian Literature is chaired by the reactionary writer Mikhail Alekseyev, with two Ukrainian vice-chairmen, I. Karabutenko and V. Krikunenko. To centralize control over non-Russian literatures still further, following the Seventh Congress in 1981 the Secretariat, apparently without consulting the Board, established a Bureau for Councils on the Literatures of Soviet Nationalities (*Byuro sovetov po literaturam narodov SSSR*); it is headed by another veteran Russian bureaucrat, Yury Surovtsev.

Politically reliable writers and literary apparatchiks also head the remaining councils, which cover all the major literary genres (except poetry). There are councils on Criticism and Literary Research (*literaturovedenie*); on Drama (*dramaturgia*) in the Theater, Film, and Television; on Literary Translation; on the Sketch and Publicistic Literature (*khudozhestvennaya publitsistika*)—a peculiar Soviet genre; on the Literature of Adventure and Science Fiction (*priklyuchencheskaya i nauchno-fantasticheskaya literatura*); and on Literature for Children and Young People. On January 14, 1987, the Council on Prose Fiction, which had ceased to function for several years, was revived under the chairmanship of Pyotr Proskurin, whose name appears among the list of released secretaries. The Union also has a Council on Working with Young Writers, and even a Council on Afghan Literature, headed by the organizational secretary Yury Verchenko. The formation of this latter council was probably motivated by the Party's desire to help the Union justify and support the Soviet occupation of Afghanistan.

There are only a handful of commissions at any one time, and unlike the councils they tend to be classified by literary topics, rather than by genres. As of the late eighties the Union had commissions on Soviet German Literature (produced by descendants of immigrants who settled originally in the Volga region under Catherine the Great, but were deported to Central Asia in World War II), and on Military Literature (*voenno-khudozhestvennaya literatura*). But there was a Council on Literature of the Sea, so it seems that a strict distinction between councils and commissions is not being maintained.

The Party uses the councils and commissions to mobilize writers for projects, hoping to avoid the potential problems involved in leaving them to their own devices. Councils and commissions try to meet their first task, agenda control, by doing a lot of the practical liaison with the writer's community. For example, the relevant council (or section on the local level) can help an author writing about a military topic to get in contact with military installations and to arrange interviews with officers and with draftees. A writer can, of course, simply call or send a letter to a scientist in a research institute, or other organization, saying "I am writing a short story and I want to interview you." But this approach may not work with a military installation or a politically sensitive institution. Councils and commissions serve the invaluable function of providing the writer with the official "paper" (*bumaga*) that will get him special treatment. The Council on the Literature of Adventure and Science Fiction might assist writers in meeting members of the scientific community, and getting permission to visit research institutes, which are normally closed to the general public.

The impact of participating in such councils and commissions is cumulative. The councils and commissions invest their time heavily in responding to Party decrees and announcements, and especially to officially sponsored anniversaries. So, for example, the Council on the Literature of Adventure and Science Fiction declared in its report to the 1981 Congress that it had devoted much of its attention to celebrating the anniversary of the birth of Felix Dzerzhinsky, co-founder with Lenin and first head of the Cheka, predecessor of the KGB. The Council had received the active support and encouragement in its celebrations from representatives of the KGB, the MVD (regular internal police), the Komsomol, the Party, and others.

The councils and commissions encourage the direct participation of citizens and other organizations in the work of writers. Thousands of joint meetings and discussions between writers and their readers are held every year. As a further encouragement for a writer to produce works on desired themes, and to fulfill "tasks," the Union can offer him or her an all-expenses paid creative trip (*komandirovka*), which aims to foster *narodnost*—a feeling for the people, their lives and their work. In a luxurious volume published in 1984 on the fiftieth anniversary of the Union, it is stressed that the writer's work begins long before he sits in the quiet of his study in front of his typewriter, and does not end with the publication of his work. He is expected to visit the sites he describes and talk to the types of people who will populate his novel. He must travel and discuss his work with them, and perhaps visit again the setting of the work to "get a better grasp of his real-life material" (*glubzhe osvoit zhiznenny material*).[15] The writer is encouraged not to lose touch with the working people or the nation.

Since it has paid the writer's research costs, the Party continues to monitor the ideological correctness of his literary works by encouraging Soviet readers to express their opinions publicly. Thus, letters to the editor are yet another layer in the Party's "defense in depth"—a form of public pressure by the collective on the individual. Because Marxism-Leninism decrees that literature is a reflection of Soviet life, there is an immense importance attached to reader complaints. Workers will write to the author, to his journal, to his local chapter of the Union, or perhaps to the local Party *obkom* about his story. In the Stalinist period, these letters often amounted to public denunciations. Now, they are far less ominous, but they will have an effect on the author and on his work. Each writer is obliged to take these comments seriously, and to report back to the readership and to the Union Secretariat, showing how he has done his best to respond to "the people and the Party." Valery Ganichev, editor-in-chief of *Roman-gazeta* (literally *Novel-newspaper*), which reprints novels and shorter fiction in a popular format every two weeks, stated that his enterprise received thousands of letters a year, and was obliged to respond to every one of them. He emphasized that there is a Soviet law which decrees that every letter must be answered, and within a specified time-frame.[16]

Readers' letters often do not address literary or artistic questions. If a book or story features a schoolteacher, then schoolteachers will take the author to task for not portraying them attractively. If an author writes about construction workers in Siberia, that group will have every right to complain and suggest helpful changes to improve the characterization. It is not only individual readers who offer criticism about the way in which they have been portrayed in fictional works, but also entire industries. It is not at all unusual for a Ministry to complain officially, but not publicly, about a literary work in which its employees or practices are shown in an unflattering light.

The Union takes *narodnost* seriously, and so must the writer who wants to enjoy further benefits of Union membership. *Narodnost* has encouraged a national army of literary vigilantes. One émigré claimed: "Everybody can kill your manuscript, even a typist. She might notice something that she interprets as an ideological mistake, and start yelling, 'This is anti-Soviet propaganda!' " Soviet authors must always remember that anyone is entitled to make a citizen's arrest of a literary work. Even under glasnost readers can and do send letters attacking writers for their works; the old custom of denunciation dies hard. The only difference in the late eighties is that the authorities generally do not follow up on such accusations of "anti-Soviet activities."

Obviously, a writer is not likely to invite public abuse by being too critical about any occupational group in Soviet society. On the contrary, he is much more likely to portray such groups favorably, particularly since there are tangible rewards for doing so. To take one example among many: the military and the security forces have long demonstrated a serious interest in literature, and not simply to censor it. Members of these elite groups like to see works written about them—in a favorable light, usually foiling nefarious plots by capitalist spies and their Soviet dupes. To inspire writers to focus on their activities, the Soviet army, navy, and air force offer several literary prizes. In addition, nearly every Soviet and Republic ministry has established prizes for literature and the other arts.

Not wanting to have its spies left out in the cold, the KGB also offers prizes for "the best artistic works about Chekists and border guards"—the latter form a major unit of the KGB, with their own heavy armor and aircraft, and their special day in the Soviet calendar, "Border Guard Day," every May. The KGB prizes are not limited to literature; indeed, the majority are awarded for feature films and television series which focus on the activities of Western spies and agents, foiled by KGB heroes—rather like Soviet James Bond movies. The KGB expects high standards; it did not award a first prize in 1986. Second prize went to a two-part film entitled "Dossier on the Man in the Mercedes." There were three third prizes, including one for another film entitled "The Barman (*barmen* in Russian) at 'The Golden Anchor.' " Several runners-up received what were described as "incentive (*pooshchritelnye*) diplomas and valuable gifts."[17]

The results of the KGB competition were published in the official Union weekly, *Literaturnaya gazeta,* on December 24, 1986. The value of the prizes was not given. However, in the spring of 1984 the KGB did announce a special competition for the best literary works and films to mark the upcoming 70th anniversary in 1987 of the founding of the Cheka. The announcement said that the KGB would award 3,000 rubles for one first prize, 2,000 each for two second prizes, and 1,000 each for three third prizes; plus the usual "incentive diplomas." Three thousand rubles is equal to $4,500 at the official exchange rate; according to Soviet statistics, the average annual per capita income is a little more than 2,400 rubles.

This system of positive incentives appears to work quite well. The rules of the game are clear—prospective applicants know what theme and authorial stance the prize committee expects. The Party does not actually give assignments; it does not have to. Several émigrés pointed out that the system has become much more sophisticated than it was in Stalin's time, when "social command" involved sending writers off to create favorable copy about various industrial projects. It can still happen that a writer will be offered the choice of going to a project or losing the chance to publish for several years, or indefinitely. However, since Khrushchev, the Party's bureaucrats have simply announced themes, linked with Party policies, and made it clear that writing about them will bring writers special favors. Everyone knows that various agencies offer prizes, so it is smart to write on officially sponsored topics.

A writer who fails to meet his responsibilities can be quickly identified by watchdogs in his council or commission. If he fails to attend meetings regularly, expresses opinions that appear unorthodox, or in any other way displays too independent a spirit, then he may not suffer much beyond being "reasoned with" by his colleagues. Beyond that, he will be put at the bottom of the list when it comes to apartments, cars, vacations, and other benefits.

The Secretariat supplements this public, collective pressure on the writer with more discreet, closed meetings at which it reprimands those writers who appear reluctant to meet their responsibilities. This kind of harassment can have a cumulative effect on a writer's health as well as on his career. In a moving tribute on the tenth anniversary of Boris Balter's death, Vladimir Voinovich in 1984 accused the Union bureaucrats of bringing Balter to an early grave through constant harassment. Voinovich spoke of

> . . . those demagogues in the Writers' Union who attacked anyone who had different ideas or who was more talented than they, and made their victims face the "firing squad" of denunciations, slander, and false charges—sometimes at open meetings, but more often at closed ones.[18]

As Voinovich points out, these sessions of cultural prophylaxis are not made public. However, one example came to light in 1983, during a speech by Union First Secretary Georgy Markov at a plenum of the Central Committee of the Party. Markov presented the episode to illustrate the triumph of the Union Secretariat in fulfilling its responsibilities to the Party. A well-known, but unnamed, author had written a play that was already in production and had received much praise. However, the Secretariat decided that the play was "profoundly flawed" (*sugubo oshibochnoi*). Markov and his fellow bureaucrats summoned the writer for a discussion, at which he arrived in a cheerful frame of mind, since he had many supporters. Members of the Secretariat realized that their job was to "unsaddle him from his white steed and lower him onto the sinful earth," as Markov put it:

> We had to overcome his outlook, change his attitude toward himself and bring him to a new understanding of his own work, while at the same time not arousing any bitterness in him; we wanted our colleague to preserve a cooperative spirit and his positive attitude toward the collective.

This took some time to achieve. The author remained unconvinced even after more than three hours of "heated debate," and announced he would simply withdraw the play and let time judge its merits. But Markov's story had a happy ending. After several weeks had passed, the repentant author came and declared with absolute sincerity: "It took too long, but I want to thank you for a memorable discussion."[19] Markov was determined to bring this author to heel in part because he had not played the game according to the rules; the playwright had tried to bypass the Union, and operate on his own, fully confident in his own ability and the popularity of his works. The collective insists on a central role in the creation and editing of a manuscript; the author should have submitted his play in manuscript to his council, the Council on Dramaturgy, for discussion and suggestions.

Incidents such as this serve not only to bring a writer into line, but to alert others to the consequences of such individualistic behavior. It comes as no surprise that in almost all cases this type of collective pressure brings the individual to his knees: it is a tactic long used in other ideologically based communities. The approach adopted by Markov and his fellow secretaries bears a striking resemblance to that of the medieval Catholic Church: first came the *attritio* (attrition), the hammer blow to smash the sinner's pride; then contrition, wherein the sinner acknowledged wrongdoing before God and man; finally, absolution was granted and the black sheep allowed back into the fold, chastened but forgiven.

If a writer persists in being uncooperative and begins to engage in what Konstantin Fedin described as "criminal activities" (*ugolovshchina*), then the council may be called upon to initiate more severe penalties, leading finally to expulsion from the Union. Lidia Chukovskaya's expulsion was formally initiated by the bureau of the section on Children and Youth Literature, to which she belonged—it was a section, not a council, because it was part of the Moscow branch. Chukovskaya had been a thorn in the Union's side for several years—prompted to speak out, as she says, because "There comes a time in your life when truth grips you by the throat, then commands your soul to obey it forever."[20] She had written open letters and supported many dissidents. She and her father, Kornei Chukovsky, a famous author of children's books, had even offered their home to Solzhenitsyn when he was under attack. But it was probably her open letter, entitled "The People's Anger" ("*Gnev naroda*"), which she had sent abroad for publication in September 1973, that caused the Party ideological apparatchiks to have her expelled from the Union. In her letter Chukovskaya deplored the vicious campaigns, supported by "professional stool pigeons" such as Vadim Kozhevnikov, who days earlier had declared, in an *Izvestia* article (August 30, 1973), that nuclear physicist Andrei Sakharov, creator of the Soviet hydrogen bomb, was hatching a plot to have Western imperialist powers intervene in the internal affairs of the Soviet Union and other East European countries. Chukovskaya declared that campaigns of hatred against Pasternak in 1958, against Solzhenitsyn in 1969, and against Sakharov in 1973 were merely continuing the work of Joseph Stalin.

Chukovskaya describes how she was summoned to appear on December 28, 1973 in the office of Yu. F. Strekhnin, a Union secretary, on the second floor of the Writers' Club. Strekhnin (yet another of those powerful figures in Soviet literary life who are totally unknown as writers, or in any other capacity) explained that her colleagues in the section on Children and Youth Literature had recommended two weeks earlier that she be expelled from the Writers' Union. Every effort was made to keep up the appearance that the Secretariat was scrupulously observing protocol and not simply obeying instructions received from the Central Committee of the Party. And yet her fellow writers had made the recommendation without informing her, and Strekhnin himself had not alerted her in advance as to the reason for this meeting.

As Strekhnin began to read out the brief written complaints and charges against her, a representative of the section, Anatoly Mednikov, walked in and sat down. As Chukovskaya remarked, the attackers all leveled virtually identical charges; she inferred that they had received instructions from Party officials. Their statements said that it was essential that she not be allowed to shame the memory of her father any longer, and that she was only interested in promoting herself in the West with anti-Soviet diatribes. None of the accusers was present, except Mednikov.

Chukovskaya was particularly angered by the written statement of Albert Likhanov, a writer of novels about the problems of youth, who argued that her behavior constituted "outright anti-Soviet activity"—a very serious charge. He declared that she had lied in claiming that some dissidents had been put illegally into psychiatric hospitals; they were genuinely ill. Likhanov added that Chukovskaya was no different from Litvinov, Yakir, and Krasin (convicted dissidents) in that she was simply trading on the name of her famous father. As Chukovskaya was able to show, Likhanov's statement was a tissue of lies and false innuendo.[21]

None of Chukovskaya's attempts to justify her behavior was allowed to halt the steady progress toward expulsion, nor were any of her many friends and admirers permitted to speak in her defense. Following the meeting in Strekhnin's office, she was summoned to attend a meeting of the board of the Moscow writers' organization on January 9, 1974. Chukovskaya has very poor eyesight and therefore had to stand by a window in order to read. Sergei Narovchatov, an orthodox poet, who became chief editor of *Novy mir*, presided. However, he did not name any of the other speakers (there were about two dozen people in the room), so Chukovskaya was obliged to walk back and forth from her place at the window in order to see who was speaking and then take down his or her statement, as well as her own replies. A guard at the door had barred any of her friends, also members of the Writers' Union, from attending the meeting. It is hard to imagine an elderly, frail woman with poor eyesight being treated in this harsh manner, particularly by fellow members of a writers' association.

The meeting, which amounted to a trial *in camera* with the accused having no rights and no legal representation, began with the reading of a bill of particulars: Chukovskaya's support for Sinyavsky and Daniel; her letter to Sholokhov; her letters in support of Solzhenitsyn, Galanskov, Ginzburg, and other dissidents; and the publication abroad of two novellas. These perfectly normal, even worthy activities were said to be "anti-social" and therefore to contravene the Union's Statutes, which had of course been contoured in 1967 precisely for use against members like Chukovskaya. As Chukovskaya herself points out, it is a strange organization indeed that regards as criminal activity the defense of one member by another, and acts as a prosecutor itself.

Almost all the speakers—inveterate Stalinists and neo-Stalinists, such as Yury Yakovlev, Anatoly Mednikov, Yury Zhukov, Nikolai Gribachev, Agnia Barto, Nikolai Lesyuchevsky, Sergei Narovchatov, Mikhail Alekseyev—mentioned Chukovskaya's letter, "The People's Anger." A second common feature was the effort to separate Chukovskaya from her celebrated father. Each speaker professed his or her eternal admiration for the works of Kornei Chukovsky, and deplored the disgrace brought to his name by his daughter, conveniently ignoring the fact that the Union had blocked the publication of several of his works.

The process continued and Chukovskaya was formally expelled from the Union—"sentenced to oblivion," as she puts it. After expulsion from the Union an author's life may be made simply very difficult, or he may be persecuted and threatened to the point where he must emigrate. In this case Chukovskaya was not forced into exile, but left in peace. Fortunately she managed to survive in the Soviet Union until the dawn of the new era of glasnost.

Chukovskaya was expelled from the Union less than a month before Alexander Solzhenitsyn was arrested in the middle of the night and put on a plane for Frankfurt, West Germany. This forcible exile capped a running battle between Solzhenitsyn and his few friends on the one side, and the Party, the KGB, and the Union Secretariat on the other. Solzhenitsyn presented by far the most serious challenge to Brezhnev's new system, in part because, in protesting "guidance," he had become a symbol for rebellion even among formerly devoted adherents to the Party line. The most notable of these converts had been Alexander Tvardovsky (1910–71), a talented poet and an orthodox Marxist who supported Khrushchev's Thaw and became one of its leaders. Tvardovsky served as chief editor of *Novy mir* from 1950 to 1954 and again from 1958 to 1970. He had joined in the condemnation of Pasternak's *Doctor Zhivago,* but made amends by finagling permission from Khrushchev to publish Solzhenitsyn's *One Day in the Life of Ivan Denisovich* in November 1962, then fought to publish the same author's stories—"Matryona's Home" and "Incident at Krechetovka Station"—when the Thaw was over. As the conservative forces gained strength, Tvardovsky suffered a series of defeats. He had Solzhenitsyn's novel *Cancer Ward* set in type in 1966, but at the last minute the Central Committee did not allow its publication. After printing 80,000 copies of an issue containing Konstantin Simonov's *War Diaries* about the appalling defeats of 1941, Tvardovsky was forced to pulp the entire print-run.[22]

A former member of *Novy mir*'s editorial board, now living in the West, reported that each issue of the journal, while Tvardovsky was editor-in-chief, would go not only to Glavlit for censorship, but also to the Central Committee of the Party. Tvardovsky was too popular a writer to be expelled from the Union, but in 1970 he was finally forced to resign as chief editor of *Novy mir* by Mikhail Suslov, the chief ideologist of the Politburo. Suslov stayed in the wings, and allowed eleven literary bureaucrats of the Union to send a joint letter to the journal *Ogonyok*, accusing Tvardovsky of "anti-Soviet activities."[23] He was followed as chief editor by his former deputy, V. A. Kosolapov. A broken man, Tvardovsky died of cancer in July of 1971.

The Union's Secretariat mounted a campaign against Solzhenitsyn at this same time, but with different results. The procedures followed by members of the Secretariat in their handling of Solzhenitsyn reflected the general approach in the Brezhnev period after the fiasco of the Sinyavsky-Daniel trial in February 1965. They did not at first try to bully or threaten. They began by trying to appeal to the writer's sense of loyalty. They argued that if he persisted, he would be giving comfort to the enemy (Western capitalist states). They used all the arguments about "service to the people"; they even tried bribery, asking the writer if he lacked anything. They hinted that a trip to the West might be in the offing—the most dazzling prize they could offer.

Solzhenitsyn has described the meeting he had with the Union bosses at the Secretariat building in the summer of 1967. Tvardovsky (who accompanied him) had urged Solzhenitsyn to discuss with them his open letter to the Fourth Congress of the Union the previous May, demanding an end to censorship, and a fundamental change in the structure and activities of the organization. The letter had been supported by nearly 100 Union members; this fact, together with Solzhenitsyn's worldwide fame, made the top secretaries uncharacteristically polite.

Solzhenitsyn was met by First Secretary Georgy Markov ("a plump fox" [*otyevshayasya lisa*]), the organizational secretary Konstantin Voronkov ("a chunky bouncer" [*korenasty vyshibala*]), and the "working secretaries" Sergei Sartakov ("ugly as sin [*murlo*], but comic too") and Leonid Sobolev—the latter arrived late "because there was no car free to bring him in and he knew no other means of travel." These and other secretaries live in a cocoon, protected from the vulgar realities of Soviet life. As Solzhenitsyn says, they are not writers at all, but clerks (*kantselyaristy*)—he uses a pre-revolutionary term, calling up images of superfluous tsarist officials.

Solzhenitsyn describes the vast offices with their sumptuous furnishings, including large tapestries portraying Leo Tolstoy (inevitably, given the building's putative associations), Pushkin, and Gorky, the founding father of the Union, who is a little out of place in being ranked with Tolstoy and Pushkin. Solzhenitsyn asked for a glass of plain tap water, whereupon:

> A maidservant appeared from some secret inner office to load the enormous polished table with fruit juices and mineral waters, followed by strong tea and expensive crumbly cakes, cigarettes and chocolate truffles (all bought with people's hard-earned money [*narodnye denezhki*]). It was time for polite drawing-room chat; I heard that this was the Rostov house, and how it was kept up, and how Countess Olsufyeva, on a visit from abroad, had asked to see it (Voronkov pronounced the word "countess" with relish [*so smakom*] and I could imagine him dancing attendance on her—or slipping into her cell to shoot her in 1917).

It was obvious that Markov and his fellow secretaries were most concerned about the foreign radio broadcasts, which had commented extensively on Solzhenitsyn's letter of the previous May and read it out repeatedly. This meant that it was widely known in the Soviet Union, where millions of people (including many among the Soviet elite) listen to foreign radio stations such as the BBC, Radio Liberty, Voice of America, Deutsche Welle, and Radio Israel. Markov had evidently been given the assignment of trying to accommodate Solzhenitsyn in some way, of persuading him to disavow his letter and thus save the Soviet authorities from further embarrassment. It did not work with Solzhenitsyn. This conversation must have been one of the few times that these "literary generals" felt at a real disadvantage. As a rule they have far greater power over less prominent writers and are used to getting their way.[24]

Following this failed attempt to have Solzhenitsyn recant, the Secretariat began to issue the carefully graduated series of reprimands which had been approved at the Fifth Writers' Union Congress just three months earlier. Once this process was initiated, the writer knew he was heading for the final punishment, expulsion from the Writers' Union. He understood equally well that, without the protection of Union membership, he would be exposed to the charge of parasitism, or worse, since he now became a legitimate target for forces external to the Union.

In Solzhenitsyn's case none of the tactics employed by the Secretariat worked, and it was obliged to resort to the final punishment. Solzhenitsyn's account of his life as a writer inside the Soviet Union, *The Oak and the Calf*, contains a vivid description of a November 4, 1969 meeting of six of the seven members of his local chapter in Ryazan (including Solzhenitsyn himself), summoned to confront and expel him. The branch's leader, its secretary, was in the hospital awaiting an operation, but a member from another local chapter was brought in to make a quorum. The Party's secretary for ideology attended; he dominated the proceedings. Frants Nikolaevich Taurin, a secretary of the Russian Republic writers' organization, presented the ostensible topic for discussion, a resolution on the need for "tighter control over writers going abroad, and further measures for the ideological indoctrination of writers." These measures had been necessitated by the recent defection in England of the writer Anatoly Kuznetsov. But the real reason for the meeting was to expel Solzhenitsyn. A resolution of expulsion had already been typed up; the Ryazan writers were expected to approve it. The resolution charged Solzhenitsyn with "anti-social behavior" and "gross violation of the basic provisions of the Statutes of the Union of Soviet Writers," and asked the Writers' Union in Moscow to confirm their request that he be expelled from the organization.

Alexander Sergeyevich Kozhevnikov, the local Party *obkom* "secretary for agitation and propaganda," attended to make sure that nobody wavered (he was not listed as a Union member in the 1966 Directory). When Solzhenitsyn began to defend himself forcefully against the vague charges and the local members seemed unable to counter his arguments effectively, Kozhevnikov simply interrupted the proceedings and laid down the law. He explained that he did not want to interfere because the writers were, of course, completely independent, but they should consider the fact that Solzhenitsyn had declined to disassociate himself from Western comments about his situation, and he had refused to acknowledge the "guiding role of the Party." The leading functionaries of the Union cooperated fully with the Party's ideological secretary, and indeed displayed considerable enthusiasm for their role in disciplining a fellow Union member.

The vote was 5 to 1 to expel, with only Solzhenitsyn himself voting against. The result was a foregone conclusion, although a young member of the Ryazan chapter, Yevgeny Markin, expressed puzzlement at the sudden switch in attitude toward Solzhenitsyn, who had only recently received such lavish praise. But when the time to vote came, Markin voted to expel—it would have been expecting too much of a minor writer in an exposed position to do otherwise.[25] A few days later, while Solzhenitsyn was still in Ryazan, the Russian writers' branch in Moscow also expelled him. The announcement was made in *Literaturnaya gazeta* (November 12, 1969). No doubt, if any actual meeting of the Russian Republic branch was held to cast a formal vote, it would have been attended by the ideological secretary of the Moscow *gorkom*, or Party City Committee. However, at the national level the Party authorities can rely upon the Union apparatchiks to take care of recalcitrant writers themselves. And the top members of the Secretariat have not been shy about carrying out their responsibilities. They summon writers to the Secretariat building at 52 Vorovsky Street to administer reprimands, and on occasion to expel members from the Union. As often as not, a writer is expelled in his absence and without forewarning, as was the case with Solzhenitsyn.

A slanderous press campaign against Solzhenitsyn was intensified. Solzhenitsyn's war record had already been falsified; it was alleged that he had served time in the camps as a common criminal (not as an innocent victim) and that he had surrendered to the enemy. Solzhenitsyn, a decorated veteran officially cited for bravery, was particularly furious about the suggestions that he had "betrayed his country" and "collaborated with the Germans."[26] Finally, on February 14, 1974 the authorities gathered sufficient courage to have Solzhenitsyn seized in the middle of the night and put on a plane to Frankfurt, West Germany. Later his wife was permitted to join him with their children, but she refused to leave until the KGB agreed to let her take all of Solzhenitsyn's papers and manuscripts. Over the next few years several other famous dissident writers were exiled in a similar manner; others were expelled from the Union. Harsh though it was, the handling of both Tvardovsky and Solzhenitsyn showed that Brezhnev had not returned to full Stalinism: neither writer was arrested, let alone sent to Siberia or executed.

Although the Union carries out the formal procedure of rebuke, reprimand, and other punishments leading finally to expulsion, it is the Party at all times which is pulling the strings. When the literary scholar Yefim Etkind was expelled from the Leningrad branch of the Union in 1974, he did not waste any time talking to his fellow writers. He went straight to the Leningrad Party Office in the Smolny Institute (Lenin's headquarters during the Bolshevik coup and formerly an exclusive girls' school). He has described his conversation there with Zinaida Mikhailovna Kruglova, the *obkom* second secretary, that is, the person in charge of ideology.

Etkind's crime was his friendship with Alexander Solzhenitsyn, forcibly exiled to the West the previous February, and with Joseph Brodsky (exiled a decade earlier to the Far North as a "parasite," but long since released and permitted to emigrate to the West).[27] As Etkind says, holding the position she did, Kruglova was "in charge of 'propaganda', i.e. the press, books, museums, education—all our cultural life in fact." She made decisions affecting everyone in Leningrad; she even refused to allow a world-famous scholar to travel to the West to receive an honorary doctorate.

Kruglova had two young men with her, presumably a couple of apprentice "responsible officials" or "instructors." They said very little but gave Etkind hostile stares. In answer to all Etkind's attempts to justify his behavior and refute the amorphous charge of "anti-Soviet" behavior, Kruglova simply repeated such phrases as, "You're evading the issue." "You're trying to wriggle out of it." "You're hiding something." "It suits you to say that."[28] These are all phrases straight out of Lenin's polemical toolbox, as shown in his 1905 article on "Party Organization and Party Literature," as well as in countless other articles and essays. Etkind, deprived of his job as a professor and also of his membership in the Writers' Union, had no alternative but to emigrate to the West (in 1988 the Leningrad branch of the Union formally readmitted him to the Union, a remarkable example of glasnost in action).

On occasion ideological specialists from the Party will also step forward when it seems that the Union secretaries cannot keep control. Emigrés stressed that generally the Party's ideological specialist is used to having his or her own way, and so as a rule is not very patient with those who express differing opinions. Such an apparatchik enjoys full membership or at least candidate membership in the Bureau, or Buro (*Byuro*), of the Central Committee of the Union Republic's Communist Party. This man (or woman, in some cases) will usually attend Union conferences, particularly those that have as guests writers from the "fraternal" socialist countries of Eastern Europe, or writers from the West. He will usually be on the reception team at the airport, meeting and greeting all foreign visitors; he will often be on a plane himself as part of a delegation of Soviet writers (or other cultural figures) going abroad. To make his presence there look natural, he usually holds the position of "Chairman of the Foreign Affairs Commission" of the Supreme Soviet of his Union Republic, although his real responsibility remains secretary in charge of ideology.

The Party's ideological specialists take a routine interest in manuscripts submitted for publication, and will step forward to threaten or punish an individual writer short of expulsion. Vadim Nechaev now lives in Paris, but when he was a member of the Leningrad chapter, he had a run-in with the Party's culture representative:

> I wrote a cycle of stories when I was a journalist in the Far East. I sent them to a journal; they were scheduled to appear in 1963. But unfortunately, Khrushchev had a meeting with writers; there was a swing to a hard line. The galleys of my

> stories, already printed, ended up at the *obkom*—galley proofs from journals are routinely read by the local *obkom*. The local *obkom* turned down the entire cycle. The editor at my journal told me to call the *obkom*. I did, and they asked me to stop by for a meeting. The secretary for culture was a middle-aged woman; she was in charge of culture, movies, literature, and so forth. (I will not name this lady—she later went on to work in the Central Committee.) She said that the stories were too gloomy, and that I described life in far too dreary a fashion. She proposed that I should go home and rework the stories and remove the pessimistic details and dark scenes.

Nechaev made the mistake of thinking he could slip a barely touched manuscript past the Party's ideologically watchdog. He was naturally reluctant to emasculate his work:

> I went home, but I decided that to follow her advice would result in stories that were not worth reading. So I just changed the punctuation, and took it back to her. She was very angry. She said, "So you think you can play games with us, do you? Well, it just takes one word from us, and at the very least not a line of what you write will be published anywhere within the Soviet Union for three years." She mentioned the example of a Leningrad writer about my age, who was sent off to work on some distant [industrial] project until he brought back some optimistic verses about the working classes. I only got two of these stories published, and nothing else of mine was published in the Soviet Union for almost three years—just as she had said.

This was only the beginning of Nechaev's problems. He was later ordered expelled from the Union by Grigory Romanov, the hard-line Party boss for Leningrad, who became furious that Nechaev had been organizing art exhibits in his own apartment without seeking official approval. Romanov, whose rule over Leningrad was named the "second Romanov period" (after the Romanov dynasty), was himself notorious for his luxurious lifestyle; he once used a priceless eighteenth-century service from the Catherine Palace at his daughter's wedding; predictably, some pieces were smashed. Later he managed to become a member of the Politburo, but was outmaneuvered and sent packing by Gorbachev. After the Leningrad chapter had done Romanov's bidding, the KGB moved directly against Nechaev, again obviously with Romanov's approval. Nechaev had no wish to emigrate, but his mind was changed one night when thugs sent by the KGB set fire to the door of his apartment, while he and his wife, and their baby, were asleep inside.[29] The Nechaev family barely escaped the dense flames and smoke; they applied for emigration shortly thereafter.

This type of physical abuse was called upon by the authorities whenever they felt it necessary, but was comparatively rare in the Brezhnev period, according to most émigrés. Anatoly Gladilin drew a sharp distinction between the position of writers in the Stalin and post-Stalin period:

> Since Stalin's time, when by his personal order writers were killed or sent to labor camps—since that time *no member of the Writers' Union has ever been liquidated*. In my time I was criticized a lot, and very severely, and many other writers were criticized even more. But I survived. I didn't die from hunger. I managed somehow. But if I hadn't been a member of the Writers' Union, then I might have been arrested. That is what happened to Joseph Brodsky—he wasn't a member and he was arrested as a parasite. . . . As long as you are a member of the Union, then the Soviet authorities cannot deal with you directly, with naked force. They must deal with your organization. Even the KGB must deal with a member of the Writers' Union through the organization.[30]

One terrible exception to the protection generally offered by Union membership occurred on the evening of April 25, 1976 when Konstantin Petrovich Bogatyryov, a well-known expert on Russian and German poetry, and a respected translator of poetry, was bludgeoned and his skull fractured just outside his apartment door in Moscow. He did not die for 52 days. A former friend said that the attack on Bogatyryov was an "enigma" to him: "For sure it was the KGB that sent the thugs. But maybe they were just supposed to frighten him. Maybe they got carried away." Since Bogatyryov was still a member of the Union at the time of this attack, the writing community was particularly shocked. At Bogatyryov's funeral on June 20, Vladimir Voinovich gave a defiant eulogy, saying that Bogatyryov had been the victim of a wholly unwarranted assault, and urging an investigation.[31] It never occurred.

As a rule, harassment takes such forms as slashing the tires and smashing the windows of the target's car (a favorite KGB warning), abusive telephone calls in the middle of the night, and the interruption of mail service. But probably the most serious, permanent result of expulsion is that the writer can no longer earn a living. One émigré termed expulsion the "Soviet version of excommunication—once you are expelled, you will never again get a single ruble for writing." He added that it would be better never to have joined the Union than to be expelled from it, because now you were a marked man.

All copies of the expelled writer's works are removed from libraries and bookstores throughout the Soviet Union, no public mention of his name is permitted, and of course there is a categorical ban on publication of his existing or future manuscripts. Chief responsibility for these actions is turned over to Glavlit, whose officials warn editors at journals and publishing houses of the prohibitions. The aim is to isolate the sinner, to "send him to Coventry," to turn him into a non-person, with no possible means of financial support. Friends are frequently warned not to try to help the writer, and are watched carefully to see that they obey—although this does not always intimidate the sturdiest allies.

In fact, the writer's main hope is the devotion and courage of friends and relatives. In contrast to the many incidents of treachery and malice among Union members, there has always been a countervailing tradition of support. Even before his expulsion, Solzhenitsyn had been befriended by Kornei Chukovsky and his daughter. Later, the distinguished cellist Mstislav Rostropovich (now director of Washington's National Symphony Orchestra) did the same. The émigré writer and translator Shimon Markish mentioned that this type of friendship toward those in trouble existed even in Stalin's time:

> Prominent literary men and women were thrown out of the Union. How would they survive? Some had real friends. These friends would say, "Look, I have a contract for a book on Pisarev [a literary critic of the nineteenth century] or some such subject. You write it. I'll publish it—unfortunately, my name will be on the cover—but the money is yours."

Although the help of such friends enabled Solzhenitsyn to live in comparative safety, it was the award of the Nobel Prize for Literature in October 1970 that secured his position. It was now impossible for the Soviet police to abuse him physically, or send him back to the Gulag or to a psychiatric prison as a "schizophrenic personality"—a tactic used with many dissidents, although not with Union members. Solzhenitsyn confesses in his memoirs that he did not realize at the time the full strength of his position or the nervousness of the Soviet authorities. He blames himself for not being bolder and seizing the advantage that his privileged position afforded him. However, it is unlikely that action on his part could have prevented the Soviet authorities (namely, the KGB, headed at the time by Yury Andropov) from forcibly expelling him to West Germany.

The post-Stalin guidance system has been a success in the sense that the great majority of writers are prepared to do what is expected of them, if not willingly, then at least without complaint. They publish vast quantities of books that epitomize the Party's ideological preferences: they are optimistic, upbeat, and show the Party as the inspiring leader of a society well on its way to full communism, in spite of domestic and foreign foes. These works of Soviet *sotsrealizm* are equivalent to the "capitalist realism" of the United States—"happy ending" paperbacks sold at supermarket checkout counters.

After the distortions of the Stalinist managerial style, the Writers' Union had come into its own under Brezhnev. But ironically, at the very moment the Party appeared to have finally contoured an effective guidance system for monitoring and channeling creative literature, the whole elaborate structure was threatened by the economic reality of supply and demand, and by the unpredictable behavior of human beings—Dostoevsky's "ungrateful bipeds"—among millions of Soviet readers. Bureaucratic greed and corruption among "literary generals," who were the main beneficiaries of the system, together with increasing reader alienation from orthodox literature, caused a steep decline in the quantity of books actually sold. Thus the Party's agenda was jeopardized, for literature could not serve its educative function if the target audience refused to read its message. The Writers' Union whole *raison d'être* was undermined by societal and economic changes the Party preferred to ignore.

6

Purity and Profit

Of course, we could make at least 5 million rubles by publishing a translation of *The Godfather* or a James Bond novel, but we refuse; and that is why we think our system is better than yours.

OFFICIAL AT GOSKOMIZDAT (*1983*)

By the late 1970s the Party and the Union had to all appearances perfected a new guidance system that ensured the obedience of the vast majority of Union members without the use of Stalinist terror. For the few remaining recalcitrants, they had put in place an effective sequence of punishments: those writers who could not be bribed or cajoled into conformity were finally expelled from the Union, and in some cases from the country. Such outcasts could be safely ignored, as statistics showed vast editions of officially approved books continued to be published in increasing number every year. What statistics did not show was how many of these volumes were actually being sold. Gradually the facts emerged: millions of copies of ideologically correct Soviet novels lay unbought on the state bookstores' shelves.

The Party had targeted the writer, but left out of the equation the Soviet reader, supposedly the *raison d'être* of the entire guidance system: according to *narodnost*, literature should be by, about, and for the people. As Ilya Ehrenburg noted at the 1954 Writers' Congress, readers had changed since Socialist Realism was promulgated; they were becoming more intelligent and sophisticated than writers. Over the next twenty-five years this process accelerated. Soviet surveys corroborated data generated by interviews with Soviet émigrés to the United States during this period: the domestic audience was avoiding contemporary Socialist Realist literature, preferring instead Russian classical literature, works written in the Soviet period but suppressed by the authorities, and almost every type of Western fiction and non-fiction.[1] The Soviet authorities could not force citizens to buy sufficient quantities of the "right" kinds of books, that is, the "classics of Marxism-Leninism," and the orthodox Soviet fiction that embodied the tenets of Socialist Realism. In the words of Oleg Bitov, a former editor at *Literaturnaya gazeta:* "These works were printed to be pulped."[2]

Thus a new literary dilemma had arisen to take the place of the one that Lenin and his followers thought they had resolved in the twenties. The Writers' Union Secretariat was happy with things as they were, but its patron, the Party, started to question the return on its investment. The whole intricate network, of which the Union was the nexus, threatened to unravel. The émigré writer Sergei Yurenen described the apparatchiks' dilemma: "They want to bring more ideology into the content of literature. But then the quality suffers. And the quantity [of books sold] drops. Because Soviet readers do not want them."[3] The post-Stalin leaders became aware of this problem and made attempts to resolve it. However, they merely tinkered with symptoms, rather than dealing directly with causes: they were reluctant to loosen their grip on writers altogether, or to give up the idea of using literature as propaganda. Thus, the fundamental nature of the system remained unchanged.

Initially, the Party attempted to breathe new life into Socialist Realism. As if in support of Ehrenburg's evaluation of growing reader sophistication, the Party had its loyal supporters at the same 1954 Congress argue that Socialist Realism was not a straitjacket, but could expand to accommodate almost any theme or approach to reality. Konstantin Simonov charged that some of his comrades viewed Soviet society through rose-tinted glasses due to "a misunderstanding of the essence of Socialist Realism." Unfortunately, noted Simonov sadly, this faulty interpretation had been expressed even at the First Writers' Congress and had developed since then, in spite of the efforts of Maxim Gorky himself and astute critics such as Alexander Fadeyev and Pavel Yudin to correct the error. (Both these men were in fact directly associated with efforts to browbeat writers into producing works to order.) As a result, instead of remaining faithful to a true Socialist Realist approach, much Soviet prose had been damaged by the "varnishing of reality" (*lakirovka*). Simonov perceived a distinct threat to Soviet literature in a "vulgarizing" tendency which he identified with specific critics—the tendency to approach Socialist Realism as a "single, unified style" that must be adopted by all writers, and to condemn anything written outside this style as "wicked and evil" (*ot lukavogo*, literally "inspired by the spirit of darkness"). On the contrary, insisted

Simonov, quoting from the Union's Statutes (which, as he knew, had been ignored from the day they were issued), "Socialist Realism guarantees all artists the clear possibility of creative initiative, of choosing a wide variety of forms, styles, and genres."[4]

In their presentations later at the 1954 Congress, two other major establishment writers, Konstantin Fedin and Leonov Leonov, followed Simonov in defanging Socialist Realism. Leonov managed not to mention it at all in a long report on the work of a special commission assigned to revise the Union's Statutes. Instead he emphasized the humanitarian role of the Union and its responsibilities to the younger generation. But Fedin, like Simonov, took up the meaning of Socialist Realism as the main focus of his speech. He recalled with amazement that fellow writers and foreigners often asked him to define Socialist Realism and, when he recommended that they take the whole varied achievement of Soviet belles lettres as their answer, they looked disappointed. Evidently, noted Fedin in surprised disbelief, these people actually expected precise recipes for cooking up Socialist Realist works. They seemed to be suggesting that Socialist Realism could be assembled according to a formula: "50 percent positive hero, 5 percent negative character, 1 percent social contradictions, 1 percent romantic enthusiasm, and 100 percent aquavit." When the laughter in the hall died down, Fedin declared boldly "Art is not created from recipes":

> A scholar can write a research paper on "How the Novel *Don Quixote* was Made," but we will not learn from it how to write a novel like *Don Quixote*. (Applause) The artist must always rely on his own talent and effort to "invent" each work of art. If he is incapable of doing so, then all he will achieve is duplicating copies of works by others.[5]

The speeches of Simonov and Fedin were the literary equivalent of Khrushchev's later attack on Stalin—the end of infallibility. If there was no definitive statement as to what constituted Socialist Realism, then where was the dogma, the Truth?

Later, in the Brezhnev period, there were continued attempts by such critics as Vladimir Markov to define Socialist Realism as an "open system" that could accommodate many types of literature. But such efforts did not get to the central issue: Socialist Realism lacked any real meaning as a *literary* term. Émigré writers and critics were unanimous on this score, and one added: "Western scholars try to give it legitimacy, but this is futile; it is really just a synonym for the grip of the state." Those who had to function under the method even after Stalin's death shared the same view. In his novel *Zhizn i sudba* (*Life and Fate*), set during World War

II, Vasily Grossman has a character compare Socialist Realism to a magic mirror that constantly reassures the leadership by saying, "You, you—Party, government, and state—you are fairest of them all."[6] Vladimir Voinovich, the satirical novelist, has given his own succinct definition: "Socialist Realism is praise of the leaders in terms they can understand." It seemed to many that the literature of Socialist Realism had degenerated into stereotypes, cardboard characters, and a focus on industrial production, rather than on human relationships.

In the post-Stalin period, Socialist Realism lost whatever literary coherence it might have originally possessed, but *partynost* and *narodnost* retained their force. Party leaders were extremely reluctant to dispense with Socialist Realism altogether, because it incorporated fundamental beliefs that lay at the heart of the Soviet social experiment. Editors still became nervous if an author painted too dark a picture of contemporary Soviet society, or if the author attempted too obvious an experimental, "modernist" style in either language or plot. The residue of Socialist Realism remained as a nexus of themes, motifs, and cliches that constituted a pattern of expectations for both the creative writer and the journalist. Literature and journalism were handled in similar fashion—following the lead of Lenin, the two professions had always been intimately related in the minds of Soviet apparatchiks. The Party trained ideological specialists in culture and media—they moved back and forth between the two—and Party leaders grouped all cultural and media people together whenever they wished to outline a new policy.

A former Soviet journalist, Leonid Vladimirov, gave examples to illustrate how the system worked in practice, at least prior to glasnost:

> There are certain laws—unwritten laws—in Soviet literature. You cannot find them published anywhere. If you take out the Statutes of the Writers' Union, or the journalist's handbook (*Spravochnik zhurnalista*), you will not find them. But anyone who spends five days in an editorial office is well versed in them. Law Number One says that no information detrimental to the Soviet Union, or to Eastern Communist countries, can be published without "soup." "Soup" goes like this: "The Central Committee of the Communist Party pays a lot of attention to providing good shoes for citizens. The last Party Congress made special provision for shoe production. Many factories provide a lot of shoes of good quality. But against this happy background, it is sad to note that factory X in region X is continuously underfulfilling its quota."[7]

A former censor from the Azerbaijan Republic, who was interviewed in the West about her job, showed that Vladimirov's remarks apply in exactly the same way to literature. She gave an example of a poem she killed:

> I once had to forbid the publication in *Literary Azerbaijan* of a poem called "The Foreigner." In it the author described a not untypical Soviet situation: someone is on a business trip to another town, where after a hard day's work, he is asleep in his hotel room. Suddenly, he is wakened and told to clear out for a foreigner. The poet has him say some bitter words about this: "I am a citizen of this country. I fought for it, and here I am thrown out into the street in the middle of the night." All true. This foreigner may well have been a fascist. But I killed the poem, because it would have made a negative impression in the West.[8]

This example demonstrated "Law Number One" in action. There was no state secret being given away, but the system was being criticized without "soup." The corollary of this law is that any information favorable to the Soviet Union can be published without "soup." Conversely, as Vladimirov explained:

> Law Number Two states that no event favorable to a capitalist country can be published as such. Whatever achievement there is in the West—if you are absolutely bound to report it—you have to paint in some black and blue. That would be its "soup."

Socialist Realism accepts the fact that everything is not yet perfect in Soviet society, and has provided guidelines for handling "negative social phenomena." Ilya Suslov, a talented writer who edited and wrote for the satirical "page 16" of *Literaturnaya gazeta*, gave an example of literary soup:

> In my time, you could discuss alcoholism—why it exists in the best country in the world, how it got there. We could explain its appearance by saying we inherited it from the past, or that it was imported from the West. We could not say that it originated in our society. No—it's not us, it is not because Soviet people are bored, and have little to do during leisure time. We could not describe the boredom of Soviet life as the root of our alcoholism.

Tension or conflict within Soviet society must be handled within the overall framework of the Party's leading role in society. Suslov again provides a typical plot:

> Say there is a director of a plant. He is a good man; he works like a horse, but his methods are stopping progress in what is

called the "scientific and technological revolution" [*nauchno-tekhnicheskaya revolyutsia*, or NTR]. The Party sends in a chief engineer. He is young. This new engineer knows not only all about the NTR, but has a "human factor." He knows that people are unhappy, and works heroically and successfully to help them.

According to the Party's canon, a good piece of literature exemplifies several formulas. Suslov described a typical example:

> [The hero] could be a soldier, or collective farmer, marshal, Party functionary, or KGB spy. It doesn't matter. This man puts his life on the line for the Party, and for the people. He must be very positive. He may have some faults, some negative points in his character, but he risks his life in the front line for the Party. He doesn't have to *be* a member of the Party—in fact, the Party loves it when people do things *for* the Party, and the KGB just loves that too. He could be a pilot or a Young Pioneer—any background will do. But from the bottom of his soul he must believe in the ideals of the revolution.[9]

In addition to these types of plot and conflict, Soviet writers and journalists must treat Lenin and the current General Secretary of the Party with reverence. Suslov ticked off what he termed "newspaper cliches" dotting the pages of a typical short story:

> "Soviet power is best," "The dream of workers is fulfilled" and "Lenin knows best." Here verbal bricks have been put in the walls of newspapers or journals or even poetry, so that everyone will remember them. It's an old propaganda trick.

These deeply ingrained "laws" vitiated the Party's attempts to update or broaden Socialist Realism. They also doomed to failure an effort to introduce more rationalism into publishing, with the creation in 1963 of the State Committee of the USSR Council of Ministers for the Press (*Gosudarstvenny komitet Soveta Ministrov SSSR po pechati*). This was one of a score of such committees (the KGB, formed in 1954, is the most celebrated) that were instituted in the decade following Stalin's death as part of the Party's efforts to deal with the increasing complexity of Soviet economic life. The Committees were ordered to place more emphasis on technical skill in plan formulation and statistical analysis; they reported to the Presidium of the USSR Council of Ministers. Some state committees acquired ministerial status; so, for example, the State Committee for the Press was given greater authority than the lowly Ministry of Culture, as the Party sought to strike a better balance between ideological control and economic efficiency.

Instead of promoting more rational decision-making, the State

Committee for the Press followed the usual Brezhnev pattern of becoming an entrenched bureaucracy that gathered into its hands increasing dominion over all publishing. It acquired a broader mandate and a longer name in 1978, becoming the State Committee for Publishing Houses, Printing Plants, and the Book Trade (*Gosudarstvenny komitet SSSR po delam izdatelstv, poligrafii i knizhnoi torgovli*), but is referred to simply as Goskomizdat. The expanding authority of this little-known, but immensely powerful institution made things worse for the writer, since it raised one more obstacle between him and his reader—yet another bureaucracy, whose job was to ensure a proper measure of ideology in Soviet literature. Publishing, alone of all Soviet industries, had to fulfill not one but *two* plans. One was an economic and a production plan, while the other was ideological, the "thematic plan" (*tematichesky plan*) or *templan*. The *templan* continues to be set for all types of publishing, not just literature, by Goskomizdat. In deciding the *templan* in literature, Goskomizdat works closely with the chief editors of major journals, who usually belong to the Writers' Union. Indeed, although Goskomizdat is part of the apparatus of the state, reporting to the Council of Ministers, its officials responsible for literature are, coincidentally, almost all members of the Union themselves. The *templan* for literature—what gets published, and in how many copies—favors the works of the Union Secretariat, that is, the orthodox propaganda that Soviet readers avoid. Taken together, the Union and Goskomizdat play a much more decisive role in Soviet literary life than Glavlit, the official censorship organization, which can only approve or disapprove manuscripts sent to it by journals and publishing houses at the end of the review process.

Saddled with a *templan*, executives at Goskomizdat in the Brezhnev period naturally believed that their job was not to produce an economically viable product, but rather to market an ideology. Soviet centralized planning had always stressed production rather than consumption. Industrial enterprises fulfilled the plan by weight, size, or some other gross measure; whether anyone purchased and was satisfied with the products was not their concern. In the case of publishing, the *templan* measured ideological content. Managers were judged by production figures, not by sales. To meet the plan each year, all that the publishers had to do was print large editions of the "classics of Marxism-Leninism," and literature that embodied the principles of Socialist Realism. As long as ideological purity meant more than financial profit, they would continue to receive good reports from their superiors. It did not take long for the secretaries at the Writers' Union to manipulate this system to their own advantage.

The Union virtually *is* the publishing industry for creative writing because it controls all major literary journals in the country—controls, that is, on behalf of the Party, and in cooperation with its ideological specialists. A Union member usually will offer his manuscript—even if it is a long novel—to a journal rather than a publishing house, since most Soviet fiction appears for the first time in one of the "thick journals" (*tolstye zhurnaly*), either complete in one issue, or serialized in two, three, or even four consecutive issues. Thus journals play a particularly significant role in the Soviet literary scene. They appear monthly rather than quarterly, and in hundreds of thousands of copies; they publish not only original verse and fiction, but also critical articles, reviews, and essays, not always limited to purely literary topics. The publication of fiction in such journals continues a tradition that goes back to the nineteenth century. Fortunately for Soviet writers, there is an impressive array of publishing outlets. Soviet presses produce a total of 5,275 periodicals in forty-four Soviet and twenty-four foreign languages (in addition to 8,515 newspapers).

All literary periodicals are subject to the authority of the Union and its Republic and regional branches. Dozens of journals have a line on their masthead, "Organ of the Union of Writers," or "Organ of the RSFSR Writers' Organization"—and this number includes almost every national and regional literary journal in the country. The Union controls another dozen weekly papers, often in conjunction with other cultural and creative organizations. In fact, the Union has under its jurisdiction 120 literary journals in the Russian language alone.[10] The Union also runs an important publishing house, *Sovetsky pisatel* (Soviet Writer), which has branches in all fifteen Republics. There are publishing houses under the jurisdiction of institutions and enterprises other than the Union. However, Party ideological specialists tend to have the same general outlook, and they are in constant touch with the Union Secretariat.

A Union member has privileged access to these journals and the Soviet Writer Publishing House. The editorial board that reviews his manuscript will be staffed by people who are themselves members of the Union; the outside reviewers will more than likely also be members. Without the entrée of his membership card, an author would have very little chance of having his manuscript reviewed or published by the journal's editorial board. However, since practically all major publishing outlets for literature fall under the jurisdiction of the Union of Soviet Writers or are subject to its veto, the author finds it difficult to avoid the authority of the Secretariat. Anyone who runs afoul of powerful Union secretaries will have a hard time publishing.

In addition, the writer faces a phalanx of bureaucrats and ideological watchdogs as he tries to get his manuscript into print. Having survived the gauntlet of meetings in the Writers' Union, the author's real fight is just beginning. The elaborate procedures he must go through bear little relationship to traditional concepts of censorship in the West. Assuming the writer is living in the Russian Republic, his manuscript would be submitted to a journal and would need to be approved by most or all of the following people or bodies, in sequence:

An editor of the journal's appropriate department; e.g., prose fiction.
The head of the journal's editorial department.
The journal's "responsible editor" (*otvetstvenny redaktor*).
The journal's first deputy chief editor.
The journal's chief editor.
The censor (or employee of Glavlit).
The District or Regional Committee of the Party.
The Russian Republic branch of Goskomizdat.
The USSR Goskomizdat.
The KGB.
The Propaganda Department (and the Culture Department) of the Party Central Committee.[11]

Thus, there are five layers of editorial review—each occupied by an individual who can change the pages in front of him or disapprove them altogether—before the manuscript even reaches an official from Glavlit, who usually sits on the editorial board of journals. With Glavlit approval the manuscript may then be considered for inclusion in the *templan* of Goskomizdat at the Republic and/or national level.

Several émigrés said that manuscripts were routinely reviewed by the Party's ideological apparatus, that is, by the secretary for ideology in the local Party Committee. If a manuscript raises no particular problems, then it will be published without further discussion. But if it does, then the author's manuscript might well have to be approved by the Party's Central Committee. Its authority is invoked only in rare instances, because the Central Committee already has its representative on the editorial board. Sergei Yurenen explained:

> In the structure of each journal, or in any other central publication, there is always a place for people who are called "the eye of the tsar," meaning "the eye of the state." Those

> people are represented by two assistants to the chief editor. One will be the responsible editor (*otvetstvenny redaktor*), who is usually the representative from the KGB. Another would be a deputy chief editor, who reports to the Central Committee.

Yurenen's comment helps explain the order in which editorial review is structured: the "responsible editor" (*nomenklatura* of the KGB) and the first deputy editor (*nomenklatura* of the Central Committee) see a manuscript before the journal's chief editor does. The chief editor is himself *nomenklatura* of the Central Committee, as one émigré explained: "The chief editors of all central publications are appointed or sacked by the Personnel Department of the Party."

Generally speaking, Soviet editors try to downplay the role of the Party ideological specialists in their work, although they are quite ready to discuss their relationship with the Writers' Union. The intertwining of the "thick journals" and the Union was emphasized by Grigory Reznichenko, "responsible editor" at *Novy mir*, during an interview in December 1985. He explained that the Ministry of Culture does not evaluate the journal's performance:

> No, absolutely not. And neither does the Department of Culture of the Party Central Committee. We don't have anything to do with them. But every two or three years we present a report about our work at a meeting of the Board of the Writers' Union. They appoint literature critics to discuss our work and conduct a general review of our journal.

The Soviet press will ordinarily carry an account of the Secretariat's or Board's report, and their criticisms and suggestions for improvement. Reznichenko's insistence that the Central Committee's Department of Culture has nothing to do with the journal may be true in a technical sense. However, the Party most assuredly does "guide" the editorial activity of *Novy mir*, as it does that of all Soviet publications.

During an interview at the editorial offices of *Literaturnaya gazeta* in December 1985, the first deputy editor, Yury Petrovich Izyumov, had less hesitation about admitting the Party's role in his newspaper:

> Yes, we have a Party organization here; I belong to it since I am a Communist. We also have a Party Bureau, which guides (*rukovodit*) its work. But the Party Bureau's tasks consist in trying to get Party members to contribute as much as possible to the general work of our newspaper. The Party Bureau does not control the running of the paper (*Partbyuro ne kontroliruyet rukovodstva gazety*). Its task is to make sure that every Communist works

> as well as possible, that he does his job properly, and that he behaves in an exemplary fashion. We are paying a lot of attention to that now; we want everyone to be not only a good worker but also, as it were, a good person.

No doubt the *Partbyuro* does watch carefully over the professional and moral behavior of Party members. However, it also works hard to "guide" the overall activity of the newspaper. Otherwise it would not be fulfilling its mandate as stated in the Party's own *Rules*. This is just as true in the editorial offices of various publications under the Union's jurisdiction as it is within the Union itself.

Émigré writers and critics supported Izyumov's general claim that the Party does not interfere directly in the operations of a Union publication. They pointed out that such interference is not necessary, because the people reviewing manuscripts at each level tend to think along similar lines. They have been brought up in the Soviet system and trained to believe in the principles embodied in *partynost*, as interpreted by the Party leaders at any given moment. In any case, chief editors and their chief deputy editors attend briefing sessions at the Central Committee every two weeks.

The Union of Soviet Writers plays a critical role in ensuring authorial compliance with the Party's wishes. The key figure in the process once the manuscript is submitted for publication is not an official from Glavlit, who sits on the editorial board, but an editor, a man or woman who works inside the offices of one of the literary journals. The editor, at least at the senior level, is virtually certain to be a member of the Union. Anthony Adamovich, an émigré of the older generation, has argued that the editor fulfils the role of censor, while the representative of Glavlit, who usually serves as a member of the editorial board, merely "recommends."[12]

Obliged as they are to function in such an intricate system of checks and balances, editors tend to be nervous about passing for publication any manuscript that might potentially raise ideologically sensitive questions, knowing that their own decisions will be reviewed at a higher level. They, not the author, will be held responsible for lack of vigilance, and for betraying the Party's trust. Editors also know that some authors will try to "slip something through," to use "Aesopian language" to make critical or satirical comments about Soviet reality. Part of the problem for both editor and author is that nobody can be completely sure at any given moment what constitutes a serious ideological error, or an "anti-Soviet" work. Anatoly Gladilin outlined the dilemma:

> Editors are called into meetings all the time where they are given instructions. They all know perfectly well that no editor, at any time, has ever lost his job for printing a dull but safe piece of

> literature. But many editors lost their jobs because they let through a "sharp" thought, a questionable hint which might qualify as a political mistake. Therefore, when they review your manuscript they check it from every possible side, because they risk their own heads. The editor will be held responsible for everything that can qualify as an ideological or political mistake, not the writer. The writer would be criticized; he might not be published for several years. But then he could be published again. This happened to me. But the editor will lose his job. And then what could he do? Could he become a worker, a plumber for instance? Therefore, the institution of censorship in the Soviet Union begins with the editors.

Since editors are the ones exposed when a mistake is made, one can understand their caution. They are not generally on the *nomenklatura* lists of either the Central Committee or the KGB, while their superiors, the "responsible editor," first deputy chief editor, and chief editor, are. If these top editors make an ideological error, they too would be subject to review, first by the Ideological Commission of the Central Committee and then by its Secretariat, which would decide their punishment. One émigré mentioned that *nomenklatura* editors do not usually suffer for their first mistake, particularly if it is committed within six months or so of their appointment. Thereafter, a mistake might be taken more seriously. But unless the mistake is of a very serious nature, the *nomenklatura* editor would not be fired, and even if he were, he would probably receive a position of similar rank elsewhere. Émigrés seemed unanimous in considering job security one of the main benefits of belonging to the *nomenklatura*.

The editorial process is lubricated with liberal doses of hypocrisy, as everyone is expected to maintain the facade of a free press. It is considered bad form to even mention the word censorship. Editors at all levels like authors to understand why a change has to be made without objecting, or even asking for an explanation. The editors do not like to be forced to say directly that something cannot be published because of outside political interference. The representative of Glavlit is never named as such, but sometimes delicately referred to as a "political editor." A rare glimpse into the sort of dialogue the writer might have with an editor was given by the Leningrad writer Daniil Granin, concerning his attempts to get the memoirs of Yevdokia Nikolaevna Glebova printed. Glebova is the sister of Pavel Filonov, a remarkable avant-garde painter who starved to death in the Leningrad blockade during World War II. His works were exhibited in Leningrad only in January of

1989—after being hidden in storage since the twenties. Granin's account of his conversations with his editor show just how futile and frustrating these literary battles can be:

"Why, you know, Daniil Aleksandrovich, it's not worth it; let's wait."

"But what are we 'waiting' for?"

"Daniil Aleksandrovich, you yourself should understand."

"But I don't understand."

"But how can you fail to understand?"

It is the editor who usually wins these battles over semantics and hidden meanings.

Soviet editorial practice is a great deal more complex than that under the tsars: gone are the one-on-one duels between writer and censor. The existence of Glavlit itself was censored from the early thirties until very recent times; the word censorship is still, even under glasnost, rarely ever mentioned in public, except with reference to the tsarist past or the capitalist present.[13] Under Soviet practice the author's manuscript—already the result of a "collective process of writers' thinking," self-censored and shaped as a result of discussions at various meetings—is then subjected to a whole network of censors. As one veteran of the system put it, "Every journal has an editorial board, and each member of the board has the power to kill your manuscript." The manuscript's passage back and forth over as many as six desks (and often more), is so slow that tiny cuts—the omission of a single word or phrase—can accumulate into massive hemorrhaging, draining the vitality from a work. Sergei Yurenen recorded a classic illustration of this gradual blood-letting from his experience as an editor in the essays section of *Druzhba narodov* (*Friendship of Peoples*). He discussed his work on a book of essays about industrial topics:

> I remember once I received an essay about oil workers in the Caspian Sea. Originally this essay was over 60 typed pages. I edited this essay for three months, because Glavlit sent over different directives which prohibited us from talking about specific aspects or numbers in the oil industry. The "responsible editor" would pass the directives on to us—nobody sees the censor.
>
> After three months, this essay had become 20 pages, which did not contain a single original thought of the author, or any figures. It was just an abstract—pure lyrics, you might say.

The surreal quality of the finished product, "pure lyrics" as Yurenen described it, is characteristic of Glavlit polishing. A former victim mentioned that he once saw one of his pieces after it came back from Glavlit: "It looked like an abstract picture. It was already in galley-proofs, and it was all crossed over and underlined with different colored pencils."

Vladimir Voinovich, the celebrated novelist now living outside Munich, confirmed the central role of the editor and the hidden presence of Glavlit:

> I always had trouble with the censorship, from beginning to end. I suppose you know that in the Soviet Union you never know your censor. All the requirements come from the editor, and even if there are specific censorship requirements, he would never be able to tell you so. He would say that all the requirements came from him. Except in *Novy mir*. There they would say openly, "The censor wants this or that." But usually the editor is much stricter and requires more than the censor does.

The editor is the conduit for Glavlit, which on a day-to-day basis has considerable "hands-on" authority; its official mandate is to guard "state secrets." There are, however, a wealth of examples where the system is not being criticized, nor are state secrets being given away, but still a work is killed. Censorship—understood in the broader sense that applies in the Soviet context—works at a petty, foolish level much of the time. Few people are trying to write or say something truly subversive, but the vast bureaucratic system of censorship must demonstrate that it is indispensable. Voinovich related an anecdote that illustrates the frustrating obscurantism that writers must face:

> I wrote a very famous song, "I believe, my friends," while I was working for Moscow Radio in their comedy and satire department. I wrote the song very fast, in one day, and the composer wrote the music the next day. The song was played the day after that, and it became famous right away.
>
> Suddenly I received a phone call from a musical editor at Moscow Radio. She said that they wanted to make a record of my song, but they had one condition. They wanted me to change one word in the following lines:
>
> > "I believe, my friends, that the caravans of rockets will take us ahead from one star to another, from far away planets, on dusty trails we will leave our footprints."
>
> And the word she wanted me to change was "dusty." She didn't like the expression "dusty trails" and wanted me to change it to "new trails." I refused, and she said they would not make a record.

> But despite this, my song was still played all the time on the radio. So that shows you how different decisions can be made by different editors. I wrote this song in September of 1960, and in April of 1961 Yury Gagarin went into space. He sang my song, but still they didn't make a record. Later, Nikolaev and Popovich [two other cosmonauts] sang my song in space, and after them, Khrushchev sang my song. Then I received a call from the same woman editor, who said to me, "Tomorrow we are going to make a record."
>
> I said to her, "OK, very good. But I want to change one word. I want to change the word "dusty."
>
> She replied: "No, that is impossible. Nikita Sergeyevich [Khrushchev] sang the song that way!"[14]

Why would she object to "dusty" and ask for the substitution of "new"? After all, Voinovich is speaking of cosmonauts leaving "footprints"; would not a "dusty" trail logically continue the metaphor? Here the objection has nothing to do with lofty matters involving affairs of state; nor is it really ideological except in a tenuous sense. The Soviet Union is future-oriented; "building communism" means creating a "new" society. The adjective "new" (*novy*) is therefore constantly used in Soviet writing: the opening sentence of the Writers' Union Statutes alludes to itself as "the literature of a new historical epoch." "New trails" fits nicely into this positive picture; "dusty trails" does not, even though the adjective accurately describes both the surface of the moon and solar dust. Voinovich's song illustrates the relative weight of each station of Soviet editorial review: if the General Secretary of the Party approves, then everyone lower down the review process can relax.

Émigré writers were quick to add that not all editors cared only for their careers; even before glasnost some were willing to resist the arguments of censors, or of the Party's ideological experts. Anatoly Gladilin's remarks were typical:

> There are some brave and good people among editors, and they will try very hard to publish your book. If you can explain everything in it to them, and they can understand all its nuances and justify them, then the clever editor will try to do it [that is, try to get it past Glavlit and the ideological apparatus].

The editor's dilemma with the censorship is thus entwined with the writer's dilemma. In their efforts to get a work into suitable shape for publication, to "get it through," editors often function not so much as censors but as co-authors of the work. Even when a work is successfully steered through the shoals, it results in something different from its original form. All too often, a published work becomes a collective effort, rather than the creation of one individual—and of course that is exactly what the Party culture and media specialists are anxious to achieve.

Even though the chief editor and the entire editorial board may be united in their desire to publish a work, their collective vote in favor may not be enough. Sergei Yurenen provided a remarkable example of just such a situation from his experiences at *Druzhba narodov*. In 1974 there occurred what he termed a "micro-thaw" in the Brezhnev regime. At this auspicious moment, Sergei Antonov, a run-of-the-mill Soviet writer, submitted a novel, *Vaska*, to *Druzhba narodov:*

> Nobody expected anything from him. But this particular novel was perhaps just as explosive in its content as Solzhenitsyn's *One Day in the Life of Ivan Denisovich*. It was about the completion of the first part of the Moscow Metro [during the thirties], about accidents and poor construction methods, and about the horrors of collectivization. . . . Our editorial board did everything we could to publish the novel. I remember at the last meeting I was leading the discussion and we had already approved it. Nobody was against publishing it. Sergei Baruzdin was, and is still, chief editor of *Druzhba narodov*. But Sergei Antonov's novel was killed at a very high level. I think it may have been on the level of the Department of Culture of the Central Committee, because in this case both the chief editor and the editorial board of our journal wanted to publish the work. But after that, it was returned to the author. It is unknown in the West, even unknown in *samizdat*, since Antonov did not give his work to anyone else to read.

Glavlit had passed the manuscript, but the Central Committee of the Party through its Department of Culture had the final say. Yurenen said that shortly after this decision, to "balance their relationship with the journal," the authorities permitted *Druzhba narodov* to publish Yury Trifonov's highly regarded novel *Dom na naberezhnoi* (*The House on the Embankment*), which revealed the moral degradation of the contemporary Soviet urban elite, traced to the same Stalinist period treated in Antonov's novel. This is an interesting example of compromise, demonstrating the Central Committee's power to reward as well as to punish. The message to the journal's chief editor, Sergei Baruzdin, was that he should not press too hard; in the future, perhaps he would be more successful.[15]

Yurenen's account and the comments of other émigrés suggest that the authority of the Union secretaries, like that of editors, is best described as the "power of the negative"—to kill manuscripts they do not like or that make them nervous. However, even if they are behind a work, they must submit to the authority of the Central Committee's ideological specialists. Anatoly Gladilin illustrated this point from his experience as a member of the Moscow branch of the Union, then headed by Sergei Sergeyevich Smirnov, best known as the author of a respected World War II novel, *Brestskaya krepost* (*The Brest Fortress*).[16] Smirnov tried to help Gladilin publish his book about a nineteenth-century Russian radical, which was to appear in the series "Fiery Revolutionaries" (not a Union publication). It would have been published in the publishing house of the Central Committee of the Party. Gladilin thought it was an honest book. Smirnov felt the same, and invited him to his office to talk over how he might help Gladilin bring it out. Also present in the room was Ilyin—at that time the secretary for organizational affairs of the Moscow branch:

> Smirnov was praising me, saying what a wonderful book I had written. Ilyin hugged me as well, and whispered in my ear, "Did you send any of your manuscripts abroad?" I answered, "No, no." Then Smirnov said that he understood that the writers' organization owed me a lot, and that he understood how much at fault they had been in all my problems. But right now, he couldn't help me. There was no one in the Central Committee whom he could talk to personally. He asked me to wait. He expected a change. If a new boss were to come in to head the Propaganda Department of the Central Committee, then he might be able to intervene. This did happen, . . . But I left, and Smirnov died [in 1976]. I just want to emphasize how difficult it is for even such a highly placed person as Smirnov to do something good for you.

The Secretariat may have to share power when it comes to deciding what will be published, but it has virtually absolute authority over what cannot be published.[17] Gladilin put the Secretariat's power into perspective:

> Let's say that I bring a book to the publisher, and they don't like my book, so they don't want to publish it. If I then go to the Central Committee of the Party, and if the Central Committee wants my book to be published, then it will be published. Or if I go to the First Secretary of the Union, and if he wants my book to be published, then maybe, just maybe, my book will be published. But if the Secretariat of the Writers Union doesn't want my book to be published, then nothing will help me.

This "power of the negative" creates special problems for writers. Every author wants to be published, and so the pressures to please the Secretariat and compromise at every stage of review are very strong, since not even the support of the First Secretary of the Union can always overcome the collective will of the Secretariat. Over and over, former Union members mentioned that "the most important thing for a writer is to be published." Soviet officials in Moscow repeated the same idea. Oleg Bezrodny, deputy chief of Goskomizdat's International Relations Department (almost certainly a post on the *nomenklatura* list of the KGB) stated that authors almost always accept their suggestions for changes or revisions in their manuscript because publishing means that "they are getting canonized."[18] A former Azerbaijani censor echoed the same sentiment: "It is better for a writer to be published censored than not at all."[19] After passing through such an elaborate editing process, it is no surprise that under Brezhnev most fiction, drama, and verse became homogenized; different genres ended up looking the same, with the same types of characters and plots.

The inducements to conform are many, not the least of which are the handsome fees authors can be paid. The substantial rewards for compromise were illustrated in an interview with Anatoly Zhukov, head of the prose fiction department, and Grigory Reznichenko at the editorial offices of *Novy mir* in Moscow in December 1985. Reznichenko held the position of "responsible editor" at the journal; hence, he was serving, in Yurenen's phrase, as one of the "eyes of the tsar"—both he and his position were on the *nomenklatura* lists of the KGB. Reznichenko stated that the previous year his journal had received "2,140 manuscripts in the prose section alone." Out of that number, only twenty-two, or 1 percent, were actually published in 1985. A large proportion of the unfortunate rejects were *samotyok*, "self-flowing," Soviet publishing jargon for "slush pile." These unsolicited manuscripts have just as forlorn a chance of ever seeing print as their Western counterparts. A large proportion of *samotyok* manuscripts, it seems, come largely from aspiring authors outside the Union.[20]

A Soviet literary journal, like a book publisher, pays the author by the "signature" or "printers' sheet" (*avtorsky list*)—about 16 printed pages. The going rate per signature ranges from about 250 rubles to more than double that amount, although a 1988 decree has promised higher rates.[21] The minimum rate of 250 rubles amounts to about $365, but since basic commodities, public transportation, and rents are heavily subsidized, a Soviet citizen could live quite handsomely on 250 rubles a month. The best authors, or the more powerful, can command top rates.[22] Reznichenko explained how the situation worked at *Novy mir:*

> Take Daniil Granin, for example, or say Ananyev—any leading writer. [Based on a 2–3 page outline] we consider that his work will be interesting. In order to attract him to our journal, we will offer a financial contract and pay him an advance of 25 percent.[23]

The 25 percent is arrived at by calculating the length of the work:

> Let's say the author tells us that his novel will be fifteen signatures long. Well, as a rule we pay 400 rubles a signature, so 25 percent would be 1,500 rubles. We would give him that amount and then wait for his manuscript.

A Soviet journal acts in much the same way as a book publisher in the West, contracting and paying advances for full-length works. However, the journal pays advances based on the length of the work, not on the estimated sales, which could only be measured by a rise in the request for subscriptions. If an author received the type of advance suggested by Reznichenko, he would be making, on the basis of a brief outline, an amount well over half the annual salary of many Soviet citizens, including white collar workers. If his book does sell well, the author can continue to receive royalties called *potirazhnye,* although at a reduced rate (usually 50 to 60 percent) per signature.

Once a writer gets himself established to the point where a leading journal will pay a 25 percent advance on his own estimate of length, then he can make a great deal of money. Soviet publishing practices encourage the production of enormous tomes, since authors are paid according to length. Moreover, authors need not care whether their books sell or not. Soviet writers are so used to this system that one, responding to a question as to how many copies had been sold of one of his books, exclaimed: "But why should I care about that? Every library will order a copy. No one knows how many are sold. Only the *tirazh* (print-run) counts for my rubles."

It is no surprise that the Union can not only generate vast quantities of approved prose and verse; it can also recruit many writers to its standard. The Union dominates the Soviet literary scene to such an extent that it has become self-generating; that is, it attracts a certain type of member. Former Soviet philosopher Alexander Zinovyev has tried to correct the mistaken Western view of the typical Soviet writer as a talented individualist struggling to publish dissident works against the efforts of the evil authorities. In fact, he says, most writers are eager to become part of the system:

> People of a certain type want to be writers. They are all products of the same kind of education and upbringing. They live and

> function according to standard Soviet conditions, that is, according to the laws of large congregations of people. They are an integral part of the Soviet social structure with its hierarchy of social positions, its distribution of privileges according to rank, and so forth. . . . They are part of the Party's ideological apparatus.[24]

Many writers are now fully integrated into the bureaucratic class that has dominated Soviet (and East European) society since the time of Stalin.[25] They can aspire to the many *nomenklatura* positions available in the enormous publishing industry.

Ironically, the Party has thus created a system that appeals to graphomaniacs and to those most willing to compromise—that is, those least concerned about outsiders tampering with their manuscripts. The Union has always had many members quite happy to write standard books according to the Party's expectations, in order to receive royalties on this generous scale. Igor Pomerantsev, an émigré critic from Kiev now living in London, said that there is no shortage of authors eager to write to order; on the contrary, journals and publishing houses are besieged with ideologically correct manuscripts.[26] But the very energy of all these authors and would-be authors seeking to fulfill the Party's tasks for literature creates a monstrous economic problem for their patron. The Party was, and still is, obliged to subsidize writers whom no one wants to read. Isaak Babel said at the 1934 Congress that he would practice "the genre of silence." Fifty years later Sergei Yurenen claimed that all orthodox writers are really being "paid for silence" because their books remain unread. And it is the state that absorbs the loss, while members of the Secretariat and their protégés enjoy the benefits.

Brezhnev exacerbated the problem with his policy of delegating power to bureaucracies on behalf of the Party; this had the unintended result that bureaucrats—notably those in the Union Secretariat—used their authority on behalf of themselves. "Literary generals" arranged to have their own works published in vast editions, and suppressed the works of other, genuinely popular writers, or permitted them to be published only in small editions and at long intervals. Hence the Party was left carrying the economic bag at the same time that the Soviet reading public was becoming more and more alienated from official cultural policies.

What then did the public want? The vast majority of the Soviet population was not interested in "anti-Soviet" works. There was a great demand for escapist literature, including adventure fiction and whodunits, both domestic and foreign. People wanted non-fiction on such politically innocent subjects as gardening, art, occultism, sex, music history, and architecture. What is more, the Soviet reading public had developed different tastes and habits according to social class and educational background. According to Victor Yenyutin, an émigré writer and former sociologist now living in California, during the seventies the higher strata of the Soviet intelligentsia wanted to read such works as the poetry of Federico Garcia Lorca, and the vast middle-brow Soviet readership was trying to read Agatha Christie.[27] Unfortunately for Soviet readers, these were precisely the types of books that the authorities were least inclined to provide, because they did not contain the correct ideological message, or contained no message at all.[28]

Unwittingly, the Party's very success in achieving near-universal literacy among the Soviet population boomeranged. Lenin's admirable insistence on educating the masses came back to haunt his successors as a "book boom" (Russians use the English word "boom"), which Party leaders seemed unable to take advantage of, either ideologically or financially. As average incomes increased, Soviet society suffered from rising cultural and intellectual inflation. More and more citizens had disposable income that they wished to spend on the "finer things of life," including sets of the major Russian authors, foreign works in translation, and children's books like *The Three Musketeers* and *The Count of Monte Cristo*. A Soviet official acknowledged the rise in the standard of living, pointing out that "people want to decorate their homes, and leave sets of classics to their children."[29]

The book boom, with the concomitant rise in the standard of living, resulted in a "book hunger" (*knizhny golod*) throughout Soviet society so widespread that books that were quite innocent politically, still became major black-market items that commanded many times their published prices. What Soviet readers found particularly infuriating was the sure knowledge that some of the most popular works were being published, but they could not obtain them, because they had been "published for export" to the West in order to acquire foreign hard currency, or else "published for the Beryozka," that is, sold in Soviet stores that only accepted Western currencies (especially the so-called Book Beryozka on Kropotkinskaya in Moscow, which underwent extensive renovation in 1985). The Soviet authorities made sure to stock the Book Beryozka with many copies of rare items—the poetry of Anna Akhmatova or Osip Mandelshtam, or lavish art books—because they could attract foreign customers with *valyuta* (hard currencies). Only privileged Soviet citizens were—and are—allowed to shop at such stores; for example, those who have worked abroad and been paid in certificates or coupons, called "golden rubles" because they are worth fifteen times as much as ordinary rubles.

Members of the Writers' Union did not feel the same hunger pangs the rest of the population did, since they could shop at their own well-stocked bookstore. Indeed, the Writers' Union contributed its own full measure to the corruption and "stagnation" (*zastoi*) of the late Brezhnev period, now being so roundly condemned under Gorbachev. However, little has changed; an editor or publishing official can arrange to publish the works of the powerful Union secretaries; in return they will approve publication of a work by him. The Secretariat's authority over publishing is so extensive that it even has its own *templan*, as one émigré related:

> If you are a member of the Secretariat, then you can be included in the *templan* of the Secretariat. If you are included in this publishing plan, then the publisher has to publish your work. He would have a very hard time refusing to do so. The basic principle is that if you are a Union boss, then you have to be published.[30]

In the late seventies, as the Brezhnev period drew to its close, Yury Andropov's KGB operations against the dissident movement and against *samizdat* and *tamizdat* became increasingly effective with the closing down of underground publications and the arrest of their editors and contributors. At the same time, liberal writers grew ever more disgusted with the repression and corruption that were debasing Russian cultural life. In frustration, a small group of writers and artists decided upon a frontal attack on Party controls and censorship. They selected their works which had been rejected for publication, and assembled them in typed form as a "literary almanac" (that is, a collaborative journal appearing at irregular intervals) under the title *Metropol*. Its contributors included writers already well-known in the West, such as Vasily Akysonov, Fazil Iskander, Andrei Voznesensky, and Bella Akhmadulina, as well as others whose international reputations are less well established, but who are also widely respected in Russian literary circles—Andrei Bitov, Victor Yerofeyev, Yevgeny Popov, Yuz Aleshkovsky, Inna Lisnyanskaya, and Semyon Lipkin. The almanac also printed lyrics from the enormously popular but then officially ignored actor and guitar singer, Vladimir Vysotsky. It ended with a poem entitled "Trammels" ("*Puty*") by G. Sapgir, with illustrations by A. Brusilovsky, showing nude male and female figures struggling to escape ropes, cages, and heavy burdens. In the final picture a couple has escaped the ropes and is running to freedom.

Unfortunately, the editors and contributors to *Metropol* were not so fortunate as the figures in Brusilovsky's final image. They did not escape from the "trammels" of the Party or the Writers' Union. The five editors of the almanac (Aksyonov, Bitov, Iskander, Popov and Yerofeyev) had not submitted their almanac to a publishing house or Glavlit, but directly to the Writers' Union—a decision which reveals clearly the fact that it is the Union Secretariat which decides on a day-to-day basis what is to be published and what is not. The almanac was the responsibility of the Moscow writers' organization, since all the authors lived in Moscow. The first secretary of the branch at that time, Felix Kuznetsov, immediately arranged a meeting of its board, at which publication was refused and Akysonov singled out as the ringleader in a project that would, it was claimed, embarrass the Soviet Union in the West, arouse anti-Soviet activities, and perhaps even damage the strategic arms limitation talks in Geneva.

In fact, there was nothing very political about any of the contents of the almanac. Certainly, some authors had fun at the expense of orthodox literary taste, and one or two contributions included mildly explicit sexual descriptions calculated to shock Soviet prudery. But the major reason for the swift counterattack of the Writers' Union was the Secretariat's determination not to permit its authority over literary life to be challenged. No doubt the Central Committee ideological specialists were also alarmed at the collective nature of the challenge. They were used to dealing with individuals such as Solzhenitsyn or Chukovskaya, but here was a whole group of writers banded together to form a united front against the rules and regulations of publishing.

It did not take long to shut down the *Metropol* affair, although at least one copy of the eight reached the West and was published in Russian, and later in English translation. The leaders of the project were punished in various ways, with Aksyonov being forced into exile. Inna Lisnyanskaya and her husband Semyon Lipkin resigned from the Writers' Union in protest, an act of courage whose significance can be fully appreciated given what has been said about the advantages of membership and the dangers of losing it. Their public letters of resignation illustrated the underlying themes of the liberal revolt during the Brezhnev period. Lisnyanskaya wrote:

> Though not prone to literary or other battles, I face a dilemma: Shall I remain a Union member or a human being? I choose the second, for in ceasing to be a human being I could not remain a writer.

Lipkin wrote:

> I leave the Writers' Union knowing that you have no need of me. You only need yourselves. I will only add that Russian literature was always my holy of holies, and I will continue to serve it until my dying day.[31]

At the time of the *Metropol* affair in 1979, Vasily Akysonov and his co-editors were taken to task for offering a political challenge to the Party's hegemony over the printed word. However, the motives of Felix Kuznevtsov, first secretary of the Moscow writers' organization, and the Union Secretariat, in stepping in to drive the *Metropol* writers out of the Union and even into exile, need to be re-evaluated in the light of contemporary efforts to make publishing more economically viable. It is just as likely that Kuznetsov and his fellow secretaries were motivated not so much by Party loyalty, or an eagerness to carry out Party directives, as by a self-serving desire to protect and preserve their own fiefdoms.

Had Yury Andropov lived longer, then it is very likely that the *Metropol* affair would have occasioned several more resignations from the Union, or kangaroo courts, expulsions, and forced exiles to the West. Instead, Andropov died (in circumstances that have yet to be explained fully) and was succeeded in quick succession by Chernenko and then by Mikhail Gorbachev in March of 1985. With Gorbachev came the age of glasnost, and a major assault on the publishing system created by Stalin and refined by Brezhnev.

The Gorbachev era, insofar as it impacts upon the Union and Soviet publishing, is an outgrowth of issues that were raised under Brezhnev. Even in the mid-seventies the Soviet press had begun to acknowledge serious problems in Soviet publishing. The enormous prices for black market items constituted speculation in the Soviet understanding of the term and certainly robbed the treasury of potential income. Soviet academics and economists began conducting a lively debate concerning the nature of the book as a "product" and its place in the economy.[32] Some scholars argued that books are indeed a product like any other, with their value to be sought not in unquantifiable ideological gains, but rather in costs of production and distribution balanced against selling price. For decades the Soviet authorities failed to take this rational economic view to their bosom. Gosplan (the State Planning Committee) always regarded *printing* as a full-fledged industry, but *publishing*—everything involved in the preparation, distribution, and selling of a text—was listed with clubs and libraries, as part of culture and education, meaning that it could not be held to the same strict accounting as a regular industry.

This tentative shift from ideology to economics, from purity to profit, actually gathered renewed strength under Andropov, though the Party's ideological assumptions made its leaders reluctant to turn over publishing completely to the cost accountants. In his report to the Central Committee's plenary session in June 1983, USSR Minister of Culture Demichev gingerly sat astride the political fence: "As research has shown, funds expended on culture can bring not only ideological benefits, but also great economic efficiency (*vysokuyu ekonomicheskuyu effektivnost*)."[33]

The new concern with balancing purity and profit was revealed during a lengthy interview conducted in December 1983 with Dr. Andrei Nikolaevich Sakharov, then chairman of the Literature Department of Goskomizdat. Dr. Sakharov explained that he and his colleagues were doing everything they could to ascertain and meet readers' demands for books. He admitted that in his own estimation, only one-third of the popular demand for fiction could be met: "We know the demand for certain books, but we cannot meet it." His explanation? "You would have to cut down all the trees in Siberia to meet the demand. You would need the printing presses of the entire world." This same phrase was used by two other officials to explain book hunger.

Sakharov stressed that his department conducts a type of "market research" chiefly through a book trade organization called *Soyuzkniga*, literally "UnionBook," which reports back requests for books throughout the country, and also sales levels. Sakharov stated that Goskomizdat collates data obtained in libraries on the frequency with which books are borrowed and requested. He mentioned that each bookstore and library has a box of cards for individual reader requests. The Editorial Council *Redaktsionny sovet*), a group of 20–30 persons, meets once a year to make final recommendations to him, which were not binding. Sakharov himself held consultations with the various institutes, translators, living authors, and editors for dead authors. All plans were sent to Sakharov; he then meshed them together. Sakharov insisted that meeting popular demand for books was his prime concern, and his answer to the question on any possible contradiction between ideological purity and financial profit was a firm "Nyet." Dr. Sakharov said nothing about making decisions based upon the views of either the top officials of Goskomizdat, the Union Secretariat, or the local Party organization.

Dr. Sakharov stated that, as in other Soviet industrial enterprises, plans are both immediate, that is, for the following year (*godovoi plan*) and long-term (*perspektivny*), meaning for the duration of the current *pyatiletka* (five-year plan). He explained that these plans are drawn up in each publishing house, which decides the economic issues within its own purview. It proposes a total budget request to him (the system of *khozraschet*, or economic self-sufficiency). Each publishing house decides on the prices it will charge for books in order to make a profit, but in some cases, as for books for children, prices are set below cost. In much the same way as if they were producing widgets, journals and publishing houses have to present a plan that shows they are going to publish a certain amount of material, and therefore need a specific quantity of paper. But in addition, they must also propose their own *templan*, which shows what sorts of writers and works are being considered for the coming year and, very important, the size of the editions proposed. Typewritten copies of the *templan* for journals and for publishing houses are identical in format.[34] Dr. Sakharov modestly described his own role as one of coordination.

Oleg Bitov, former editor for foreign literature at *Literaturnaya gazeta*, painted a rather different picture.[35] He stated that a Soviet publishing executive does not regard profit as his most important goal. Rather, he is more preoccupied with two other objectives. The first is to protect his own fiefdom. Consequently, he constantly asks himself, "What does my own immediate supervisor want?" His second objective is to be "safe" from an ideological point of view. Only after assuring himself on these counts would profit come into play.

Both the Soviet official and the Soviet defector acknowledged the special importance of the *templan*, but disagreed on the role played by reader demand in its formulation. In a sense each was right in his emphasis; Sakharov as a senior official was announcing official policy, while Bitov as a middle-rank editor was telling the story as he had experienced it over several years. As it happened, the future lay with Sakharov, but Bitov's down-to-earth remarks about the practical realities of Soviet publishing served as a warning of the difficulties that lay ahead of the reformers.

In the age of glasnost open discussion in the Soviet press has revealed considerable dissatisfaction with the cozy arrangement through which top officials in Goskomizdat and in the Union Secretariat have manipulated the *templan* system to their own advantage, robbing the treasury of money and preventing readers from finding books they want to buy. As one investigative journalist complained bitterly in the liberal weekly magazine *Ogonyok*, it is not the reader who decides what books to read: "These decisions have been made by officials at Gozkomizdat and officials of the Union of Writers."[36]

The *Ogonyok* article produced extensive statistics showing exactly how the Writers' Union-Goskomizdat cartel benefits the Secretariat. The size and frequency of the editions of works by the "literary generals" is staggering, whereas the editions of genuinely popular writers are much smaller and much less frequent. The article points out, quoting figures from another source (Sergei Shvedov of the Book Institute in *Voprosy literatury*), that in five years (1981–85) works by Yury Bondarev, a Litburo member and leading conservative Russian nationalist, were published in no less than 50 editions, with a total print-run of 5,868,000 copies! This figure even exceeded the print-run of 4,129,000 copies enjoyed by Georgy Markov, the Union First Secretary, over the same period. The most interesting statistic is still missing. How many copies of these vast editions were actually sold and how many were simply "printed to be pulped"? And what was the overall cost to the state of printing them? It must have been very great because Bondarev would have received the top rate per signature as a powerful Union secretary.

At the Eighth Union Congress in 1986, several writers felt emboldened to criticize this corrupt practice, thus confirming reports by many émigrés. The most outspoken attack on the Secretariat bosses was the speech by Yulian Semyonov, himself a popular writer of Soviet *detektivy* (crime and spy thrillers) and a close friend of the KGB (for many years it was impossible to criticize him in print). He ridiculed "a cult of literary emperors who, on closer inspection, prove to be naked, and whose books, which are printed in gigantic editions, are a principal source of income to recycled-paper dealers."[37] Semyonov also attacked the Secretariat's stranglehold over publishing:

> Wastepaper is still being published. . . . Book editions are determined by the Writer's Union and Goskomizdat, whereas Gosplan and the Ministry of Finance, which are interested in real money for the state treasury, are excluded from this process—to say nothing of the reader himself. I have a concrete proposal. . . . Since we have paper problems and young writers have problems getting published, we should request permission to publish writers' books by xerographic reproduction.

As he must have known, Semyonov's "modest proposal" is not likely to be followed, if only because of strict control over all copy machines in the Soviet Union. Unauthorized copying of material or possession of a copy machine can bring a Soviet citizen two or three years in jail.

The Union-Goskomizdat cartel has worked out a *quid pro quo* that benefits each, and keeps the Politburo happy much of the time. For example, Oleg Bitov related that Konstantin Chernenko, while General Secretary of the Party, had written a book (or much more likely had it written for him) on the Soviet Union's "leading role" in fostering human rights. It had an enormous print-run, which enhanced his prestige. It did not matter that the entire print-run, according to Bitov, was pulped immediately after it was printed. The authorities had not even waited for citizens to take copies to official pulping centers, where they receive in exchange certificates for use in purchasing books they really want. The publishers of this volume may have lost economically, but they gained in return the gratitude of the Central Committee. Now the publishing house was entitled to print a large edition of its chief editor's latest work, or the works of his friends.

Lenin had prophesied that Soviet literature would become "truly free" because Soviet writers would produce ideologically correct works "voluntarily." Unfortunately for the Soviet treasury, he did not anticipate that the least talented writers would be only too willing to produce works to order, while the most talented would resist writing to a formula. Furthermore, he did not foresee that Soviet readers would voluntarily refuse to buy officially approved works. Unwittingly, the Party's reward system and ideological preferences had encouraged this outcome. Power within the Union, that is, the ability to make and implement publishing decisions, was locked up within the Secretariat. A small group of men were thus able to do exactly what Lenin insisted—in "Party Organization and Party Literature"—he and his colleagues would never permit: turn Soviet literature into "a means of enriching individuals and groups." Against all expectations, and contrary to Lenin's goals, the system has been manipulated by individuals who make themselves ruble millionaires in the process. Ironically, the Union membership as a whole has come to resemble the very same "upper 10,000" that Lenin had condemned so roundly in his 1905 article.

Under Mikhail Gorbachev, the contradiction between purity and profit, which had already opened a fissure in the motto "Ideology is our most important product," was further called into question. The Party's subsidy of writers whom no one wanted to read had become enormously expensive. The main thrust of the campaign for glasnost and perestroika was economic—and it should come as no surprise that among its most ardent, if cautious foes, were the "literary generals" of the Union Secretariat. They realized immediately that economic rationalism threatened their cosy cartel.

7

The Threat of Glasnost

No society can exist without glasnost.

MIKHAIL GORBACHEV

For Mikhail Gorbachev, glasnost (bringing things out into the open, making them public) was a means to an end, not an end in itself. He called for glasnost in literature and the media as a prelude to his main agenda, perestroika, or the restructuring of the Soviet economy; it is economics which lies at the basis of the whole reform movement, although Gorbachev has obviously used his reform campaign to embarrass Brezhnevites and potential rivals.[1] This focus on economics is made more obvious by two key terms introduced by Gorbachev. First, *uskorenie* (acceleration within the Soviet economy) replaced the Brezhnev notion that Soviet society had already achieved a state of "advanced socialism" (*razvitoi sotsializm*), and was well on the way toward communism. The revised Party Rules as approved at the 27th CPSU Congress in March 1986 speak of "perfecting socialism" rather of "building communism." Second, *novoe myshlenie* (new thinking) is viewed as essential in the social and political sphere to encourage initiative and improve productivity—this influential argument has been advanced by an important Gorbachev adviser, the distinguished sociologist, Academician Tatyana Zaslavskaya. To put it schematically, Gorbachev has tried to use glasnost to create the appropriate climate (*novoe myshlenie*) in which perestroika can take place.

Gorbachev's reforms amount to a revolution; typically for Russia, this is a "revolution from above" (*revolyutsia sverkhu*); the Soviet historian Natan Eidelman has called such revolutions "a Russian peculiarity" (*osobennost*).[2] To succeed in this vast economic and social revolution, Gorbachev needs writers, as well as other professionals in the mass media. As products of the Thaw period, he and his supporters are well aware of the social and psychological power wielded by creative writers. The criticism of Stalinist methods in the fifties and sixties was produced chiefly by novelists and poets, who seized upon the opportunities offered by Khrushchev's politically-motivated policy of increased liberalism.

The policies of the Gorbachev generation are a delayed response to Khrushchev's reforms; they are making up for nearly 20 years of lost time. Most of Gorbachev's supporters are bright men and women who were held in check and removed from their positions in the mid-sixties, as Brezhnev secured his power base. Members of the Gorbachev generation have all had to make compromises; to attend endless, boring Party meetings; to make enthusiastic speeches about each change in Party policy, regardless of their real feelings; to play the Komsomol activist by reporting fellow students. Such is the typical career path of the future Party apparatchik. Similar compromises are not unknown among ambitious employees in the West. This Western kind of sycophancy is, however, quite different from denouncing others and sending them to a living death in the Gulag or to immediate execution. Such were the compromises made by Brezhnev's generation, the so-called "generation of '38," whose members rose rapidly by taking the positions of those arrested and killed in the Great Purge, and thus felt both gratitude and respect for their patron Stalin.

There is some justification for Yevgeny Yevtushenko's rather brash claim that the new leaders were brought up on his poems and those of his contemporaries. Certainly, Gorbachev and his fellow reformers came to maturity at an exciting time, when Khrushchev's anti-Stalin campaign shook the foundations of the system, and many people thrilled at the chance to discuss new ideas and approaches. Theirs is the first real post-Stalin generation. They have had no adult experience with their country's two most searing events, Stalin's purges and the German invasion. They have no career connections with the Stalinist system, and they have no military ax to grind: they were children during the war and are less vulnerable to nationalistic appeals by old comrades-in-arms than are members of the Brezhnev generation and some of their younger supporters. Gorbachev and his allies belong to the fourth generation in the Soviet period that has enjoyed the benefits of higher education. Gorbachev himself has a law degree from Moscow University, making him the first lawyer to lead the Soviet government since Vladimir Lenin.[3] The Gorbachev cohort is the first to have been exposed on a large scale to Western literature and ways of doing things.

Once again, as in Khrushchev's day, it is the established bureaucracy in the Writers' Union Secretariat that has become a major obstacle to a reform movement initiated by the Kremlin. The Union is typical of the kind of bureaucratic organization established by the Party which has very little to gain from glasnost or perestroika. As early as 1970, a book by Soviet legal scholars on the creative unions contained criticism of "bureaucratism" and red tape (*volokita*), and called specifically for the introduction of more glasnost in the administrative affairs of the Writers' Union.[4] But the Union Secretariat made as little effort to change its ways as did other bureaucracies. Now Gorbachev is trying to persuade officials, whom the Party itself has put into power, to embrace reforms that will in effect oblige them to relinquish their authority.

The "literary generals" have two major, unspoken objections to glasnost. The first is that old sores will be reopened, and their own role in the destruction of careers, suppression of works, and overall crushing of the Thaw itself will be brought out into the open. The second is that, if glasnost leads to perestroika in the Writers' Union, then their own privileged position in Soviet literature will be threatened. Until now they have enjoyed material advantages (money, houses, cars, prizes, travel) as a result of playing the bureaucratic game according to the Party rules. Glasnost and perestroika threaten them with a new social revolution, one which would require them to place their works in the open market to be judged according to merit—with sales depending on supply and demand, and not on Goskomizdat's rewarding projections. They have noted that Gorbachev's supporters spend almost as much time attacking the "stagnation" (*zastoi*) of the Brezhnev era, and indirectly the ensconced apparatchiks, as they do the "assault on socialist legality" under Stalin.

The Union may include some of the most determined opponents of glasnost and perestroika, but the membership also contains many of Gorbachev's most ardent supporters. In a lead article to a volume of essays by proponents of perestroika, *Inogo ne dano* (*There Is No Other Way*), published in 1987, Academician Tatyana Zaslavskaya attempted to identify attitudes toward Gorbachev's reforms among various social and occupational categories. Her conclusion was that the "intelligentsia in the social sciences and the humanities" (*sotsialno-gumanitarnaya intelligentsia*), in which she counted writers and artists, is unique in Soviet society because it ranges to both extremes across the whole gamut of attitudes toward perestroika. It includes not only "initiators" and "supporters" at one end of the scale, but also "conservatives" and "reactionaries" at the other, with "quasi-supporters" and "observers" occupying a centrist position.[5] Zaslavskaya's conclusions suggested that the

Union would become a major battleground in the struggle for glasnost and perestroika. Her prediction has proven to be correct.

Attitudes toward glasnost and perestroika began to crystallize only in 1987 and 1988, as the radical nature of Gorbachev's reforms became clear. Initially, conservatives were not particularly concerned about Gorbachev. Many assumed, mistakenly, that he was following Yury Andropov's policy decision to attack corruption and to administer yet more "discipline" to the demoralized workforce. As with Khrushchev's anti-Stalin campaign, the first suggestion of Gorbachev's real agenda came with a change in literary policy. It was signalled as early as September 1984—six months before Gorbachev took power—in a long speech delivered by General Secretary Chernenko to assembled writers, on the fiftieth anniversary of the Union's First Congress. Since Gorbachev was already serving as ideological secretary, the number two position in the Politburo, he may well have supervised the writing of Chernenko's speech, although it would have required general Politburo approval. Chernenko stated: "We resolutely reject petty tutelage over people working in the arts. Art is art because it is free: one will not create anything really new and beautiful by using force [literally, 'the stick']."[6] George Orwell would have appreciated the irony of the Politburo proposing such a liberalization of cultural policy in 1984.

Once he himself took over the post of General Secretary, Gorbachev moved quickly to enlist the support of writers and the media. He displayed little concern that criticism either in the press or in literature would seriously threaten the Party's hegemony in Soviet society. This attitude represented a startling departure from the standard outlook of Gorbachev's predecessors. As Vasily Aksyonov has said: "[Soviet leaders] are so afraid of books; they exaggerate terribly the importance of books. They fear that a writer will instigate an uprising."[7] Although there is no way of knowing for sure, some émigrés stated their firm belief that it was Alexander Yakovlev who helped Gorbachev understand that glasnost need not threaten the political foundations of the regime.

Yakovlev's career, like that of many members of the Gorbachev team, was put on hold during the Brezhnev years. In 1973 he lost his position as acting head of the Central Committee's Department of Propaganda for criticizing the Russian nationalist movement, and was sent off to serve as ambassador to Canada. Ten years later, and just two years before he took over as General Secretary, Gorbachev made a successful visit to Canada and was very impressed by Yakovlev. Within a month of that visit Gorbachev had him appointed director of the prestigious Institute for International Relations and the World Economy (IMEMO) in Moscow.

Yakovlev, trained as an economist, became a corresponding member of the Academy of Sciences in 1984. After serving one year as head of the Central Committee's Department of Propaganda, the same position from which he had been removed a decade earlier by Brezhnev (a sweet revenge), Yakovlev was promoted to the position of Central Committee Secretary for Propaganda at the 27th Party Congress in March 1966. He became a candidate member of the Politburo the following January, and a full member six months later.

Alexander Yakovlev's hand could be seen in two events before the year 1985 was out, and both laid out the overall Gorbachev strategy in dealing with the Brezhnev opposition: attack Stalin, including his role in World War II (which had been unassailable even during the Thaw), and use the Writers' Union as a major ally in promoting glasnost. To rub salt into the wound, criticism of Stalin's actions in the early years of World War II was initiated in 1985, which marked the 40th anniversary of the Soviet entry into Berlin. Anastas Mikoyan's memoirs were published, accusing Stalin of central responsibility for the catastrophic Soviet defeats in the first year of the war: at Kiev in 1941, the Germans took more than 600,000 Soviet soldiers prisoner—twice the number of Germans who surrendered at Stalingrad in February 1943.

As Gorbachev's chief of ideology, Yakovlev made a tactical push for the new policy at the Sixth Congress of the Russian Republic Writers' Organization in December 1985. At this congress, Yakovlev revealed his plan to introduce glasnost by urging reform within the creative unions. The choice of the Russian Republic Writers' Organization as the site for such a policy change might appear rather surprising, since this was the very branch dominated by the time-servers and hacks that had been created in 1958 to serve as a counterweight to the "liberalism" of the Moscow chapter. However, the Russian Republic branch does include the Moscow and Leningrad chapters, and represents nearly half of the total Union membership (4,318 as of December 1985, out of a total of 9,584 as of June 1986). As such, it offered a stage big enough to send a signal that would reverberate throughout the country, and prepare the ground for the national congresses of the Union of Cinematographers and the Writers' Union, both scheduled to take place in 1986.

The most significant speech at the Congress was given by Yevgeny Yevtushenko, who may well have been briefed by Gorbachev's aides, perhaps even by Yakovlev himself. As a man who has a keen sense for the sources of power, Yevtushenko would have been unlikely to cast his net so wide, well beyond the bounds of literature, without some assurance that he had support in the Politburo. Significantly, not a single writer followed Yevtushenko's lead. Many of his statements were daring enough to have been cut from the version published in *Literaturnaya gazeta*.[8]

As if to show that the opening campaign for literary glasnost had a larger agenda, Yevtushenko attacked "the shortage of paper for the books that people want to read, while half the timberlands are being cut down for boring pseudo-scholarly brochures." Yevtushenko was arguing from a safe Party position, being careful not to point out the real reason for the shortage of paper to print books people want to read: paper is used to print vast editions of "the classics of Marxism-Leninism," and of what Russians call "bricks" (*kirpichi*); that is, weighty tomes of fiction by the top bureaucrats in the Writers' Union. He contrasted the plight of the average Soviet citizen to the privileged existence of members of the Union, who have special access to restricted stores; and he even mentioned "the special coupons for souvenir kiosks that every delegate to this Congress, myself included, has in his pocket."

Yevtushenko argued for a loosening of restrictions on the publication of literary works, and for the publication of older works that had been banned for decades. He seemed to be following Tvardovsky's 1967 line of argument, by insisting that it would be better to publish certain works in the Soviet Union, rather than let them be published in the West, to be used as anti-Soviet propaganda on radio stations beamed back at Soviet citizens: "How long are we going to go on helping all those foreign 'Maria Alekseyevnas' who happily concoct at least half their poisonous radio menus from things that we hide and hush up?" Yevtushenko was not arguing that works should be published if someone wants to publish them, or that censorship is inherently bad. He was tailoring his appeal to Party sensibilities: let us prevent the hostile West from using our own literature to attack us. This is a particularly sensitive point, since the Soviet authorities have long been very concerned about the information that reaches the population through Western radio broadcasts, which attract a large audience across the country.

There is a pleasing symmetry in the fact that Yevtushenko's publications and speeches led the charge for glasnost. He had played a prominent part in the anti-Stalin campaign during the Thaw. In fact, he had taken a leading role in the anti-Stalin campaign (notably in his poem "The Heirs of Stalin," which was published in *Pravda* in 1962). In Krushchev's time literary change had been the harbinger of an important shift in the political wind. Now, scarcely had the delegates departed from the Russian Republic Writers' Congress, their pockets stuffed with souvenirs purchased with their special coupons, when Gorbachev made important personnel changes in the Party. He moved quickly to replace his predecessors' appointees at all key positions, from the Politburo down, notably Romanov, the former Leningrad Party boss, and Grishin, who held the same position in Moscow. This changing of the guard demonstrated that he had sufficient support at the top for his policies, and also showed his skill as a political infighter.

In 1986 Yakovlev began making important appointments in pursuit of glasnost within the Party ideological apparatus in the Central Committee, as well as in Goskomizdat, the Ministry of Culture, and the editorial boards of some leading literary journals and publishing houses. The people replaced were all holdovers from the Brezhnev regime. One of the most important appointments was that of Sergei Zalygin as chief editor of the Union's leading literary monthly, *Novy mir*. Zalygin, now in his seventies, promptly restored it to its traditional eminence. Other appointments of note were those of Grigory Baklanov as chief editor of the journal *Znamya;* Vitaly Korotich, former first secretary of the Ukrainian Writers' Union, as chief editor of the weekly magazine, *Ogonyok;* Albert Belyaev, formerly a deputy head in the Central Committee's Department of Culture, as chief editor of *Sovetskaya kultura;* and, in 1987, Dmitry Urnov, a senior researcher at the Institute of World Literature, as chief editor of a major critical journal, *Voprosy literatury*. Some appointees are former hardliners, such as Belyaev and Korotich, who have changed their views dramatically and become ardent supporters of glasnost.

Gorbachev's appointment of Alexander Yakovlev at the top of the Politburo's ideological apparatus continued to have a ripple effect throughout the entire system. Yakovlev's appointees have in turn ratcheted change through their own chains of command. In many cases, the underlings who have been reassigned or demoted were those responsible for reassigning and demoting current members of Gorbachev's team during the Brezhnev years. Yakovlev's appointee as head of the Central Committee's Department of Culture, Yury Voronov, is a case in point. He had been chief editor of the youth paper, *Molodaya gvardia,* during the brief Thaw under Khrushchev. He fell into disgrace in 1966, after earning the hostility of Politburo ideologist Mikhail Suslov by defending a fellow editor; he has now been brought back into power. So far, his tenure has witnessed a significant loosening of controls in literature and publishing, a repeat of the Thaw he actually participated in as a young man more than twenty years ago. In December 1988, following Gorbachev's sweeping perestroika of the Politburo and Central Committee the previous September, Voronov was appointed chief editor of the important weekly newspaper and official organ of the Union Board, *Literaturnaya gazeta*. Alexander Chakovsky, Brezhnev's old campaigner, has been—"at his own request" according to the Soviet media—retired so he can begin collecting his pension.[9]

The 27th Party Congress in early March 1986 witnessed an affirmation by Gorbachev and by Moscow City Party chief Boris Yeltsin of the need for openness. But, simultaneously, the first indications of resistance to the new ideas appeared as well. Perhaps it was inevitable that hesitation about glasnost should be expressed by a writer, or rather by an official of the Union—none other than Georgy Markov, the longtime First Secretary. He stated outright from the Party Congress podium that he did not see the need for more glasnost in Soviet society. He followed his formal speech with a news conference, opposing specifically the possible publication of Pasternak's *Doctor Zhivago,* which had been advocated by Yevtushenko, Voznesnesky, and others. The resistance of men such as Markov to literary openness derives not only from their conservative beliefs, but also more directly from their complicity in the suppression of the writers and works now being revived. In the case of Pasternak, for example, Markov had joined the attack on the novel as a slander against the Soviet people. Thus, resistance to glasnost came precisely from the very organization the Party had originally set up to carry out its will in literary matters.

However, the following month, a sister creative union, the Union of Cinematographers, held its national congress, and the liberals managed to vote the old guard out of office—a major organizational coup. Elem Klimov, a director who had had problems with the authorities, was elected the new First Secretary. Klimov reported later that he had been nominated by Alexander Yakovlev himself. By all accounts, this was a tumultuous congress—quite unique. Why did Yakovlev, obviously with Gorbachev's approval, launch an assault on the old guard at this Union, and also specifically on Goskino, the equivalent for the movie industry of Goskomizdat? The motive appears to have been at least partly economic; films cost a great deal and take many months to plan and produce, so the state has a large investment in every film that is made. If Goskino shelves a film, refusing to permit its distribution—and it has done this on many occasions—then the state absorbs a considerable loss of income—not solely the cost of making the film, but the potential theater receipts in the Soviet Union and abroad.[10] Goskino's actions in this instance parallel those of Goskomizdat in restricting publication of books in demand, while authorizing massive editions of "bricks."

The Cinematographers' Congress marked a major step forward

in the campaign for glasnost and perestroika, because it involved organizational change, specifically a change in the leading personnel of a creative union. However, it had tipped off the Writers' Union bureaucrats on what was planned for their own Eighth Writers' Congress in late June of 1986. Their suspicions were confirmed on June 19, a few days before the Congress opened, when about thirty writers and editors, including several members of the Secretariat, were summoned to the Kremlin for a personal chat with Gorbachev himself. This extraordinary meeting set the tone for all the speeches and discussions at the Congress that followed. It also presented in sharp relief the role that creative writers (and the media in general) were expected to play in the preparatory campaign for perestroika.

Paradoxically, Gorbachev sought help for his proposed reforms and restructuring from the very group which had the most to lose if his policies were implemented: Georgy Markov (then First Secretary of the Union), Sergei Mikhalkov (then and now President of the Russian Republic organization), Alexander Chakovsky (then chief editor of *Literaturnaya gazeta*), Nikolai Gribachev (chief editor of *Sovetsky Soyuz*), Vladimir Karpov (then chief editor of *Novy mir*, and soon to be given the position of Union First Secretary), Felix Kuznetsov (then First Secretary of the Moscow organization, now Director of the Academy of Sciences' Institute for World Literature, IMLI), Yegor Isaev (producer of reams of rhymed gibberish), Anatoly Ananyev (a deputy chair of the Soviet Committee for the Defense of Peace, and chief editor of *Oktyabr*), longtime bureaucrat Valery Dementyev, and Genrikh Borovik, a journalist with known KGB connections. An odd-man-out in this group was the poet Andrei Voznesensky, although later at the Writers' Union Congress it became clear that he had been chosen (probably by Yakovlev) to be a major spokesman for literary openness, in which he undoubtedly believes personally.

Pravda reported the meeting, saying only that it involved "an open exchange of opinions." However, a partial transcript of Gorbachev's remarks reached the West; it revealed that the *Pravda* version had been censored—whether with Gorbachev's knowledge or not it is impossible to say.[11] The transcript makes fascinating reading. Gorbachev covered a wide range of topics, generally those that he had addressed in earlier speeches, but his language was more colorful and direct. He confessed that it had taken some time to get the reform movement started; that there had been "clashes and arguments" in the Politburo, which had "just put everything on hold for two or three years"—perhaps this comment referred to Andropov's long illness and the year-long transition under Chernenko. But now he wanted to make it clear that the Politburo would be guided by two major considerations. First, the new leadership would persevere in dealing with serious problems that had been neglected under Brezhnev. He told of having seen sacks of documents on scientific and technological problems; Brezhnev had ordered that a special plenum be held on the subject and then just forgot about the whole matter. Second, the Politburo was determined to reform the Party from top to bottom, "from General Secretary to rank and file members," because the Party must lead the new policy (Gorbachev began to make good on this promise with the shake-up of the Politburo and Secretariat on September 30, 1988). He said there would be no "dual morality in the Party, nor two sets of laws," one for the Party and the other for everyone else—a brief nod to Andropov's policy of tough moral and professional discipline.

He complained about the damage being done by alcoholism, which he called "our national tragedy." He understood very well that, because of his efforts to restrict the use of alcohol by raising the price and limiting the hours of liquor stores, people made jokes about him and called him *Mineralny sekretar*, that is, "Mineral (water) secretary," instead of *Generalny sekretar*.[12] He was also well aware that writers "like to drop by the Writers' Club and have a few drinks." He noted that alcoholism was a Russian and a Slavic problem, which did not affect the other nationalities (the "Muslims") to nearly the same extent. He said that the statistics on alcoholism are frightening (*strashny*).

Gorbachev referred in harsh terms to a "layer of apparatchiks" (*upravlenchesky sloi*), located in both the ministries and the Party apparatus, which he said separated the people from the leaders. He knew perfectly well what these folk were saying and that they were trying everything they could to prevent reform. He singled out for special criticism Gosplan (the State Planning Commission), saying that the bureaucrats there are a law unto themselves; they enjoy having everyone come and beg them for things, while they control the allocation and distribution of raw materials and capital. He also noted that the bureaucrats want above all to protect their own privileges: "In our country nothing is exploited quite so much as official position (*dolzhnostnoe polozhenie*)." Old campaigners that they are, Markov, Chakovsky, and the rest probably nodded vigorously at this point or shook their heads in disbelief. The transcript has at this moment an indication that shocked exclamations equivalent to the Western "No! Really?!" were heard. But the apparatchiks must have been getting very nervous as Gorbachev's free-wheeling lecture continued.

Since his audience consisted of writers and editors, Gorbachev spent a great deal of time talking about their role and importance. He explained that he viewed the writing community as a substitute for the missing "loyal opposition" in Soviet society.

> We have no opposition [party]. How then are we going to control ourselves? Only through criticism and self-criticism; but most importantly through glasnost. No society can exist without glasnost.

Gorbachev's remark contains a fascinating echo of an idea first adumbrated by Leo Tolstoy and introduced by Solzhenitsyn in his novel, *The First Circle*. Here a character argues that Russian writers constitute "a second government" and that is why they make the authorities so nervous. It is a fact that the finest creative writers in Russia have traditionally performed the role of loyal opposition, but not in quite the way Gorbachev was suggesting; they have acted independently, not under instructions from the tsarist or Soviet government. What Gorbachev was trying to do in this speech was to co-opt the writers, encourage them to abandon their role as a second (and rival) government, and instead act as a loyal opposition within bounds set by the Party. He told the assembled writers in the Kremlin that he needed their help in creating more openness, which in its turn would establish a more democratic atmosphere in the country—the prerequisite for restructuring. This makes quite clear where literature and the media fit in Gorbachev's overall policy agenda.

But while Gorbachev advocated more democracy, more criticism, and more self-criticism, he warned that too much democracy could lead to anarchy. He cautioned specifically against raking up old problems, and seemed to be apologizing for not addressing the Stalinist past in a more forthright manner:

> If we had started trying to deal with the past, we would have wasted all our energy. It would have been like hitting people over the head. And we must move forward. We will deal with the past. We will put everything in its place. But right now we have to direct our energies forward.

He declared that "generations will have to pass before we will have genuine restructuring." He also made it clear that weapons and military might will not help the Soviet Union in its eternal struggle with the capitalist West:

> Our enemy has figured us out. They are not frightened by our nuclear weapons. They are not going to start a war. They are

> worried about one thing: if democracy develops in our country, if we can pull it off, then we will win. Therefore, they [the Western powers] have started a campaign against our leadership using all available means, even terror. They write about the apparatus that crushed (*slomal sheyu*, lit. "broke the neck of") Khrushchev, and that will now do the same to the current leadership.

The transcript does not contain any further explanation of these points, or the charges against the West. It is tempting to think that these were the sorts of arguments Gorbachev and Yakovlev had used in the Politburo. Gorbachev's remarks do make abundantly clear the seriousness of the Party's problems, as he and his supporters view them. The inference is that Party leaders are trying to resume where Khrushchev left off domestically, but without the global "adventurism" (the Cuban Missile Crisis) that helped bring Khrushchev down.

Gorbachev concluded by mentioning the Congress of Cinematographers, which had taken place the previous month, noting that "certain comrades" within the Politburo had been upset and had charged that the Union was "out of control, it was like guerilla warfare." But he was firm in his belief that changes had to be made in the film industry to improve quality. As an illustration of the low level of Soviet films being produced, Gorbachev referred to a very poor film on the Russian poet Lermontov, but did not mention, since everyone understood this very well, that the film was fiercely Russian nationalist in tone and deliberately anti-Semitic. Gorbachev did not pursue the subject further, but the pointed reference to the Lermontov film made clear his awareness that Russian nationalists formed a significant part of the opposition to his campaign for glasnost and perestroika. They see Gorbachev's reforms as inspired by alien Western notions.

In sum, Gorbachev's remarks indicate that he and his fellow Party leaders have a slightly different agenda than do the liberal writers and editors. While each side is trying to get as much as it can from glasnost, each side interprets the term in a rather different fashion. Gorbachev is changing the "tasks" assigned to writers. He made a point of quoting a question first asked by Gorky, a pillar of the regime, but anathema to most writers: "Who are you with, masters of culture?" Echoing the magic mirror in Grossman's novel, *Life and Fate*, men like Georgy Markov and Alexander Chakovsky would naturally respond in tandem: "With you, dear Party, with you." But the writers and critics brought up on the heady promises of the Thaw a generation ago want to escape the clutches of the Party, and seek to revive older traditions that specifically exclude Maxim Gorky and his literary ancestors, the radical critics of the nineteenth century. However, the liberals seized with both hands Gorbachev's invitation to follow the lead of their sister organization, the Union of Cinematographers.

The Eighth Writers' Union Congress, which followed shortly after Gorbachev's Kremlin chat, was a lively affair with a host of speeches attacking the many faults of the "literary generals" (some of them by name) and calling for a variety of reforms.[13] On this occasion it was the poet Andrei Voznesensky, rather than Yevgeny Yevtushenko, who took the lead in proclaiming the need for glasnost and arguing for the publication of forbidden works. His speech included the phrase: "Glasnost is the sister of literature." Such remarks result from what Russians call politely Voznesensky's "complicated position" (*slozhnoe polozhenie*), and occasionally earn him harsh criticism among both Soviet Russians and émigrés, who are suspicious of his close ties with high officials.

The celebrated cellist and conductor Mstislav Rostropovich is willing to be more generous, and perhaps gets closer to the essential problems of the liberal writer in the Soviet Union today:

> He is trying to be honorable. He has a difficult life. I know that only too well. All the time he is testing where the limits are. What else might he dare do? Perhaps they [the authorities] won't understand what he is up to. Or maybe they will, but pretend they don't. He is walking along the edge of a precipice.[14]

At the Eighth Congress, Voznesensky seemed to be striding confidently along the center lane of a major highway, and must have felt that he had official backing: perhaps, as was likely in the case of Yevtushenko, he had received an official nudge from Alexander Yakovlev. This possibility is suggested not only by the boldness of Voznesensky's remarks, but also by a photograph published in *Pravda* during the Congress (June 25, 1986), showing Voznesensky speaking in a group of rather bored literary apparatchiks, including Markov himself. There was no indication as to who the people photographed were, and the caption simply read "In the corridors during the Congress." But the message was clear to all seasoned *Pravda* readers: the old guard might not want to listen to people like Voznesensky, but he had the ear of the new Party leadership, and his voice was going to carry a lot of weight in the future.

Nevertheless, the old guard proved they can withstand a charge and fight back. They managed to resist efforts by liberals to follow the lead of the Union of Cinematographers and make radical changes in the Writers' Union hierarchy. Although Markov did not last as

First Secretary, and was given the vacant and purely honorary post of President at the Eighth Congress, he retained his position as a member of the new nine-man Litburo formed shortly after the Congress. Even more important, the conservative and effective second secretary of the Union, Yury Verchenko, retained his position as *orgsekretar* in the Litburo.[15] Since the Writers' Congress, the maneuvering between the old guard and the liberals has sometimes seen its invective spill over into the Soviet press, but organizational power is still held by the conservatives.

The new First Secretary, Vladimir Karpov, must be a great disappointment to both Gorbachev and Yakovlev, who would have expected him to support their campaign for glasnost and perestroika, since he spent time in the Gulag under Stalin. Although he is not distinguished as a writer, Karpov's record as a human being is unassailable. During World War II he served as a scout and captured for interrogation no less than 79 German officers and soldiers. Karpov received his country's highest award for bravery in battle, being named a Hero of the Soviet Union—this award is equivalent to the Congressional Medal of Honor.

Far from supporting reform, Karpov has tended to side with the conservatives. He seems more concerned about material questions than freedom of speech. Like an American politician trying to get more pork-barrel projects for his district, or a union boss pressing for better rates for his members, Karpov has given several speeches arguing for a re-examination of copyright regulations, which have not been updated since before World War II. He insists that writers should receive far higher rates for their work, and also urges more generous pensions in view of the large amounts of revenue that many writers bring to the Soviet budget. He objects strenuously to suggestions that writers should be taxed at higher rates (part of the new economic reforms), and he rejects outright any suggestion that Union members are privileged, and expresses concern that glasnost and perestroika might be used to rake up "ancient grudges" (*davnie obidy*) and to settle "old scores" (*starye schety*). Such remarks endear Karpov to the conservatives in the Union, particularly the powerful secretaries and chief editors of various journals in the capital. But his campaign for better economic conditions has probably earned him broad support among the Union membership.

The continuing strength of anti-reform elements in the Writers' Union was revealed in October 1987, when the Litburo and the Secretariat combined with conservative Party elements in the Union to prevent Yevgeny Yevtushenko's election to the position of first secretary of the Moscow writers' organization. The circumstances surrounding this election, and the frank account of the debate and vote in the Moscow board that was published in *Literaturnaya gazeta,* give a fair picture of the conflicting forces now at work in Soviet literary politics. Something like a genuine debate and open election appear to have taken place. The press reported that discussions went on for five hours, and published a shortened version of the three final candidates' "campaign speeches." The paper even gave the votes cast for each candidate. However, past experience suggests that the Party organization must have had its meeting first to decide on a candidate that would be acceptable, then voted for him in a bloc. The conservatives were quite determined to prevent Yevtushenko's election to such an important position. The winning candidate was Alexander Mikhailov, who happens to be a "released secretary." Mikhailov's actions to date have demonstrated that Gorbachev's pleas in his Kremlin chat prior to the Eighth Union Congress failed to cause any change in his heart.

The resistance of the conservatives has not, however, prevented many articles and letters to the editor from appearing in the Soviet press, attacking the Union's privileged status and its resistance to glasnost. Critical remarks about the Union and the literary situation made at the 1986 Congress were published in full. *Literaturnaya gazeta* (July 2, 1986) printed unusually outspoken speeches by the elderly writer Sergei Zalygin (who soon after became chief editor of *Novy mir*), and the writer Olzhas Suleimenov, who is first secretary of the Kazakh branch of the Union, and therefore a member of the Board and Secretariat.

Zalygin complained about the concentration of power in too few hands at publishing houses, journals, and at Litfund. He suggested a revival of candidate membership so as to improve standards in the Union. He wanted to slow down the rapid increase in membership, which was diluting standards and threatening to add to the Union's already large administrative apparatus. He stated that most of the Board's meetings were a waste of time, and urged it to play a more active role, recalling the more lively atmosphere at the First Congress of Writers in 1934.

Suleimenov's remarks were even more pointed. He complained about "the relations between writers' organizations and the local ideological leadership." With heavy irony, Suleimenov said:

> We bow down before you, Party intelligentsia, true patriots and internationalists! The local writers' organizations cannot defend a book if an ideological bureaucrat has criticized it. His opinion is, as it were, an evaluation by the whole Party, no less. The book's fate is decided—and often the author's fate as well. When

> you meet such old hands, you think: "He ought to be a gardener, but he's working as a lumberjack."[16]

The threat of such comments is echoed in complaints about the favorable reviews that books by "literary generals" receive. In fact, nearly all book reviews are favorable; books that the Secretariat does not like are simply ignored altogether. *Literaturnaya gazeta* or *Literaturka,* the weekly newspaper of the Union Board, has been one of the main culprits in this area. Editors and literary officials are known to call reviewers and instruct them to give a work a positive or negative review.[17] The respected critic Igor Zolotussky has complained of the initial neglect and then negative review of Alexander Bek's long-suppressed novel *A New Assignment* (*Novoe naznachenie*), which deals with the Stalin era; his speech was published in *Literaturnaya gazeta* itself:

> Nobody is interested in literary criticism that circles around going nowhere, but this is the type of criticism that still predominates in the first part of the newspaper. While the second part deals with real life and people speak aloud, in the first part, which evaluates literature, voices are reduced to a whisper. It is still the same old story: praise for bad books, "theoretical" articles full of [orthodox] quotations. It is all the same typical Litgazeta fence-sitting (*firmennoe litgazetovskoe vzveshivanie*).[18]

Gradually, published criticism of the Union's leadership became more intense and began to be voiced by the general public. An article appeared on the front page of *Komsomolskaya Pravda* in August 1988, deploring the broad gap in various cultural institutions, including the creative unions, between their pledge to "serve the people" on the one hand, and the actual "dearth of information" (*informatsionny golod*), and the continued use of "telephone law" by Moscow bureaucrats who ignore the wishes of people out in the provinces. In a harshly worded letter published in *Sovetskaya kultura* in June 1988, two readers charged that the creative unions were ignoring glasnost and perestroika altogether. They argued that the unions were obsolete creations of Stalin, still reflecting "the spirit and the word of Stalinist authoritarianism and its pyramidal bureaucratic structure." Why is it, they wondered, that the creative unions should still retain this structure, when so much is changing in Soviet society? They condemned the unions for suppressing individual creativity, robbing art of its mystery, and substituting merely "the metallic aftertaste of bureaucratic redtape" (*metallichesky privkus kantselyarshchiny*).[19]

In spite of such harsh criticism, the main fruit of glasnost, thus far, has been the publication for the first time in the Soviet Union of several works that are widely known in the West, but were previously suppressed: Pasternak's *Doctor Zhivago;* Anna Akhmatova's poem about the Great Terror, *Requiem;* Zamyatin's anti-utopian satire, *We,* and his article "I Am Afraid . . ." ("Ya boyus . . ."), which forecast accurately enough the destruction of Russian literature under Stalin;[20] Bulgakov's short novel, *Heart of a Dog* (*Sobachye serdtse*); and two novels by Vasily Grossman: *Life and Fate* (*Zhizn i sudba*), a work that revolves around the Battle of Stalingrad but expands into a major indictment of Stalinist Russia, which it compares to Hitler's Germany, and *Forever Flowing . . .* (*Vse techet . . .*)—a harsh indictment of Lenin as the precursor of Stalin.

The publication of these works demonstrates that a fundamental change has occurred in the Party's *verboten* list; so does the publication of a collection of prose fiction by Vladimir Nabokov, not only an émigré who fled Russia after the Bolshevik coup, but a writer who made relentless fun of Nikolai Chernyshevsky, of Marxism-Leninism, and of Soviet cultural pretentions. In addition to these works by authors now deceased, journals have been competing frantically to publish works by living authors (including another merciless satirist, Vladimir Voinovich), which had previously been banned or simply never submitted for publication. Most of these works focus on the Stalin period: for example, Anatoly Rybakov's long novel on the thirties, *Children of the Arbat* (*Deti Arbata*),[21] and Anatoly Pristavkin's *A Small Golden Cloud Spent the Night* (*Nochevala tuchka zolotaya*)—the title is borrowed from a famous poem by Mikhail Lermontov, the Romantic poet; the novel tells the story, through the eyes of two young boys, of Stalin's destruction of ethnic minorities.

The paradox of glasnost is that the Party is now much more willing than many conservative editors and "literary generals" to authorize publication of formerly forbidden as well as challenging new works.[22] The Party has changed its "tasks" for writers, but the Secretariat is unwilling to pass these along and support them. The main resistance to the reforms is to be found in the Russian Republic writers' organization, which is dominated by conservatives and extreme Russian nationalists. Their attitude emerged clearly from a printed account of a meeting of the Secretariat of the Board of the Russian Republic Writers' Union.[23] Present at the meeting were many of the "old guard" who clearly see that their print-runs will ebb to zero once the journals start publishing previously forbidden fruit. Pyotr Proskurin, a "released secretary" whose artistic skills are valued most clearly by himself and other literary apparatchiks, spoke from the heart:

> The magazine *Ogonyok* has been behaving very strangely lately. This magazine is considered to be a "weekly socio-political, literary, and art magazine," that is, an organ that one assumes is for a national readership. Then why is it that recently a spirit of cliquishness [echoes of Fadeyev!], even a kind of caste exclusiveness such as has not been seen for a long time in our country—not since the 1920s, I think—has been manifesting itself more and more tangibly in this national organ, especially in its basic assumptions regarding literature and art? . . . Our criticism must react sensitively to every such incident, otherwise God knows where we will end up, if such incidents come to prevail more and more. . . .

Proskurin is worried about the fate of his own fiction. Who would publish it if ideological correctness were not considered to be an important principle of selection, indeed, the most important principle? Proskurin is particularly angry about the growing popularity of formerly suppressed writers and the publication of their works; he dismisses this development as "literary necrophilia (*nekrofilstvo*)." Proskurin's allusion to the literary debates of the twenties itself recalls the Dostoevsky-Chernyshevsky debate, which was rehashed then as well. Now, sixty years later, the liberals are carefully not attacking Chernyshevsky by name, but they have ridiculed many of his notions by undermining the ideological foundations of Socialist Realism, and they have also quoted Dostoevsky with great frequency as a model writer and critic. In an extraordinarily blunt article, which attacked corruption and greed among Union secretaries, the widely respected writer and critic Natalia Ilyina noted: "It was Dostoevsky who declared that, however noble an author's intentions might be, if he does not succeed in expressing them in an artistic manner, then his work will never achieve its objective."[24] The insistence on the priority of art over social message is a direct contradiction of Chernyshevsky's credo, and of Socialist Realism itself. Natalya Ivanova and Stanislav Rassadin have also complained about the appallingly low level of literary criticism in the Soviet Union, and blame Socialist Realism (by implication) and the conservatives (explicitly) for it.[25]

The critic Benedikt Sarnov ridiculed the pretensions of orthodox Soviet literary views, beginning in the twenties, and quoted the infamous declaration by Leonid Sobolev, "The Party and government have given the Soviet writer absolutely everything he needs.

They have taken only one thing from us—the right to write badly." Sarnov notes that Gorky quoted this statement in his speech to the First Congress of Writers in 1934, and adds wryly that orthodox writers have been struggling to recover the right to write badly ever since.[26] Sarnov was severely criticized in the press, but sources within the Soviet Union report that he also received many letters praising his courage in writing this essay.

The publication of forbidden works, and salvos of scorn levelled at Stalin and at "stagnation" (*zastoi*) during the Brezhnev period, might not appear too serious at first sight, but they constitute a direct attack on the current Union leadership, who were responsible for the "illegalities" now under fire. Liberal critics have used the fate of Alexander Tvardovsky as a club with which to thump the current Union leaders, and the chief editors of some journals who gained their positions by helping the Party end the Thaw. These "literary generals" in the Union Litburo and Secretariat established the neo-Stalinist style of rule that prevailed for nearly twenty years.

However, it is not only the hard-line bureaucrats who are offended by the liberals' criticism of the old ways of doing things, or their attempts to promote pluralism and variety. Many of the older writers look back to World War II as a sort of golden age, when they began to rise in the hierarchy. Like Vladimir Karpov, the Union First Secretary, they write exclusively about World War II, in which many of them served, either as combatants or as correspondents, often with great distinction. Their wartime experiences serve as a bond. As is the case for some men in other nations, the war contoured and defined their political and cultural outlook. Their understandable pride in having helped defend their country and their firsthand experience of agony, brutality, and death have gradually turned them into fierce Russian (and sometimes Soviet) nationalists. And they have retained a faith in Stalin as the great wartime leader, whose name was on the lips of so many soldiers as they charged into battle and died.

Like other powerful emotions, the veterans' feelings of pride and nostalgia can be readily manipulated. Some of the leading conservative bureaucrats, whose main agenda is to protect their own fiefdoms, have had success in portraying the liberals as unpatriotic, even though many liberal writers served with great distinction in the war, and spent time in the Gulag too. One of the leading conservative writers, Yury Bondarev, has likened the current debate to "a civil war in literature" and suggests that he and his admirers, now being attacked by hordes of hostile forces, are in much the same position as the defenders of Stalingrad in those dark days of late 1942. He seems undisturbed by the fact that this comparison places those who disagree with him in the uniforms of Nazi invaders—the most hated image in the Soviet Union today.

Some literary conservatives have thus linked arms with members of the Russian nationalist movement, already the most potent force in Soviet political and cultural life, to form a neo-Stalinist opposition to Gorbachev's reforms. These disparate groups have joined forces because they see the Gorbachev reforms as inspired by alien notions from the capitalist West. Such fears have been part and parcel of opposition to modernization throughout Russian history, but Gorbachev's Western style, his stress on productivity, bottom-line economics, market measurements, and his acceptance of the possibility of unemployment—all these have heightened their fears and provoked a new wave of intense xenophobia.

What Gorbachev's opponents may not have perceived is that his aim is not to become "Western," but to become more competitive with the West; in other words, to make the Soviet system stronger. In this, Gorbachev is following in the footsteps of many "reforming" tsars of the past, most notably Peter the Great. Like him, Gorbachev is using cultural renewal to complement and validate essentially economic reforms. Seweryn Bialer, a leading Soviet specialist at Columbia University, in speaking of Alexander Yakovlev, has summed up equally well the stance of Gorbachev:

> He is a modernizer, but I wouldn't call him a Westernizer. Westernizer implies somehow a desire to transplant the Western system of values into Russian conditions. That is not Yakovlev. He wants to borrow, but in a very selective way.[27]

Russian nationalists across a broad spectrum remain unconvinced. The Russian nationalist movement is a complex phenomenon, one that responds to widespread concerns about the destruction of the environment and national treasures, and to the need for a meaningful community of like-minded people. The National Society for the Protection of Historical and Cultural Monuments (*Vserossyskoe obshchestvo okhrany pamyatnikov istorii i kultury*, or VOOPIK), founded in the late sixties, has millions of members. Russians dominate the Society and do much good work in protecting old churches and other pre-revolutionary buildings and sites. Under Gorbachev, a new and lavishly endowed organization called the Soviet Culture Fund (*Sovetsky fond kultury*) has been established. It is headed by Academician Dmitry Likhachev and includes Raisa Gorbachev as a member of its Presidium. The Soviet media gave wide coverage to the Fund and its inaugural conference in November 1986.[28] The Fund has attracted an enthusiastic response from Soviet citizens, especially Russians, many of whom evidently intend to turn the new organization into a more active version of VOOPIK. They are making substantial cash contributions to the Fund, and are eager to repair the damage that has long been done to the Russian national heritage by the Soviet regime.

The Soviet Culture Fund may help to defuse some of the intense feelings of anger and frustration among many Russians, but they are just beginning to tap their strength. Russian nationalists and environmentalists, led by writers, have already mounted a successful campaign against a vast scheme to reverse the Siberian rivers in order to irrigate the deserts and other dry regions of Soviet Central Asia. This scheme would have involved flooding certain areas of Siberia (the Russian Republic), and at the same time threatened to rob these areas of resources to enrich non-Russian regions of the country. In this campaign, concern for the environment turned into anger at the favoritism being shown the despised *natsmen*, or non-Russian and non-Slavic peoples of Central Asia, who many Russians feel enjoy a privileged position in Soviet society. Russians frequently complain, even to foreigners, that too high a proportion of the Soviet GNP goes to the non-Russian Republics.[29] Many Russians also display violent anti-Semitic feelings, whenever they discuss "un-Russian activities."

The alliance between extreme Russian nationalists and conservative neo-Stalinist bureaucrats made its major assault on glasnost and perestroika in March 1988. Yegor Ligachev, increasingly frustrated by Gorbachev's appointments and by Yakovlev's leading role in ideology and culture, made a serious blunder by trying to embarrass both men, and by timing his attack while Gorbachev was out of the country. It is assumed that Ligachev personally promoted or at least approved the reworking of a letter from a Leningrad chemistry teacher, Nina Andreyeva, into a full-page article, published on March 13, 1988 in the Russian nationalist paper, *Sovetskaya Rossia*, under the title "I Cannot Give Up My Principles" ("Ya ne mogu postupatsya printsipami"). Andreyeva (or her high-placed editors) focused her attention on the role being played by Jews in the current Western-inspired reforms of Soviet culture and the abandonment of Stalinist principles. She even mentioned Trotsky (a former Menshevik) and the Menshevik leader Martov (who did become an opponent of Lenin), in an obvious effort to link Gorbachev and Yakovlev to "hostile elements" of the past, particularly those of Jewish origin, who were trying to undermine the achievements of the October Revolution.

The whole letter reeked of Stalinist assaults on "cosmopolitans" and the Jewish "doctors' plot." The use of the concocted letter from "an outraged citizen" recalled an old Stalinist technique, and the word "principles" has long been a favorite rhetorical device: Party ideologists always like to describe their opinions as "principled" (*printsipialny*), as though opponents could have no principles; the word has come to mean little more than "dogmatic, orthodox, following the current Party line." The liberal intelligentsia held its breath for an entire month until April 15, when *Pravda* published a long rebuttal, reportedly written by Yakovlev, entitled with deliberate emphasis "The Principles of Perestroika" ("Printsipy perestroiki"). Yakovlev, an experienced ideological infighter, was obviously not going to allow Ligachev to occupy the semantic high ground. The *Pravda* editorial rejected all Andreyeva's arguments, focusing on her crude attempts to whitewash Stalin and the Stalinist record, and her efforts to dress up the neo-Stalinists as Russian patriots, and to tar Gorbachev and his reforms with the brush of Jewish and Western anti-Soviet activities. While Ligachev's tactical blunder has not ended his political ambitions, it has given a great boost to the reform movement. Andreyeva's letter, as a statement by anti-reformists, revealed them to have no real platform, since the only argument they can advance against perestroika is that it is part of a Jewish conspiracy—a suggestion that links them to the so-called "Black Hundreds" of the late tsarist period, who advocated and carried out officially condoned pogroms against the Jewish population.

Many conservative writers and critics, such as Vadim Kozhinov, remained undeterred by this rebuff to Ligachev. They continued to publish articles linking support for Stalin with a defense of Russian national virtues. While protesting attacks on the Stalin era, they often charged Jews and Western capitalism with attempts to undermine the Soviet system, which paradoxically (given its appalling record) they credit with preserving Russianness.[30] Yury Bondarev exemplifies the type of intellectual opposed to glasnost and perestroika. He occupies the influential position of vice-president of the Russian Republic writers' organization. Under his leadership this organization has become the headquarters for all Russian nationalists and conservatives opposing Gorbachev's reforms. The Russian Republic branch's official publication, *Nash Sovremennik* (*Our Contemporary*), has likewise become the opposition's chief organ. In a speech reported in both *Pravda* and *Izvestia*, Bondarev characterized his opponents as writing "extremist criticism" and accused them of declaring:

> Let the weeds flourish and all evil forces compete; only with chaos, confusion, disarray, intrigues and epidemics of literary scandals, only by shaking faith, will we be able to sew together

> a uniform of thinking advantageous to us personally. Yes, this criticism lusts for power, and casting off morality and conscience, it may push ideology to the brink of crisis.[31]

Bondarev dismissed sarcastically the publication of most of the masterpieces others have hailed: "Aren't we looking at the sun and the sky through ruble notes obtained from increased print-runs?" Bondarev further stated that "trust in history has been largely undermined, as has trust in almost all of the past, in the older generation."

Bondarev lists the "remarkable talents" now being "slandered": Vasily Belov, Viktor Astafyev, Pyotr Proskurin, Valentin Rasputin, Anatoly Ivanov, Mikhail Alekseyev, Sergei Bondarchuk, and Ilya Glazunov. These names offer a carefully balanced collection of Russian nationalists and reactionaries; Astafyev and Rasputin are respected as writers, although both have permitted themselves to be associated with extreme nationalists. Bondarchuk is the old movie director, who ruled with an iron fist, until he was removed in the "coup" at the Union of Cinematographers' Congress in May 1986. Glazunov is an orthodox painter, much favored by the elite because of his idealized portraits of old Russia (although he tried some more "daring" works in earlier times).

In its turn, one of the main bastions of glasnost, the weekly magazine *Ogonyok*, which is edited by the Ukrainian Vitaly Korotich, has subjected Bondarev and his allies to merciless ridicule and savage personal criticism.[32] The abusive tone of these exchanges reached a new level in the first issue of *Ogonyok* for 1989, which contained an open letter submitted by a former ally of Bondarev, Mikhail Kolosov, chief editor of *Literaturnaya Rossia* (a conservative, Russian nationalist paper), accusing Bondarev of interfering in the work of the paper, of pushing his own cronies into positions of authority in the Russian Republic writers' organization, and of feathering his own bed by using influence to have his works published in large editions.[33]

A group of nationalists and conservatives rallied at once to Bondarev's defense in an open letter that was published in *Pravda* just a week or so later. The letter was signed by Mikhail Alekseyev, Viktor Astafyev, Vasil Belov, Sergei Bondarchuk, Sergei Vikulov, Pyotr Proskurin, and Vasily Rasputin.[34] All, except Vikulov, had been praised by Bondarev the previous year as major cultural figures being viciously attacked by liberals. Vikulov is chief editor of the Russian nationalist and extremely conservative journal *Nash Sovremennik* (*Our Contemporary*). He is also the author of unreadable prose and verse, but will be remembered in Russian literary history as one of the signers of the notorious 1969 letter attacking Alexander Tvardovsky, entitled "What Is *Novy mir* Against?" This is also likely to be the fate of two other signers of that 1969 letter, Mikhail Alekseyev, chief editor of the neo-Stalinist journal *Moskva*, and Pyotr Proskurin, another major opponent of Gorbachev's reforms. To add insult to injury, Proskurin was appointed to the memorial panel charged with commemorating Alexander Tvardovsky's famous wartime poem, *Vasily Tyorkin*. Proskurin has never recanted the vituperation and abuse heaped on Tvardovsky in that letter. Tvardovsky's widow has protested, so far in vain, the obscenity of naming her husband's tormentor to this post.[35]

Only ten days after *Pravda* published the letter defending Bondarev and attacking *Ogonyok* (Korotich's name was not mentioned), a *Pravda* editorial appeared (January 28, 1989), demanding greater tolerance for differing opinions and a willingness to listen to the arguments of others in the spirit of "socialist pluralism." The editorial also mentioned that the newspaper had been bombarded with letters, including some by distinguished cultural figures, protesting the belligerent tone of the letter sent in Bondarev's defense. In evaluating the significance of this editorial, it should be remembered that all *Pravda* editorials are written by specialists in the Central Committee. Thus it was a criticism of those signing the January 18 letter, but also of *Pravda*'s editorial board in publishing it without comment or a rejoinder. Significantly, the new chief editor of *Literaturnaya gazeta*, Yury Voronov (a Gorbachev supporter), has quickly instituted a regular column entitled "Dialogue of the Week," which allows sharply differing opinions on various cultural and social issues to be aired side by side. One "Dialogue," carried over several issues of the paper in March 1989, pitted the extreme Russian nationalist (some would say, anti-Semite), Vadim Kozhinov, against the outspoken liberal, Benedikt Sarnov, who is Jewish. No doubt Yakovlev's earlier counter-attack against Nina Andreyev's "letter" encouraged Voronov to bring the views of Kozhinov out into the open and subject them to immediate scrutiny.

The attacks on Korotich in 1988 were part of a growing pattern of Russian chauvinism and anti-Semitism, hauntingly similar to widespread sentiments at the beginning of this century in tsarist Russia, and in Nazi Germany in the thirties. Unfortunately, the revival of interest in the Russian Orthodox Church has also been accompanied by similar reactionary behavior. At a meeting in January 1989 Vyacheslav Gorbachev (no family relationship as far as is known), an editor at the reactionary journal *Molodaya gvardia*, received cheers and applause when he recited statistics showing the large number of Jews receiving higher education and among the membership of both the Academy of Sciences and the Writers' Union—membership in the latter is a sign of special privilege, as we have pointed out. Given the prejudice against Jews in higher education, it testifies to their intelligence and energy that so many of them do make successful careers.

Although Korotich was under such fierce attack, he was finally selected as a candidate for the National Congress of Deputies, in spite of conservative opponents in the *Pamyat* organization, who physically threatened him and shouted anti-Semitic slurs at him and his supporters.[36] Korotich's magazine *Ogonyok* in February (No. 7, 1989) reported that it had been overwhelmed with letters and telegrams, including a total of about 900 in one day alone, offering support against the January 18 letter in *Pravda*.[37]

The final scene in this battle between the forces of glasnost and conservatism has not been written. It seems that Bondarev, Proskurin, and their colleagues have many friends among the Russian nationalists, as well as in high places such as the editorial offices of *Pravda*. And they also control editorial policy in several other monthly journals, including Anatoly Ivanov's *Molodaya gvardia*. Mikhail Nenashev, Gorbachev's appointee to head Gozkomizdat, has made some efforts to put the organization's book publishing policies on a more rational basis.[38] However, thus far his main achievements have been the "unrestricted" publication of Russian classical literature, that is, the printing of vast editions (20 million copies) of Pushkin and Tolstoy. It is not clear yet whether he (or his successor) will be able to prevent the continued publication of large editions of works by "literary generals," which as we have seen wastes scarce paper and prevents publication of works the public really wants to read. The allocation of paper is another of the hidden censorship mechanisms in Soviet publishing.

The "commanding heights" of cultural policy are still owned by Gorbachev, and the Union Secretariat does not control all of culture. So, for example, the Union of Cinematographers has been reformed, and theater workers finally received approval to form their own creative union in 1986, against strenuous objections by Yegor Ligachev and other conservatives. Theaters in Moscow have taken advantage of glasnost and their newfound independence to demonstrate an obvious fascination with twentieth-century European drama, staging plays which had not been seen in the Soviet Union for many years, and sometimes not at all. Since 1986 there have been several performances of plays by Eugene Ionesco, Samuel Becket, Jean Cocteau, and Arthur Miller.

But perhaps as important as the actual plays that are being produced in Moscow, and throughout the country, is the economic impact of the new law that went into effect at the beginning of 1987, which permitted 69 theaters across the country to operate in a more advanced style of *khozraschet* (economic self-management), and to actually select their own repertoires. The Western reader will doubtless wonder what other way there could be of doing things. But in fact, for almost the whole of the Soviet period theaters have been given a *templan* (just like publishing houses and journals and other institutions), which told them what plays or categories of plays they could produce in any given season. The *templan* always contained a healthy assortment of orthodox Soviet potboilers. The result has been that for many years theaters have been empty, as increasing numbers of Soviet citizens become better educated and more sophisticated in their literary tastes. As a rule only selected theaters in Moscow, such as the famous Taganka under its director, Yury Lyubimov (now in the West), were able to produce anything startling or challenging. Now, with the new 1987 law, at least 69 theaters throughout the Soviet Union will have an opportunity to try new and daring productions, which should certainly attract much bigger audiences. Of course, they will have to meet higher production costs, because theaters have also been permitted to raise actors' salaries by a maximum of 30 percent and to make other financial decisions formerly reserved for bureaucrats in the Ministry of Culture apparatus. The new options for theaters will certainly encourage greater diversity and innovation in dramatic literature.

The tentative reforms at Goskomizdat and the more sweeping changes in the theater suggest that, having won the battle over glasnost, Gorbachev might yet win the war to introduce perestroika into Soviet cultural life. The real test still remained—could the conservative Union Secretariat and the Russian Republic branch be persuaded to accept Gorbachev's new cultural policies? He had tried gentle persuasion and changes in personnel; in 1989 it seemed he was preparing to apply to the Writers' Union the strategies he had used in the Party and government structures in the fall of 1988.

8

The Promise of Perestroika

Whither is fled the visionary gleam?
Where is it now, the glory and the dream?

WORDSWORTH

By the spring of 1989, Mikhail Gorbachev and his advisers were at long last ready to make the transition from glasnost to perestroika in literature. Gorbachev had outmaneuvered his main conservative opponent, Yegor Ligachev, in his "coup from above" (*perevorot sverkhu*) of September 30, 1988. Some Russians and some Western commentators expressed concern that Gorbachev's reshuffling of the Central Committee and Politburo involved a damaging compromise, since Yakovlev was moved from ideology to foreign affairs. But Gorbachev had already shown considerable skill in blunting opposition by appearing to give something away, most notably when he sacrificed Boris Yeltsin in the fall of 1987—this cost him nothing politically, even though Yeltsin continues to be extremely popular among the people of Moscow. Similarly in this case, the main point was that Ligachev had lost authority over ideology, and hence his ability to oppose glasnost and perestroika. Yakovlev's replacement as head of the new Commission for Ideology, Vadim Medvedev, served in the seventies as Yakovlev's deputy in the Department of Propaganda.[1] We must assume that he is a supporter of glasnost and perestroika, although he will obviously have his own style and preferences.

The reshuffling of the ideological apparatus in the Central Committee had no immediate impact on the Union, even though it abolished all Central Committee departments.[2] The departments were consolidated into six so-called commissions, which exercised supervision over smaller units, called departments (*otdely*), as in the old regime. Vadim Medvedev jumped directly to full membership in the Politburo and took charge of the new Commission for Ideology. A Ukrainian, Alexander Semyonovich Kapto (b. 1933), became head of the new Department of Ideology and automatically a member of the Commission for Ideology. The remaining personnel in the new Commission were not listed, but it seemed very likely that there would be several holdovers from the old Departments of Culture and of Propaganda. In fact, V. K. Yegorov, former assistant deputy head of the Department of Propaganda, was mentioned in January 1989 as "deputy head of the Party Central Committee's Department of Ideology" (*zamestitel zaveduyushchego Ideologicheskim otdelom TsK KPSS*).[3]

Gorbachev's attempts to make similar institutional changes in the Union had achieved little more than did the frustrating attempts at liberalization made by Tsar Alexander II, the "Tsar Liberator," in the nineteenth century. In 1859, John Stuart Mill wrote on "the melancholy condition of the Russian empire," which he attributed to the fact that

> . . . the Czar himself is powerless against the bureaucratic body: he can send any one of them to Siberia, but he cannot govern without them, or against their will. On every decree of his they have a tacit veto, by merely refraining from carrying it into effect.[4]

Gorbachev decided not to resort to sending conservatives to Siberia; if nothing else, such actions would be a denial of the principles he had embraced. And so, conservative bureaucrats in the Secretariat and in the Union membership had managed to resist all attempts at true reform in the organization. However, Gorbachev's electoral reforms in the government apparatus in late 1988 presaged a similar restructuring in other bureaucracies, including the Writers' Union.

The 1988 "Law on Elections" mandated the creation of a new Congress of People's Deputies (*Syezd narodnykh deputatov*), consisting of 2,250 people. By all accounts, the resulting elections were often free in the Western sense of the term—citizens were able to defeat many Party candidates running unopposed, simply by crossing out their names on the ballot. But the Party was able to maintain a guiding hand even in these new-style Soviet elections. Fully one-third of the deputies (750) were elected by "social organizations" such as the Party itself (which elected 100 deputies), the Komsomol (75), Trade Unions (100), the Committee of Soviet Women (75), and Veterans (75), among others. The Union of Writers, along with the other creative unions (the Union of Designers elected only five), elected 10 members to the new Congress of People's Deputies.[5] It was as though the Writers' Guild or the American branch of PEN were given the authority to elect, from within their rolls, several members to the U.S. Congress.

The choice of "two-step elections" (*dvukh-stupenchatye vybory*), instead of direct universal suffrage, illustrated Gorbachev's reluctance to proceed without giving organizations, not simply the Party itself, special privileges. At the same time, this tentative approach to political reform showed Gorbachev's skill in gaining sufficient support for his policy of perestroika, which threatened Party and government bureaucrats with the loss of their power to rule by fiat and without accountability. The open debate during the sessions of the Congress of People's Deputies, all televised live throughout the country, carried glasnost to high levels, although institutional reform proceeded more slowly. The election of candidates to the new Supreme Soviet revealed signs of behind-the-scenes management by Gorbachev and his supporters. As at all meetings within the Writers' Union, the Party delegates would have held separate, closed meetings during the Congress in order to decide upon candidates, for whom they then voted *en bloc*. The result was that fully 90 percent of the 542 delegates elected to the Supreme Soviet were Party members. However, the televized debates of the new body, which ended its initial session on August 4, 1989, showed once again that deputies took their responsibilities seriously and could not be cajoled into voting timidly and automatically for proposals handed down from the top.

The Congress of People's Deputies marked a significant step forward in Gorbachev's campaign for political reform, and was apparently designed to serve as a model for other "voluntary" organizations, including the Union. On March 22, 1989, just a week before the Congress opened, *Literaturnaya gazeta* published a draft of the new Union Statutes. The draft embodies Gorbachev's strategy, already evident in electoral reform, of using legal codes and parliamentarianism to outmaneuver staunch opponents of perestroika, while at the same time trying to maintain the Party's guiding role in the whole process. Thus the draft can be viewed as a general policy statement as well as a charter for the Writers' Union. The proposed Statutes are nearly twice as long as the 1971 version they would supersede, and the language is less ideological and grandiose. Much effort must have been expended on selecting terminology that would accommodate the varied constituencies represented in the large commission that prepared the draft.

The draft repeats a few phrases from the existing Statutes and follows the same format: a preamble and five sections (*razdely*). But there the similarities end. Each section has undergone substantial revision and expansion.[6] Section III from the 1971 Statutes on admissions procedures has been sharply cut back and incorporated into Section IV (the former Section II) on members' rights and responsibilities. The draft now simply states that new members are admitted according to special regulations passed by the Board; it adds that new members pay an initiation fee of 5 rubles and annual dues of 10 rubles (the graduated dues of up to 3 percent of monthly income are to be dropped). An entirely new and lengthy Section II has been added on Union activities in various cultural and social areas. The five sections now read: I. The Aims of the Union of Soviet Writers and Its Areas of Competence; II. The Basic Activities of the Union of Soviet Writers; III. The Organizational Structure of the Union of Soviet Writers; IV. The Rights and Responsibilities of Members; V. The Legal Rights of the Union of Soviet Writers, of the Republic Unions of Writers, of Union Organizations with Equal Status (meaning Moscow and Leningrad), and Other Local Branches.

The preamble of just one sentence sets the tone for the whole document:

> The Union of Soviet Writers is a voluntary, self-governing social and creative organization of professional writers, which operates on the basis of the Soviet Constitution and its own current Statutes, and grounds its activities in the principles of socialist democracy, openness, and the personal initiative and responsibility of each member.

Gorbachev's new legalism is reflected in the prominent reference to the Constitution and the Statutes. The obligatory mention of glasnost, together with an insistence on individual professional responsibilities, presents a strong contrast to the Union's proud claims in the much longer 1971 preamble that it was assisting in the creation of "the most just society on earth," as well as to its ex-cathedra pronouncements about "Soviet patriotism and socialist internationalism" and its global objectives of world peace and social justice. The 1989 document places emphasis on familiar Gorbachev buzzwords and phrases, not all of them new to Soviet political discourse: "pluralism" (*plyuralizm mneny*), "dialectical contradictions," "an atmosphere of candor and truthfulness," "democratization." Some of the phrases used are so shopworn that they have to be propped up with the word "genuinely" (*podlinno*): "genuinely humanistic and universal ideals," "genuinely creative competition among comrades"—an echo of the old Stalinist phrase "socialist competition" (*sotsialisticheskoe sorevnovanie*).

Subtle changes in tone and language run through the document, but they usually leave the Party's authority undiminished. For example, the word "tasks" (*zadachi*) in the title of the first section of the 1971 Statutes, "Tasks of the Union of Soviet Writers," is dropped in favor of the less imperative *tseli* ("aims" or "purpose") in Section I, Clause 1 of the new draft.[7] However, the Union is still said to be "guided" (*rukovodstvuetsya*) by the programmatic aims of the Communist Party and commits itself to accomplishing "the tasks of revolutionary perestroika." Significantly, the old Stalinist term *zadachi* creeps back into the draft when the current Party leader's main policy objective is mentioned.

The new Statutes may promise Union members more of a say in their affairs, but they still give writers assignments, even if those assignments are presented in less ideological terms. The old Section II on members' responsibilities and rights becomes Section IV, but with the order reversed: the word "rights" comes first. The list of rights repeats those of the 1971 version, but adds a new one that reflects the reality mentioned by several émigrés: the Union will protect members against any infringements on their creative or authorial rights and against "insults (*oskorblenia*) to their honor and dignity" (IV, 6). The latter phrase in its nineteenth-century flavor seems to confirm the comparison of the Union with the tsarist nobility (*dvoryanstvo*), and serves as a reminder that the Union includes many members of the Soviet elite.

The list of responsibilities (IV, 7) is very brief; it calls upon members not only to obey the Statutes and maintain lofty artistic standards, but also to carry out the decisions and "public service assignments" (*obshchestvennye poruchenia*) of the Union's ruling organs. Members are also obliged to overcome a bizarre combination of literary vices: "cliquishness (*gruppovshchina*), mutual back-scratching (*komplimentarnost*), and any manifestations of nationalism and chauvinism." This grouping may reflect some give-and-take in the commission: some members were willing to accept cliquishness if others would grant chauvinism. Failure to fulfill these responsibilities could expose a member to the same sequence of rebukes and reprimands that have existed since 1967. The draft still threatens expulsion for a grab-bag of sins including "failure to observe the principles and tasks (*zadachi*) of the Union," and "anti-social behavior" (IV, 9).

In spite of these atavistic phrases, throughout the draft there is an effort to disassociate the Union and its mission from Stalin and Brezhnev, although neither is mentioned by name. Instead of "struggling against bourgeois and revisionist influences" (1971), writers are now called upon to "struggle against routinism, inertia, and stagnation"—*rutina, kosnost,* and *zastoi* are all code words for the Brezhnev era. Although Brezhnev has been targeted by

Gorbachev and his supporters as the main cause of Soviet society's economic woes, in some cases the new draft simply reflects trends that developed in the late sixties and the seventies. The most notable example has been the slow decline of Socialist Realism, the method that had officially guided Soviet writers since 1934. Yury Verchenko, *orgsekretar* and co-chair of the special Union commission charged with reviewing the Statutes, had announced at the plenary session of the Board, held on March 1 and 2, 1988, that Socialist Realism would be kept as a requirement in the draft of the new Statutes. In fact, Socialist Realism is not mentioned anywhere in the draft, although the reluctance of some conservatives to see it disappear without a trace apparently led to the admonition that the Union should encourage works that are "realist in method and socialist in their ideals."

Both *partynost* and *narodnost* are retained, albeit "in their genuinely Leninist interpretation" (*v ikh podlinno leninskom ponimanii*). Socialist Realism can now be thrown overboard since it is associated with Stalin, while *partynost* and *narodnost* remain obligatory for Union members because they derive from two of Lenin's most seminal statements, *What Is To Be Done?* (1902), and "Party Organization and Party Literature" (1905). The third element of the Leninist trinity is also retained in the draft, when the Union's basic aim is said to include raising the "ideological and esthetic potential" (*ideino-estetichesky potentsial*) of Soviet literature. The compound word *ideino-estetichesky* has long been employed by orthodox Soviet critics as a strategy for giving *ideinost* artistic standing. The reaffirmation of these Leninist principles is key to Gorbachev's overall strategy for perestroika.[8]

In one important aspect the new draft continues a tradition begun by Stalin and expanded by Brezhnev: it reinforces the authority of the Union. The first section discusses not only the "aims" of the organization, but also its "areas of competence." It lays claim to overall responsibility for developing, financing, and legislating all of Soviet literature, including the book-publishing industry. It establishes the Union's authority to represent writers in disputes with other government agencies and institutions. A new clause (I, 3) asserts the right of the Union to take all available steps to curtail decisions by other government bodies that might threaten literature, publishing, or the individual rights of Union members. This new clause reflects the status of the Union as a powerful organization with both the desire and the clout to protect its fiefdom against potential interference by other bureaucracies.

An entirely new second section, "Basic Activities of the Soviet Union of Writers," and the revised Section V on the Union's legal rights, provide detailed evidence of the vast expansion of the Union's jurisdictional prerogatives that gained momentum during the Brezhnev era. Section V confirms the Union's legal right to sign contracts, create self-financing and cooperative enterprises, use credit, maintain the equivalent of checking and savings accounts, file suits, and respond to court action by others. Section II is, with Section III on organizational structure and procedures, the longest in the draft. It is divided into seven subsections designating various spheres of authority and influence: The Development of Soviet Literature, The Study and Formation of Public Opinion and the Scientific Interpretation of the Literary Process, Publishing and the Book Trade,[9] The Coordination of the Activities of Republic Branches, International Relations, Social and Public Activities, and Economic and Financial Activities.

The framers of the draft display considerable linguistic ingenuity in the wide variety of verbs they use to describe the Union's activities: create, develop, devise, organize, facilitate, publish, stimulate, encourage, establish, determine, confirm, recommend, decide, institute, carry out, dispatch, contract, and even control. Furthermore, the various activities of the Union are now organized functionally and suggest that the Union is creating new divisions within its organizational structure. For example, "creative trips," stipends and loans, and literary prizes and awards are all included under the first subsection, The Development of Soviet Literature, but a statement on the "construction of writers' clubs and other establishments in accord with the statutory aims of the Union" is located in the second subsection, The Study and Formation of Public Opinion and the Scientific Interpretation of the Literary Process. Litfund's activities are reviewed in the sixth subsection, "Social and Public Activities." The fifth subsection, on International Relations, establishes the Union's legislative and executive authority in this restricted and prestigious area. It sets policy, negotiates agreements with foreign groups, receives and sends delegations, recommends Soviet literary works for translation into foreign languages and decides which should receive prizes, and works with the Soviet Copyright Agency (VAAP) to defend authors' rights abroad. The Union is able to carry out its responsibilities in international relations in part because it has been granted access to foreign currency; at the end of the seventh subsection, brief reference is made to the fact that the Union conducts economic activities abroad with the use of its own hard currency fund (*valyutny fond*). This appears to be the first time that the existence of this fund has been officially acknowledged.

The equally long third section, "The Organizational Structure of the Soviet Union of Writers," leaves the basic structure of the Union unchanged, with one exception: there is no mention of the Litburo by name. The 1989 draft states:

> For the efficient resolution of everyday issues and of those issues that arise as a result of decisions taken by the Board (or the Secretariat), the Secretariat creates from its own membership a working secretariat (*rabochy sekretariat*), whose decisions, within its area of competence, are binding upon all organizations, institutions, and enterprises that fall under the Union's jurisdiction (III, 7).

Perhaps the *rabochy sekretariat* is designed to fulfill the same functions as the Litburo, but it more likely refers to the released secretaries, that is, full-time functionaries linked to the Party's Central Committee. Until there is further commentary and explanation available, it will be hard to tell how profound a change is being contemplated at the apex of the organization. Following past custom, the draft makes no reference to the appointment or election of a "secretary for organizational and creative work," nor to the *nomenklatura* or the Central Committee—all of which have played such a decisive role in the Union's affairs. These omissions should not be interpreted as meaning that they will disappear from the Union's affairs. Indeed, since Yury Verchenko still occupies his position, the draft's silence on the key elements that make up the Party's guidance system provides a useful reminder of the limits of glasnost, and perhaps of perestroika too.

The new draft repeats the claim that the national congress, held every five years, holds supreme authority, and that the Board serves in its place between congresses, but it gives much more detail on procedures than the 1971 Statutes. It also outlines new policies that are clearly aimed at wresting control of the Union from the hands of the "literary generals" without recourse to wholesale removal of personnel by the Politburo. There appears to be a deliberate effort to build up the Board's authority by listing its rights and responsibilities, some of which are new (III, 6). The Board determines the Union's annual budget, monitors the work of Republic branches and the Moscow and Leningrad organizations (which enjoy Republic status), decides on the number of people serving in the Secretariat, and two years after they are elected decides whether secretaries should continue in office or be replaced. The Board also has the new job of selecting candidates for the Congress of People's Deputies—the Union is entitled to send ten.

The draft suggests an increased role for the Board in its relationship to the Secretariat. The Board is given the assignment of implementing new procedures for the election of the Union's chief officers and "ruling organs." The draft speaks of "candidates" for the post of First Secretary being obliged to present a "program of activities" before the Board, as though in an election campaign. In an important switch, the vote for the First Secretary and other members of the secretariat is to be "direct and secret" (not open as always in the past), and there will be no restriction on the number of candidates. This provision appears specifically aimed at curtailing the manipulation of elections by a small group of top secretaries. Furthermore, the First Secretary and other members of the Secretariat may only serve for two consecutive five-year terms.

The draft proposes that the same ten-year limit be imposed "as a general rule" on all other executive officers: the president of Litfund, the president and vice-presidents of the Central Auditing Committee, the director and board of the "Sovetsky Pisatel" Publishing House, the rector of the Gorky Literary Institute, and the chief editors of all Union journals, newspapers, and periodicals. This Soviet version of the "Roosevelt rule," also used in Gorbachev's electoral reform, is evidently designed to bring about the early retirement of longtime Brezhnevites in the Union apparatus and to legalize the periodic removal of Union executives in the future. If approved, and if implemented, the ten-year limit would be a severe blow to the conservatives, who would lose control not only in the Secretariat but over several major journals. Without privileged access to the pages of these periodicals, they would have a hard time getting their works published, since few people want to read them.

The new voting procedures should create a more democratic atmosphere in the Union and encourage more accountability to the membership. They should serve also to give Gorbachev much greater control over the Union, since a few top secretaries could not arrange to have themselves "re-elected" to high office over long periods of time. Gorbachev, or his ideological advisers on cultural affairs, may be hoping to have the Board function more like the Central Committee, which plays a decisive part in the daily life of the country through its departments and agencies. Both bodies are about the same size with around 300 members (the Central Committee has additional candidate members who are not permitted to vote). However, in the draft, the Board is still required to meet "not less than once a year." To play a bigger role and to exercise its statutory authority over the Secretariat, it would have to hold plenums on a more frequent schedule, and meet for more than two or three days at a time.

Unless the Board is able to exercise much greater authority than in the past, it seems that the Secretariat will continue to dominate the Union to an equal if not greater extent than the Politburo dominates the Party. The draft for the first time refers specifically to the Secretariat as the Union's "executive body" (*ispolnitelny organ*). It exercises control (*osushchestvlyaet kontrol*) over all Union activities between congresses and plenums of the Board. The Secretariat is said to be subject to the Board, and yet it is given the authority to make and confirm all administrative appointments, as well as appointments of the chief editors and editorial staff of all Union publications, and of executive officers of all other Union organizations. This control over appointments is decisive and will present a problem for those who wish to make the Union function in a more democratic fashion. Both liberals and conservatives know well Stalin's lesson: "Cadres determine everything."

The 1971 Statutes close with the statement: "The Union of Soviet Writers may be abolished (*likvidirovan*) by order of a national congress." (A similar statement guaranteeing the right of a Soviet Republic to secede from the federal union is included in the Soviet Constitution.) The 1989 draft repeats this same idea, but suggests that the Republic, Moscow and Leningrad, and other local branches, are independent by stating that the decision that each cease operating must be taken by a congress of the relevant branch. It goes on to decree that all property belonging to such a branch should be returned to a designated government or public agency.

Gorbachev's ideological specialists in the Central Committee may have had to do some arm-twisting to ensure the inclusion of certain provisions that threaten to limit the authority of the "literary generals." But the question remains as to what effect this exemplary document will have on the Union's operations and the daily life of its members. Is this the beginning of a brave new world, or will it become yet another example of a utopian dream that gets lost in the Party's refusal to allow Soviet writers to seek their own way? Perhaps the performance of the Congress of People's Deputies and the new Supreme Soviet offer some hope for the future. The spirit of freedom manifested by deputies may prove infectious and encourage writers to stand up for their rights in the Union.

A spark was lit, even before the elections to the Congress of People's Deputies took place, and before the Union published the draft of the new Statutes, by a small group of writers in the Moscow branch of the Union. On March 10, 1989, "Writers for Perestroika" (*Pisateli v podderzhku perestroiki*) held the inaugural meeting of a new "April Committee," dedicated to changing the way the Union functions and to gaining more independence for its members. The

April Committee (the reference is to the critical plenum of the Central Committee in April 1985, a month after Gorbachev became General Secretary) met in the Union Club and Vladimir Karpov, the First Secretary, attended. He could not have been pleased with what he heard, because Anatoly Pristavkin, the chief figure behind the new movement, gave a speech declaring that the Union was undergoing a severe crisis, that its leaders seemed incapable of changing with the times.[10] He admitted that writers were no longer expelled, but charged that the Secretariat still treated writers according to the old Stalinist principle, as mere appendages to the Union's "iron organism." He suggested that not much had changed since the twenties, when Zamyatin said: "Other countries are proud of their writers, here they smash them in the face."

Pristavkin deplored the fact that Litfund still kept its income and activities a deep secret, and denounced a system in which some writers became millionaires, while others, celebrated throughout the country, were forced to "live on handouts" because they could not get their works published. Pristavkin declared that he and his colleagues had decided to fight against the lack of democratic procedures and elections; the April Committee would demand human rights for its members and also the freedom to offer opinions, whether or not they agreed with those of the Party. He chided the Union leadership for not assisting in the founding of "Memorial" and urged the need for a truthful history of the Union, including a complete accounting of the Union's role in suppressing its own members under Stalin and Brezhnev.

The inaugural meeting of the April Committee appears to have been well attended, and its mission popular with many writers. As of March 14, 1989, it had already attracted 305 members of the Moscow branch and also 17 non-Union writers. The Committee's Manifesto, very brief and informal (perhaps a deliberate contrast to the new draft of the Union's Statutes, which was published just a few days later), states that both Union members and nonmembers are welcome to join the new group without any statement as to qualifications or eligibility—dues are 10 rubles per year. The Manifesto is divided into four parts: Principles, Structure, Working Groups, and Membership. It speaks of the Union as no more than a government Ministry of Literature, which is incapable of achieving perestroika, and declares that the Union does not belong to its apparat any more than Soviet literature belongs to the Union. The purpose of the April Committee is to raise the reputation of writers and to restore their dignity.

As is the case of the Union itself, the highest organ of the new Committee is its general meeting, which elects a Provisional Council for one year. The size of this Council is not mentioned in the Manifesto, but at the inaugural meeting a group of 15 Moscow writers was elected to serve for the first year.[11] In addition, the Manifesto announced the election of 7 working groups, whose members all serve without compensation (clearly a hint at the highly paid and privileged "released secretaries" in the Union). The working groups are called: Rights and Responsibilities, Quick Reaction (to defend writers who are subjected to harassment or abuse of any kind), Publishing, Press Center, Cooperation (with other creative unions, religious groups and others, including PEN), Treasury (accounts), and Creative Reserve (to help beginning writers). The April Committee gives every appearance of taking a business-like approach; it has already obtained space in the Union Club building (room 207) and lists telephone numbers for those interested in joining or requesting information.

Some Western press accounts suggested that the April Committee had been established outside the Union and that its main purpose was to bring about the Union's demise. During the Thaw an unknown number of writers were reported to have urged that the Union be abolished. Under glasnost, calls for the Union to wind up its affairs have been renewed. At the March 1988 plenum of the Union Board, Vladimir Karpov, the First Secretary, ended a very long speech by mentioning that "some comrades" had made this modest proposal. Karpov defended the Union's existence by quoting the section in Lenin's 1905 article on "Party Organization and Party Literature" which argues that freedom of association is superior to freedom of speech, and asserts the right of the Party to control literature and to collectivize it.[12] By appealing to these particular words, Karpov was trying to outmaneuver his maverick comrades, because belief in Lenin is the crucial article of faith of the Party itself.

As long as the Union is perceived as a central part of the Leninist legacy, even though it was actually established by Stalin, then it can never be abolished, any more than the Party itself. But it is not just the Party that would object to any serious effort to abolish the Union; so too would the vast majority of Union members. They would lose their livelihood. How indeed would most Soviet writers manage without the Union? In March 1985, as Gorbachev took over the reins as General Secretary, Anatoly Gladilin was not very optimistic about their prospects in a hypothetical post-Union world of free enterprise in Soviet literature:

> If the Writers' Union were to disappear along with the Soviet system, it would be a real tragedy for the majority of writers.

> They would not be able to survive in a system of free competition. You see, in the Writers' Union they know whom to visit, whom to ask for help. But here [in the West] where would they go, whom could they ask for help in selling their books, and whom would they ask to publish them? None of them would know. The members of the Writers' Union know the rules of the game. If you suddenly dumped them here [Paris], they would be very unhappy people. They would run to President Mitterand or maybe to President Reagan, asking for help, demanding that the White House recommend their books for publication because they would not be able to understand why a publisher prints some books but not others.[13]

Gladilin stressed that since the Soviet system is bound to continue, it was important that the Union continue to exist also, not so much because of perks and privileges, but rather because it provides protection for its members against "naked" interference by the KGB, even possible arrest and execution in periods of severe repression.

Anatoly Pristavkin and his colleagues are perfectly well aware of these realities. A reading of the Manifesto and Pristavkin's speech should dispel any suggestion that the purpose of the April Committee is to dissolve the Union. The April Committee describes itself as an "independent grouping" (*nezavisimoe formirovanie*) within the Moscow organization of the Russian Republic branch of the Union. In a personal interview in August 1989, Anatoly Pristavkin made no mention of trying to close down the Union. On the contrary, he encapsulated the main aim of his group as an effort to reform the organization, to make it more responsive to the membership. He said that the secretariat of the Moscow branch had raised many obstacles to the formation of the April Committee, and admitted that he and his colleagues had had to struggle for a long time to overcome them; many problems still remained. But Pristavkin pointed out that the Committee was getting ready to publish its first almanac, full of "fascinating material." Furthermore, he and his fellow "writers for perestroika" were planning to put out a weekly newspaper and also a journal. In this way the Committee would try to break the monopoly of the Union over publication, and provide all writers, not simply those favored by the Secretariat, with a chance to see their works in print and to make a living as professional authors.

The April Committee is fighting an uphill battle, but has already made considerable progress. Its leaders must be receiving some support from the Party because the Committee is dedicated to perestroika and offers a way of embarrassing and perhaps outmaneuvering the established literary bureaucrats in the Union, who succeeded in resisting change much longer than their brethren in all the other creative unions. Nevertheless, some writers, including those who have joined the April Committee, remain nervous about its long-term prospects. During a visit to the United States in May 1989, the respected Soviet writer Tatyana Tolstaya linked the Committee's fate with that of the whole democratic movement:

> April could be a force if, if, if—If it develops a strategy, if it is based on common sense, if writers stop quarreling. That is many ifs. But Russians always go to extremes. This is the difficulty of building a democracy out of nothing. It is like a cat becoming a dog. It may be possible, but it will take a long time. And there will be a stage when the cat can no longer catch mice, and when she still can't bark.[14]

Whether the April Committee can help the Union make such a magical transformation remains to be seen. Since writers have as much to lose as the Party if the Union were abolished, then it seems logical that the destinies of both organizations will continue to be entwined. The one constant throughout the Union's history has been its close link with the Party. The Union's structure and procedures have been altered several times to respond to changes in the Party itself and its policies. The measured loosening of ideology's stranglehold in the Union's proposed Statutes parallels the democratization that has already taken place in the political sphere. The April committee is seeking to ride this wave.

Whatever impact the new Statutes might have on the democratization of the Union's operations, it is quite clear that they reinforce its power and prestige. Of the three pillars of the Soviet guidance system for literature, the Union alone has survived and even gained authority since the early thirties. Socialist Realism has now faded from view; and Glavlit and comparable censorship agencies have lost much of their earlier authority. *Glavrepertkom* (the theater censorship) has been instructed to keep a very low profile and permit the performance of plays which could not have taken place prior to Gorbachev's arrival. In much the same way Glavlit has taken a back seat in order to allow daring publications to appear.

The defanging of Glavlit has been a difficult process, with much backsliding. However, it has continued steadily. The First Secretary of the Writers' Union, now Vladimir Karpov, and the chief editor of *Ogonyok*, Vitaly Korotich, were quoted as saying during a debate on Soviet culture at the Edinburgh Festival in 1987 that censorship is virtually over in the Soviet Union. Apart from strategically sensitive subjects, nothing was forbidden anymore. Both said, however, that works by exiled writer Alexander Solzhenitsyn would remain unpublished. Karpov said (AP, August 11, 1987) that "Solzhenitsyn is too much of a politician and his politics are just untrue."

More promising comments about the reduced activities of Glavlit were made by the chief editor of *Novy mir*, Sergei Zalygin, when he met with specialists in Russian philology in Paris on March 5, 1987. The Radio Liberty correspondent, F. Salkazanova, reported Zalygin saying that

> . . . since he became chief editor of *Novy mir*, questions of publication . . . have been decided by the editorial board, not by other departments. Glavlit, which with the support of the Central Committee used to be able to block publication, . . . no longer decides this question. The censorship now examines works only to determine whether they divulge military secrets."[15]

Shortly thereafter, additional information about the place of censorship under glasnost came from an impeccable source in Moscow, namely, a member of Zalygin's own editorial board. This information was revealed in a talk given on May 15, 1987 by Anatoly Ivanovich Strelyany to the Komsomol *aktiv* of Moscow State University.[16] During the lively exchange with the audience, all of whom were of course Komsomol members, some very candid admissions were made. Such openness is customary at meetings of this kind, since many things can be spoken, but not published, in Soviet society:

QUESTION FROM THE FLOOR: Is it true that Zalygin, the editor of *Novy mir*, spoke in France about the removal of censorship?

STRELYANY: He anticipated things a bit. It's still there, only there's less of it. Every publishing house has a political editor [the Glavlit representative]. They are nice people and sympathize with us, they complain about how hard it is for them. But every single one of them has an enormous book of "what-you-can'ts" (*chego nelzya*) from the Council of Ministers, compiled on the basis of recommendations from ministries and departments. . . .

The book of "What-you-can'ts" to which Strelyany alludes is the notorious "Talmud"—the Glavlit censors' nickname for their index of forbidden topics, names, facts, books, and so forth.

The works of Alexander Solzhenitsyn became a test case of the determination of the new Soviet leadership to move from glasnost to perestroika. The sticking point was not so much Solzhenitsyn's portrayal of the Gulag, since its existence had already been acknowledged and condemned as part of the growing anti-Stalin campaign. The chief problem was the exiled writer's criticism of Lenin and his assault on many of the cherished notions of the Soviet regime. On the other hand, it was very much in Solzhenitsyn's favor that he was a Russian nationalist, and hence enjoyed the support of many established literary figures.

Vadim Medvedev, the new Party ideology secretary, said at a news conference in March 1989 that publication of Solzhenitsyn would do nothing less than "undermine the foundations on which our present life rests."[17] He was referring chiefly to *The Gulag Archipelago,* in which Solzhenitsyn argues that Lenin laid the foundation for Stalin by making use of terror against opponents, both actual and potential. For some liberal writers, however, Solzhenitsyn remains a great writer, and they wanted to test the outer limits of glasnost by "rehabilitating" his works. In late 1988 Sergei Zalygin, chief editor of *Novy mir,* was one of several prominent intellectuals, including members of the Union of Cinematographers, who began a campaign to restore Solzhenitsyn's official reputation. Although Solzhenitsyn in September 1988 refused an invitation to become a member of "Memorial," the voluntary organization established in Moscow to explore the Stalinist repressions of innocent victims, Zalygin went ahead with plans to publish Solzhenitsyn's "Nobel Lecture" in the December 1988 issue of *Novy mir* and extracts from *The Gulag Archipelago* in the January 1989 issue.[18] The back cover of the October 1988 issue of *Novy mir* announced these planned publications. Suddenly, high Party officials, bypassing Zalygin and his editorial board, ordered printers to destroy the cover and replace it (much the same thing had happened to Tvardovsky at *Novy mir* in the mid-sixties). The emotions of Zalygin, the man who had previously declared that since he became chief editor of *Novy mir* all editorial questions had been decided internally without interference from the Central Committee, can be imagined. A man of courage and great prestige, he requested and was granted an audience with Gorbachev. A *samizdat* account of this meeting shows Gorbachev in an uncharacteristically angry mood:

> The boss (*vozhd*) of perestroika stamped his feet in the Khrushchev manner and used the familiar form of address with the seventy-five-year-old prose writer [Zalygin], who had entered into an unequal battle for the interests and honor of Russian literature.[19]

The reference to Khrushchev is particularly appropriate. It seems that one or more Party apparatchiks had told Gorbachev that Zalygin was planning to publish sections of *The Gulag Archipelago* that attacked Lenin, although this was not true. Gorbachev took the bait, just as Khrushchev had done when he attended the exhibit of modernist paintings at the Manezh Exhibition Hall in December 1962.

Many highly placed intellectuals of all shades of opinion wrote to Gorbachev protesting the decision to prohibit the publication of Solzhenitsyn's works. At first, Gorbachev would not relent, but finally he was persuaded to change his mind. Sergei Zalygin was able to announce that *The Gulag Archipelago* would be published after all. What is more, in June 1989 the journal *Oktyabr* published, as promised, an even more direct assault on Lenin's role as Stalin's predecessor and the destroyer of Russian freedom—Vasily Grossman's part-novel, part-essay, *Forever Flowing . . .* (*Vse techet . . .*).

With the publication of *The Gulag Archipelago* and *Forever Flowing . . .*, it would seem that Glavlit has finally been defanged. Given the apparent certainty that the Union will continue to exist and flourish, and be closely linked to the Party, what are the chances that the next Russian winner of the Nobel Prize for Literature will be a member in good standing of the Writers' Union, since 4 of the first 5 winners were not?[20] Will the Union, as an agency of Party "guidance," continue to prevent writers of genuine talent from publishing their works within a reasonable time and without interference or gratuitous censoring? Or will Russian literature be obliged to pursue its underground existence, with publications in *samizdat* and *tamizdat*? It is very difficult, and perhaps unwise, to attempt definite answers to such broad questions. Western forecasters of change in Soviet society have about as good a track record as the economic managers in Gosplan. Only a dyed-in-the-wool pessimist would argue that the future of Russian literature will closely resemble its past over the first seventy years of Soviet rule, and only a Marxist would argue that it must develop according to a specific blueprint. But what evidence there is suggests qualified hope.

The revival of Russian literature does not depend on the immediate publication in the Soviet Union of Solzhenitsyn's works, either in part or in whole; conversely, the decision to publish his works is no guarantee for the future of Russian literature. Nor is it necessary for serious authors to attack Lenin in order to write good fiction or poetry. What is necessary is to remove the Union insofar as it is a barrier between writer and reader. The Union does not have to cease being an organization, but it must cease being the Party's organizational weapon. This process may have already begun. Socialist Realism, described by one émigré as the "grip of the state," has been omitted from the new Statutes; perhaps that grip may be loosening. Even more startling and promising is the formation of the April Committee—a rival group in the Union, with access to the media and the potential ability to attract members and money to its cause. We can expect the April Committee to follow up on the commitment in its Manifesto to "take an active part" in discussing the new draft of the Union's Statutes, and perhaps also to monitor compliance with its democratic provisions.

It remains to be seen, however, if the "method of collective work on literary material," prescribed by Gorky at the First Congress, will be quietly abandoned. This method is the meeting, and it is in meetings that creativity drains away. Many literary masterpieces have been written in isolation, even in prison: Paul's Letter to the Thessalonians, Boethius' *Consolation of Philosophy*, and Milton's *Paradise Lost* are but a few. Nothing of note in literature has ever been created in a meeting.

The proposed Statutes are a significant step in the direction of individual freedom. The great skill with which they were written is evident when one considers that they simultaneously reinforce the Leninist principles of *partynost* and *narodnost* while quietly abandoning Lenin's dream of utopia. The end of what the British scholar Terry McNeill has termed "violent utopianism" and the abandonment of a "hopeless utopian experiment" are having a serious, and probably lasting impact, on Soviet literature.[21] A great majority of Soviet intellectuals perceive that Marxist-Leninist theories and pronouncements have as little value in literature as they do in economics. Socialist Realism is in tatters as an artistic credo and has finally been officially abandoned.

Perhaps the Soviet "cultural intelligentsia" is at long last relearning the lessons taught by the great Russian writers of the past, particularly Dostoevsky, who warned that a utopian socialist experiment would inevitably fail because it was based on a false conception of human nature. In *Notes from Underground* Dostoevsky ridiculed Chernyshevsky's utopian vision in *What Is to Be Done?*, but his most extensive examination of the inherent contradiction of trying to bring about a brave new world through "violent utopianism" is *The Devils* (*Besy*), which appeared in 1871. Unfortunately for the Russian people (and many of their neighbors), Dostoevsky's lessons were lost on a radicalized reading public that was diverted the following year by the publication of a Russian translation of Karl Marx's *Das Kapital*. Undaunted, writers, more than any other group, have tried to prick the Marxist-Leninist balloon. Yevgeny Zamyatin wrote his anti-utopian novel *We* in 1920, even before the Soviet Union came into existence as a state (1922).

And as early as 1921, during his farewell address on Pushkin, Alexander Blok argued that poets would always be at odds with the Soviet regime, because it sought to rob them of their "secret inner freedom." Perhaps the Party now itself has realized that such freedom does not threaten its own political hegemony.

Soviet Russian writers are no longer bound by the Statutes of their organization to "struggle for the construction of communism, for social progress, for peace and friendship among nations." It would seem that they are free once again to address the "accursed questions" of human existence that bedevil twentieth-century men and women as much as they did those who lived under the tsars. If and when they return to their cultural roots, Russian writers will recapture their Soviet and foreign audience, and return their country's literature to its rightful place on the world stage. The Soviet writer and the Soviet reader will not be the only ones to benefit from this change in focus: the Soviet government will find its coffers immensely enriched as well. And that will mean that not only glasnost but also perestroika have occurred in Soviet publishing. Lenin's utopia, the land envisaged by the Radiant Beauty, will still lie beyond the horizon, but such an arrangement might be an acceptable compromise here on earth, where human beings must live in Plato's "mixed elements."

APPENDIX

Facts and Figures

Union Membership

Year	Total	Male	%	Party	%	Educ	%	51+	%	61+	%
1934	2194										
1954	3695										
1959	4801										
1967	6567	5687	89.3	3592	54.7	4116	62.7	3352	51.0	1352	20.6
1971	7270	6271	86.3	4048	55.7	4880	67.1	3903	53.7	2101	28.9
1976	7833	6736	85.9	4550	58.1	5663	72.3	4604	58.8	2550	32.6
1981	8669	7392	85.2	5157	59.5	6686	77.1	5498	63.4	2943	33.9
1986	9561	8075	84.5	5636	58.9	7785	81.4	6219	65.0	3395	35.5

Note 1. Breakdown of total membership was not published for first three congresses.
Note 2. "Educ" means those with higher education (post-secondary school).
Note 3. "51+" and "61+" indicates all members who were 51 years or older, or 61 years or older, at the time of the congress.
Note 4. Membership for 1954 includes 553 candidate, or probationary, members. At the 1954 congress, the admission of candidate members to the Union was discontinued. However, many candidate members still remained in the Union.
Note 5. Party membership for 1967 includes 39 candidate members. Candidate members of the Party are usually included as full members for statistical purposes in Soviet publications. Not included in the 1967 figures are 83 members of the Komsomol.

SOURCE: Statistical data ("Statisticheskie spravki") provided in verbatim reports of Writers' Union congresses.

Congress Delegates

Year	*Total*	*Male*	%	*Party*	%	*Educ*	%	*51+*	%	*61+*	%
1934	597	570	95.5		52.8						
1954	738	654	88.6	522	70.7	359	48.6	228	30.9	53	7.2
1959	497	464	93.4	377	75.8	251	50.5	252	50.7	64	12.9
1967	525	493	93.9	403	76.8	310	59.0	380	72.4	170	32.4
1971	527	488	92.6	432	82.0	335	63.6	321	60.9	159	30.2
1976	567	527	92.4	462	81.5	401	70.7	381	67.2	189	33.3
1981	588	552	93.9	496	84.3	445	75.7	427	72.6	235	40.0
1986	567	523	92.2	475	83.8	461	81.3	432	76.2	248	43.7

Note 1. Not all delegates actually attend the congresses, due to health or other problems.
Note 2. Delegates in 1934 included 377 with voting rights (*s reshayushchim golosom*) and 220 with non-voting rights (*s soveshchatelnim golosom*), since at that time the Union admitted both full members and candidate, or probationary, members. There is some confusion about the number of delegates, since Soviet sources state there were 590; this does not jibe with the listed names of voting and non-voting delegates. At the 1934 congress 7.6% of the delegates belonged to the Komsomol, and were grouped with Party members and candidates to form a total of 60.4%.
Note 3. No figures for higher education or age were given for 1934. However, the congress report states that at least 420 of the 597 delegates were 40 or under.
Note 4. By 1967 the Union no longer admitted candidate members. However, no less than 112 candidates admitted in previous years were delegates to the congress, although without voting rights.
Note 6. The sudden jump in older delegates in 1967 (both those 51 years or older and 61 years or older) probably results from efforts under Brezhnev to consolidate the Party's authority and to exclude younger delegates, who had risen to prominence during the Thaw. These efforts may also explain the unusually low number of delegates, and the fact that 16 members of the Secretariat, not elected as delegates, were said to be "taking part in the work of the congress."

SOURCE: Reports of the Accreditation Committee (*Mandatnaya komissia*) at the Writers' Union congresses.

Repressed and Liquidated Writers

We may never have a complete list of members of the Writers' Union, let alone of all professional writers, who were "repressed" under Stalin (and at other times in Soviet history). Under glasnost, various Soviet individuals and institutions have been trying to assemble accurate lists; these expand considerably the names of more famous literary victims mentioned in Western histories of Russian literature, most notably by Gleb Struve, *Russian Literature under Lenin and Stalin 1917–1953*, p. 282.

The following lists, which include writers of all Soviet nationalities, sometimes overlap. They do not always distinguish between members and non-members of the Union, or between those writers who died and those who survived the Gulag. However, the lists are valuable contributions to the final goal of a complete accounting. All names are transliterated directly from the Cyrillic; non-Russian names may not therefore reflect correct spelling in the original language.

1. Professor I. Eventov, who attended the First Congress of Writers, provided two lists which distinguish between those who attended the 1934 Congress and those who were not delegates, but not between those who died and those who survived. Eventov implies that most of the people he mentions were members of the Writers' Union. Perhaps because their fate is common knowledge, he does not include a few of the most famous victims: the poet Osip Mandelshtam, the theater director Vsevolod Meyerhold, the literary critic Dmitry Mirsky, the poet Nikolai Klyuev.

Delegates at the 1934 Congress:

I. Babel, R. Bauze, Yu. Berzin, D. Bergelson, N. Brykin, N. Bukharin, A. Vesyoly, Ya. Virtanen, D. Vygodsky, A. Gorelov, D. Gofshtein, A. Zorich, A. Kamegulov, I. Kataev, L. Kvitko, V. Kirshon, M. Koltsov, B. Kornilov, I. Kulik, A. Lebedenko, I. Nusinov, I. Lezhnev, G. Lelevich, Z. Lozinsky, M. Maizel, I. Makaryev, A. Makedonov, P. Markish, I. Mikitenko, N. Nakoryakov, B. Pilnyak, K. Radek, M. Rozental, N. Svirin, A. Selivanovsky, L. Subotsky, T. Tabidze, A. Tarasov-Rodionov, S. Tretyakov, I. Fefer, Ye. Charents, M. Shkapskaya, B. Yasensky, R. Eideman, P. Yashvili.

Others (presumably members of the Union):

D. Al, G. Belykh, O. Berggolts, G. Venus, A. Voronsky, S. Galkin, M. Gerasimov, T. Gnedich, I. Grossman-Roshchin, G. Gukovsky, V. Dneprov, S. Dreiden, A. Zhigulin, N. Zabolotsky, A. Zonin, V. Karpov, V. Kirillov, S. Klychkov, V. Knyazev, S. Kolbasyev, D. Kugultinov, K. Kuliev, B. Lifshits, D. Likhachev, A. Leskov, I. Mashbits-Verov, P. Medvedev, P. Oreshin, A. Piotrovsky, L. Radishchev, L. Razgon, S. Rodov, G. Serebryakova, Ya. Smelyakov, V. Stenich, S. Spassky, Ye. Taratuta, D. Kharms, V. Shalamov, V. Erlikh.

SOURCE: I. Eventov, "Spor o poezii i sud istorii," *Literaturnaya gazeta*, November 9, 1988, p. 3.

It is not clear whether "V. Karpov" refers to the current First Secretary of the Writers' Union; rumor has it that he was arrested and spent some time in the camps.

Some of these victims survived the camps, including Dmitry Likhachev, a member of the Academy of Sciences and the leading authority on early Russian literature. Likhachev outlines his experiences prior to the Great Purge in the far north camp at Solovki and later on the White Sea Canal (1928–32) in his letter to *Ogonyok*, no. 28 (July 1988). Likhachev's letter serves as a salutary reminder that many thousands of people were being arrested and sent to the camps and projects (where they often died) well before Kirov's assassination. The difference after December 1, 1934 was that the victims included Party officials and other loyalists.

The Soviet *Kratkaya Literaturnaya Entsiklopedia* includes entries on most of the writers on Eventov's lists, mentioning the date (but usually not the place) of death of the following writers, adding the ritualistic phrase: "Illegally repressed, posthumously rehabilitated" (*Nezakonno repressirovan, posmertno reabilitirovan*):

> Babel (1941), Bergelson (1952), Vesyoly (1937), Gerasimov (1939), Gofshtein (1952), Gukovsky (1950), Zorich (1937), Kamegulov (1937), Kataev (1939), Kvitko (1952), Kirillov (1943), Kirshon (1938), Klychkov (1940), Knyazev (1937 or 1938), Koltsov (1942), Kolbasyev (1942), Kornilov (1938), Kulik (1941), Lelevich (1945), Markish (1952), Medvedev (1938), Mikitenko (1937), Nusimov (1950), Oreshin (1938), Pilnyak (1937), Piotrovsky (1938), Svirin (1944), Selivanovsky (1938), Stenich (1939), Tabidze (1937), Tarasov-Rodionov (1938), Tretyakov (1939), Fefer (1952), Kharms (1942), Yashvili (1937).

Virtanen (1939), Voronsky (1943), Charents (1937) and Shkapsaya (1952) are not listed as having been either repressed or rehabilitated. In no case does the KLE mention the arrest and imprisonment of those writers who survived.

2. The most complete list of literary victims has been compiled by Eduard Beltov, an editor at the journal *Druzhba narodov*. Over many years he has assembled data of 17,000 public figures in culture, politics, and the military. During an interview he mentioned several names of well-known writers in Russian who had died or been killed during the Stalin era, noting that they represented all possible esthetic and political viewpoints. Again, like Eventov, Beltov does not bother to mention the most famous names:

> Arkady Bukhov, Ivan Vasilyevsky, Vladimir Narbut, Alexander Vorovsky, Aleksei Gastev, Leopold Averbakh, Illarion Vardin, Sergei Dinamov, Aleksei Selivanovsky, Rodion Akulshin, Gleb Alekseyev, Sergei Budantsev, Ivan Vasilyev, Alexander Zava-

lyshin, Victor Kin, Sergei Klychkov, Ivan Kasatkin, Ivan Kataev, Vladimir Kirillov, Vasily Knyazev, Pyotr Oreshin, Ivan Pribludny, Sergei Tretyakov, Sergei Amaglobeli.

Beltov also lists groups of writers from non-Russian literatures who lost their lives. The major target among these appear to have been Ukrainian writers, whose continued persecution over several decades he describes as "indescribable." Beltov estimates that as many as 500 Ukrainian writers and critics were arrested and 150 of these died or were shot. He only mentions three names: Dmitry Falkovsky, Oles Dosvitny, Aleksei Vlyzko.

Belorussian literature suffered similar blows; in fact, after a promising start in the 1920s and early 1930s, it practically disappeared. Beltov says that those few surviving Belorussian writers, such as Yakub Kolas, wrote almost nothing, expecting that their turn would come next.

Beltov says that Jewish literature suffered "a crushing blow" with writers being arrested both before and after World War II. He lists the following victims: David Bergelson, Perets Markish, Itsik Fefer, Lev Kvitko.

Among Armenian writers who died were 41 members of the Union: most of them were founding members and many were of an advanced age. Beltov mentions the following: Sarkis Mubladzhyan (pseud. Atrpet), Abraam Zamenyan, Gevorg Karadzhyan, Arutyun Chuguryan, Sogomon Melik-Shakhnazaryants, Emin Ter-Grigoryan, Konstantin Melik-Shakhnaryan (pseud. Khachan Tmblachi).

Beltov lists the following victims from the smaller literatures, some of them barely starting to emerge:

Udmurt literature lost Kuzma Chainikov (pseud. Kusebai Gerd), Mitrei Kedra, Mikhail Konovalov, Grigory Medvedev;

Altai literature lost Pavel Chagatstroev, Ivan Toltok, Nikandr Chevalkov;

Bashkir literature lost Abdula Amantai, Gusei Davletshin, Ivan Nedolzhi, Afaal Tagirov;

Kabardinian literature lost Mukhamed Afaunov, Karachai Blaev, Tutu Borukaev, Pshemakhs Keshokov, Sosruko Kozhaev, Dzhansokh Naloev;

Kazakh literature lost Saken Seifulin, Yalzhas Bekenov, Mozhit Dauletbaev, Ilyas Dzhansugurov, Sattar Yerubaev, Magzhan Zhumabaev, Turmagambet Iztleuov;

Tajik literature lost Rashid Abdulo, Ali Khush, Guzhyan Zafari, Said Rezo Ali-zade;

In addition, more than twenty Ossete writers died, but Beltov does not list any names. Nor does he mention the names of Georgian writers, although he is aware that Georgia lost two of its best-known authors, Titsian Tabidze and Paolo Yashvili.

SOURCE: "Eto nuzhno ne myortvym—zhivym . . . ," *Knizhnoe obozrenie*, June 17, 1988, p. 7.

Members of the Litburo (1970–86)

1970: K. A. Fedin, president; G. M. Markov, first vice-president; S. V. Sartakov, vice-president; S. A. Baruzdin; Yu. N. Verchenko; S. V. Mikhalkov; V. M. Ozerov; N. S. Tikhonov; A. B. Chakovsky.

SOURCE: *Pyaty syezd* (Moscow, 1972), p. 178.

1971: G. M. Markov, president; Yu. N. Verchenko, V. M. Ozerov, S. V. Sartakov, vice-presidents; A. P. Keshokov; V. M. Kozhevnikov; M. K. Lukonin; S. V. Mikhalkov; S. S. Narovchatov; K. M. Simonov; N. S. Tikhonov; N. T. Fedorenko; A. B. Chakovsky.

SOURCE: *Shestoi syezd* (Moscow, 1978), p. 639.

1976: G. M. Markov, president; Yu. N. Verchenko, V. M. Ozerov, S. V. Sartakov, vice-presidents; A. P. Keshokov; V. M. Kozhevnikov; M. K. Lukonin; S. V. Mikhalkov; S. S. Narochatov; K. M. Simonov; Yu. I. Surovtsev; N. S. Tikhonov; N. T. Fedorenko; A. B. Chakovsky, O. N. Shestinsky.

SOURCE: *Sedmoi syezd* (Moscow, 1983), p. 548.

1981: G. M. Markov, president; Yu. N. Verchenko, V. M. Ozerov, S. V. Sartakov, vice-presidents; M. N. Alekseyev; A. A. Ananyev; Ye. A. Isaev; V. M. Kozhevnikov; A. P. Keshokov; F. F. Kuznetsov; V. V. Karpov; S. V. Mikhalkov; Yu. I. Surovtsev; A. B. Chakovsky; N. T. Fedorenko; O. N. Shestinsky.

SOURCE: *Vosmoi syezd* (Moscow, 1988), p. 455.

1986: Ch. T. Aitmatov; G. Ya. Baklanov; Yu. V. Bondarev; V. V. Bykov; A. T. Gonchar; S. P. Zalygin; V. V. Karpov; G. M. Markov; Yu. N. Verchenko.

SOURCE: *Pravda*, July 2, 1986.

Executive Personnel in Central Committee Departments of Culture and of Propaganda (1987)

The following chart of Central Committee Department of Culture and of Propaganda identifies apparatchiks charged with the responsibility for the Union as of mid-1987.

Central Committee Department of Propaganda:

Head	Yury Aleksandrovich Sklyarov
First Deputy Heads	Pyotr Yakovlevich Slezko
	Albert Ivanovich Vlasov
Deputy Heads	Nail Barievich Bikkenin
	Vladimir Nikolaevich Sevruk
	Nikolai Vladimirovich Shishlin
	Vyacheslav Ivanovich Zarubin

All these men were appointed or else first identified in their positions in 1986, except for Bikkenin (identified in 1985) and Sevruk (identified in 1976).

Central Committee Department of Culture:

Head	Yury Petrovich Voronov
First Deputy Head	Yevgeny Vladimirovich Zaitsev
Deputy Head	V. K. Yegorov

The first two were also appointed in 1986, while Yegorov was first identified in 1987 [*Literaturnaya gazeta,* August 26, p. 2]; he had replaced Yury Afanasyev, who had first been identified in 1974, meaning that he was a Brezhnev appointee.

SOURCE: Alexander Rahr, "The Apparatus of the Central Committee of the CPSU," RL 136/87 (April 10, 1987). Mr. Rahr has produced several very useful tables and biographies of leading Soviet officials over the years. Zaitsev replaced a rare top female apparatchik as First Deputy Head: Z. P. Tumanova served in that position for at least a decade, being listed as a member of the Presidium at the Fourth Congress of the RSFSR Writers' Organization. See *Chetvyorty syezd pisatelei RSFSR. Stenografichesky otchet* (Moscow, 1977), p. 7.

Notes

PROLOGUE
52 Vorovsky Street

1. A visit in August 1989 revealed that the beautiful mansion had been left to deteriorate to such an extent that scaffolding was necessary to lend support to the pillars of the central complex. Apparently, the building will be retained for ceremonial occasions, but the Secretariat is planning to move to more modern and more sturdy quarters lower down on Vorovsky Street within two or three years.
2. A detailed discussion of the Republic and other regional branches of the Union lies beyond the scope of this book. For a brief introduction to this important topic, see Paul Goble, "Readers, Writers, and Republics: The Structural Basis of Non-Russian Literary Politics," in Mark Beissinger and Lubomyr Hajda, eds., *Soviet Nationality Problems* (Boulder, CO: Westview Press, 1989).
3. For detailed statistics on Union membership and congress delegates, see the Appendix, "Facts and Figures," at the end of the book.
4. Maya Ganina took the floor at the Eighth Union Congress to complain to the delegates: "There is not a single woman on the Presidium of our congress! The Writers' Union treats women as an evil force: it pretends they don't exist, but it fears them." *Literaturnaya gazeta,* July 2, 1986.

   Alexandra P. Biryukova became a candidate (or non-voting) member of the Politburo in the fall of 1988. She is only the second woman to approach these heights in the Party hierarchy. For a few years during the Khrushchev period, Yekaterina Furtseva served as a full member of the Politburo; she resigned in 1961. Women have not fared much better in the government apparatus. However, Biryukova herself argues that women's lack of representation in the upper echelons of power results from their "natural" inclination toward children and family. See Annette Bohr, "Resolving the Question of Equality for Soviet Women—Again," *Report on the USSR,* vol. 1, no. 14 (Radio Liberty, April 7, 1989), pp. 10–16.

5. So, for example, a 1987 reference work on members of the Moscow branch of the Union was simply titled *Pisateli Moskvy*, that is, *The Writers of Moscow*, as though non-members could not be considered writers and were not worth including.

6. See *Spravochnik Soyuza Pisatelei SSSR* (Moscow, 1986), pp. 759–81 and 764–83. These lists of what are called *pechatnye organy* ("printed organs") include periodicals published not only in Russian, but in many other languages of the Soviet Union. The *Spravochnik* or *Directory* is published every five years in connection with the national Congress of Writers.

   For a composite list of Union newspapers, journals and almanacs, see *Vosmoi syezd pisatelei SSSR. Stenografichesky otchet* (Moscow, 1988), pp. 495–97.

7. Yu. D. Severin, ed., *Kommentary k Ugolovnomy Kodeksu RSFSR*, 3d. ed., revised and expanded (Moscow, 1984), pp. 44–45. Perhaps it is a sign of the times that Article 21 was amended in 1987 to include, under "other forms of parasitical existence," failure to pay alimony or child support, as well as disobeying the passport system; that is, failing to carry the internal passport required of all Soviet citizens from the age of sixteen; it shows among other things the citizen's marital status and nationality—Russian, Jewish, Ukrainian, and so forth. See *Vedomosti RSFSR* (Moscow, 1987), no. 43, item 1501, p. 927.

8. *Tvorcheskie soyuzy v SSSR* (*Organizatsionno-pravovye voprosy*) (Moscow, 1970), pp. 174–76. This is the only book-length analysis in any language dealing with the Writers' Union and similar organizations established for the "creative intelligentsia."

9. The Soviet Union has exported the "creative union" concept throughout Eastern Europe, as well as to the People's Republic of China, Cuba, Nicaragua, Afghanistan, and other countries where it has, or had, influence.

10. In late 1988, Soviet newspaper articles suggested that schoolteachers and lawyers should form their own unions. It is not always made explicit whether these would be creative unions, but it is almost certainly what these professionals have in mind, because of the professional prestige and material benefits that creative unions are known to provide. See, for example, V. Nastichenko, "Byt li soyuzu sovetskikh advokatov?" *Sovetskaya kultura* (December 8, 1988), p. 2.

    Under glasnost, Mikhail Gorbachev (himself trained as a lawyer at Moscow State University) has encouraged a broad re-examination of the Soviet Constitution and legal system, with a view to removing some of their unusual aspects. The Soviet press now contains articles advocating the "presumption of innocence" (*prezumptsia nevinnosti*)—the word *prezumptsia* has been borrowed, as well as the concept.

11. Personal interview in Paris, March 1985.

12. The root meaning of *rukovodstvo* is "leading by the hand." We translate the term as "guidance," but other meanings in English are "leader-

ship" and "direction." The term was probably used so as to avoid the harsher word "control" (*kontrol*).

13. *KPSS o kulture, prosveshchenii i nauke* (Moscow, 1963), pp. 181–82.
14. *Tvorcheskie soyuzy v SSSR*, p. 36, quoting with approval a book by I. F. Volkov, *Partynost iskusstva* (Moscow, 1966).
15. These arguments and quotations are taken from Yury Surovtsev, "The Union of Soviet Writers as a Professional Public Organisation," in *The Union of Soviet Writers: Aims, Organisation, Activities* (Moscow: Progress, 1981), pp. 5–12. Hereafter cited as *Aims*.
16. Quoted in *The Writers' Union of Canada: A Directory of Members* (Toronto: Writers' Union of Canada, 1981).
17. *Tvorcheskie soyuzy v SSSR*, p. 18.
18. *Aims*, p. 8.
19. *Ustav Soyuza Pisatelei SSSR* (Moscow, 1971). The draft of the proposed revised version of the Statutes, published in *Literaturnaya gazeta* (March 22, 1989), p. 3, lays out the Union's objectives in a less global manner. The new version is reviewed in Chapter 8.

CHAPTER 1
Organizing Utopia

1. Objective writing about the political situation did get into print in other areas—for example, in philosophy and theology—but it did not reach nearly as broad an audience as literature.
2. For an excellent discussion of these issues, see Rufus W. Mathewson, Jr., *The Positive Hero in Russian Literature*, 2d ed., enlarged (Stanford University Press, 1975).
3. N. G. Chernyshevsky, *Chto delat? Iz rasskazov o novykh lyudyakh* (Moscow, 1959), p. 294. All quotes are taken from this edition, published for use in Soviet secondary schools.

   The exhortatory tone and the repetition of phrases are typical of Chernyshevsky's style, a style that Dostoevsky parodied to great effect in *Notes from Underground*. However, Chernyshevsky's purpose demanded this kind of rhetoric, which is also typical of Lenin's polemics. Dostoevsky was parodying Lenin before the event.
4. Russians generally shared the favorable nineteenth-century European view of America as a great land of opportunity. Later in the novel a character says:

   > In America a man can be a cobbler's apprentice or be ploughing fields one day, become a general the next day, and president the day after that; then again a clerk or a lawyer. Americans are a peculiar people (*osoby narod*). All they want to know about a man is how much he earns and how much he knows. (p. 327)

5. Chernyshevsky gives an extensive portrait of Rakhmetov in Chapter 29, entitled "An Unusual Man" (*Osobenny chelovek*), pp. 202–18.

6. The work's great success continued to infuriate political conservatives well into the twentieth century, but it found defenders even among exiles in the West who had been defeated and driven out of Russia by the Bolsheviks. When Vladimir Nabokov satirized Chernyshevsky in a chapter of his novel, *The Gift* (*Dar*), leftwing exiles refused to publish the offending chapter; it only appeared in an English edition.

7. In many instances women abandoned their husbands and children; this was the case with the captivating Frenchwoman, Inessa Armand, whose action was directly inspired by her favorite revolutionary book, *What Is To Be Done?* She became a close, and some say intimate, associate of Lenin. At one time, before the Revolution of 1917, he lived with Armand and his wife Nadezhda Krupskaya in a *ménage à trois* reminiscent of that described in Chernyshevsky's novel. See Bertram D. Wolfe, "Lenin and Inessa Armand," in Bertram D. Wolfe, *Revolutionary and Reality: Essays on the Origin and Fate of the Soviet System* (Chapel Hill: University of North Carolina Press, 1981), pp. 81–97.

8. As quoted in *Lincoln Day by Day: A Chronology 1809–1865*, ed. Earl Schenck Miers (Washington, DC, 1960), vol. 3, p. 121.

9. On the role of utopianism in Marx and in Soviet thinking, see Jerome M. Gilison, *The Soviet Image of Utopia* (Baltimore: Johns Hopkins University Press, 1975).

10. Philip Selznick pointed out in his book, *The Organizational Weapon* (New York: McGraw-Hill, 1952), p. 6:

> For Lenin, organization was an indispensable adjunct to ideology. He did not believe that he could win power by propaganda alone. Rather he urged the need to forge a group which, beginning with an ideological commitment, would use whatever means were available to influence decision in society. For him, the task was not so much to spread the "truth" as to raise to power a select group of communicants.

This view is shared by Merle Fainsod in his benchmark work, *How Russia Is Ruled* (Cambridge: Harvard University Press, 1953). See section "Organization: The Elite Party," in the revised edition (1963), pp. 39–48.

For a dissenting opinion, see Robert C. Tucker, "Lenin's Bolshevism as a Culture in the Making," in a collection of articles: *Bolshevik Culture*, ed. Abbott Gleason, Peter Kenez, and Richard Stites (Bloomington: Indiana University Press, 1985), pp. 25–38.

11. See the second section of *Chto delat?*, entitled "Stikhynost mass i soznatelnost sotsialdemokratii," in *V. I. Lenin, Polnoe sobranie sochineny*, 5th ed., Vol. 6 (Moscow, 1959), pp. 28–53. This "brochure" (as Lenin himself called it) was originally published in Stuttgart and then smuggled into Russia. For a good translation into English, accompanied by an informative introduction and notes, see *V. I. Lenin's What Is*

To Be Done?, edited and translated by S. V. and Patricia Utekhin (London: Oxford University Press, 1963).

12. Unlike *What Is To Be Done?* and almost all Lenin's other writings, the article was not published outside Russia in the clandestine revolutionary press, but in St. Petersburg and legally. It was allowed because Tsar Nicholas II loosened press restrictions in an attempt to defuse the widespread unrest that had followed Russia's humiliating defeats in the Russo-Japanese war. Lenin laid out Bolshevik policy under the changed conditions, arguing for an end to "Aesopian language" and for open "partisanship" in the media.

    Lenin's article appeared in issue No. 12, for November 13, of the newspaper *Novaya zhizn* (*New Life*). The paper was shut down in December after the Bolsheviks, led by Trotsky, attempted a premature armed uprising in the capital.

13. All translations are our own and are taken from the text of the article included in *Russkaya literatura XX veka: Dooktryabrsky period. Khrestomatia* (Moscow, 1980). For an English translation of the whole article see the useful volume edited by C. Vaughan James, *Soviet Socialist Realism: Origins and Theory* (New York: St. Martin's Press, 1973), pp. 103–6.

14. In earlier times the term *klassovost*, or class-consciousness, was frequently used. However, when Stalin declared in the thirties that the Soviet Union had become a truly socialist state, one without class conflicts, the term declined in value and has since practically disappeared.

15. Lenin believed that if you declare your intentions, then they must be honorable. The assumption, which underlies much of Soviet polemical writing, is that opponents are wicked in large part because they conceal their beliefs; they are unwilling to state them boldly.

16. All translations are our own and are drawn from *Vesy*, no. 11, 1905, pp. 61–66. The review initiated a section in the journal headed "Landmarks" ("Vekhi"), written by Bryusov under the pseudonym of Mr. Aurelius. Bryusov co-edited the journal.

    As if to emphasize the different cultural world he and his colleagues inhabited, Bryusov's critique of Lenin's article was punctuated with a reproduction of Aubrey Beardsley's elegant, saucy portrait of Mrs. Pinchwife—dressed as a man. Lenin would have doubtless seen this as a deliberate insult and proof of his arguments about bourgeois culture.

17. *Lenin on Literature and Art* (Moscow: Progress, 1967), p. 275.

18. Toward the end of his life Lenin began to have grave doubts about the ruthless brutality of the new state. He wrote a series of letters, known as his "Testament," which included a warning about Stalin's harsh personality. George Kennan has offered a judicious evaluation of Lenin's, and the Party's, relationship to terror:

    > Lenin scarcely appreciated the extent to which he, by his own ruthlessness, intolerance, and lack of scruple in the conduct of Party affairs in earlier years, contributed to the creation of the problem with which,

on his deathbed, he saw the Party faced. So long as he lived, his personality was sufficiently powerful to contain and conceal the problem, even though he had helped to create it. But with his death, and with Stalin (to whose darkly mistrustful mind no political issue was ever without its personal implications) in the dominant position within the Party, nothing could prevent these weaknesses from coming to the fore.

See Kennan's Introduction to the collection of essays by Boris I. Nicolaevsky, *Power and the Elite* (New York: Praeger, 1965), p. xvii.

Under glasnost, tentative criticism of Lenin's role in laying the groundwork for Stalin's use of mass terror has been published in the Soviet Union, and the Cheka, founded by Lenin, has also come under attack. Official history books insist that the Cheka acted only in the best interests of the people; the term *chekisty* is still widely used to describe members of the KGB as they heroically defend the Soviet state against its enemies, foreign and domestic. However, a very different picture of the Cheka appeared in early 1989. The literary monthly *Sibirskie ogni* published a harrowing account of a mass execution by the Cheka, written already in 1923 and discovered in the manuscript division of the Lenin Library in Moscow: Vladimir Zazubrin, "Shchepka. Povest o nei i o nei," no. 2, 1989, pp. 3–41. Zazubrin was himself shot in 1938. In his eyewitness account, men and women are taken in groups of five, forced to strip naked and turn to face a wall, then shot in the back of the head.

19. *Lenin on Literature and Art* (Moscow: Progress, 1978), pp. 282–83.

20. A facsimile reproduction of the resolution or decree (*postanovlenie*) from the April 24, 1932 issue of *Pravda* is printed in *Istoria russkoi sovetskoi literatury*, vol. 2 (Moscow, 1967), p. 7. For an English translation, see C. Vaughan James, p. 120.

    The term used for "restructuring" was *perestroika*, revived in 1986 by Mikhail Gorbachev to describe his economic reforms—an interesting example of the Party's terminological consistency.

21. Quoted by Herman Ermolaev, *Soviet Literary Theories, 1917–1934: The Genesis of Socialist Realism* (Berkeley and Los Angeles: University of California Press, 1963), p. 114.

22. For a vivid account of Soviet literary politics on the eve of the First Congress of Writers in 1934, see Max Eastman's *Artists in Uniform* (New York: Knopf, 1934). Eastman takes a strong anti-Stalin line, but as a socialist he portrays Stalin as anti-Leninist. For Eastman, Lenin was a great lover of literature and culture who would have adopted a much more liberal policy than Stalin, had he lived longer.

23. The authoritative collaborative volume, *Sovetskoe literaturovedenie za 50 let* (Leningrad: "Nauka," 1968), p. 15, states that at the time Socialist Realism was promulgated:

    Fundamental statements by Marx and Engels on literature and art remained not only unexplored but in some cases quite unknown. Even Lenin's contributions to the resolution of issues in Marxist esthetics and criticism had not been examined. It was only in the early thirties that the first serious general works to treat these issues began to appear.

24. Gorky's motives in cooperating so enthusiastically with Stalin, and his responsibility for what happened to many Russian writers, continues to be a subject of great disagreement. Alexander Solzhenitsyn in his *Gulag Archipelago* and other writings can hardly contain his hostility toward Gorky, whom he considers a despicable traitor, a man who went out of his way to whitewash Stalin's crimes out of vanity and ideological fanaticism. On the other hand, Nikolai Bukharin, the presumed author of "Letter of an Old Bolshevik" (written shortly after Gorky's death in 1936), argues that Gorky was absolutely convinced he was protecting the old Russian intelligentsia and its traditions; see Boris I. Nicolaevsky, *Power and the Elite*, ed. Janet D. Zagoria (New York: Praeger, 1965).
25. Quoted by Nina Gourfinkel in her biography, *Gorky* (London: Evergreen Books, 1960), p. 178.
26. *Pervy vsesoyuzny syezd sovetskikh pisatelei 1934: Stenografichesky otchet* (Moscow, 1934), p. 717. Hereafter cited as *Pervy syezd*.
27. *Pervy syezd*, p. 669.
28. *Pervy syezd*, p. 663. Yudin gives the following breakdown of members from the seven Republics in the Soviet Union at that time:

RSFSR	1,535
Ukraine	206
Belorussia	about 100
Georgia	158
Armenia	90
Azerbaizhan	79
Turkmenia	26
These figures give an overall total of	2,194

29. See *Svod Zakonov SSSR*, vol. 3, section 2, pp. 692–63. The Litfund Statutes, presented by the Union Board and confirmed by the Council of People's Commissars on February 20, 1935, are reproduced on pp. 693–97. Similar funds were formed for the Union of Composers in 1939, and the Union of Artists in 1940.
30. There is a complete table of congresses of the national and Republic writers' organizations through 1971 in *Kratkaya Literaturnaya Entsiklopedia*, vol. 7 (Moscow, 1972), p. 293.
31. *Pervy syezd*, pp. 673–74. The Union Board of 101 members included several well-known writers, not all of them enthusiastic supporters of the Soviet regime: Mikhail Zoshchenko, Boris Pasternak, Boris Pilnyak, Mikhail Prishvin, Yury Tynyanov, and Ilya Ehrenburg. The Auditing Committee also included some unlikely names: Isaak Babel, Yury Olesha, and Perets Markish; the latter became secretary of the Committee's three-member Bureau. Babel and Markish became victims of Stalin's purges; Olesha survived but alcoholism destroyed his career.

32. *Pervy syezd*, p. 4. Zhdanov attributed the phrase "engineers of human souls" to Stalin; it soon became a standard description of writers in the Soviet press. Without mentioning either Zhdanov or Stalin, Valentin Katayev in a brief reminiscence published in 1984 says that it was Yury Olesha who first used the phrase in an article published just a few days before the Congress opened. See Valentin Katayev, "Sobytie nebyvaloe," *Novy mir*, no. 5, 1984, p. 216.

33. The session in question is reported on pp. 170–91 of *Pervy syezd*.

34. In spite of the mutual hostility between Soviet Russia and Nazi Germany, the approaches of Stalin and Hitler toward culture were mirror images of each other. On September 22, 1933, a law established the Reich Chamber of Culture (*Reichskulturkammer*), which was closely linked to the Ministry of Propaganda and Enlightenment, headed by Goebbels, in much the same way as the Union of Soviet Writers and other creative unions were tied to the Central Committee's Department of Culture and the Propaganda of Leninism. The Reich Chamber was divided into seven sub-chambers for literature, music, film, fine arts, radio, theater, and the press. The close link between the creative arts and the press in Nazi Germany again echoed the traditional Soviet approach. Just as in the Soviet Union, membership in one of the Chambers was essential for any professional career in the arts or mass media. Not surprisingly, the type of officially approved art and literature produced by Nazi Germany was strikingly similar to that engendered by Socialist Realism. For a useful review and anthology of writings, see George L. Mosse, ed., *Nazi Culture* (New York: Schocken Books, 1981).

35. The speeches of Andrei Zhdanov, Gorky, Karl Radek, Nikolai Bukharin, and A. I. Stetsky (head of the literature section of the Central Committee's Department of Culture and Leninist Propaganda) are included in *Soviet Writers' Congress, 1934* (London: Lawrence & Wishart, 1977); this is a facsimile reprint of *Problems of Soviet Literature*, ed. H. G. Scott (London: Martin Lawrence, 1935).

Bukharin was by this time in a very precarious position politically. Stalin ran him on a loose rein and allowed him freedom to make speeches and go through the motions of being an important member of the Party. Bukharin tried desperately to show that he was willing to fit into the new régime and could be useful to it, but his fate had already been decided.

36. *Pervy syezd*, p. 287.

37. *Pervy syezd*, p. 190.

38. *Pervy syezd*, pp. 154–55.

39. *Pervy syezd*, p. 236.

40. *Pervy syezd*, pp. 203–4, 206. Sobolev's remark in Russian reads as follows: "Partia i Gosudarstvo dali pisatelyu vsyo, otnyav u nego tolko odno—pravo pisat plokho."

41. *Pervy syezd*, p. 225. In his reminiscence of the First Congress Valentin Katayev says that Gorky paused for effect and raised his finger in warning

as he said "That is all, nothing more." See "Sobytie nebyvaloe," *Novy mir*, no. 5, 1984, p. 217.

42. *Pervy syezd*, pp. 280.

43. "Syezd byl prazdnikom sovetskoi literatury—prazdnikom raskreposhchenia ot rappovskikh dogm." See I. Eventov, "Spor o poezii i sud istorii," *Literaturnaya gazeta* (November 9, 1988), p. 3. Eventov's view of the First Congress as "a holiday to celebrate our emancipation from RAPPist dogma" was widely shared, as was the general enthusiasm of the occasion. See the series of reminiscences on the 50th anniversary of the First Congress under the heading "Soyuzu pisatelei—50" in *Novy mir* for 1984: no. 5, pp. 214–21; no. 6, pp. 227–33; no. 7, pp. 215–29; no. 8, pp. 205–45.

44. *Pervy syezd*, p. 675.

45. One of the most bizarre parts of Gorky's speech occurred when he called upon all the foreign writers present to band together to produce a collaborative volume about "one day in the bourgeois world . . . just an ordinary, working day showing all its insane, fantastic variety." From the examples Gorky gave it was clear he had in mind a negative portrait. There is no evidence that any of the foreign writers responded to Gorky's assigned task.

46. *Hand on the Heart. Scandinavian Writers on the Soviet Union* (Moscow: Progress, 1967), pp. 16, 24. Nexo, completely unknown in North America, has recently received considerable attention because of the successful film "Pelle the Conqueror," based on one of his novels. The film won the Palme d'Or in Cannes in 1988, and the Oscar for Best Foreign Film in 1989.

47. Ilya Ehrenburg, *Memoirs: 1921–1941* (New York: Grosset and Dunlap, 1966), p. 278.

48. The First Congress of Writers was held in the splendid Hall of Columns, but the show trials were held elsewhere in the Assembly Mansion of the Nobility.

    This famous building, located in central Moscow near the Bolshoi Theater, was built in the 1780s by the noted Russian architect, M. Kazakov. See M. A. Ilyin's useful volume, *Moskva* (Moscow, 1963), pp. 234–35; there is a photograph of the building on page 228 and one of the Hall of Columns on page 230. See also P. V. Sytin, *Iz istorii moskovskikh ulits* (Moscow, 1958), pp. 154–55.

CHAPTER 2
Whip and Gingerbread

1. Harold Swayze, *Political Control of Literature in the USSR, 1946–1959* (Cambridge: Harvard University Press, 1962), p. 42. Swayze uses the phrase with reference to the post-war period, but it applies equally well to the thirties.

2. While the Union ignored its own Statutes calling for regular congresses

every three years, a semblance of organizational life was maintained at the Republic level during Stalin's reign. The Georgian organization met in 1939, as did the Uzbek and Kazakh organizations. The Tajik writers met in 1947 and the Ukrainians in 1948. The Belorussian writers' organization held a congress in 1949 that was attended by Boris Pasternak. The three newly created Baltic organizations met during World War II, shortly after the Soviet Union annexed Estonia, Latvia, and Lithuania. All these Republic congresses are listed in the *Kratkaya Literaturnaya Entsiklopedia*, vol. 7, p. 293.

3. *Pervy syezd*, Prilozhenie VII.

4. See the detailed review of the Union's activities during the Stalin period by Jack F. Matlock, Jr., "The 'Governing Organs' of the Union of Soviet Writers," *American Slavic and East European Review*, vol. 15 (October 1956), pp. 382–99.

5. See Table 5 in John Murray's unpublished doctoral thesis, "The Union of Soviet Writers: Its Organization and Leading Personnel, 1954–1967" (University of Birmingham, England, 1973), p. 167.

6. Stavsky had fought in the Civil War as a commissar. He had been an important official in RAPP, then served on the Organizational Committee that established its successor, the Union of Writers. Stavsky wrote heroic stories about the Civil War and also about the brutal commandeering of grain during collectivization, in which he also participated as a commissar. In 1937 he became chief editor of *Pravda* and died in 1943 at the front in World War II.

Kulik, president of the Ukrainian branch of the Writers' Union, was arrested in 1937 and died in 1941, presumably in the Gulag. See *KLE*, vol. 3, p. 887. He spent three years (1914–17) in the United States, as an organizer for the Social Democratic Party, and served as Soviet Consul in Canada from 1924 to 1926. His many proletarian poems included one devoted to the harsh existence of American blacks, called *The Black Epic* (*Chernaya epopeya*, 1929).

7. Of the five members of the Secretariat, all except Ivanov were members of the Party. Kulik and Lakhuti were appointed to provide non-Russian representation.

Lakhuti is remembered in Russian literary history for one gesture of kindness. In the fateful year of 1937 he arranged, through the Writers' Union, for Osip Mandelshtam, just returned from three years' exile, to visit Stalin's White Sea Canal project. His idea was that Mandelshtam would write some enthusiastic poems about the canal, which was being built with slave labor at a great cost of life, and thus extricate himself from trouble with the authorities. Mandelshtam went on the trip, but could only write general nature poetry; he was arrested and died in Siberia in 1938.

8. *Khrushchev Remembers*, ed. and trans. by Strobe Talbott, with an Introduction, Commentary and Notes by Edward Crankshaw (Boston: Little, Brown, 1970), pp. 171–72. Shcherbakov continued to rise high in the Party apparatus, becoming a member of the Politburo, Moscow

Party boss, and chief commissar of the Red Army in World War II. He died in 1945. In an eerie reprise of the accusation of "medical murder" that surfaced after Gorky's death, several Jewish doctors in January of 1953 were accused of murdering Shcherbakov. Khrushchev had no doubt that Shcherbakov, like Zhdanov in 1948, died from an enormous consumption of alcohol.

9. "It is certain that Gorki's death finally untied the hands of those in Stalin's immediate entourage who demanded haste in the contemplated crucifixion [of the Old Bolsheviks]." See "Letter from an Old Bolshevik" in Boris I. Nicolaevsky, *Power and the Soviet Elite* edited by Janet D. Zagoria (New York: Praeger, 1965), p. 62.

   The Soviet defector Igor Gouzenko wrote a fascinating novel about Gorky entitled *Fall of a Titan* (New York: Norton, 1954), in which he suggests an elaborate plot to kill the writer, who is given the name Mikhail Gorin. The French writer Romain Rolland is satirized as the gullible pro-Stalinist Romain Rouen, who visits Gorin not long before his death and returns to Paris full of enthusiasm for Soviet progress, maintaining silence about his doubts and suspicions.

10. *Ogonyok*, no. 18 (April 1989), pp. 12–14.

11. See Lev Ozerov, "Trudy i dni Nikolaya Zabolotskogo," *Ogonyok*, no. 38 (September 1988). Interrogators usually invoked the name of Gorky to justify their demands on writers.

12. The non-Russian Republic branches of the Writers' Union have taken the lead in investigating and publishing facts about Soviet atrocities. For example, the weekly newspaper of the Belorussian Writers' Union revealed the discovery of a mass grave in the Kuropaty Woods, a popular recreation area just outside Minsk. The grave contained thousands of skeletons buried in layers one on top of the other. Investigators, through interviews with old people in the area, learned that mass executions had taken place over a period of five years, from 1937 until 1941, that is, until the Germans overran Belorussia, and soon began to conduct similar mass executions. See Kathleen Mihalisko, "Mass Grave of Stalin's Victims Discovered in Minsk," RL 288/88 (June 26, 1988).

   A few months later the Ukrainian Republic Writers' Union published information about a similar mass grave outside Kiev. The authorities finally accepted the fact that the grave concealed victims of Soviet (and not German) atrocities. However, they continue to deny responsibility for the mass grave of more than 4,000 Polish officers in the Katyn woods near Smolensk, and have offered no explanation as to the fate of another 11,000 arrested Polish officers.

   Many other mass graves must exist, but are located in remote areas. In one of his stories about the Gulag, collected as *Kolymskie rasskazy* (London: OPI, 1978), Varlaam Shalamov relates that he was with a work party deep in the forests of Siberia when a bulldozer, sent as part of Lend-Lease to help the Soviet war effort, pushed some surface earth off a large hill. The hill turned out to be a gigantic pile of frozen human bodies—prisoners who had been shot in 1938.

13. R. A. Medvedev, *K sudu istorii: genezis i posledstvia Stalinizma* (New York: Knopf, 1974), p. 445. "Almost one third" is a slight exaggeration, since the membership in 1934 was about 2,200, and would have been somewhat higher by 1936. Even so, this is a staggering proportion of the membership.
14. See the interview with Eduard Beltov, "Eto nuzhno ne myortvym—zhivym . . . ," *Knizhnoe obozrenie,* no. 25 (June 17, 1988), p. 7. We are grateful to Martin Dewhirst for bringing this interview to our attention. Beltov refers to the figure of 600 writers as appearing "in some Western publication," without mentioning Roy Medvedev, whose book was only published abroad.

    Among the sources used by Beltov was the *Kratkaya Literaturnaya Entsiklopedia,* published in nine volumes between 1962 and 1978. It lists the date of birth and death of all writers and often mentions that a writer was "illegally repressed and posthumously rehabilitated" (*nezakonno repressirovan i posmertno reabilitirovan*). See the Appendix, "Fact and Figures," for details.
15. Beltov's even-handedness is a useful corrective to the tendency promulgated by individual nationalities that they were victims, and others were villains. See the response to the Beltov interview by Sergei Serebryakov, a senior researcher at the Shota Rustaveli Institute of Georgian Literature (part of the Georgian Academy of Sciences), "Razvenchivayutsya li mify: Ili kak oni zarozhdayutsya," *Zarya vostoka,* July 14, 1988, p. 3.

    Leningrad, always suspect in Stalin's eyes, suffered unusually high losses. See "Oni vernutsya iz nebytia," *Literaturnaya gazeta,* December 28, 1988, p. 5. This same article states that 150 writers disappeared without trace in the Gulag, half of them members of the Union. Both estimates seem low.
16. For a complete listing of names of victims provided by Eduard Beltov, see the Appendix "Facts and Figures."
17. *Kratkaya Literaturnaya Entsiklopedia,* "Syezdy pisatelei SSSR," vol. 7 (1972), p. 290.
18. "Oni vernutsya iz nebytia," *Literaturnaya gazeta,* December 28, 1988, p. 5.
19. In November 1988 Professor I. Eventov, a survivor of the First Union Congress, provided a list of 45 participants of the First Congress who had been "repressed" beginning in 1935. Eventov added a second list of 40 non-participants, other writers who had also suffered "repression" during the Stalin period. See I. Eventov, "Spor o poezii i sud istorii," *Literaturnaya gazeta,* November 9, 1988, p. 3.

    Eventov's lists are reproduced in the Appendix, "Facts and Figures."
20. *Ogonyok,* no. 32 (August 1988) and no. 37 (September 1988). The weekly magazine started collecting private and institutional donations to erect a series of monuments to Stalin's victims and organized an exhibit of photographs and documents, where family members and friends of those who disappeared without trace sought and exchanged information.

The Union of Composers was absent from the list of founding institutions probably because it was still under the control of a devout Stalinist, Tikhon Khrennikov, who denounced many of his colleagues to the NKVD.

By 1989, less than two years after a small group first thought of the idea in August 1987, "Memorial" has grown into a national organization with chapters in 103 Soviet cities and towns. The Ministry of Culture and Moscow City Council have tried to take over the movement by announcing a competition for the memorial monument. However, "Memorial" has decided to expand its mission to create a series of information and archival centers. See the fascinating interview with a member of the Executive Collegium of "Memorial," Arseny Roginsky, in RS 43/89 (May 12, 1989).

21. *Literaturnaya gazeta*, December 7, 1988 and December 28, 1988.
22. *The Union of Soviet Writers: Aims, Organisation, Activities* (Moscow: Progress, 1981), p. 43. This volume is also silent on the denunciations by Vsevolod Vishnevsky. Instead, there are several laudatory photographs of him in uniform during the war, one showing him on May 5, 1945 at the Reichstag in Berlin.
23. On the eve of his suicide in May 1956, Alexander Fadeyev revealed the existence of the secret Politburo resolution of 1937 to a close friend. See *An End to Silence: Uncensored Opinion in the Soviet Union*, ed. Stephen F. Cohen (New York: Norton, 1982), p. 116. This volume consists of extracts from the magazine *Politichesky dnevnik*, a *samizdat* publication compiled and edited by the Marxist historian Roy Medvedev.
24. The following account is based on Ivan Uksusov, "58-aya statya za 58 knig s avtografami," *Literaturnaya gazeta*, November 16, 1988, p. 5. Article 58 of the Russian Criminal Code became notorious as the legal justification for sending Soviet citizens to the Gulag; it speaks in vague terms of "anti-Soviet activities."
25. *Hope Against Hope: A Memoir*, translated by Max Hayward (New York: Atheneum, 1970), p. 352. This is a translation of the first part of Nadezhda Mandelshtam's *Vospominania* (New York: YMCA-Press, 1970). Her account remains our best source for the situation among writers and the Writers' Union during the Stalin period. It has not been published in the Soviet Union, but has been widely read in *samizdat* editions.
26. Nadezhda Mandelshtam, *Hope Against Hope*, pp. 352–56. This chapter is entitled "The Accomplice" (*Soprichastny*), showing that she held Fadeyev partially responsible for her husband's fate.
27. *Hope Against Hope*, p. 159.
28. *Hope Against Hope*, p. 150.
29. *Hope Against Hope*, p. 279.
30. Personal interview, Geneva, September 1988.
31. See Yulia Neiman's poem, "1941," in *Literaturnaya Moskva*, vol. 2 (Moscow, 1956).

32. An interview with an elderly woman neighbor in Tashkent does not mention the presence of Nadezhda Mandelshtam, but gives vivid details of the Akhmatova's life at the time. See "Akhmatova v Tashkente," *Literaturnaya gazeta* May 3, 1989, p. 7.
33. See the memoirs of a Russian emigrant, who was a boy living in Chistopol during the winter of 1941–42: Vladimir Golyakhovsky, *Russian Doctor* (London: Robert Hale, 1984), pp. 89–90.

    See also Alexander Gladkov, *Meetings with Pasternak: A Memoir*, edited with an introduction by Max Hayward (New York: Harcourt Brace Jovanovich, 1977), p. 41.
34. See *Kratkaya Literaturnaya Entsiklopedia*, vol. 7, p. 111.
35. Alexander Fadeyev and Mikhail Sholokhov went to work for *Pravda*. Arkady Gaidar worked for *Komsomolskaya Pravda*. He was with the Red Army at Kiev when it was surrounded by the German Panzer commander Guderian; he refused to be flown out to safety (unlike Marshal Budyonny whose dispositions of his troops had caused the encirclement), and died at the front.
36. *Izvestia*, May 2, 1988; quoted in *CDSP*, vol. XL, No. 23 (July 6, 1988), pp. 16–18. It is quite clear from the transcript that Stalin and Zhdanov had made a calculated decision to end the liberal atmosphere of the war years and to signal that the Kremlin was going to reassert its control over all cultural and intellectual life. This domestic crackdown was paralleled by a harsh foreign policy that helped create the Cold War.
37. Vera S. Dunham, in her book *In Stalin's Time: Middle Class Values in Soviet Fiction* (New York: Cambridge University Press, 1976), reminds us that no account of the post-war period can be complete without a recognition of the fact that novels were being published in vast quantities, in spite of threats and ideological intransigence, and that these works were read and enjoyed by a surprising number of people. Dunham enlivens her account of these mind-numbing works with wit and humor.
38. Alexander Werth, *Russia: Hopes and Fears* (New York: Simon and Schuster), p. 281. Werth's point was that Glavlit played an ancillary role in Stalin's time; manuscripts were in effect "censored" by Fadeyev, since they never even reached Glavlit. Werth correctly describes the Writers' Union and Glavlit as "a pair of Siamese twins."
39. Discussing the rewriting of works by Fadeyev and Sholokhov, Arkady Belinkov notes that in the late Stalin period a man named Yury Lukin became "the editor of *Tikhy Don* [*The Quiet Don*], and practically the author," since he made so many changes and additions to Sholokhov's celebrated novel. See *The Soviet Censorship*, ed. Martin Dewhirst and Robert Farrell (Metuchen, NJ: Scarecrow Press, 1973), p. 13.
40. The terms "liberal" and "conservative" are used here, but others prefer "reformers" and "dissidents" or "hardliners" and "reactionaries." The debate between liberal and conservative writers continues into the Gorbachev period and has spread more openly into the political arena.

41. *Vtoroi syezd pisatelei SSSR. Stenografichesky otchet* (Moscow, 1955), p. 3. Hereafter referred to as *Vtoroi syezd*.
42. *Ogonyok,* no. 22 (May 1987), p. 23. These previously unpublished excerpts from Ehrenburg's memoirs might well have been given the same title, since they appeared twenty years after the writer's death in 1967.
43. *Vtoroi syezd,* p. 344.
44. Ehrenburg's speech is printed in *Vtoroi syezd,* pp. 142–46.
45. *Vtoroi syezd,* pp. 248–52. Neither Ovechkin nor Ehrenburg actually used the phrase "whip and gingerbread," but it clearly lay behind their remarks. The first writer to object to the policy by name was Alexander Kron in the second volume of the almanac *Literaturnaya Moskva* (Moscow, 1956), p. 789: "Neobkhodimo reshitelno pokonchit s retsidivami politiki knuta i pryanika v iskusstve." Kron's use of the word *retsidivy* suggests that he consider "whip and gingerbread" as a policy left over from Stalin's times.
46. *Vtoroi syezd,* pp. 248–49. Like a number of speakers, Ovechkin ridiculed Simonov for his attempt to please all sides: "One can certainly not accuse Konstantin Simonov of ignoring any specific question. His report contained equal measures of criticism, self-criticism, boldness, and caution—everything in its proper place (applause)." Ilya Ehrenburg also received applause for noting that Simonov had spoken about the suppression of critical letters in other publications, but neglected to say that he had done the same thing as chief editor of *Literaturnaya gazeta.* In his speech Sholokhov poked fun at Simonov for producing similar works in all genres at a record speed so that he could receive as many awards and medals as possible.
47. *Vtoroi syezd,* p. 506. Fadeyev's claim that bourgeois writers are "secretly" beholden to capitalist forces comes straight from Lenin's 1905 article.
48. The position was revived later and now serves as a way of letting former First Secretaries down gently when it comes time for them to move on—Konstantin Fedin occupied the position for several years until his death in 1977. It then remained vacant until Georgy Markov was moved up to the presidency in 1986; his request that he be relieved of the responsibility of the position was accepted by the Union Board in January 1989. It will now remain open until it comes time to replace the current First Secretary, Vladimir Karpov.
49. The speech was made part of the U.S. Congressional Record, 84th Congress, 2nd Session, vol. 102, part 7, pp. 9389–9402. It is reproduced, together with many other important documents, in Basil Dmytryshyn, *USSR: A Concise History,* 3d ed. (New York: Scribner's, 1978), pp. 494–537.
50. See the transcript entitled "Party Writers Discuss the Past," in *An End to Silence,* pp. 105–114. Sholokhov's remark recalled the title of Gogol's famous novel *Dead Souls,* which refers both to the spiritual

lifelessness of the landowning gentry and to their dead serfs (also known as "souls"); the rascally Chichikov is trying to buy the names of the "dead souls" on the cheap in order to use them as collateral to purchase his dream estate. The harsh contrast between ends and means has such obvious application to Soviet conditions that the phrase "dead souls" continues to be widely applied under glasnost, this time to the elderly, conservative members of the Central Committee who were removed by Gorbachev in April 1989.

51. Mikhail Shkerin, "Shtrikhi tragedii. Vspominaya Aleksandra Fadeyeva," *Literaturnaya gazeta* (April 12, 1989), p. 5. Shkerin, who knew both Fadeyev and Sholokhov, says that it is high time Fadeyev's suicide letter was published. The publication of such remarks often hints that future action is contemplated.

52. See Nikita Khrushchev, *Vospominania. Izbrannye otryvki* (New York: Chalidze Publications, 1979), p. 268.

Stalin never worried very much about drunkenness and debauchery among his subordinates; in fact, he found such behavior reassuring, and even encouraged heavy drinking at late-night parties in the Kremlin and at his suburban dacha. Beria was a particularly vicious womanizer; Bulganin a little less threatening; Vyshinsky, chief prosecutor at Stalin's Show Trials, maintained several mistresses.

53. Mikhail Shkerin, "Shtrikhi tragedii," cited above. An American equivalent would probably be: "Go ahead, hit me!" Shkerin learned of this incident with Fadeyev through Sholokhov, who was a longtime foe of Fadeyev. Shkerin's account seems designed to portray Sholokhov in a favorable light, but he also shows the positive side of Fadeyev—his charm and dynamism.

CHAPTER 3
Party Guidance

1. The phrase "organized consensus" is borrowed from Victor Zaslavsky's book *The Neo-Stalinist State: Class, Ethnicity and Consensus in Soviet Society* (New York: M. E. Sharpe, 1982).

2. Merle Fainsod, *How Russia Is Ruled*, revised and enlarged edition (Cambridge, MA: Harvard University Press, 1963), p. 225.

3. Shimon Markish, personal interview, Geneva, Switzerland, September 1988.

4. Personal interview, Geneva, September 1988.

5. Among many informative accounts of the Khrushchev period available in English are: Merle Fainsod's *How Russia Is Ruled;* an expanded and revised version co-authored by Jerry F. Hough, entitled *How the Soviet Union Is Governed* (Cambridge: Harvard University Press, 1979); C. A. Linden, *Khrushchev and the Soviet Leadership 1957–1964* (Baltimore: Johns Hopkins University Press, 1966); Mikhail Heller and Aleksandr M. Nekrich, *Utopia in Power* (New York: Summit Books, 1986).

6. *Chetvyorty syezd pisatelei SSSR. Stenografichesky otchet* (Moscow, 1968), p. 209. Hereafter cited as *Chetvyorty syezd.*

Levi was almost certainly making a veiled reference here to the trial of the writers Andrei Sinyavsky and Yuly Daniel in February 1966; they had been sentenced to seven and five years of hard labor respectively for sending their works abroad surreptitiously.

Other foreign guests, many of them from the Soviet Union's Third World allies or longtime sympathizers in the West, behaved with more circumspection. Lillian Hellman, the only official American guest (official guests have all their expenses paid), did not address the delegates. However, another American, the artist Rockwell Kent, presented the Union with a painting he had made of the house in upstate New York where Maxim Gorky had lived in 1905 (and where he had written the novel *Mother,* a revered Soviet classic). *Chetvyorty syezd,* p. 111.

7. *Tvorcheskie soyuzy v SSSR (organizatsionno-pravovye voprosy)* (Moscow: Yuridicheskaya literatura, 1970).
8. *Pyaty syezd pisatelei SSSR. Stenografichesky otchet* (Moscow, 1972), p. 34. Hereafter cited as *Pyaty syezd.*
9. *Shestoi syezd pisatelei SSSR. Stenografichesky otchet* (Moscow, 1978), p. 19. Hereafter cited as *Shestoi syezd.*
10. *Literaturnaya gazeta,* July 1, 1981.
11. The same is true of the title *otvetstvenny redaktor* or "responsible editor." The liberal historian Yury Afanasyev, introducing a collection of essays by supporters of glasnost and perestroika, wrote that he was at ease with the title "responsible editor" for the first time in his life. He noted that it had always meant "responsible to the authorities" (*nachalstvo*) rather than to the reader, and expressed the hope that the term would soon become an anachronism. See *Inogo ne dano* (Moscow: Progress, 1988), p. 5.
12. *Voprosy literatury,* no. 12, 1987, p. 186.
13. Solzhenitsyn recounts the story of how "Kostya" Voronkov rose to power in the Union—he started as a clerk, by replacing a girl "picked out" (for reasons which probably had little to do with her typing skills) by Alexander Fadeyev. Solzhenitsyn also states that Voronkov was the Union's link to the Central Committee in his time, illustrating that the job description has not changed. See Solzhenitsyn's *The Oak and the Calf: Sketches of Literary Life in the Soviet Union* (New York: Harper & Row, 1979), pp. 199, 281. This is a translation of *Bodalsya telyonok s dubom: Ocherki literaturnoi zhizni* (Paris: YMCA-Press, 1975).
14. Personal interviews, Moscow, August 1989.
15. In his book, *Political Elite Recruitment in the Soviet Union* (New York: St. Martin's Press, 1984), pp. 154–55, Bohdan Harasymiw says that in addition to the *nomenklatura* list of actual appointees there is a second list (*uchetnaya nomenklatura*) of those men and women being considered for promotion into the *nomenklatura.*

See also *The Soviet Nomenklatura: A Comprehensive Roster of Soviet Civilian and Military Officials*, comp. Albert L. Weeks (Washington, DC: Washington Institute Press, 1987).

16. See Alexander Rahr, "Turnover in the Central Party Apparatus," Radio Liberty Research: RL 256/87 (July 9, 1987), pp. 1–10. Also M. Voslensky, *Nomenklatura: Gospodstvuyushchy klass Sovetskogo Soyuza* (London: OPI, 1984); translated into English as *Nomenklatura: The Soviet Ruling Class. An Insider's Report* (Garden City, NY: Doubleday, 1984).
17. Personal interview, Geneva, August 1985.
18. See interview with Yury Verchenko, "Soyuz Pisatelei: Rabota i zaboty," *Nedelya*, no. 28, 1988, p. 14. Questions were put to Verchenko in response to a hostile letter about Union privileges, sent by an irate engineer to this weekly supplement to the government's daily *Izvestia*.
19. "Po nakazam syezda," *Literaturnaya gazeta*, July 23, 1986.

    In a general discussion of the administrative apparatus of creative union Secretariats, the 1970 volume *Tvorcheskie soyuzy v SSSR* mentions "released secretaries and other governing officers" as having the greatest authority (p. 91), but does not go on to define their responsibilities.
20. As of 1988 the Secretariat had 15 consultants on the literatures of the Soviet Republics (presumably one for each Republic), and 8 consultants on general literary questions, apparently assigned according to genres. See "Soyuz pisatelei: rabota i zaboty," *Nedelya*, no. 28, 1988.
21. The operation of the councils and commissions is discussed in Chapter 5.
22. Personal interview with Anatoly Gladilin in Paris in 1985. This is an interesting comment, suggesting a very un-Marxist lack of respect for the cultural activities of the working class.
23. Stalin made changes on three occasions which left the monitoring agencies for culture and media pretty much where they were originally. The 1934 reorganization established a Department of Culture and the Propaganda of Leninism; in 1939 this became the Propaganda and Agitation Administration; and in 1948 the Department of Propaganda and Agitation. In 1935 the Department of Culture and the Propaganda of Leninism were split into five departments: Party Propaganda and Agitation, Press and Publishing, Schools, Cultural and Educational Work, and Science. This arrangement was reversed in 1939. At some time, probably in the Khrushchev period, the Department of Culture and Propaganda was split into two departments, one of Culture, and the other of Propaganda. On September 30, 1988, as part of his sweeping "restructuring" of the top echelons of the Party, Gorbachev again melded the two departments into one, called the Department of Ideology, which is subordinate to a Commission for Ideology in the Politburo, headed by Vadim Medvedev.
24. See the Appendix, "Facts and Figures," for lists of personnel.
25. Neither Yevgeny Vladimirovich Zaitsev, his first deputy (who moved

over from the position of First Deputy Minister of Culture of the USSR), nor Yury Sergeyevich Afanasyev, his former deputy, was listed as a member of the Union in the 1981 or 1986 Union Directories, nor is V. K. Yegorov, the latest official to be identified in the Central Committee Department of Culture.

26. For example, Alexander Yakovlev held the position briefly before his own rapid promotion to full membership in the Politburo in 1987.

Nail Bikkenin, a First Deputy, was appointed in the summer of 1987 to the influential position of chief editor of the Party journal *Kommunist*, which has become a leading supporter of Gorbachev's reforms. This fact demonstrates the importance of the Department of Propaganda as a training ground for future high Party officials in the area of ideological guidance.

There was no parallel path from the Department of Culture to the upper echelons of the Party hierarchy. However, in the reorganization that took place on September 30, 1988, Yury Voronov was appointed to the important position of chief editor at *Literaturnaya gazeta*, and V. K. Yegorov, appointed as Deputy Head of the Department of Culture in 1986, was vaulted to the position of Deputy Head of the new Commission for Ideology.

27. *Literaturnaya gazeta*, March 11, 1987. Among several decisions taken by the Litburo was one to create a cooperative, that is, semi-autonomous, publishing house for a group of Moscow writers. This was part of Gorbachev's glasnost campaign. The publication of brief accounts of Secretariat meetings, and even more of Litburo meetings, is of recent origin. It echoes the regular publication of accounts, usually expressed in bland terms, of the weekly meetings of the Politburo itself, held every Thursday, but by 1989 only every two weeks.

28. This is a piece of Soviet jargon which has passed into ordinary Russian language, although not yet into Russian–English dictionaries. In his book on the *nomenklatura* system, Michael Voslensky says the word is used specifically of second-echelon officials who do all the work, while the actual head of an organization or unit "exercises general supervision." See *Nomenklatura*, p. 393.

29. For some examples of "telephone law" see the fascinating account by Barry Norman in *The Wall Street Journal*, May 26, 1988, "Soviet Legal System Offers Most Citizens Swift, Cheap Justice." As he says, "As long as nobody picks up a telephone, the legal system works." One of the cases cited clearly shows the superior authority of the Party over the KGB in a personnel dispute.

30. Personal interview, Paris, March 1985.

31. Personal interview, Paris, March 1987.

32. Yegor Ligachev held that position from March 1985, when the Gorbachev administration began, until the fall of 1988, when an unexpected one-hour meeting of the Central Committee made sweeping changes in the top echelons of the Party: Ligachev himself was given prime responsibility for agriculture. (Gorbachev himself once occupied this

post and managed to use it as a platform to launch his career; however, it has never been considered very prestigious.) Ligachev's place as secretary in charge of ideology was taken by Vadim Medvedev, who rose to full membership in the Politburo without being a candidate member.

33. See the latest version of the Party Statutes, as approved by the 27th CPSU Congress, *Ustav KPSS* (Moscow: Politizdat, 1986), Section VI.

34. Shimon Markish, Geneva, September 1988.

35. See Solomon Volkov's Introduction to his edition of the composer's memoirs, *Testimony*, trans. Antonina W. Bouis (New York: Harper & Row, 1979), p. xxxix. This is a fascinating book, which provides nuggets of information on the literary scene as well as the musical world of Stalinist Russia and the Khrushchev period.

36. *Pervy syezd*, p. 663.

37. There appears to be general agreement among Western scholars that the influence of the PPO secretaries has been declining steadily since Stalin's death, chiefly because of the higher training and professional standing of the people they have to deal with in factories or other enterprises. It has not been possible to plot any similar change in the Writers' Union, although it is our impression that the Party relies much more heavily on the top apparatchiks in the Litburo and Secretariat to exercise overall supervision, and uses the PPOs for grassroots guidance.

38. See the report of this meeting in *Literaturnaya gazeta*, November 27, 1985.

39. At the Fourth Congress of the RSFSR Organization in 1975 M. A. Dudin proposed a slate of ninety-nine people for the Congress Presidium "on behalf of the Moscow, Leningrad, Daghestan, Primorsky, and Kaliningrad writers' organizations." See (*Chetvyorty syezd pisatelei RSFSR. Stenografichesky otchet* (Moscow, 1977), p. 4.

At the Sixth Congress of the RSFSR Writers' Organization in 1985, Daniil Granin used the phrase "Po porucheniyu partynoi gruppy syezda predlagayu izbrat. . . ." G. A. Akhunov used the phrase "Po prosbe partynoi gruppy syezda predlagaetsya izbrat. . . ." It all comes to the same thing. See the *Stenografichesky otchet* (Moscow, 1987), pp. 9, 10.

40. See the draft of the Statutes (III, 17) in *Literaturnaya gazeta* (March 22, 1989).

41. We also owe to Prokofyev the immortal lines: "We could not be poets outside the Soviet system. Our debt to this system is enormous. I think it would take a whole lifetime and more to repay our debt." Quoted in *Pyat desyatilety. Soyuz pisatelei SSSR, 1934–1984* (Moscow, 1984), p. 160.

42. Naum Korzhavin, in *Strana i mir*, no. 6, 1985, pp. 88–90. This short recollection was published as one of five brief but fascinating essays about the Writers' Union under the suggestive title, "Union of Reptiles"

(*Soyuz reptily*). The other former members to contribute were Vasily Aksyonov, Kirill Kostsinsky, Igor Yefimov, and Mark Popovsky.

CHAPTER 4
Soviet Parnassus

1. See *Tvorcheskie soyuzy v SSSR*, p. 176, footnote 1.
2. L. Avdeyeva, "Krysha?" *Sovetskaya kultura*, August 15, 1987, p. 3.
   The abolition of the *profkomy* on March 25, 1988, is reviewed in Julia Wishnevsky, "Writers' Trade-Union Committees in Moscow Dissolved," RL 157/88 (April 7, 1988).
3. For the Party's dues see Section X of the current *Ustav* (Moscow, 1986). They range from 10 kopeks per month for those earning 70 rubles per month and less, to 3 percent of monthly income for those earning 300 rubles or more per month.
   The use of such a scale provides tacit recognition that the income of members in both Party and Union varies very widely. At the same time, the scale makes sure that those who earn large sums will contribute a commensurate amount to the organization. The rate of exchange for rubles and dollars, set artificially high by a Soviet government hungry for "hard currency," or *valyuta*, is roughly $1.50 to 1 ruble, as of 1989. The ruble is a non-convertible currency; in real terms it is worth less than 10 percent of a U.S. dollar, but within the Soviet Union it buys more than this true exchange rate suggests.
4. For several years the Statutes themselves were not reprinted or distributed to members. Many émigrés said that they had never seen a copy, but it hardly mattered since they were not followed. Nowadays each member is said to receive a copy of the Statutes in the form of a miniature pamphlet, roughly 3″ × 4″ in size.
   We have a copy in our possession. It is undated, with a print run of 5,000 copies. That would have been enough for each member to have a copy in 1971, but since then the membership has increased to nearly 10,000.
5. *Chetvyorty syezd*, p. 79.
6. There has been a curious reaction to this in the glasnost era. A writer from Rostov with strong Party connections complained about the abuse of the secret ballot by members who paid applicants many compliments in speeches, but then blackballed them in the actual vote. The writer had suffered this particular humiliation himself. He reminded his readers that Party votes are always open and suggested that a change to open voting should be made in the planned revision of the Writers' Union Statutes. A. Agafonov, "Slova Dobrye—Shary Chernye," *Literaturnaya gazeta*, August 27, 1986.
7. As stated by Yury Verchenko in an interview in *Nedelya*, no. 28, 1988.
8. The *anketa* has come under close scrutiny as part of legal reforms

during glasnost. See Konstantin Simis, "Kommentary yurista k statye 'Yeyo velichestvo anketa'," RS 94/88 (October 10, 1988).

9. A glance at the reference work *Pisateli Moskvy*, published in 1987, makes it clear that there have been many cases of writers being admitted even before the date their first book was published.

10. Again, it is always possible that such information is readily available to the membership in the weekly publication of the *partkom* and board of the Moscow branch of the Union, *Moskovsky literator*. Since 1971 the Union Secretariat has also been issuing, irregularly but free of charge, a newsletter called *Informatsionny byulleten*. We have seen copies of the former, but not the latter. Judging from a report on the *Byulleten* for the period 1981–86, given by the deputy "responsible editor" Ye. Smotritsky, its pages have been given over to routine statements about Party plans and declarations. See *Vosmoi syezd*, p. 491.

11. For an official history, see the memorial volume on its fiftieth anniversary: *Vospominania o Litinstitute* (Moscow, 1983). For some interesting sidelights from a former student, see Anatoly Gladilin, *The Making and Unmaking of a Soviet Writer* (Ann Arbor, MI: Ardis, 1979).

12. In our interviews with both émigrés and with writers and critics in Moscow we noticed a total lack of interest in, and even disparagement of, cultural life in the provinces. Cultural and intellectual activity is heavily centralized, with few exceptions (such as Yury Lotman's investigations of structuralism in Tartu, Estonia; or the highly-regarded Siberian Branch of the Academy of Sciences in Novosibirsk). The general outlook is reminiscent of the attitude of Parisians towards the rest of France, or of New Yorkers to everything West of the Hudson.

13. Personal interview, Munich, June 1984.

14. Z. Ibragimova, "Daleko-daleko ot Moskvy . . . ," *Literaturnaya gazeta*, Nov. 5, 1986.

    As early as the 1954 Union Congress, Vladimir Ovechkin had complained about provincial writers wanting to live in the capital.

15. "Trevoga," *Novoe Russkoe Slovo*, July 28, 1985, p. 4. The word *kormushka* means literally a feeding trough for animals. KGB is of course the acronym for the secret police, the Committee on State Security (*Komitet gosudarstvennoi bezopasnosti*). MVD stands for *Ministerstvo vnutrennikh del*, or Ministry of Internal Affairs, which monitors the regular police force, the *militsia*. Some MVD troops wear the same uniforms as the regular army and have been used for crowd control; they are notorious for their brutality.

    The Writers' Union has long enjoyed an enviable reputation as a comfortable setting in which various loyal servants of the state may spend their twilight years. Membership provides a valuable addition to their pensions, and the Club is an attractive spot for a drink or a meal with friends.

16. *Hope Against Hope*, p. 277. Several of the writers, including Valentin Kataev, Viktor Shklovsky and Konstantin Fedin, had just moved into

the first building constructed specially for writers on Lavrushinsky Pereulok.

17. Mikhail Bulgakov, *Master i Margarita* (Ann Arbor, MI: Ardis, n.d.), p. 52. The building and facilities described by Bulgakov are not those of the present day Writers' Union, but an earlier location on Tverskoi Boulevard (the building still exists). Bulgakov also mentions a place called Perelygino which has many dachas; this refers to the celebrated writers' colony outside Moscow, called Peredelkino.

 Bulgakov's original target was the Russian Writers' Association, but as he continued the novel in the late thirties he switched his focus to the new Union of Writers.

18. The traditional word for police was avoided in the Soviet period since it had tsarist associations; it is now only used for capitalist police forces.

19. See "Parasites Never" in Vladimir Voinovich, *The Anti-Soviet Soviet Union* (New York: Harcourt Brace Jovanovich, 1986), p. 178. This is an excellent translation by Richard Lourie of *Antisovetsky Sovetsky Soyuz* (Ann Arbor, MI: Ardis, 1985).

20. This is a term that needs to be explained in the Soviet context. Corruption and speculation are terms often used for activities that would be regarded as perfectly normal anywhere outside the Soviet bloc. For example, buying something and then selling it later for a higher price than the official one is automatically speculation. Since the state owns everything, then it alone will decide its value. The new 1988 law on "cooperative enterprises"—which means basically the legal, limited introduction of private enterprise into the Soviet economy for the first time since the twenties—may well lead to a fundamental change in attitudes, but the resistance to all forms of "speculation" is deeply ingrained in the population.

21. Personal interview, September 1988. Action taken in three weeks amounts to breakneck speed in the Soviet Union.

22. The official continuity is based on Lenin's "two streams," and therefore depends on a privileged interpretation of nineteenth-century Russian culture.

23. On the history of old Moscow streets and neighborhoods, see the splendid book by P. V. Sytin, *Iz istorii moskovskikh ulits (ocherki)*, 3d. edition, revised and expanded (Moscow, 1958).

24. Sad to say, the Church of Saints Boris and Gleb was demolished and replaced by the Pedagogical Institute of Music, while the Supreme Court of the USSR now sits on the site of the former Church of the Holy Mother of Rzhevsk. The wanton destruction of thousands of churches and other old buildings under Lenin and his successors has recently come under increasing attack in the Soviet press, although most of the blame is laid at Stalin's door.

25. This is just one of many examples of such renaming of streets and places, without regard to their long historical associations. The practice

helps explain in part the rise of the Russian nationalist movement, a very important social and political phenomenon in contemporary Soviet society. Many Russians, including the celebrated writer Yury Nagibin, have been urging that old Moscow streets be given back their original names. In late 1988 and early 1989 Andrei Zhdanov's name began to be removed from towns, universities, and streets. Mariupol, a town in the Crimea, received its old name back, and there is talk of renaming the Zhdanov University of Leningrad.

26. On one occasion, we wished to purchase a new volume of Anna Akhmatova's poetry. It could be found only here, but we had to ask a Union member to go to the restricted second floor of the bookstore. Later we had a chance to see this second floor; it is a jumble of unopened cartons, piles of books, where harassed assistants struggle to meet the special requests of Union members.

27. The American Litfund is based in New York City and its president is Alexander Fainberg, who is concerned about the organization's declining reserves. See his article "Speshite delat dobro!," *Almanac-Panorama*, February 5–11, 1988; reprinted from the New York City paper *Novoe Russkoe Slovo*.

The Washington, DC Litfund is also very active, with Helen Yakobson, Professor Emerita of George Washington University, playing a leading role.

28. "O Literaturnom fonde Soyuza SSR," *Svod Zakonov SSSR*, vol. 3, section II (Moscow, 1987), p. 692. This section also contains the statutes of Litfund, and details of the founding of similar funds for artists and composers (members of all "creative unions" receive benefits from such funds).

29. See the draft of the new Statutes (II, 5) in *Literaturnaya gazeta* (March 22, 1989).

30. *Literaturnaya gazeta*, June 25, 1986, p. 5.

31. Both the CPSU and the Soviet government apparatus continue to struggle with this chronic problem. Gorbachev has made great efforts to improve the situation, in part by encouraging newly married couples to work together to construct what are called "young people's residential complexes" (*molodyozhnye zhilishchnye kompleksy*), but the demand for housing remains unsatisfied throughout the country. See the interesting essays by Aaron Trehub, "New Party-Government Resolution on Cooperative Housing," RL 164/88 (April 18, 1988), and "The USSR Supreme Soviet Looks at Housing: Background," RL 217/88 (May 24, 1988).

32. See Karpov's speech, *Izvestia*, November 19, 1987, p. 5; quoted in *CDSP*, vol. 38, no. 51 (January 21, 1987), p. 15.

33. The poor quality of this mass-produced housing has been the source of countless jokes and even cartoons published in the Soviet press for many years. The apartment blocks are put together with pre-fabricated slabs and without proper structural support. In Moscow this is not a

serious problem, but the weak construction was revealed tragically in the Armenian earthquake of November 1988.

34. Pensions are calculated at half the most recent monthly salary. It seems that pensions are fixed (with no inflation rider), so that many older people receive pensions that are very low, even below the official poverty line of 70 rubles per month.

35. Workers in other enterprises usually have similar privileges; that is, the opportunity to place orders for foodstuffs (*zakazy*), for which they pay ahead of time at their place of work. Their orders are then brought to them so that they are saved the inconvenience of spending endless hours shopping. Various factories and enterprises provide this service to attract good workers, to keep them happy, and to prevent them from absenting themselves during working hours to shop. One of the ways a Russian will decide to work in one institution or plant rather than another is by comparing which has better *zakazy*.

36. Fedin was never known particularly for his concern with children; a far more appropriate name would have been that of the beloved children's writer, Kornei Chukovsky, who also lived nearby. Perhaps the growing concern among writers for restoring former names to streets in Moscow will extend to the renaming of the Club and other Union facilities. In addition to naming the Club, Peredelkino, and literary prizes after Alexander Fadeyev, who consigned many of his fellow writers to the Gulag, the Soviet authorities also erected a large monumental complex to him, consisting not simply of a statue of the writer, but additional statues representing characters in his works.

37. The exact amount of the Union's foreign currency account is not known. Its existence was first mentioned publicly in the Draft Statutes. See *Literaturnaya gazeta*, March 22, 1989.

38. As stated in an interview in *Nedelya*, no. 28, 1988.

39. *Literaturnaya gazeta*, December 10, 1986.

40. I. Konstantinovsky, "Chto takoe Litfond?," *Literaturnaya gazeta*, August 19, 1987; and the response by N. Gorbachev in the same issue.

41. Boris Yeltsin, who has survived disgrace and removal from the Politburo in 1987, recently revealed some interesting salary figures for Party apparatchiks. During a talk on November 12, 1988 to students at the Higher Komsomol School in Moscow, Yeltsin stated that the average monthly salary for a full-time Party worker is 216 rubles. He added that a Party *obkom* "instructor" receives 240 rubles per month, a department head 380, and a secretary (presumably still in an *obkom*) receives 450 rubles per month. A first secretary receives 550–600. These are quite handsome salaries, but not outrageously high. The transcript of Yeltsin's talk was published in the Perm newspaper *Molodaya gvardia* (December 4, 1988). See also Aaron Trehub, "Boris El'tsin Speaks Out Again," RL Report, vol. 1, no. 2 (January 13, 1989), pp. 6–7.

In an interview with the *Washington Post* on January 31, 1989, Vitaly Korotich, chief editor of the liberal weekly magazine *Ogonyok*, said that Gorbachev himself receives 1,500 rubles per month, while other Politburo members receive 1,200–1,500. Top military officers may earn more: as much as 2,000 per month. Of course, such salaries give only a sketchy idea of the actual standard of living enjoyed by the Soviet elite, especially those in and around the Politburo. Their "total compensation" is many times higher than their cash income, because of hidden fringe benefits ranging from free housing, vehicles, travel, medical care, servants, and so forth—and all of these goods and services are of the highest quality, usually imported, and unobtainable by ordinary Soviet citizens.

42. See Natalia Ilyina, "Zdravstvui, plemya mladoe, neznakomoe . . . ," *Ogonyok*, no. 2, 1988, pp. 23–26. Ilyina remarks that there is something disgraceful about all this fuss over a living writer [and, one might add, of such limited talent], while Russia still lacks a museum to the great poet Alexander Blok, who died in 1921. She also relates the story of seeing a woman crying in desperation in the editorial offices of a publishing house as she struggled to rewrite a text by one of the powerful secretaries; this work would then be published in a vast print-run, with great profits accruing to the "author." Print-runs and royalties are discussed in Chapter 6.
43. Personal interview in Munich, June 1984.
44. See Vladimir Voinovich, "Shut Up and Eat!" *New York Times*, May 15, 1983.
45. *The Anti-Soviet Soviet Union* (New York: Harcourt, Brace, Jovanovich, 1985), p. 198.
46. "Soyuz reptily," *Strana i mir* [Munich], no. 6, 1985, p. 95.

CHAPTER 5
Crimes and Punishments

1. An English translation of the letter is included as Appendix II in Robert Conquest, *Courage of Genius: The Pasternak Affair* (London: Collins and Harvill, 1961), pp. 136–63.
2. *Mladost*, Belgrade, October 2, 1957.
3. This account was given by the émigré literary critic, Arkady Belinkov, at a conference held in Munich in 1970 shortly before his death. See *The Soviet Censorship*, p. 13.
4. Demichev's account is paraphrased by Yevgeny Yevtushenko in *Ogonyok*, no. 19 (May 1989), p. 19. This issue contains a long statement by Yevtushenko on the circumstances surrounding the arrest of Sinyavsky and Daniel, excerpts from the testimony at the trial and contemporary articles in the Soviet press, together with recollections from several writers. All in all, this publication of materials is a remarkable example of glasnost.

In his recollections, Yevtushenko repeats his claim, first reported in *Time* (February 9, 1987), that in November 1966 Robert Kennedy had taken him into the bathroom of his Manhattan apartment and told the Soviet poet in the utmost secrecy that American agents had revealed the identity of Sinyavsky and Daniel to the KGB. The reason for this action, according to Robert Kennedy, was that the American intelligence community wanted to create a scandal in the Soviet Union that would divert world attention from increased U.S. military involvement in South Vietnam.

5. *On Trial* [revised and enlarged edition], translated and edited by Max Hayward (New York: Harper & Row, 1967), pp. 280 and 283. See also *Sinyavsky i Daniel na skamye podsudimykh* (New York: Inter-Language Literary Associates, 1966).

Arkady Vasilyev (1907–72) was an undistinguished writer of heavy-handed satires directed against "bourgeois survivals." He will be remembered only for his participation in the trial. The same is true of Zoya Kedrina, a writer of humdrum, orthodox criticism, who was born in 1904, graduated from the Gorky Literary Institute in 1938 (a fateful year), and became a member of the Writers' Union in 1941; she did not become a member of the Party until very late, in 1978.

6. See *The Soviet Censorship* (1981), p. 44.

7. Personal interview, London, March 1983.

8. See "Proudly, a Soviet Dissident is Buried," *New York Times*, January 3, 1989, A3. In a kind but belated gesture, Daniel's old comrade in adversity, Andrei Sinyavsky, was suddenly given a visa to visit Moscow and attended the funeral of his elderly mother, but may have attended Daniel's also. The funerals of celebrated literary figures who have been persecuted by the Soviet regime have become major public events. Their graves continue to be places of pilgrimage for large numbers of Russian people, and not simply intellectuals.

In the months prior to his death, the Soviet authorities permitted some of Daniel's works to be published, and he was interviewed in September 1988 by *Moscow News*. This is a familiar pattern; when a dissident author is near death, the authorities set about beginning his or her rehabilitation, with a view to "recapturing" after death the very person they persecuted during his lifetime.

9. See Alexander Werth, *Russia: Hopes and Fears* (New York: Simon & Schuster, 1969), pp. 277–78.

10. *On Trial*, edited by Max Hayward (New York: Harper & Row, 1967), p. 292.

11. *On Trial*, pp. 288–89.

12. *Chetvyorty syezd*, p. 80.

13. Lidia Chukovskaya, *Protsess isklyuchenia: Ocherk literaturnykh nravov* (Paris: YMCA-Press, 1979), p. 51. The title has multiple meanings, since *protsess* means process and procedure as well as court case, and *isklyuchenia* means exclusion as well as expulsion. The list of punishments in Russian reads as follows: *predupredit; strogo predupredit; postavit na vid; vygovor; vygovor s zaneseniem v lichnoe delo; strogy*

vygovor s zaneseniem v lichnoe delo. The extraordinary fine-tuning of these punishments reveals the well-developed bureaucratic thinking of the Secretariat and the ideological apparatchiks.

14. Yuri Surovtsev, "The Union of Soviet Writers as a Professional Public Organisation," *The Union of Soviet Writers: Aims, Organisation, Activities* (Moscow: Progress, 1981).
15. *Pyat desyatilety. Soyuz pisatelei SSSR 1934–1984* (Moscow, 1984), p. 345. This volume contains some fascinating photographs and reproductions of sketches and paintings. The extraordinary luxury of the book, printed on silk paper and obviously at very high cost (in Yugoslavia, not Moscow) provoked a lot of anger and ridicule among Russian writers, who felt it was a terrible waste of money and yet another boondoggle of the Union Secretariat to promote its privileged members.

    It is not unusual for special volumes of this type, art books, even journals, to be published abroad, because (as Soviet publishing executives themselves admit) Soviet printing presses are not able to handle high-quality jobs. The new journal *Nashe Nasledie* (*Our Heritage*) of the Soviet Culture Fund is being published by British media tsar Robert Maxwell in England.
16. Personal interview, Moscow, December 1983. Emigrés confirmed that the letter department of every journal is busy. In fact, answering letters is a job that many aspiring authors take on to get their foot in the door.
17. The word "chekist" is taken from Cheka, an acronym of the initials of the Extraordinary Commission (*Chrezvychainaya komissia*), founded by Lenin immediately after the Bolshevik Revolution of 1917. The Cheka was abolished in 1922, but its functions and personnel were taken over by various successor organizations.
18. "The Tenth Anniversary of the Death of Boris Balter," RL 226/84 (June 6, 1984).
19. *Plenum Tsentralnogo Komiteta KPSS. Stenografichesky otchet* (Moscow, 1983), pp. 95–96. Mikhail Gorbachev, then a member of the Politburo, was chairing the very session at which Markov spoke. Just over two years later, he became General Secretary of the Party. Markov resigned as First Secretary of the Union in June of 1986.
20. Lidia Chukovskaya, *Protsess isklyuchenia*, p. 27. In this book Chukovskaya provides an account of her dealings with her colleagues in the section on Children and Youth Literature, and with the secretariat of the Moscow branch of the Union.
21. *Protsess isklyuchenia*, p. 77. Likhanov's career was not harmed by his performance in this matter. He received the Komsomol Prize for Literature in 1976, and later became chief editor of the youth journal *Smena*. In 1987 he was named president of a new Soviet Children's Fund by Mikhail Gorbachev. He has continued to publish extensively, and some of his works on Soviet youth have received wide praise.
22. According to Zhores Medvedev, *Ten Years after Ivan Denisovich* (New York: Macmillan, 1973), p. 62.

23. The open letter, entitled "Protiv chego vystupaet *Novy mir?*," was published in the weekly magazine *Ogonyok*, no. 30, 1969. The signatories, all influential members of the Writers' Union, although undistinguished as writers, were: Mikhail Alekseyev, Vladimir Chivilikhin, Anatoly Ivanov, Sergei Malashkin, Alexander Prokofyev, Pyotr Proskurin, Sergei Smirnov, Nikolai Shundik, Sergei Vikulov, Sergei Voronin, and Vitaly Zakrutkin.

There is no doubt that Tvardovsky earned the special hatred of the hard-line Soviet writers because he opened up the pages of *Novy mir* to critical articles on their boring, poorly written novels and poems.

During glasnost Tvardovsky has become a major hero for the liberals, who constantly remind their readers that the current leaders of the conservative opposition to perestroika include several of those who signed the 1969 letter against him.

24. See his memoir, *The Oak and the Calf* (New York: Harper & Row, 1979), pp. 168–74; we have altered this translation slightly. For the original Russian, see *Bodalsya telyonok s dubom*) Paris: YMCA-Press, 1975), pp. 177–78. On the mores and materialistic outlook of the Secretariat members and their wives, see the blunt article by Natalia Ilyina, "Zdravstvui, plemya mladoye, neznakomoye . . . ," *Ogonyok*, no. 2, 1988, pp. 23–26; also the brief article by another leading critic, Benedikt Sarnov, in *Ogonyok*, no. 3, pp. 5–8.

25. *The Oak and the Calf*, pp. 484–93. For Solzhenitsyn's record of the Ryazan meeting in the original Russian, see pp. 527–39.

26. See his letter to the Fourth Congress of Soviet Writers, cited in *Aleksandr Solzhenitsyn: Critical Essays and Documentary Materials*, edited by John B. Dunlop et al. (Belmont, MA: Nordland, 1973), p. 469.

27. A transcript of Brodsky's trial has now appeared in the Soviet Union: F. Vigdorova, "Sudilishche," *Ogonyok*, no. 49 (December 1988), pp. 26–31.

28. Yefim Etkind, *Notes of a Non-Conspirator*, trans. Peter France (London: Oxford University Press, 1978), pp. 208–17. Etkind was fired from his position at the Herzen Pedagogical Institute in Leningrad and left without any way of earning a living. He was therefore obliged to emigrate to Paris, where he now teaches at the University.

To balance the portrait of Kruglova given here, we should point out that in 1976 she was replaced by Yevgeny Zaitsev, who reportedly carried out his office in a much less boorish fashion; Zaitsev was brought to Moscow by Yakovlev and served as First Deputy Head of the Central Committee Department of Culture, where he was reputed to be a supporter of glasnost, as was Yury Voronov, the Department's Head (another old colleague of Yakovlev).

29. Personal interview, Paris, March 1987.

30. Personal interview, Paris, March 1985.

31. For a description of the mood and events surrounding the assault on Bogatyryov and his death, see L. Chukovskaya, *Protsess isklyuchenia*, pp. 171–82.

CHAPTER 6
Purity and Profit

1. See John and Carol Garrard, "Soviet Book Hunger," *Problems of Communism* (September–October, 1985), pp. 72–81. Data from the Soviet Interview Project revealed the following reader preferences in fiction in the late Brezhnev period (p. 75):

Type of Fiction	*Percent*
Classic foreign fiction	53.8
Classic Russian fiction	48.2
Detective/mysteries	42.8
Modern foreign fiction	41.8
Soviet fiction	32.1
World War II fiction	28.4
Science fiction	28.0

These figures are significant, given the overwhelming amount of orthodox Soviet and World War II fiction published in the Soviet Union, and the corresponding lack of the types of fiction most preferred by respondents.

Further on reading habits and preferences, see John Garrard and Amy Corning, "The Soviet Reader: New Data from the Soviet Interview Project," *Solanus* [New Series], vol. 2 (1988), pp. 3–38.

On the popularity of Western fiction in the Soviet Union, see Maurice Friedberg's fascinating book, *A Decade of Euphoria* (Bloomington: Indiana University Press, 1977).

2. Personal interview, London, June 1984.
3. Personal interview, Munich, June 1984.
4. *Vtoroi syezd,* p. 89.
5. *Vtoroi syezd,* p. 502.
6. Vasily Grossman, *Zhizn i sudba* (Lausanne, Switzerland: L'Âge d'Homme, 1980), p. 187. The novel was completed in 1961, but then "arrested" by the KGB; copies of the manuscript were later smuggled to the West. It was finally published in the Soviet Union in 1988. Grossman himself died in 1964.
7. Personal interview, London, December 1985.
8. *Infrared,* no. 6, July 1983 [Canterbury, England], p. 4.
9. Personal interview, Washington, DC, September 1984.
10. For a list of Writers' Union periodicals published in all the official languages of the Soviet Union, see the *Spravochnik Soyuza Pisateli SSSR* (Moscow, 1986), pp. 759–83. For an excellent survey of the role that these periodicals (and a few that do not belong to the Union) are playing in the campaign for glasnost, see Julia Wishnevsky, "A Guide to Some Major Soviet Journals," *RL Bulletin* 2/88 (July 20, 1988), 29 pp.
11. This list is adapted slightly from one included by Yefim Etkind in

his *Notes of a Non-Conspirator* (Oxford University Press, 1978), p. 172. Etkind is a literature professor and former member of the Leningrad branch of the Union, who now lives in Paris. In 1988 the Leningrad branch voted to reinstate Etkind as a member.

12. *The Soviet Censorship*, edited by Martin Dewhirst and Robert Farrell (Metuchen, NJ: Scarecrow Press, 1973), p. 19.
13. Thus it is quite appropriate for the *Bolshaya Sovetskaya Entsiklopedia* (*Large Soviet Encyclopedia*) in its entry on "tsenzura" not to mention censorship of writers; it considers censorship only in Western history and pre-revolutionary Russia. "Controls" are mentioned in the Soviet Union, but justified simply as a means of maintaining national security (the function of Glavlit). *Rukovodstvo* or "guidance" is not mentioned.
14. Personal interview, Munich, Germany, June 1984.
15. Yurenen felt that a "Soviet classic" had died, but his story had a happy ending under glasnost: Sergei Antonov's novel finally appeared in 1987.
16. From 1959 to 1960 he edited *Literaturnaya gazeta*. He should not be confused with Sergei Vasilyevich Smirnov, an orthodox poet and notorious persecutor of liberal writers.
17. Stalin interfered personally on frequent occasions to decide what should or should not be published, or who should or should not receive a prize. However, since his death it seems that a Soviet leader has only intervened once to order publication of a work rejected by the Union Secretariat: As part of his anti-Stalin campaign, Khrushchev gave his personal permission for Solzhenitsyn's *One Day in the Life of Ivan Denisovich* to be published in *Novy mir* in November 1962.
18. Personal interview, Moscow, December 1983.
19. *Infrared*, no. 6, July 1983 [Canterbury, England], p. 3.
20. The Union's own publishing house, Sovetsky Pisatel, reports the same enormous volume of unsolicited manuscripts, also called *pritok*. Between 1981 and 1985 Sovetsky Pisatel received a total of 5,000 manuscripts, of which 4,000 came from writers in Moscow. See *Vosmoi syezd pisatelei SSSR. Stenografichesky otchet* (Moscow, 1988), p. 485. It was not stated what percentage of these came from Union members, but it should be remembered that the Moscow branch only has 2,000 members.

    Over roughly the same period, the press put out 2,458 titles in editions totalling 118 million copies. However, it was not clear how many manuscripts in the *pritok* were included in those impressive numbers, nor how many successful authors belonged to the Union.
21. The decree, entitled "Ob uporyadochenii stavok avtorskogo voznagrazhdenia za izdanie, publichnoe ispolnenie i inye vidy ispolzovania proizvedeny literatury i iskusstva," covers all the arts. Its impact on literature was discussed in an interview with Union First Secretary Vladimir Karpov ("Novy stimul dlya tvorcheskoi raboty," *Literaturnaya gazeta*, August 3, 1988). Karpov became quite testy at one point when

the interviewer implied that writers have a pretty good life already and wondered what these increases in royalties had to do with quality.

It seems that VAAP, the Soviet copyright agency, will be required to pay authors more, and more promptly, for translation and sale of their works abroad—something the agency has not done in the past, much to the chagrin of many writers. See "Avtorskoe voznagrazhdenie: novy poryadok," *Sovetskaya kultura,* December 20, 1988, p. 8.

22. When we received a VAAP contract for our article published in *Inostrannaya literatura* (May, 1988), we were pleasantly surprised to see that we would be paid 330 rubles per signature, and that each monthly issue of the journal was printed in 490,000 copies. The experience offered a good lesson in understanding better the Soviet professional writer's situation and his desire to be published, whatever changes might be made to his manuscript. Our article was edited in a completely professional manner, with no hint of political pressure, even though it contained some critical comments on Socialist Realism and orthodox Soviet literature.

23. The linking of the names of Granin and Ananyev was diplomatic, rather like balancing a political ticket in the United States. Granin, a Russian, has occupied important administrative positions in the Leningrad branch of the Writers' Union, but he is a respected author and an enthusiastic supporter of glasnost and perestroika. Ananyev, a Kazakh, is not a distinguished author, but an important "literary general" and editor. He has displayed great political skill in retaining his position as chief editor of the journal *Oktyabr* since 1953, the year of Stalin's death. Quick as ever to adjust, Ananyev turned his journal under glasnost into a leading publisher of formerly forbidden works, most notably two novels by Vasily Grossman, who died in official disgrace in 1964.

24. Alexander Zinovyev, *Ni svobody, ni ravenstva, ni bratsva* (Lausanne: L'Âge d'Homme, 1983), pp. 37–38.

25. In this connection see the fascinating book by the Hungarian sociologists George Konrad and Ivan Szelenyi, *The Intellectuals on the Road to Class Power: A Sociological Study of the Role of the Intelligentsia in Socialism* (New York: Harcourt Brace Jovanovich, 1979).

26. Personal interview, London, December 1983.

27. Personal interview, Monterey, California, July 1984.

28. Under glasnost some effort is being made to cater to this demand for escapist literature. The Literature Department of the popular weekly magazine *Ogonyok* (no. 7, February 1989) announced the establishment of a "Library of Foreign Detective Novels" (*Biblioteka zarubezhnogo detektiva*), which will provide Russian translations of an admirably wide range of authors, beginning with Arthur Conan Doyle, Agatha Christie, Dashiel Hammett, and Georges Simenon, and moving on to John Le Carré, Dick Francis, and Frederick Forsyth. Russians are as avid readers of these authors as are readers in the West. John Le Carré is apparently popular among the Soviet elite; he was feted in Moscow during a visit of British writers in 1988.

In 1983 officials at Goskomizdat told us that they planned mass editions (20 million copies) of Russian classics, such as Pushkin and Tolstoy, and were making a special effort to "meet the demand" for other politically innocent works that have been virtually unobtainable through most of the Soviet period.

29. Dr. Andrei Sakharov, then head of the belles lettres section of Goskomizdat. Moscow, December 1983. The authors are indebted to Dr. Sakharov for his unfailing courtesy during a lengthy interview. He is not responsible for the conclusions expressed in this chapter.
30. Anatoly Gladilin, personal interview, Paris, March 1985.
31. Lisnyanskaya and Lipkin are among only a handful of writers who have voluntarily resigned from the Union. Another is Georgy Vladimov, who sent a harsh indictment of the Union bosses, dated October 10, 1977, as he put it, "excluding them from his life."

    Under glasnost and perestroika, Lisnyanskaya and Lipkin have been readmitted to the Writers' Union, as have Yerofeyev and Popov. Other authors readmitted in recent months are Vladimir Kornilov, Boris Pasternak, and Alexander Galich—the last two posthumously.
32. On these issues, see Gregory Walker, *Soviet Book Publishing Policy* (Cambridge: Cambridge University Press, 1978).
33. *Plenum Tsentralnogo Komiteta KPSS 14–15 iyunya 1983 goda. Stenografichesky otchet* (Moscow, 1983), p. 72.
34. The typical *templan* has a series of headings: No./ Author and Title, brief/ No. of sheets/ Print-run/ Status/ Compiler/ Description/ Author-Publisher (000s). In the "Status" column the usual entries are "application" (*zayavka*), "manuscript," and "partial manuscript."
35. Personal interview, London, June 1984. We interviewed Bitov a few months before he disappeared from the West and re-surfaced in Moscow, claiming to have been kidnapped by agents of Western intelligence. At his Moscow press conference, sitting next to him, was the same Izyumov, from *Literaturnaya gazeta,* whom we interview in December 1985 and quote earlier.
36. Vladimir Vigilyansky, " 'Grazhdanskaya voina' v literature, ili o tom, kak pomoch chitatelyu Lva Nikolaevicha," *Ogonyok,* no. 43 (October 1988), p. 7. The "Lev Nikolaevich" of the title is Tolstoy, whose works are still hard to find in any Soviet bookstore, even in Moscow. The use of the phrase " 'Civil War' in literature" refers to a comment made by the reactionary writer and Litburo member Yury Bondarev (b. 1924). He claimed that decent, patriotic writers like himself were being attacked by the enemies of socialism. He also argued that the situation of loyal Soviet writers (that is, himself and his friends) had become similar to that of the defenders of Stalingrad during the German attack in World War II. Bondarev participated in the war as a very young man and received medals for service, but so did many of the writers he has been attacking.
37. *Literaturnaya gazeta,* July 2, 1986, p. 9. Quoted from *CDSP,* vol. 38, no. 35, p. 10. Semyonov is the son of Nikolai Bukharin's personal

secretary, who was arrested and sent to the Gulag when Bukharin fell from power in 1938. Semyonov is one of many successful Soviet public figures whose fathers (and mothers) were arrested, and often executed under Stalin.

CHAPTER 7
The Threat of Glasnost

1. Perestroika ("restructuring") has been a more common term than glasnost in the Soviet glossary because of the system's need to mount frequent campaigns, to declare past policies and their proponents to be "anti-Party," and to initiate brave new beginnings—always based on Leninist principles. Stalin used the word perestroika in 1932 when announcing the decision to disband all proletarian writers' organizations and establish the Union of Soviet Writers; the term has cropped up many times since then.

2. See the interview with Natan Eidelman in *Ogonyok*, no. 44 (October 1988). Eidelman, a Jew, had a fiery exchange of correspondence in 1987 with the Russian nationalist author, Viktor Astafyev, whose remarks were suffused with anti-Semitism. Because he has opened his pages to Jewish writers and scholars, *Ogonyok*'s chief editor, Vitaly Korotich (himself a Ukrainian), has been accused of being a Jewish cosmopolitan, of being "a homegrown Goldstucker"—Eduard Goldstucker was president of the Writers' Union of Czechoslovakia and a leading supporter of the "Prague Spring" in 1968.

3. Gorbachev's law degree was earned, as far as we know—this is by no means always the case with Party officials, who have their academic work done for them and their books ghost-written.

   Academician Tatyana Zaslavskaya states that degrees and diplomas are awarded often simply to fulfill the plan, and are even purchased. This custom has become so extensive that she suggests the possession of a diploma or degree should no longer be used to define the Soviet intelligentsia. See T. Zaslavskaya, "O strategii sotsialnogo upravlenia perestroikoi," *Inogo ne dano*, ed. Yu. N. Afanasyev (Moscow, 1987), p. 14. Her comments should be of interest to Western scholars attempting to establish class boundaries in Soviet society based on educational achievement.

4. *Tvorcheskie soyuzy v SSSR*, p. 58.

5. See the table in Zaslavskaya's article "O strategii sotsialnogo upravlenia perstroikoi," *Inogo ne dano*, p. 39.

6. The text of Chernenko's speech was printed in *Izvestia*, September 26, 1984.

7. Interview in *Washington Post Magazine*, April 10, 1983.

8. See the issue of December 18, 1985. The full text of Yevtushenko's speech (as far as we can tell) was reproduced in the *stenotchet* of the Congress: *Shestoi syezd pisatelei RSFSR: Stenografichesky otchet* (Mos-

cow, 1987), pp. 106–10; the account records that the speech was followed by "prolonged applause," one of the very few speeches so honored. For an English translation of his speech, see the *New York Times*, December 18, 1985.

9. Julia Wishnevsky provides a lucid review of the circumstances surrounding Voronov's appointment in Radio Liberty's *Report on the USSR*, vol. 1, no. 1 (January 6, 1989).
10. For an excellent account of the Soviet film industry see Val Golovskoy (with John Romberg), *Behind the Soviet Screen* (Ann Arbor, MI: Ardis, 1986). The book retains its value, even though it has been overtaken to some extent by recent events.
11. The transcript was published in the New York émigré newspaper *Novoe Russkoe Slovo* (November 16, 1986); on the censoring of Gorbachev's remarks, see the monthly *Posev* [Frankfurt, West Germany], no. 2, 1987, p. 23.
12. Gorbachev is also referred to as "GenSok" instead of "GenSek"; *sok* is Russian for "juice," that is, a soft drink.

    Gorbachev's anti-alcohol campaign has provoked a new *chastushka*, or rhymed jingle on a contemporary topic, as quoted by V. Senderov in *Posev*, no. 5 (1988), p. 20:

    V pyat utra poyot petukh,
    V vosem—Pugacheva;
    Magazin otkroyut s dvukh,
    Klyuch—u Gorbacheva.

    A rough translation: "The cock crows at five in the morning, [the pop singer, Alla] Pugacheva sings at eight; The [liquor] store is opened [only] at two in the afternoon, Gorbachev has the key."
13. For the complete stenographic record see *Vosmoi syezd pisatelei SSSR. Stenografichesky otchet* (Moscow, 1988).

    The Russian émigré press covered the Eighth Congress quite extensively. Two of the most balanced and incisive accounts were those by R. Bakhtamov, "Partynaya organizatsia i partynaya literatura," *Strana i mir* [Munich], no. 8, 1986, pp. 13–27, and by Mikhail Lemkin, "O vosmom syezde pisatelei SSSR—vzglyad izdaleka," *Russkaya mysl* [Paris], August 22, 1986, pp. 8–9. These two publications are among the very best in the Russian émigré community.
14. Bella Yezerskaya, ed., *Mastera* (Ann Arbor, MI: Hermitage, 1982), p. 12.
15. At the conclusion of the Eighth Congress in June 1986 a new Litburo was formed: Ch. T. Aitmatov, G. Ya. Baklanov, Yu. V. Bondarev, V. V. Bykov, A. T. Gonchar, S. P. Zalygin, V. V. Karpov, G. M. Markov, and Yu. N. Verchenko as "secretary for organizational and creative work" (*sekretar po organizatsionno-tvorcheskoi rabote*). Although Karpov became First Secretary, replacing Markov (kicked upstairs as Board President), neither man was named to head the new Litburo. Presumably

either Karpov or Verchenko chairs the meetings, now that Markov has retired (January 1989).

16. Translated in *Current Digest of the Soviet Press*, vol. 38, no. 33, p. 10.

17. Yury Antropov, "Vsenarodnaya nasha zabota," *Literaturnaya gazeta*, July 1, 1987, p. 3. The similarity of Yury Antropov's name to that of the KGB chief, and later General Secretary, occasioned countless jokes in the Writers' Union, and now and then a moment of panic, until members realized that it was not the Party boss who had decided to come and address a meeting.

18. *Literaturnaya gazeta*, March 18, 1987.

19. Vyacheslav Rodionov, "Kultura i struktura," *Komsomolskaya Pravda*, August 2, 1988, p. 1; "O tvorcheskikh soyuzakh," letter from A. Shiropaev and S. Naumov, *Sovetskaya kultura*, June 7, 1988, p. 2.

20. For Zamyatin's article and a favorable commentary, with extensive notes, see "Vechny otritsatel i buntar. Ye. Zamyatin—literaturny kritik," *Literaturnoe obozrenie*, no. 2, 1988, pp. 98–100.

21. For two thoughtful reviews of this novel, see M. Shneyerson, "Partia Lenina-Stalina: O romane A. Rybakove 'Deti Arbata'," *Posev*, no. 8, pp. 47–53; and Roman Redlikh, "S leninianoi pora konchat," *Posev*, no. 7, 1988, pp. 46–48. Both reviews recognize the novel's importance in presenting a psychological portrait of Stalin, but they also analyze, correctly in our view, its artistic weaknesses and Rybakov's failed effort to turn Kirov into a hero as a way of salvaging the Leninist tradition.

22. The Moscow literary critic Igor Vinogradov, who refused on principle to publish during the Brezhnev period, gave a vivid account of the current conflict of attitudes among Soviet writers and editors during an interview conducted with Radio Liberty in 1988. See "Intervyu s literaturnym kritikom Igorem Vinogradovym," RS 61/88 (July 20, 1988). Vinogradov suggested that Proskurin and other conservatives had a lot of support.

23. See *Literaturnaya Rossia*, March 27, 1988, pp. 2–4.

24. Natalia Ilyina, "Zdravstvui, plemya mladoe, neznakomoe . . . ," *Ogonyok*, no. 2, 1988, p. 23. See also Ilyina's fascinating literary reminiscences, which involve Alexander Tvardovsky, another central hero of the liberals today, "Moi prodolzhitelnye uroki," *Ogonyok*, no. 17, 1988, pp. 26–29.

25. See, for example, a series of articles by Natalya Ivanova in *Ogonyok*: "Chem pakhnet tormoznaya zhidkost" (no. 11, 1988), "Perekhod cherez boloto" (no. 25, 1988), " 'Zvezda zheny soseda Mitrofana' " (no. 34, 1988); also her review of leading literary monthlies in "Zhurnaly v fokuse mneny," *Literaturnoe obozrenie*, no. 4, 1988.

In his article "Koe-chto o professionalizme," *Ogonyok*, no. 48 (November 1988), Stanislav Rassadin notes that until very recently literary critics were not permitted to write negative reviews or even comments about top literary bureaucrats and other protected writers. He mentions the fact that, as Tvardovsky was being removed from his post as chief editor at *Novy mir*, an article critical of the reactionary hack rhymer, Yegor Isaev, was banned. Isaev remains a "released secretary" in the Union apparatus.

26. Benedikt Sarnov, "Borba za pravo pisat plokho," *Ogonyok*, no. 23, 1987, p. 11.
27. Bill Keller, "Moscow's Other Mastermind," *New York Times Magazine*, February 19, 1989, p. 41.
28. The Statutes of the Fund were published in *Sovetskaya kultura*, September 4, 1986, and in *Literaturnaya gazeta*, September 10, 1986; *Literaturnaya gazeta* printed a series of articles and readers' letters about the Fund (October 22, 1986); the inaugural conference was covered in all central newspapers—see *Sovetskaya kultura*, September 13 and 15, 1986.
29. For a useful range of views on the Russian nationalist movement in the Soviet Union, see the essays by John B. Dunlop, Darrell P. Hammer, Andrei Sinyavsky, Ronald Grigor Suny, and Alexander Yanov in *Russian Nationalism Today* (Radio Liberty Research Bulletin: Special Edition, December 19, 1988).
30. For an example of Kozhinov's literary and historical outlook, see his article "Pravda i istina," *Nash Sovremennik* (April 1988); for a response to Kozhinov's defense of Stalin and playing down of the purges, see Vladimir Lakshin, "V kilvatere," *Ogonyok*, no. 26 (June 1988). *Nash Sovremennik* is a Russian nationalist, extreme rightwing journal, while *Ogonyok* is very liberal, and a leading supporter of Gorbachev's campaign for glasnost.
31. *Pravda* and *Izvestia* July 1, 1988, pp. 3–4. Condensed in *Current Digest of the Soviet Press*, vol. 40, no. 29 (1988), pp. 21–22.
32. See the satire on the special session of the Russian Republic writers' secretariat in the provincial town of Ryazan, which was signed by the magazine's Literature Department, "Provintsialnye anekdoty: O 'ryazanskom desante,' Petre III i chistote krovi," *Ogonyok*, no. 52, 1988, pp. 13–15. The Russian word *desant* means a jump by paratroopers or an amphibious landing by marines; Korotich and his colleagues were responding to Bondarev's comparison of their disagreement to the military conflict at Stalingrad.
33. "Otkrytoe pismo Yuriyu Bondarevu," *Ogonyok*, no. 1 (January 1989), p. 8. In a remarkably candid article, detailing a whole series of abuses by conservative and reactionary writers, including Bondarev, the critic Yury Burtin had expressed the hope that Mikhail Kolosov, and others, would demonstrate increasing independence and move away from the literary bosses; Kolosov has certainly fulfilled that hope. See Yury Burtin, "Vozmozhnost vozrazit (Iz lichnogo opyta)," *Inogo ne dano* (Moscow, 1988), p. 489.
34. "Pismo v 'Pravdu,' " *Pravda*, January 18, 1989, p. 6.
35. See Julia Wishnevsky, "Tvardovsky's Tormentor Appointed to Poet's

Memorial Panel," Radio Liberty Research Bulletin, RL 152/88, April 13, 1988.

36. See Bill Keller, "New in Moscow: More Hymns to Old Russia," *New York Times*, February 22, 1989.

37. This same issue also reported that the number of letters received by the weekly magazine had increased from 4,261 in January 1988 to 13,193 in January 1989. What is more, this issue included a letter from 26 writers announcing the creation of a committee of "Writers in Support of Perestroika." Among the signatories were Vladimir Dudintsev, Natalia Ilyina, Fazil Iskander, Bulat Okudzhava, Anatoly Pristavkin, Mikhail Roshchin—the latter was the same playwright who supported Sergei Yurenen and helped him gain admission to the Writers' Union in the seventies.

38. See, for example, his comments in "Nuzhna kontseptsia knigoizdania," *Literaturnaya gazeta*, March 23, 1988, p. 1.

CHAPTER 8
The Promise of Perestroika

1. Undoubtedly, Yakovlev will retain a good deal of influence as a Gorbachev adviser. In November 1988, Tass announced that Yakovlev had been appointed to replace retired Politburo member Solomentsev as chair of the special commission investigating Stalin's crimes, particularly the murder or imprisonment in the Gulag of countless innocent victims. Other members of the commission are: Vadim Medvedev (head of the new Commission for Ideology), Victor Cherbrikov (former head of the KGB), Vladimir Khryuchkov (new head of the KGB), Valery Boldin, Anatoly Lukyanov (an old law school friend of Gorbachev), Boris Pugo, Georgy Razumovsky, and Georgy Smirnov.

2. See the excellent analysis of these changes in A. Ryadnov, "Perevorot sverkhu," *Posev*, no. 11, 1988, pp. 35–38. Ryadnov argues persuasively that the real reason for the changes was Gorbachev's determination to destroy Ligachev and to assert himself in a position of supreme authority. In the process Gorbachev seems to have downgraded the power of the Central Committee Secretariat, and perhaps of the Politburo itself. On October 1 he had himself named as President of the Presidium of the Council of Ministers, adding to his title of Party General Secretary.

3. In familiar fashion, Yegorov is described as having "taken part in the work" of a plenum of the Union Board. See *Literaturnaya gazeta*, January 25, 1989.

   In addition to Central Committee personnel, Gorbachev also has a personal aide who specializes in ideological issues: Ivan Timofeyevich Frolov (b. 1929). He has served as chief editor of *Voprosy filosofii* and *Kommunist*, and is president of the Soviet Philosophical Society. See Alexander G. Rahr, comp., *A Bibliographic Dictionary of 100 Leading Soviet Officials* (Radio Liberty Research, Munich, January 1989), pp. 62–64.

4. *On Liberty;* quoted by Aaron Trehub in RL 399/86. Of course, we

should remember that two years after this remark was made, Alexander II did indeed manage to push through the Emancipation of the serfs and some other reforms. However, they were too little, too late, and merely sowed the seeds for further radical activity and, finally, revolution.

5. See "Zakon o vyborakh narodnykh deputatov SSSR," *Pravda*, December 4, 1988. For a good review of the new election laws, see Sergei Voronitsyn, "Nachata perestroika struktury vysshikh organov vlasti," RS 117/88 (December 20, 1988), and Viktor Yasmann, "Quota of Seats in Congress of People's Deputies for Public and Professional Organizations," Radio Liberty *Report on the USSR*, vol. 1, no. 4 (January 27, 1989), pp. 9–11.

6. A juxtaposition of the 1989 draft with the 1971 document shows that of the original five sections the first and fifth retain their positions, but the second is moved to fourth place and replaced by a completely new section; the third is dropped and replaced by the original fourth section.

7. All quotations are taken from "Ustav Soyuza pisatelei SSSR: Proekt," *Literaturnaya gazeta*, March 22, 1989, p. 3. Further references in our text are to the section (Roman numeral) and clause (Arabic numeral). Note that in the Soviet text Roman numbers are used for the subsections of the second section. The sections are not numbered, but the clauses within sections are (in Arabic numerals).

8. Of the many incidents reported in both the Soviet and Western press in which Gorbachev has urged a return to the lessons of Lenin, one of the most striking occurred in Krakow, Poland, and was reported by the AP on July 13, 1988. Speaking at Wawel Castle, he repeatedly emphasized that Lenin was still a hero of our time. "Lenin's life and struggle constitute a splendid example to be followed by young people . . . a lesson in pursuing one's goals and being faithful to the ideal born out of love for people." Asking rhetorically, "Has socialism fallen through?" he answered his own question, "No . . . not at all." The subtext throughout his speech recalls Lenin's own language and style in *What Is To Be Done?*

9. Here the Union appeared to be claiming jurisdiction over an area that was still formally part of Goskomizdat's responsibilities. In July 1989 Goskomizdat lost part of its name and returned to its original title of State Committee for the Press (Goskompechat), under a new chairman, Nikolai Ivanovich Yefimov, who moved over from his position as head of the Propaganda Sector of the Central Committee's Department of Ideology.

   It is too early to say whether Goskompechat will retain all the authority of Goskomizdat, or assume a more modest role, surrendering some of its power to the Writers' Union.

10. The following account of Pristavkin's speech and of the April Committee's Manifesto is drawn from *Moskovsky literator* (March 17, 1989). This weekly newspaper is published by the *partkom* and board of the Moscow writers' organization.

Whether or not by design, the Manifesto is printed next to an announcement declaring that the secretariat of the Russian Republic branch had revoked Vladimir Voinovich's expulsion from the Union and readmitted him officially to the organization.

11. *Moskovsky literator* lists the following members elected at the inaugural meeting: A. Gerber, I. Duel, A. Zlobin, S. Kaledin, Vl. Kornilov, A. Kurchatkin, A. Latynina, Yu. Morits, N. Panchenko, A. Pristavkin, V. Sokolov, A. Strelyany, S. Ustinov, Yu. Chernichenko, and Z. Yuryev.

12. *Literaturnaya gazeta,* March 9, 1988, p. 3. This is one of the sections from Lenin's article quoted in our first chapter. In a curious omission from the full text, Karpov neglected to include the brief sentence in which Lenin ridiculed objections about workers making decisions by majority vote on what should be done in culture and philosophy. Karpov, or an editor, evidently felt this would weaken his argument.

13. Personal interview, Paris, March 1985.

14. Celestine Bohlen, "A Soviet Author's Strong Views on PEN," *New York Times,* May 9, 1989.

Tatiana Tolstaya was turned down for Union membership by the Russian Republic branch because of critical remarks she had made about a novel by the conservative Russian writer Vasily Belov. However, in October of 1988, she was admitted by the Moscow branch, which had just acquired, with the Leningrad branch, independent status within the Writers' Union equivalent to that of a Republic organization.

15. RL Bulletin 321/87 (August 4, 1987), p. 6.

16. *Posev,* the Russian journal published in Frankfurt, which has collected the most remarkable archive of *samizdat* materials in the West, managed to obtain a transcript of this supposedly "closed" meeting, and published it. See "Diskussia v MGU," *Posev,* no. 9, 1987, pp. 2–5. Strelyany's outspokenness apparently cost him his job as an editor of *Novy mir,* but he is in no personal danger, and has in fact been appointed to the influential position of director of the "Sovetsky Pisatel" Publishing House.

17. Bill Keller, "Obscure Soviet Magazine Breaks the Ban on Solzhenitsyn's Work," *New York Times,* March 20, 1989. After *XX vek i mir* (*Twentieth Century and Peace*) printed the 1974 essay, "Live Not by Lies," it found itself once again having to submit all work to Glavlit.

18. Solzhenitsyn, understandably, was reluctant to become involved in Soviet affairs until and unless the standing charge of treason against him is dropped. It is no criticism of Solzhenitsyn to point out that, in declining the invitation to join "Memorial" and perhaps visit Moscow, he may have inadvertently weakened his supporters' case.

19. Quoted from Lev Timofeyev's journal *Referendum* by John Dunlop in his account, "The Almost-Rehabilitation and Re-Anathemization of Aleksandr Solzhenitsyn," *Working Papers in International Studies of The Hoover Institution* (February 1989), p. 20. The term *vozhd* was used for Stalin. The "familiar form of address" can only be used politely

to very old friends, children, animals, and God; it is extremely rude in other contexts, and particularly when addressing an older person.

20. With the publication of Solzhenitsyn's works in his homeland has come the final accolade—readmission to the Writers' Union. See "Otmeneno reshenie ob isklyuchenii A. Solzhenitsyna iz SP SSSR," *Literaturnaya gazeta,* July 5, 1989, p. 1.
21. See Terry McNeill's brisk analysis of the current Soviet political and economic scene, "The USSR and Communism: The Twilight Years," RL 428/87 (October 29, 1987). McNeill joins a number of Western observers in suggesting that, in the end, what has brought the Soviet experiment to a halt is, ironically enough, economic reality.

Attacks on utopianism are becoming a central feature of critical articles on Soviet history and the need for new initiatives. See, in particular, L. Popkova, "Gde pyshneye pirogi?" *Novy mir,* no. 5, 1987, pp. 239–41; and Vasily Selyunin, "Istoki," *Novy mir,* no. 5, 1988, pp. 161–89. The latter article contains some searching comments on Lenin's utopian views and his fanatical faith in terror as a means of improving the living conditions of workers.

A Bibliographical Essay

The first epigraph at the front of the book is drawn from W. H. Auden's Introduction to Penguin Books' *Portable Greek Reader* (1948), which he compiled and edited; it is published by Viking in the United States. Auden's analysis of the Greek political mind would appear to have relevance to the Russian context. He says:

> Through identifying the active source of the Good with Reason not with Will, they [the Greeks] doomed themselves to the hopeless task of finding the ideal form of society which, like the truths of reason, would be valid everywhere and for everyone, irrespective of their individual character or their historical circumstance.

The search of certain Russians for an "ideal form of society" has cost their country very dear. It continues to be a central issue of Russian literature.

The second epigraph is quoted from an August 1989 interview with Vitaly Korotich, chief editor of the weekly magazine, *Ogonyok*, in his office in Moscow.

There have only been two book-length studies on the Writers' Union published in the USSR. The first is a collection of essays by members of the Union Secretariat, published in English and entitled *The Union of Soviet Writers: Aims, Organisation, Activities* (Moscow: Progress Publishers, 1981). The book is quite informative, but presents a highly favorable view of the Union's activities, rather like the annual report of an American corporation—an analogy that is not so far-fetched as it might seem at first sight. The second is a collaborative volume on the "creative unions" as whole, *Tvorcheskie soyuzy v SSSR* (*Organizatsionno-pravovye voprosy*) (Moscow, 1970), published by the Academy of Sciences' Institute of State and Law.

The Soviet periodical press, especially the weekly paper *Literaturnaya gazeta*, an official organ of the Writers' Union Board, provides much useful information about the Union's activities. Important statements of policy, occasional signs of conflicts, news of appointments, and statistical data are also available in the verbatim reports (*stenograficheskie otchety*) of each national congress of the Union and of Republic organizations. In connection with each national congress since 1959, the Union has published a *Spravochnik*, its directory of members, which includes addresses and telephone numbers.

For the Moscow branch of the Union, which has more than 2,000 members, we have *Pisateli Moskvy. Biobibliografichesky spravochnik* (Moscow, 1987). This important volume contains useful background information on each living member, and a list of major publications and awards. Similar directories are available for a few other regions; for example, *Pisateli Dona*, 2d. edition (Rostov-on-Don, 1986), and *Pisateli srednego Urala* (Sverdlovsk, 1986).

Two valuable insider views, published in translation, are: Alexander Solzhenitsyn, *The Oak and the Calf* (New York: Harper & Row, 1979), and Miklos Haraszti, *The Velvet Prison: Artists Under State Socialism* (New York: Basic Books, 1987). Haraszti's book shows that the Soviet system has been replicated exactly in Hungary.

Additional sources of information on the Union include articles and books published in Russian by émigrés in the West, particularly those of the so-called Third Wave of the seventies and early eighties. Particularly valuable for the contemporary Soviet scene is the weekly *Radio Liberty Research Bulletin*, a model of objective, informed writing produced by the staff of Radio Liberty in Munich. As of January 1989, this weekly publication was renamed *Report on the USSR*.

The Western focus on censorship (Glavlit) and on Socialist Realism has tended to push the Writers' Union into the background, with the result that the following list of Western works dealing specifically or substantially with the Union is not very long, and they mostly deal with the Stalin or Khrushchev periods.

For the earlier period, see Jack F. Matlock, Jr. (as of 1989 the American Ambassador to the Soviet Union), "The 'Governing Organs' of the Union of Soviet Writers," *American SEER*, vol. 15 (October 1956), 383–99; Harold Swayze, *Political Control of Literature in the USSR, 1946–1959* (Harvard University Press, 1962); Ernest J. Simmons, "The Writers," in H. Gordon Skilling and Franklyn Griffiths, eds., *Interest Groups in Soviet Politics* (Princeton University Press, 1971), pp. 253–89; John Murray, "The Union of Soviet Writers: Its Organization and Leading Personnel, 1954–1967," Ph.D. thesis (U. of Birmingham, England, 1973); A. Kemp-Welch, "The Union of Soviet Writers, 1932–36," Ph.D. thesis (London School of Economics, 1982). In addition, Ronald Hingley's *Russian Writers and Soviet Society 1917–1978* (New York: Random House, 1979) offers a lively and informative overview of the literary situation, including a discussion of the Writers' Union.

Although they are concerned more with text than context, general histories and surveys of specific periods in Soviet literature contain many valuable insights into the Soviet literary scene. The following list of books is necessarily selective: Vera Alexandrova, *A History of Soviet Literature*,

1917–1962: From Gorky to Yevtushenko (New York: Doubleday, 1963); Edward J. Brown, *Russian Literature Since the Revolution,* revised and enlarged edition (Cambridge: Harvard University Press, 1982); Deming Brown, *Soviet Russian Literature Since Stalin* (Cambridge University Press, 1978); Katerina Clark, *The Soviet Novel: History as Ritual* (University of Chicago Press, 1981); Vera S. Dunham, *In Stalin's Time: Middleclass Values in Soviet Fiction* (New York: Cambridge University Press, 1976); George Gibian, *Interval of Freedom: Soviet Literature during the Thaw, 1954–1957* (University of Minnesota Press, 1960); Geoffrey Hosking, *Beyond Socialist Realism: Soviet Fiction since Ivan Denisovich* (New York: Holmes & Meier, 1980); Robert A. Maguire, *Red Virgin Soil: Soviet Literature in the 1920's* (Princeton University Press, 1968); Gleb Struve, *Russian Literature under Lenin and Stalin, 1917–1953* (Norman, OK: University of Oklahoma Press, 1971).

The following reference works contain much useful information, but those published in the Soviet Union should be used with caution because entries are sometimes incomplete and/or biased (not always through the fault of the authors, but because of censorship and ideological editing):

Literaturnaya entsiklopedia, 9 volumes [not completed] (Moscow, 1929–39).

Kratkaya Literaturnaya Entsiklopedia, 9 volumes (Moscow 1962–75). This is a major source, with entries on the Union and congresses, and most of the better-known writers. Many of the entries are very informative and balanced; see, for example, "Literaturnye diskussii," in volume 9, pp. 441–72, which provides a good account of debates during the twenties and thirties.

Literaturny entsiklopedichesky slovar (Moscow, 1987). See the entry on Party decrees in literature, pp. 291–92; the short chronicle of Soviet literary life from 1917 to 1983 on pp. 392–406; and the annotated directory of writers (not only Soviet) on pp. 536–751.

Victor Terras, ed., *Handbook of Russian Literature* (Yale University Press, 1985).

Wolfgang Kasack, comp., *Lexikon der russischen Literatur ab 1917* (Stuttgart: Kroner, 1976); and a supplemental volume, *Lexikon der russischen Literatur ab 1917* (Munich: Sagner, 1986).

Volfgang Kazak, *Entsiklopedichesky slovar russkoi literatury s 1917 goda* [Russian edition] (London: OPI, 1988).

Index